Savoring
Philadelphia

By Craig LaBan

ISBN 1-58822-011-7

Published by The Philadelphia Inquirer, 400 N Broad St., Philadelphia, Pa. 19130. To purchase additional copies of this book, visit http://newsstand.pnionline.com/

2d Printing

Table of Contents

FEATURES

THE RESTAURANTS

THE GUIDE

The 76 Favorites, by Bell Rating

SUPERIOR

Fountain Restaurant
Le Bec-Fin
¡Pasion!
Susanna Foo
Vetri

EXCELLENT

Birchrunville Store Cafe
The Blue Angel
Brasserie Perrier
Buddakan
The Capital Grille
Country Club Restaurant
Deux Cheminees
Dilworthtown Inn
Django
Fuji Japanese Restaurant
Happy Rooster
The Inn on Blueberry Hill
Jake's
John's Roast Pork
Margaret Kuo's Peking
Max's
Moonlight
Morimoto
Nan
The Prime Rib
Restaurant 821
Savona
Shiao Lan Kung
Strawberry Hill
Striped Bass
Tangerine

VERY GOOD

Alma de Cuba
Audrey Claire
Azafran
Bistro St. Tropez
The Black Sheep
Cafe Spice
Carambola
Carmine's
Chlöe
Citrus
Dmitri's
Effie's
Ernesto's 1521 Cafe
Felicia's
Fork
Friday Saturday Sunday
Horizons Cafe
Judy's Cafe
Khajuraho
Kristian's
La Encina
Lakeside Chinese Deli
Las Cazuelas
Le Castagne
Lee How Fook
London Grill
Los Catrines Restaurant & Tequila's Bar
Morning Glory Diner
Ms. Tootsie's Soul Food Cafe
New Wave Cafe
Opus 251
Penang
Pif
Porcini
The Red Hen Cafe
Ritz Seafood
Rose Tattoo Cafe
Rouge
Rx
Sansom St. Oyster House
Standard Tap
Tierra Colombiana
Tre Scalini
Vietnam
White Dog Cafe

Introduction

What's your favorite restaurant?

Philadelphians are obviously obsessed, because I am asked this question at least five times a day. It makes sense to ask me, of course, since I eat here for a living, grazing menus from Center City to New Hope, Wilmington, Lancaster and the Jersey Shore in search of a memorable meal. But I am always stumped for that quickie response. Because I don't have a single favorite restaurant. I have 76.

Believe me, it wasn't easy being so brief.

In the four-and-a-half years since I returned to Philadelphia from New Orleans, I've formally reviewed and rated nearly 200 restaurants and written about hundreds more. In the process, I've tasted somewhere near 12,000 separate dishes, ranging from cheesesteaks to live scallops to flaming chocolate cigars. It's a good thing I like variety. Then again, that is the pure joy of my job, to experience the stunningly deep pool of talent and diversity that is the Philadelphia flavor.

Deciding on the perfect place for dinner is never easy. It all depends on what you crave when. Do you want to taste an ethereal spinach gnocchi bathed in brown butter at Vetri? Get ready for at least a month's wait. Or how about being pampered by the Four Seasons hotel? A drive to the Birchrunville Country Store in bucolic Chester County for garden-grown French cuisine may be more your speed. Or perhaps you are amongst the legions of sexy, black-clad diners who worship Stephen Starr's golden Buddha as if it were the real thing. Or maybe your poodle has just been bugging you to go back to Rouge. The azaleas and glamour crowd of Rittenhouse Square await.

People usually assume I'd be gorging myself on snails and foie gras at Le Bec-Fin every night if I could. And there's nothing wrong with an occasional celebratory visit to that gold-plated temple of gastronomy. But far more often, I find myself craving the down-to-earth pleasures of everyday foods, of thoughtful seasonal fare at neighborhood prices, of comfort food in all its guises, of standards done to classic perfection, of adventurous ethnic flavors and, yes — even especially — a great cheesesteak.

That's why this list of favorites doesn't necessarily include every fine dining spot that has scored a 2- or 3-Liberty Bell review. There were so many excellent restaurants that simply didn't quite resonate when I asked myself: Is it one of my absolute favorites?

Each of those that did occupies a unique place for me, which is why this book is simply organized from A-Z rather than ranked in any false order of importance.

I will always have room, for example, for the best pork sandwich in town, or an authentic Mexican mole. I treasure the last of our disappearing traditions, whether it's a bowl of sherried snapper soup, a classic Italian red gravy, or an old-fashioned chicken croquette at the diner. Want to know where to get fabulous salt-baked shrimp, dim-sum and congee in Chinatown at 2 a.m.? I know where to send you. This is important stuff.

It has been a golden age for Philadelphia's dining scene, with an energy similar to the great renaissance that jump-started the 1970s, but with far more talent and sophistication and variety driving its jaw-dropping growth. In just the last decade, the number of restaurants in Center City has tripled, and it shows little sign of slowing. Stephen Starr's group of eight restaurants alone can attract as many people to the city in a single week as would fill the Kimmel Center during a week of sold-out performances. Our restaurants have become the region's most vital cultural pursuit.

The bounty, though, has been a mixed blessing. Good food has appeared in more unlikely places than ever before, from the previously underserved suburbs to a slew of inexpensive but ambitious BYOBs that are redefining the way our neighborhoods eat.

On the downside, the local talent pool has been watered down, especially with service. Even more problematic, the constant flow of new venues has a way of overshadowing the excellent cast of existing restaurants. What's new this week may be exciting, but it also has a way of narrowing our appreciation of the big picture.

Writing a regular restaurant review column for the Sunday Inquirer Magazine only emphasizes that flavor of the week, since I can only tell the story of the region's dining scene one restaurant and one issue at a time. In compiling this list of favorites, though, I've been able to step back and draw on restaurants from my entire four-and-a-half years here, to snare our local food scene in a much larger net. There are plenty of great restaurants I still haven't gotten to, and that aren't included here, but this should do for starters — 76 full reviews plus suggestions on 240 more you should know, many of which have yet to be formally rated.

Of course, the restaurant world is constantly in flux, shuffling menus, decors and chefs. So I'd encourage you to consider these more as detailed reports of my visits rather than exact predictions of what you will find. That said, every featured review has been updated to reflect my most recent meals, and all but a handful of the 76 have been revisited within the last eight months. It is amazing how well some of the old standbys have held up. A couple have slipped a notch. But more often than not, they have improved over time. So, which one is my favorite? Well now, that depends ...

— *Craig LaBan, November 2002*

About the Ratings

There is no science to rating restaurants. There is no secret math or official list of do's or don'ts. There are no particular china patterns or personal prosciutto preferences that somehow land a restaurant that elusive top rating of four Liberty Bells.

What I care most about is how well a restaurant "works," whether it satisfies the most basic function of delivering a pleasant meal and fair value, or whether it goes beyond to offer something more unusual, more daring or sublime. Is it worth sending readers to spend their hard-earned money?

Hopefully, over four-and-a-half years, these ratings have been able to give readers a consistent sense of context for how well restaurants are achieving. But I understand it can seem like ratings often try to reconcile apples versus oranges.

How can a luxury restaurant be rated the same or lower than a pork sandwich shack? Here is a straight-talk primer:

These ratings and reviews are live, based on several real meals at each restaurant that have been paid for by The Inquirer. And they have a life of their own. As a critic, I have always done my best to remain incognito and discreet, to best replicate the kind of experience any other diner might have. My cover has occasionally been blown, but I've noted that when it seemed to be a factor.

SUPERIOR
Rare; sets fine-dining standards.

EXCELLENT
Excels in every category of the dining experience (or the best of its genre).

VERY GOOD
Interesting, with above-average food.

AVERAGE
Hit or miss.

The rating, then, is based largely on how that restaurant fits into the context of the dining scene at large, but also how it meets its own ambitions. It simply doesn't make sense to judge a bare-bones BYOB serving homey comfort food versus the polished silver pomp of Le Bec-Fin. Their personalities and aspirations are completely different. And, probably, so are the prices and the expectations that follow.

As a result, The Inquirer's ratings have evolved over the years to become a hybrid of the traditional luxury-based scale and another school that says the very best in each genre should be rewarded. I've never been one to throw Liberty Bells around, but I have acknowledged a few of those — a Chinatown nook, a classic diner, a cheesesteak and pork sandwich joint — by including them in the three-bell "excellent" tier, a rare rating that means what it says. However, the most exclusive top tier of four-bell "superior" restaurants — there are only five — inevitably still comprises fine-dining spots.

There has been considerable flexibility, especially, in the lower tiers. The two-bell "very good" category has been the broadest of all, a base line for recommendability that has seen both decently performing upscale restaurants as well as more modest places that are cooking at a high level. The one-bell "average" category (and "no bells," below) is open to any restaurant that doesn't deliver the consistency, quality or value it should. Many of those haven't been included in this book since it is, after all, dedicated to my favorites, although several have been cited with specific recommendations.

It should also be noted that numerous restaurants mentioned in this book have no rating because they haven't undergone a lengthy, formal review. This is not at all the same standing as the ignominious "no-bell" prize. For the sake of breadth and interest, I've chosen to include them nonetheless.

— *Craig LaBan, November 2002*

Alma de Cuba

The innovator of Nuevo Latino cooking brings ceviches and flaming chocolate cigars to Stephen Starr's chic and moody Restaurant Row townhouse.

'**ve** never been a big barnacle man. Then again, I had never tried to eat one until Douglas Rodriguez came to town, teaming the high-voltage creativity of his Nuevo Latino cuisine with the scene-savvy of self-proclaimed El Conquistador Stephen Starr, who wears his crown (on the menu, at least) with tongue in cheek.

Rodriguez doesn't joke about his barnacles, though. And there they were at Alma de Cuba, genuine pico rocos. (That's a gooseneck barnacle in the waters off Vancouver Island, Canada, the only place other than Chile where the mollusk lives.)

Displayed in all its terrifying intrigue, what looked like a tiny clamshell with a beak attached to one side trailed a plume of crab-like meat out the other and was perched on a hollowed-out "rock" filled with flan. The rock, in fact, was the barnacle's shell, and the mildly sea-flavored flan (made with barnacle juice) hid a few sweet surprises — dates and caramelized onion — in its custard.

It is thrilling when a chef brings diners to the brink of something scary and then reveals its beauty. Many cooks slip clumsily over the edge, especially when riding the tricky wave of a trend such as Nuevo Latino. Creativity can blossom only after the traditional ingredients are understood.

VERY GOOD

1623 Walnut St.
Philadelphia
(215) 988-1799

NEIGHBORHOOD
Rittenhouse Square

CUISINE
Nuevo Latino/Cuban

Guillermo Pernot gets it right at ¡Pasion!, where Philadelphians have discovered how elegant and ornate ceviches can be, as well as the wonders of tamarind-sauced fish and pig-shaped hibachis. Other local chefs have been less impressive. But Rodriguez, 36 — the New York-born godfather of Nuevo Latino cuisine, who made his mark at Yuca in Miami — has brought the real thing to Walnut Street from Manhattan, where he owns Chicama and Pipa.

The menu draws inspiration from Cuba — Rodriguez's parents are Cuban-born immigrants — though his palette often reaches beyond the island. (Hmmm ... no truffled mojos in Cuba? No foie gras mousse for Fidel?) No matter. When it works — and under chef de cuisine José Garces, it usually does — this food can be stunning, blazing with vibrant flavors, sparkling textures, and some of the most beautiful presentations in town.

Taco-like boats made of malanga root chips bear smoked marlin salad that tingles with pickled jalapenos and exudes the irresistible sweetness of its rum-vanilla marinade. The most tender octopus I've tasted comes sliced and dusted with smoked paprika. The black bean soup is pristine bean, a bowl of darkness with a croquette of creamy rice bobbing on the surface.

Pumpkin-seed-crusted scallops pair marvelously with a silky puree of gingery pumpkin sauce. A musky adobo spice rub gives Colorado rack of lamb an exotic zing. The lechon asado, or roast pork, is not only fairly priced at $19, but also has the perfect combination of cracker-crisp skin and butter-soft meat. The twice-cooked vaca frita ("fried cow") steak was meltingly tender and hauntingly infused with Cuban oregano and allspice.

Crushed plantain chips are the perfect Nuevo crust for a moist cut of halibut. Fufu — a soft mash of sweet plantain — is the ideal base for oysters Rodriguez, a play on oysters Rockefeller that tops a fufu-filled shell with horseradish-creamed spinach and a divinely fried oyster.

The ceviches are a study in complicated simplicity, the art of spotlighting the natural flavors of each fish (or shellfish) through intricate little contrasts.

Tiny citrus-cured scallops soft as pillows slip against crackly fried shallots and a drizzle of creamy mustard, while sweet orange segments burst into a tart lime marinade. The rainbow ceviche, inspired by the sushi roll, is made with a Peruvian marinade of lime juice, soy, ginger and cilantro. But the length of time each fish is marinated creates three distinct flavors in colorful tiers: a ruby dice of sesame-dusted tuna atop wide ribbons of well-cured orange salmon atop firm, white chunks of Chilean merluza bass.

Considering the effusive colors and other visual pleasures of Rodriguez's cooking, it's perplexing to experience the dreary darkroom spaces that Starr and New York designer David Rockwell took

Or Try These

Nobody blends quality food with fanciful concepts like Stephen Starr. Here are some of his best restaurants:

Buddakan

325 Chestnut St., Philadelphia
(215) 574-9440

Stephen Starr's first megarestaurant in Old City remains wildly popular with its giant golden Buddha and top-notch Asian fusion cuisine.

Tangerine

232 Market St., Philadelphia
(215) 627-5116

Inventive Mediterranean-inspired cuisine is served in a fabric-draped, votive-lit, fantasy room fit for a harem.

Blue Angel

706 Chestnut St.,Philadelphia
(215) 925-6889

Gorgeous Belle Epoque-style French bistro with polished renditions of the classics.

Smoked marlin boats at Alma de Cuba.

so much time and money to concoct. After months of resisting, Starr finally did agree recently to open the white townhouse curtains that had been permanently been drawn shut for effect. And there are plenty of nice architectural details inside — the tobacco-leaf-printed glass partition in the vestibule, the red mosaic that glows from the bar front like the tip of an embering cigar.

But the black-and-white photos of Cuban faces projected on the walls don't have much impact; they hover more like ghostly cliches — banging drums, rolling cigars, posing like the Mambo King.

And the dining rooms' minimalist decor is so dimly lit (and the music so loud) that the space fades into a netherworld of anonymous design, a vanilla look that could so easily have been mango or dulce de leche.

Rodriguez's food was not entirely the saint to Rockwell's design sins, but at least those missteps were bold. Pairing the foie gras with salty bacalao instead of something sweet was a challenge to foodies, but the salt cod was too chewy and brackish.

The "shrimp, shrimp, shrimp" would have been better as a less-complicated solo act. And the truffled mojo (sauce) with seared merluza sea bass was a gratuitous waste of truffle oil.

But the food nearly always succeeded, especially the desserts. The chocolate "cigar" mousse cake is brilliant, served with a sugar-pastry "matchbook" that the server sets afire. Rodriguez's chocolate bombe ("dats da bomb") is sublime in its disguise as a mushroom. The fresh coconut filled with tapioca is wonderful.

Or I could easily do a passion-fruit-flavored Alma Colada cocktail for dessert. I tried not to drink the whole coconut-shaped cup at the bar, but it was so rich and icy and glazed with dark rum. Then, as I munched through the nest of shaved coconut tousled on top, the front door swung open, and, for an instant, the late-afternoon light flooded the room. It was indeed, I realized then, a beautiful day in Philadelphia.

■ **MENU HIGHLIGHTS** Black bean soup; rainbow ceviche; scallop ceviche; pico roco barnacle; octopus salad; smoked marlin salad; oysters Rodriguez; vaca frita ("fried cow"); adobo lamb; lechon asado (roast pork); plantain-crusted halibut; scallop-pumpkin combo; chocolate cigar; "dats da bomb."

■ **WINE LIST** A concise but interesting list of Latin American and Spanish vintages with several fine selections, including a refreshing white albarino from Castel de Fornos and a versatile, cedary rioja from Spain's Martinez Lacuesta. The cocktails are expensive, but the classic mojito is potent and the Alma Colada irresistibly tasty.

■ **IF YOU GO** Dinner served Monday-Thursday 5-11 p.m., Friday-Saturday 5 p.m.-midnight, Sunday 5-10 p.m. Late-night menu served Monday-Thursday 11 p.m. to 12:30 a.m., Friday-Saturday midnight-1 a.m., Sunday 10-11 p.m. Dinner entrees $18-$31.

■ **RESERVATIONS** Reservations recommended.

■ **CREDIT CARDS** All major credit cards accepted but Discover.

■ **SMOKING** Smoking in the bar only (no cigars).

■ **HANDICAP ACCESSIBLE** Wheelchair accessible.

■ **PARKING** Valet parking costs $14.

Audrey Claire

The hip neighborhood BYOB has appealingly simple neo-Med comfort food.

udrey Taichman — a.k.a. Audrey Claire — commands the northwest corner of 20th and Spruce Streets with a cordless phone in one hand and a waiting list in the other.

The sidewalk in front of her hip little bistro is thick with young and beautiful would-be diners, waiting alongside some older Rittenhouse Square regulars with wine bottles in hand.

"Somebody's phone is ringing!" one says, sending half the crowd diving to the bottom of giant designer purses.

It's just another call for Taichman, who cheerily tells the caller, "The wait's about 45 minutes."

There is a hint of perky seduction in her voice that tames the hungry hordes around her. She calls herself "The Ringleader" and has

VERY GOOD

276 S. 20th St.,
Philadelphia
(215) 731-1222

NEIGHBORHOOD
Rittenhouse Square

CUISINE
Mediterranean

the political pluck of a Middle East peace negotiator. And so they will wait — happily — until she leads them through the austere and noisy little dining room to a narrow table made of planks, or the concrete counter that looks like a sidewalk, or to one of the outdoor cafe seats on the sloping Spruce Street sidewalk.

The menu here is appealing in its simplicity, with flavors borrowed from Italy to Israel adding a pomegranate spark or giant couscous kick to grilled fish, seafood or chicken. Salads

are light and creative. Entrees are almost always under $20. And desserts have a homespun goodness that is impossible to resist, down to the last crumb of Bubby's apple cake, made by Taichman's mom.

But Audrey Claire's success is as much about timing, niche and buzz as it is about food. If there were an untapped need in Center City for stylish but affordable neighborhood places, as well as sidewalk dining, Audrey Claire has filled it with aplomb since 1996. That's when the Toronto-born Taichman (whose middle name is Claire) used a small-business loan to rehab a dingy five-and-dime into this unlikely hot spot. Add just a smidgen more pretention, as Taichman subsequently did at her more polished second restaurant, the black-leather-clad Twenty Manning across the street, and it loses some of its appeal for me.

The bare-bones 45-seat room here, with an exposed kitchen at one end and inviting wrap-around windows, plays its minimal look to advantage. The passing street life, the tony Rittenhouse guests, the simple Mediterranean comfort food all took on an extra luster. A bucket of brilliant yellow flowers or a bowl of stacked lemons give this reclaimed corner the look of an interactive still life. No wonder Audrey Claire was an instant success.

Worthy competition has blossomed in Center City over the last three years, but this trend-setter has managed to sustain an overall quality and magnetic appeal that ranks it still among the city's best neighborhood spots.

The little restaurant does have some shortcomings. The service is pleasant but inconsistent, with a young staff that takes its casual jean and T-shirt attire a little too literally. They know the menu well, but have problems paying serious sustained attention to diners.

The kitchen, too, has its ups and downs. But it has made some noticeable improvements under Michael Salvitti, who took over the kitchen nearly three years ago. The ingredients seem a little finer, the flavors a little sharper, with more attention to local organic farms, but the menu has largely remained the same.

Salads are among the best in town, from the smoky romaine leaves of the odd-but-intriguing grilled Caesar to the tangle micro arugula dolloped with warm goat cheese studded with lentils. Bruschetta toasts came topped with grilled haloumi cheese, whose saltiness is matched by kalamata olives and capers. Luscious grilled shrimp had a lusty flavor against warm slices of creamy avocado.

Straightforward entrees were the best bets, with simple fillets of pepper-rimmed tuna coming out perfectly grilled. Herb-marinated chicken breast was moist and full of flavor. A pair of large soft-shell crabs brought an ideal taste of summer, surprisingly sweet and meaty, crisply sauteed with a garlicky wine butter rife with scallions, cilantro and mint. And the zuppa di pesce was one of the best variations on seafood stew I've tasted in a while. The heaping bowl of herby tomato broth filled with nicely cooked shrimp, scallops, mussels, squid and fish was also a fair value

Or Try These

Here are three other restaurants owned and run by women.

Susanna Foo

1512 Walnut St., Philadelphia
(215) 545-2666

Susanna Foo's exquisite French-Chinese cuisine set the city's long-standing benchmark for creative but natural fusion cooking.

Fork

306 Market St., Philadelphia
(215) 625-9425

This definitive Old City bistro has been through a series of good chefs, but it is the constant presence of co-owner Ellen Yin that gives Fork its professional polish.

White Dog Cafe

3420 Sansom St., Philadelphia
(215) 386-9224

Judy Wicks is the force behind this trailblazing University City institution, which blends social activism with creative organic cooking.

Audrey Claire is still among the city's best neighborhood spots.

at $18.50. A nest of pappardelle noodles brought an earthy saute of mushrooms and arugula in a delicate tan sauce.

The kitchen sometimes slipped. A pork tenderloin glazed in delicious pomegranate molasses was overcooked. And the feta-crusted lamb chops could have done with far less feta-crusting, which overwhelmed each delicate chop with a thick and tangy breading.

Those mistakes were easily forgotten, though, when it came to the desserts, which have an irresistible old-fashioned draw. Intense chocolate puddings ("pot de creme"), moist apple cake, caramelized, fruity upside-down pineapple cake, blueberry risotto rice pudding, and ethereally light white chocolate mousse. They all come accessorized, of course, with a cloud of home-whipped cream and a great corner view.

■ **MENU HIGHLIGHTS** Grilled Caesar salad; shrimp and avocado napoleon; arugula salad with figs and warm goat cheese; sauteed squid; grilled fish; grilled chicken breast; soft-shell crabs with herb and garlic butter; zuppa di pesce; pappardelle with mushrooms; chocolate pot de creme; white chocolate mousse; Bubby's apple cake; blueberry risotto.

■ **WINE LIST** BYOB.

■ **IF YOU GO** Dinner served Tuesday-Thursday 5:45-10 p.m., Friday-Saturday 5:45-10:30 p.m., Sunday 5:15-9:30 p.m. Closed Monday. Dinner entrees, $10.50-$19.

■ **RESERVATIONS** Accepted every night but Friday and Saturday.

■ **CREDIT CARDS** Not accepted.

■ **SMOKING** Entire dining room is nonsmoking.

■ **HANDICAP ACCESSIBLE** Yes.

■ **PARKING** Street parking only.

Azafran

The warm BYOB off South Street draws its inspiration from Latin America — even occasionally a hint of Italy, France and Asia.

 tiny strand of saffron, hand-plucked from the yawn of a purple crocus, is the world's most precious spice.

Just a pinch of this ancient Mediterranean ingredient, used in everything from paella to bouillabaisse, will spread its brilliant orange hue like a beam of warm sunlight. Though its own flavor is elusive, its presence magnifies the richness of anything it touches. Energizing. Exotic. Seductive.

It is little wonder, then, that a former florist named Susanna Goihman would want to name her restaurant Azafran, the Spanish word for saffron, as she learned to say it growing up in her mother's kitchen in Caracas, Venezuela.

VERY GOOD

617 S. Third St.
Philadelphia
(215) 928-4019

NEIGHBORHOOD
South Street

CUISINE
Nuevo Latino

What's surprising is how well Goihman, a first-time restaurateur, succeeded in conjuring the warmth of that spirit. Her charming little restaurant, a South American-flaired BYOB at Third and South Streets, fairly radiates the glow. Its walls are buffed a deep pumpkin orange, the terra cotta luster of pure, undiluted saffron. From the tiled floors to the mustard-colored tables painted with flowering vines, to the brick-oven hearth in the corner and the rhythmic, flamenco guitar of Gypsy Kings wafting in the air, the scene is set for the rustic Latin flavors to follow. Much of them, of course, will be tinted with azafran.

Moist shreds of pulled chicken bask in a piquant tomato-saffron marinade, plump with sweet raisins, olives and capers and ideally tangy next to a crisp and cheesy cornmeal arepa cake. Ground sirloin takes a similar cue inside the deep-fried empanada, a stuffing roused with cumin, and a Cuban sofrito of sauteed peppers, onions and garlic.

Azafran's kitchen was one of Center City's first restaurants five years ago to serve "Nuevo Latino" cooking, a wave that had its roots in Goihman's previous home base of Miami, where tropical products and the exotic flavors of Latin America whirled into the blender of contemporary culinary currents. The often-exciting results can compromise authenticity for the mainstream palate: a lighter egg-roll wrapper instead of the traditional empanada pastry; sweeter yellow plantains in the mashed fufu instead of the starchier green ones; healthier pulled chicken instead of beefy ropa vieja.

This would be a problem if Azafran were just another watered-down theme restaurant. But it isn't. The restaurant's wide-reaching menu, drawing inspiration from Venezuela, Cuba, Puerto Rico, Colombia, Argentina — even occasionally a hint of Italy, France and

Tres leches dessert served at Azafran.

Asia — reflects the diverse tables of Goihman's youth, the things she likes to eat.

The food has always been earnest and from the heart rather than trendy, with a focus on good flavors and fresh products. The addition of chef de cuisine Scott McLeod one year ago, however, represents a clear step up for this kitchen. A veteran of ¡Pasion!, McLeod has brought a polish and sophisticated vocabulary to the menu that Azafran's food never previously had.

A thick and juicy cut of blue marlin, for example, came crusted in coriander-scented rice then sauced in a light cream brushed with lemongrass. The garnish was a meal in its own, a delicate scallion crepe wrapped around Asian ratatouille. McLeod obviously learned a few advanced ceviche moves at ¡Pasion! One recent night's ceviche tasting brought house-smoked shrimp tossed with sweet Chinese black rice doused with a tangy vinaigrette. Tiny bay scallops cured in a citrus marinade infused with Thai basil also came with wedges of grapefruit that added bursts of sweet and sour juice to the mix.

The lemongrass-marinated grilled shrimp, which came skewered on a stick of sugar cane, was one disappointment. The shrimp were strangely mushy. But most of McLeod's offerings were a delight. A fine filet mignon, perfectly seared in a cast-iron pan, came topped with an tangy chimichurri cilantro puree to contrast the rich red wine demiglace. His anticuchos of grilled pork were impressive, the tender medallions of meat rubbed with a flavorful peanut adobo, then served with crunchy threads of green and red roasted pepper rajas. On the side, aioli sauce streaked across rounds of Peruvian potatoes stained vibrant yellow by a bouillon steeped with saffron. Of course.

McLeod has kept several of the standard dishes that made this restaurant a success to begin with, offering decent value for interesting food, and a lively, casual atmosphere — which also moves outdoors in the warm weather to Azafran's charming torch-lit back patio.

Azafran still serves a whole grilled fish with black beans and rice. The excellent citrus-marinated tuna steak remains, served with smashed sweet plantain fufu. The crisp calamari with simple pico de gallo salsa were as addictive as ever. And the pulled chicken with arepas were right on target, as were the excellent empanadas, which came with a sour cream greened with chopped cilantro.

I do miss the wonderful fried chicken breast topped with fresh arugula and tomato salad. But at least some of the restaurant's best desserts have remained. There are the churros, long, ridged sticks of deep-fried beignets that come with a dip of intensely dark bittersweet chocolate. And the tres leches is a must, a simple round of sponge cake soaked in a dairy elixir of heavy cream, condensed milk and evaporated milk. Topped with a cloud of hand-whipped cream, the cake — flavored with chocolate, banana or coffee — melts slowly on your tongue.

Fancy? No. But even as the kitchen here matures, this has always been the essence of Azafran. The simple pleasures of Goihman's heritage brought to your flower-painted table in proud, homey goodness. Like a tiny strand of saffron, its value can be far greater, and far more precious, than you'd ever expect.

Or Try These

Here are three other Nuevo Latino restaurants.

¡Pasion!

211 S. 15th St., Philadelphia
(215) 875-9895

A gorgeous addition has doubled the size of this Nuevo Latino gem, where Guillermo Pernot has evolved into one of the region's most virtuosic culinary creators

Alma de Cuba

1623 Walnut St., Philadelphia
(215) 988-1799

Douglas Rodriguez, the nation's godfather of Nuevo Latino cuisine, has paired with Stephen Starr to bring his culinary fireworks to this chic and dark Walnut Street space.

Cuba Libre

10 S. Second St., Philadelphia
(215) 627-0666

A fantasy dining room built to resemble an old Havana streetscape and an awesome rum list make this Old City nightspot worth a try, although the food has been inconsistent.

■ **MENU HIGHLIGHTS** Grilled pork anticuchos; empanadas; pulled chicken and arepa; tuna con fufu; filet mignon with chimichurri; rice-crusted blue marlin; churros with chocolate; tres leches.

■ **WINE LIST** BYOB.

■ **IF YOU GO** Dinner served Sunday, Tuesday-Thursday 5-10 p.m., Friday-Saturday 5-11 p.m. Closed Monday. Dinner entrees, $13-$22.

■ **RESERVATIONS** Not accepted.

■ **CREDIT CARDS** All major cards but Discover.

■ **SMOKING** Dining room is nonsmoking.

■ **HANDICAP ACCESSIBLE** One small step at the entrance.

■ **PARKING** Street parking only.

Birchrunville Store Cafe

The charming country-store-turned-restaurant is a sunny and sophisticated expression of its chef's French and Italian roots.

I know of many great chefs who tire of the urban pace, the relentless hours and churning volume and bureaucratic headaches of managing staff.

Wouldn't it be nice to find a little place in the country? A spot where life is calm, the hours are human, and the focus once again is on creating lovely food? An herb garden out back and a pleasant porch in the front, where regulars can sway on rocking chairs and smell the crisp and starry night air. And there you have the Birchrunville Store Cafe. At least, when it isn't also in use as the local post office.

At 40, Francis Trzeciak might seem a little young to be retiring to Chester County, to a BYOB cash-only cafe limited to serving five nights of dinner each week. But Frenchmen begin their trade early, at age 14. So, after more than two decades in kitchens from his native Aix-en-Provence to northern Italy, to Philadelphia's Monte Carlo Living Room, Taquet, and most recently Provence, Trzeciak can hardly be blamed for falling into a bucolic trance three-and-a-half years ago.

EXCELLENT

Hollow and Flowing
Spring Roads
Birchrunville, Pa.
(610) 827-9002

NEIGHBORHOOD
Chester County

CUISINE
Modern French

Even in the early darkness of a winter afternoon, it's easy to sense the rustic allure of this far-flung idyll, 40 or so miles from Center City. Stone walls line the curling roads. Pretty churches landmark the route. Alleyways of tall trees cast their shadows over rolling fields of moneyed, horsey land. And when you descend the final hairpin onto Flowing Spring Road, darned if you don't hear that spring a-babbling.

A trip to Birchrunville, though, is more than a pleasant drive. More even than a cozy seat at a wooden table in a lace-trimmed dining room painted the color of pumpkin, where the air is perfumed with candles melting in sconces. Trzeciak's cooking, a sunny and sophisticated expression of his French and Italian roots, is absolutely the best part of the journey.

Highlighting good natural flavors and quality seasonal ingredients, the menu is limited to the daily variations on some classic rustic flavors.

On a recent summer visit, his plates burst with exuberance and warmth. A leg of rabbit was stuffed with an herby green mousse, then sliced into succulent medallions over lightly creamed matsutake mushrooms. A dainty fillet of bronzino was set atop ratatouille flambeed with bourbon.

The delicate local greens that festooned his plates were so fresh, they barely needed dressing. Just a swab of mache leaves in a tart vinaigrette made of dried tomatoes added a gentle leafy crunch to the quivering puff of a goat cheese souffle and a caramelized chunk of roasted pear. A nest of tiny herbs delivered a more peppery, bitter pique, striking the right contrast to the lemony emulsion that glazed a pristine carpaccio of tuna, salmon and grouper.

An old gas pump in front of the Birchrunville Store Cafe is a reminder that the city is miles away.

Fresh figs arrived roasted, like tiny volcanos oozing molten gorgonzola out of their tops. I sliced them open, and savored the salty cream as it basted the warm and pulpy sweet fruit.

With his garden in full summer bloom, Trzeciak's powers seemed at their height. But late fall is game time, and as I recall from earlier visits, the chef offered some keepers then too. A tender chop of venison came on an elegantly bending bone, glazed with black currants steeped in shiraz wine. Thick rounds of moist wild boar were stuffed with soft roasted garlic, then ringed in a crisp collar of pancetta that brought out just the right hint of herby pig. Mussels infused the brandied saffron cream of a silky bisque with a flavorful but measured reminder of the sea.

Trzeciak is fond of painting plates with colorful oils and vinegar, swirling red pepper purees and vibrant green streaks beneath splatters of balsamic black. But these vinaigrettes were usually more than frivolous decoration, adding layered tones of freshness to otherwise simple dishes.

At times, though, the kitchen's plates were a little too precious. A salad of watercress and shrimp, mounded into a crisped parmesan cheese tuile basket with crumbled goat cheese and raspberry vinaigrette was so overconstructed, it tasted less than the sum of its parts.

More often, however, this kitchen offered familiar flavors that sang in true harmony.

A thick pink slice of foie gras terrine baked in Sauternes wine, richer and more creamy than any butter, was sparked by a honeyed marmalade of onions in red wine.

Mustard-brushed rack of lamb was a tender vision of moist meat, sided with interesting risottos, greened with herby mint or touched with earthy truffle and porcini. Excellent cuts of filet mignon received equal respect. On one occasion, it arrived glazed with slices of melted brie and ringed with herby oil; on another, it was mounded with meaty wild mushrooms and Dijon cream.

While a talented chef such as Trzeciak can carry a kitchen this size with barebones help, finding skilled service in the country can be an insurmountable challenge. Considering this, he has found and trained an excellent group of young servers from the area, whose down-to-earth demeanor meant casual service, but in no way compromised these refined dishes.

They knew the menu well, and even had a charming manner of stripping unnecessary pretense from the meal. When we asked to hear the desserts again, our server said it more clearly: "Basically, this one's a fancy Butterscotch Krimpet and that one's a fancy Kit-Kat bar."

Homespun and right on. I could not better describe these favorite confections myself. Except to add that the moist butterscotch cake was crowned with delicious homemade butterscotch gelato and that the Kit-Kat's hazelnut crunch was padded with a silky chocolate ganache.

Of course, there can be no pretense when the rest rooms are locat-

Or Try These

Here are three other restaurants in Chester County.

La Encina

2 Waterview Rd., East Goshen, Pa. (610) 918-9715

Authentic and elegant Spanish cuisine in a pleasant Chester County BYOB.

Gilmore's

133 E. Gay St., West Chester, Pa. (610) 431-2800

A charming converted townhouse in downtown West Chester is now home to the French cuisine of former Le Bec-Fin chef Peter Gilmore.

Simon Pearce on the Brandywine

1333 Lenape Rd., West Chester, Pa. (610) 793-0948

Watch the artisan glass-blowing, then head upstairs for creative regional American cooking with some Irish accents that has improved over time.

Venison chop with a reduction of blackberries and shiraz.

ed through the door across the front porch, beside a wall of postal boxes.

"Do you suppose it's a real post office?" said one curious woman, charmed by what in Center City would no doubt be a prop.

Hey, the chef has moved to a small country town. How else is he going to get mail?

■ **MENU HIGHLIGHTS** Goat cheese souffle salad; fish carpaccio with citrus emulsion; foie gras pate; butternut squash bisque; mussel bisque; stuffed rabbit leg; rack of lamb; venison chop; garlic-stuffed boar; chocolate-hazelnut crunch tort; butterscotch cake.

■ **WINE LIST** BYOB.

■ **IF YOU GO** Dinner served Wednesday-Saturday 6-9 p.m. Entrees, $22-$25.

■ **RESERVATIONS** Required.

■ **CREDIT CARDS** Not accepted. Cash or check only.

■ **SMOKING** Dining room is nonsmoking, except late at night if no one objects.

■ **HANDICAP ACCESSIBLE** No. There are three steps at the entrance and the bathrooms are not handicap accessible.

■ **PARKING** Free lot.

Bistro St. Tropez

The continued appeal of this upbeat bistro is understandable, and not just for its Schuylkill view.

t is 7:22 p.m., daylight saving time, and the blue whales that float to my right above the Schuylkill are turning golden as the sun begins to dip behind 30th Street Station.

From this perch in the Hudson Room of Bistro St. Tropez, glassed in behind the wide fourth-floor windows of the Marketplace Design Center, friends have told me wistfully that you can see Paris if you squint.

I take another chilly sip of my dry martini and put this vista to the test: The river shimmers Seine-like in the dimming dusk, edged by a double-decked expressway blur of red taillights speeding home; commuter trains glide across a stony, arched bridge and disappear behind the 30th Street Station's billowing flags and stately columns; and in the distance, the Museum of Art sits on a leafy rise, radiating the warmth of sandstone-colored walls still hot from the afternoon.

VERY GOOD

Marketplace Design
Center, 2400 Market St.
Philadelphia
(215) 569-9269

NEIGHBORHOOD
Center City

CUISINE
French Bistro

It is a glorious view. But I am not thinking now of Paris. After 18 months away from this city, I've come to this perch and am struck by how beautiful Philadelphia can be. Its monuments as grand as ever. Its arteries pulsing with gritty, urban life. Another workday drawing to a close.

So I down the martini and wait skeptically for my meal. Too often, a view is just about the only decent thing a well-posed restaurant has served.

But what follows is a surprise. A cup-size tower of lobster souffle arrives topped with a marvelous black crust of minced olives. A thick fillet of wild striped bass is sheathed in thin shingles of potato, sandwiching a layer of olives and goat cheese against the moist white fish. Homemade nougat glace for dessert is just as good, dense and ice-cream-like, with finely chopped praline and candied fruit inside, echoing a bright raspberry sauce spooned on the plate. Even the stainless-steel cup of espresso, a perfect shot of crema-topped La Colombe, is on the mark.

On this weekday evening, St. Tropez's trapezoid-shaped tables are sparsely populated, lending the restaurant's two stylish dining rooms

— a vivid collage of '70s retro, silver lame curtains, and the vivid colors of Provence — the air of a secluded enclave. In fact, just finding the restaurant at night amid the vast corridors of Marketplace's darkened showroom windows demands a certain sense of adventure. That might explain the two prosecutors at the bar, indiscreetly blabbing the juicy details of their wiretapping case. But it could have been their glasses of Lillet talking.

Or Try These

Here are three other restaurants with a view.

La Veranda

Pier 3, N. Columbus Blvd.
Philadelphia (215) 351-1898
Sit with a dockside view of a Delaware River marina at this upscale, old-world Italian restaurant, where salt-baked whole fish and Tuscan wood-fired steaks are specialties.

Rouge

205 S. 18th St.(Rittenhouse Claridge), Philadelphia (215) 732-6622
The poodle people and the glamour crowd come to nibble chef Michael Yeamans' surprisingly fine modern bistro fare, but the sights of Rittenhouse Square are the biggest draw to this see-and-be-seen cafe.

Founders

Park Hyatt at the Bellevue, 200 S. Broad St., Philadelphia (215) 790-2814
The rotunda-topped dining room has spectacular penthouse views, weekend dancing, and some excellent upscale fare, from crab cakes to bouillabaisse. Institutional service, though, can make the *grande dame* feel flat.

For the bustling lunchtime set, you're more likely to spy your decorator among the nibblers, waving swatches of taffeta or flipping through sofa catalogs gathered from the purveyors downstairs. Lured by abundant Nicoise salads with fresh grilled tuna, plates of sweet roasted red peppers, and sandwiches stuffed with everything from fresh mozzarella to filet mignon with almond brie, the designer crowd has been at the heart of the bistro's success ever since owner-chef Patrice Rames, a St. Tropez native, opened for lunch and catering here almost 16 years ago.

Dinner soon followed, and the Hudson Room was added, named in honor of the automobile factory that once operated in the building (the old car ramp, by the way, still winds its wide way down to the ground floor.) But a main ingredient to Rames' success has been the consistency with which his kitchen turns out his thoughtful take on French bistro fare at fair prices, whether it is duck confit, cassoulet, or a wide range of deftly prepared seafood.

After a couple of satisfying revisits this summer, the continued appeal of this upbeat bistro is understandable. A cream of asparagus soup du jour was light, but completely infused with the fresh flavor of green spring. The cool gazpacho was crunchy and refreshing, zippy with a spark of garlic.

Freshly peeled baby artichoke hearts were stewed barigoule-style, glazed in an intriguingly spiced dark gravy over grilled croutons. A

The dining room of Bistro St. Tropez provides a view that can remind a visitor how beautiful Philadelphia can be.

fricassee of mushrooms came in a lidded oblong crock, bathed in a frothingly rich cream sauce fragrant with truffle. Tender tubes of squid were flashed on the grill then scattered over mixed greens with a simple dressing of olive oil and lemon juice.

The entrees were also impressive. A hearty bowl of bouillabaisse brought a bounty of shellfish, head-on shrimp, monkfish and a boney cross-section of whole red snapper, a rustic touch that I appreciated in such a stylish spot. The garlicky rouille mayonnaise on the side was laced with threads of saffron. The braised fennel with the tuna could have been more tender, but the coriander-crusted fish was so delicious with its tangy tomato confit, we devoured it fennel and all.

The crab omelette, however, was one of the stranger egg dishes I've seen, an all-white disk wrapped around unadorned crab and undercooked spears of asparagus. It was clearly missing a sauce to bind the flavors, but I hesitated to complain. Our server had already cheerfully replaced the first omelette — an even stranger one stuffed with fish — that had been brought to us by mistake.

I've had mixed luck with the service here in the past, especially on busy weekend nights. But the present lunch crew couldn't have been more delightful. They were attentive and very helpful with the menu and wine list, a largely French selection that boasts some lesser-known producers.

St. Tropez's beautifully presented desserts were among the most satisfying dishes we encountered. Favorites included the cold Grand Marnier souffle, a simple cousin to the wonderful nougat glace, but laced with an irresistible dose of orange liqueur. An individual pear tarte came over buttery puff pastry topped with irresistible praline ice cream.

It is not until we clean these final plates, though, that I realize our inspiring river view has slipped away. But for a restaurant as well posed as Bistro St. Tropez, the fact that we'd hardly noticed it happen was a very good sign indeed. The dining room's wide picture windows now reflected like mirrors the tantalizing tableau of a vibrant and well-fed world inside.

■ **MENU HIGHLIGHTS** Galette decrabe; artichokes barigoules; pate; duck confit; gazpacho; cream of asparagus soup; grilled squid; mushroom fricassee; nicoise salad; coriander-crusted tuna; potato-crusted striped bass; bouillabaisse; Grand Marnier souffle; pear tarte with praline ice cream.

■ **WINE LIST** Well-stocked with several interesting and affordable French vintages.

■ **IF YOU GO** Lunch served Monday-Friday 11 a.m.-3 p.m.; dinner served Wednesday-Thursday 5:30-9:30 p.m., Friday-Saturday 5:30-10:30 p.m. Entrees: lunch, $7.25-$14.95; dinner, $15.95-$23.95. A three-course $20.02 prix-fixe menu is available before 6:30 p.m.

■ **RESERVATIONS** Recommended for weekends about two weeks in advance.

■ **CREDIT CARDS** All major cards but Discover.

■ **SMOKING** Smoking in the bar dining room only.

■ **HANDICAP ACCESSIBLE** Yes.

■ **PARKING** Parking costs $5 in Red Cross parking lot at 23d and Market. Validated discounts in adjacent parking structure.

The Black Sheep

The handsomely upscaled Irish pub serves great, updated pub fare, premium whiskeys, and the city's best Guinness.

have yet to find an Irish pub that didn't claim to draw the best pint of Guinness. But the classically handsome Black Sheep on South 17th Street is not just bragging.

Over the years, I've heard talk of wooden kegs versus steel, special basement cold rooms, state-of-the-art cooling towers, pure nitrogen infusers, and hotshot bartenders whose stout was so creamy they could sign their names in the foamy head.

I had also heard of old-country doctors prescribing pints for iron deficiency. And, come to think of it, I was feeling a wee bit anemic the other night.

So as I waited and waited and waited for a table, mulling the possibilities of a hearty lamb stew or a fragrant bowl of mussels or a pastry-topped crock of chicken pot pie, I put the Black Sheep's Guinness to the test.

VERY GOOD

247 S. 17th St.
(at Latimer)
Philadelphia
(215) 545-9473

NEIGHBORHOOD
Rittenhouse Square

CUISINE
Updated Irish Pub

The head of my pint was an ivory blank slate, no signatures or clover stamps. But the midnight-dark elixir that filled the tall glass had me brimming over with words. Cool and rich, the thick liquid washed down with an extra creaminess that defied its ebony color. Its flavor reminded me of coffee, chocolate, and the woody cream of a root-beer shake. Its subtle effervescence lingered, and I was a believer — cured, if only momentarily, of that small iron problem.

I was also ready for dinner. But our table wasn't ready. Shall I get another? Why not?

One can expect such excellent stout from the two Irish barkeeps, Matt Kennedy and James Stephens, who teamed with Gene LeFevre to open this pub near Rittenhouse Square. Kennedy's long tenure at the Dickens Inn (now the Dark Horse) is also evident in the impressive whiskey collection the bar has acquired, including some rare Irish, to go with its high-end single-malt Scotch.

The crowds that continue to swarm the Black Sheep are as much a testament to its good looks as to its quality draft. Renovated from the vacant shell of an old gay bar, the gorgeous brick townhouse has been transformed with a solid red door and window trim to match,

One of the owners, Matt Kennedy, draws a pint of Guiness beer.

warm oak wainscoting, an antique fireplace mantel, glowing mica sconces, and lacquered walls that feel like old tooled leather.

There are Celtic knots scrolling under ceiling beams, but hardly a neon shamrock to be found. There aren't any leprechauns, either, but plenty of well-coiffed Wharton students looking like Minnie Driver or Gwyneth Paltrow, flipping hair in the corner booths.

Up to the calmer second-floor dining room, a more diverse neighborhood crowd finds its way, often still in post-work corporate garb. But they are just as guilty as the students of nursing their drinks as we hungrily look on from the bar, coveting their tables.

No doubt, what has set the Black Sheep a notch higher than most pubs is food far better than might be expected. But what's the point of finding a good chef when the drinkers crowd out the eaters? When the servers have a hard enough time remembering to bring you water, let alone smile on occasion? Ours was so sullen, I hesitated even to ask for the check.

The solution can be a delicate one for the Sheep to manage as it juggles being both a drinking and dining destination, but for now, a few extra pints did fine, smoothing a wait that was worth it.

The kitchen does a fine job of bridging the divide between pub grub and fine dining, with a menu that pays as much quality attention to onion rings as it does to the slow-roasted chicken, which emerges from the gentle heat crisp and succulent over a medley of root vegetables.

While the kitchen is hardly perfect — the crab cakes are consistently bready, the steak salad chewy, the desserts somewhat uninspired — the majority of my meals were a delight. And almost always at less than $20 an entree, they were also fairly priced.

Little details made the difference in bar foods I had long taken for granted. Calamari and shrimp were crisped in a greaseless cornmeal crust with deep-fried leaves of basil. But it was the homemade tartar sauce, thick with minced capers and onions, that made the calamari impossible to stop eating.

Homemade mayonnaise enlivened with red pepper fed my onion-ring addiction. Or perhaps it was the golden beer-batter crust, which also graced hand-sliced cod for fish and chips with its satisfyingly sweet crunch.

The "hot, hot" chicken wings were meaty but merely "hot," with a gentle tingle that lingered on the lips. But the jalapeno mussels did the trick, causing my head to sweat without totally burning flavor out of the shellfish. Another rendition of mussels, these pooled in a delicious coconut-milk curry, have an addictive balance of spice and sweetness that makes them a candidate for the city's best.

A garnish of spicy pickled carrots gave the silky hummus dip an extra dimension. A light hand on the dressing made the blue cheese salad a success. A hint of garlic sneakily infused the juices of the Black Sheep's big burger.

The lamb carbonnade was probably one of the ugliest dishes I've been served, a platter of brown stew gravied over a mountain of garlic potatoes. But it was a meal in itself that I've come to crave, with tender chunks of lamb softened in ale with morsels of melting root vegetables.

Other entrees were as handsome as can be. A rich crock of chicken pot pie was topped with a golden brown lid of flaky puff pastry. A perfect chop of tender pork was marked with a

Or Try These

These are three other restaurants with Irish accents.

The Plough and the Stars

123 Chestnut St.,Philadelphia
(215) 733-0300

Great Guinness and Irish-influenced French cuisine are the draws to this beautifully rehabbed, dramatic Old City bank space.

The Bards

2013 Walnut St., Philadelphia
(215) 569-9585

Fabulous brown bread, shepherd's pie and stuffed chicken anchor the menu, and live Celtic music fills the Sunday morning air at this pleasant wood-trimmed pub.

Twenty21

2005 Market St., Philadelphia
(215) 851-6262

The old Cutter's has been purchased by its former managers and redesigned into an upscale American grill with Irish notes, from barley risotto to whiskey creme brulee. The room is still huge, but excellent service and a fine bar soften the corporate edge.

crisscross grill, then splashed with a rosemary-orange glaze.

Early problems with dessert seemed to be making up ground. A recent slice of chocolate layer cake was a stunningly moist eight-layer knockout.

Fortunately for this pub, though, there's already plenty of icing on the Guinness to make any evening happily sip away.

■ **MENU HIGHLIGHTS** Mussels in either coconut-milk curry or spicy pepperoni sauce; fried calamari; hummus; onion rings; burgers; chicken pot pie; slow-roasted chicken; grilled pork chop; lamb chops; lamb carbonnade; fish and chips.

■ **WINE LIST** Stick with beers such as the exceptionally creamy Guinness or the lemony, clove-scented Paulaner. The Black Sheep's whiskey selection is also superb, with more than 25 single-malt Scotches and a collection of premium Irish whiskeys, from single-malt Bushmills to an awesomely smooth 15-year-old Jameson.

■ **IF YOU GO** Lunch served Monday-Friday 11:30 a.m.-2:30 p.m. Dinner served Sunday-Thursday 5-10 p.m., Friday-Saturday 5-11 p.m. Bar menu available Sunday-Thursday 2:30 p.m.- midnight, Friday-Saturday 2:30 p.m.-1 a.m. Sunday brunch served 11:30 a.m.-3 p.m. Dinner entrees, $7.50 to $21

■ **RESERVATIONS** Accepted only for parties of eight or more.

■ **CREDIT CARDS** All major cards but Diners Club and Discover.

■ **SMOKING** Second floor is nonsmoking until 11 p.m.

■ **HANDICAP ACCESSIBLE** No. There are four steps to the first-floor dining room, and the rest rooms are not handicapped accessible.

■ **PARKING** Street parking only.

Blue Angel

The gorgeous Belle Epoque-style French bistro occupies an unusually elegant place in Stephen Starr's lineup of concepts.

My real estate agent — true to form — has rustled us from table to table in the Blue Angel as if conducting a whirlwind open-house tour.

First there was the booth in front (intimate, but too close to the door). Then there was the cozy red banquette beneath the train-car luggage rack that runs along the wall (cute, but drafty). Then, finally, there was the table we settled on, a modest wooden round centered on the mosaic-floored throat of this gorgeous hall.

Even on the previously doornail-dead 700 block of Chestnut Street, this was prime real estate. Surrounded on all sides by polished tiles and mirrors, lit from above by a stained-glass ceiling that shimmered with tiny lights, the dining room strummed around us with an almost cinematic energy. Air-kisses and frites for everyone!

EXCELLENT

706 Chestnut St.
Philadelphia
(215) 925-6889

NEIGHBORHOOD
Washington Square

CUISINE
French Bistro

My agent is waving "hi!" to a swath of ladies in matching fur and Prada. Meanwhile, through a Gauloise haze at the end of the zinc bar, denizens of the La Colombe coffee cartel are settling into a booth, lending their hip Gallic stamp to the Frenchness of the place.

Heads turn to gossip when former Nicky Scarfo lawyer Bobby Simone walks in. Then they swivel again when Stephen Starr makes his entrance — out of breath on a mad dash, practically panting to keep up with a restaurant empire that seems to be growing weekly. Two of those restaurants — Morimoto and Jones — he would subsequently build on this block.

While there is no disputing its heavy theme, the Blue Angel occupies an unusually elegant place in Starr's lineup of concepts. The decor is beautiful without too many design gimmicks — much of it was renovated from the space that was Stan's King of Sandwiches. And not only is this one of his few non-Asian-inspired menus, it has always been rooted in a classical culinary repertoire rather than a fusion fantasy.

This has been somewhat limiting to the ambitious chefs that have manned the stoves here, from Peter Dunmire and Shola Unloyu to Francesco Martorella. But Starr may have found the perfect match with his present chef, Michael Kanter.

I first encountered the Kanter at the super posh La Jonquille in Devon, the now-closed French/Persian palace where his inventive haute-cuisine and brasserie fare was among the most refined I've seen from a young chef. But it is obvious from my recent meals at Blue Angel that Kanter, who worked several years on the line at Le Bec-Fin, is comfortable in the milieu of traditional French cooking, where a few well-placed tweaks and a nose for good ingredients goes a long way toward giving the bistro fare here an uncommon polish.

Kanter's rendition of frog's legs, for example, brought those plump little nuggets smartly deboned, tempura fried, and napped with a truffled cream. His escargot, served in a miniature copper pot with hazelnuts and a chartreuse-champagne butter, was an obvious nod to the Georges Perrier standard.

I didn't love the croque monsieur – too much brioche and ham, not enough oozy cheese. But usually, he knew just when to play the standards straight. His French onion soup was ideal, a crock of rich brown broth filled with sweetly caramelized onions and sealed beneath a lid of molten cheese.

Twin fillets of trout meuniere were as perfect as I've tasted, delicately crisped and set beside a raft of asparagus in lemon caper butter. Steak-frites, the quintessential bistro pop-quiz, rose on the flavor of an amazing cut of l'onglet, a char-kissed chunk of hanger steak that melted beneath a pat of herby maitre d' butter. Salmon-frites gave the standard a lighter modern take, subbing a perfectly sauteed piece of fish to equal effect. A glaze of grainy mustard-flecked cream and an unruly fistful of amazingly delicious fries were the perfect one-two garnish.

It would be wrong, however, to label this menu boring simply because it is rooted in the bistro canon. Kanter has a number of dishes that indulge his creative contemporary impulses nicely. A recent

Or Try These

Here are three other French bistro-inspired restaurants.

Bistro St. Tropez
Marketplace Design Center,
2400 Market St., Philadelphia
(215) 569-9269
An upbeat bistro with a fantastic Schuylkill view, St. Tropez has a stylish, retro decor befitting its location in the Marketplace Design Center and a creative take on French cuisine at reasonable prices.

Pif
1009 S. Eighth St., Philadelphia
(215) 625-2923
A charming little BYOB serving French bistro fare inspired by the chef's daily shopping in the nearby Italian Market.

Beau Monde
624 S. Sixth St. Philadelphia
(215) 592-0656
A Queen Village cafe that offers authentic buckwheat crepes in a beautiful room with gilt paneling, mosaic hearth and sidewalk seating.

Tuna au poivre, with a shadow in the background spelling out "Blue Angel."

special salad of fresh baby bok choy leaves topped with saffron vinaigrette and tempura-fried calamari was a wonderful tableau of fresh ingredients and clever contrasts. His variations on ravioli have been sublime, stuffing those delicate pasta skins one day with silky butternut squash, then turning in mid-summer to an airy, mousse-like stuffing of crabmeat sauced with a delicate tomato provencale.

His fish preparations have also been superb, dusting a special sea bass with a "crust" of citrus zest that added a lemony zing without overwhelming the fish, and siding a nicely crisped red snapper with creamy polenta and a rich red zinfandel sauce.

The apron-clad servers have been consistently pleasant and attentive, although some surprising inexperience was obvious at a recent lunch when our server awkwardly read us specials and descriptions of the wines by the glass verbatim from handheld notes.

With talented pastry chef Sonjia Spector filling our table with sweet wonders, though, I couldn't be bothered to nit-pick the service. Strawberry crepes were topped with lemony ricotta ice cream. A layer of apricot jam added a ribbon of tartness through the decadent chocolate of Sachertorte. A round of bread pudding filled with pears and sundried cherries basked in an addictive white chocolate sauce. And those flaky, buttery, sugar-glazed triangular pastries known as turnovers absolutely seduced me with their country fruit comfort – a luscious stuffing of spiced dark cherries.

In a room full of diversions, this must be the ultimate test. Look up for the first time in two hours and notice once again the stunning twinkle of the restored glass ceiling. Scan the banquettes for another eyeful of glitz. Know that you are sitting on a block of Chestnut Street that never promised much until Stephen Starr walked into a sandwich shop one day and waved his wand, turning dead space into a real estate coup. And still, my greatest satisfaction at the Blue Angel doesn't come from snagging the perfect table. It comes from polishing off a classic meal well done.

■ **MENU HIGHLIGHTS** Escargots; wild mushroom and asiago tart; frogs legs fricassee; lump crab ravioli; French onion soup; raw bar; trout meuniere; pan-seared salmon; steak frites; seared snaper; citrus-crusted sea bass; cherry turnovers; sacher torte; pear and cherry bread pudding; petit fours plate.

■ **WINE LIST** The one-page list of exclusively French bottles is largely under $40, with a wide variety of affordable wines — Chablis, Sancerre, Chinon, Gigondas — that typify a bistro cellar. There is also a nice selection of Belgian and French beers.

■ **IF YOU GO** Lunch served Monday-Friday 11:30 a.m.-4 p.m. Dinner served Sunday-Wednesday 5-11 p.m., Thursday-Saturday 5-midnight. Sunday brunch served 11 a.m.-3 p.m.

■ **RESERVATIONS** Highly recommended on weekends.

■ **CREDIT CARDS** All major cards but Discover.

■ **SMOKING** There is a nonsmoking section.

■ **HANDICAP ACCESSIBLE** Yes.

■ **PARKING** Lot across the street costs $5 with validated ticket.

Brasserie Perrier

Top-notch upscale contemporary dining in back
and a more casual French brasserie menu in the
lively front lounge both spell quality.

They met over a perfect omelette.

A fluff of beaten eggs may not sound like the sort of haute-cuisine acrobatics a legendary chef would take note of. But Georges Perrier is an omelette connoisseur, a man who knows that perfection is sometimes hardest to achieve in the simplest things.

So when Perrier had lunch at the Germantown Cricket Club in 1995 and saw before him The Ideal Omelette — light and puffy, with two nicely rounded folds and not a speck of brown — he marched into the kitchen to shake the hand of a young chef named Chris Scarduzio.

Scarduzio would help launch Brasserie Perrier six years ago this January as executive sous-chef to then-chef Francesco Martorella. Now heading up the kitchen himself, he handles the job in much the same way he approached his omelettes, quietly but with a proficiency that dazzles by understatement.

EXCELLENT

1619 Walnut St.
Philadelphia
(215) 568-3000

NEIGHBORHOOD
Rittenhouse Square

CUISINE
Modern French

The house-smoked salmon is a study in micro perfections, with just the right texture, an elegant touch of smokiness, and a garnish of heavenly potato blinis that melts on the tongue. A choucroute steeped in beer and juniper berries and topped with crispy duck confit and wonderful sausages is one of the best versions of the Alsatian sauerkraut dish I've ever had.

Meanwhile, a lobster-risotto appetizer avoids becoming an Asian fusion cliche. Chinese five-spice powder adds only an exotic whisper to the succulent sauteed lobster tail, harmonizing with the squash that enriches the sublimely light rice.

Going easy on the Asian accents has been one of Scarduzio's mandates as Brasserie Perrier continues to emerge from an identity crisis that has hampered it from the beginning. Perrier may have desired an $18-entree French restaurant when he conceived of the project. But the restaurant that debuted with jagged art-deco rooms, fancy leather booths, crackle-glass mirrors, and a $30-plus fusion menu was far too upscale and trendy to be an honest French brasserie.

It has since undergone a slow but steady retrofitting, with an affordable under-$20 bistro menu installed in the lounge and a recent renovation that finally opened the front windows (à la Rouge).

I sense that Perrier has finally found the brasserie he desired in this bar — boisterous, affordable and distinctly French — and that the fine dining in the back rooms merely pays the bills. Yet that notion doesn't do justice to the achievements of the restaurant, which through it all has remained one of the city's finest, even as it searches for the perfect balance of its homey and "haute" impulses.

The lobster-risotto appetizer avoids becoming an Asian fusion cliche. Chinese five-spice powder adds only an exotic whisper to the succulent sauteed lobster tail.

It hasn't always been easy to carve a clear identity for this restaurant in the shadow of Le Bec-Fin down the street, and it lost a bit of the spotlight two years ago when Perrier opened his third restaurant, Le Mas Perrier, in Wayne.

But that hasn't affected quality. The service is consummately professional, with smart, personable servers who seem to enjoy what they're doing, whether passing free hors d'oeuvres during happy hour ("Foie gras dumplings, anyone? Tuna tartare?") or pondering a perfect wine pairing from the excellent (though pricey) cellar.

With a few exceptions — some chewy steamed clams and an overwrought napoleon of hot scallops atop cold crab salad — Scarduzio's cooking during my visits was divine.

Pillowy gnocchi came scattered with fistfuls of lobster meat one night; another night they mingled with delicate bolognese meat sauce. Excellent ravioli tempered the luxury of their truffled mushroom cream sauce with the rustic oomph of smoked mozzarella and a crisped sheet of salty prosciutto. A thickly sliced terrine that layered goat cheese between thin sheets of potato offered the perfect contrast of richness to peppery arugula salad.

The restaurant's lounge menu is a great bargain, but with some caveats. For one, you have to ask for it. And the lounge often has a thick cigarette haze (which gives it that authentic French brasserie touch). But I'd brave a little smoke for the superb $14 steak frites, or the succulent ham-and-pesto-stuffed chicken breast over rosemary-sauced spaetzle, or the gingery crab sui mei dumplings that are a legacy of Brasserie's fusion roots.

The Asian flavors haven't entirely been banished. Scarduzio is simply determined to use them as accents rather than main themes. And some of his best efforts make the case.

The duck-leg confit and seared breast entree, for example, is basically a French dish perfumed with star anise and served over coconut sticky rice. The flavors are evocative but not cloying. A fillet of black bass is seared crisp with a soy-cornstarch crust, posed over nutty purple rice, and then ringed by a deeply flavored ginger sauce.

Scarduzio's more traditional French dishes are equally refined. The juicy veal chop is served with a translucent ring of buttery potatoes Anna. Tender braised beef short ribs practically melt into mashed potatoes and their soulfully dark gravy. Butter-soft filet mignon is regally paired with a potato cake and wild mushrooms.

The Friday night special of bouillabaisse is a cornucopia of perfectly cooked seafood in a rich saffron broth. Another special brought two fillets of turbot, seared golden, over a bed of creamy chive polenta that I still dream about.

The desserts do a nice job of carrying the dual theme forward, his menu marrying perfect classics such as creme brulee and molten chocolate cake with more inventive creations. Coconut panna cotta. Caramelized banana tart. Chocolate ice cream spiked with fresh ginger juice. Strawberries stuffed with tomato-apple marmalade.

Perhaps my most serious complaint is the restaurant's habit of sending on-time parties into the bar with the "your table will be ready

Or Try These

Here are three other French-influenced restaurants with contemporary cooking.

Blue Angel
706 Chestnut St., Philadelphia
(215) 925-6889
Gorgeous Belle Epoque-style French bistro with polished renditions of the classics.

Rouge
205 S. 18th St. (Rittenhouse Claridge), Philadelphia
(215) 732-6622
The poodle people and the glamour crowd come to nibble chef Michael Yeamans' surprisingly fine modern bistro fare, but the sights of Rittenhouse Square are the biggest draw to this see-and-be-seen cafe.

Caribou Cafe
1126 Walnut St., Philadelphia
(215) 625-9535
This handsome cafe convenient to the theater district has had a steady string of inconsistent chefs. But the bar and sidewalk seating are irresistibly attractive, and several recent menu items boded well for a promising pre-theater nibble.

in 15 minutes" line. Then again, when the wait stretched to nearly half an hour and the host offered us drinks on the house, I opted for a 30-year-old Macallan Scotch. And I was grateful that this brasserie-in-progress maintains its top-shelf pleasures so nicely.

■ **MENU HIGHLIGHTS** Five-spice lobster over butternut squash risotto; potato and goat cheese terrine; smoked-cheese ravioli; seafood plateau; steak frites; choucroute; crispy black bass; stuffed chicken; coconut panna cotta.

■ **WINE LIST** A substantial cellar of French and California vintages leans more toward big-ticket expense-account wines than the versatile, affordable selections of a true brasserie.

■ **IF YOU GO** Lunch served Monday-Saturday 11:30 a.m.-2:30 p.m. Dinner, Monday-Tuesday 5:30-10 p.m.; Wednesday-Thursday 5:30-10:30 p.m.; Friday-Saturday 5:30-11 p.m.; Sunday 5-10 p.m. Lounge menu served Monday-Thursday 11:30 a.m.-11 p.m.; Friday- Saturday 11:30 a.m.-midnight; Sunday 5-10 p.m. Three-course lunch, $26. Entrees: dinner, $22-$38; lounge, $14-$19.

■ **RESERVATIONS** Strongly recommended.

■ **CREDIT CARDS** All major cards accepted.

■ **SMOKING** Smoking in the bar only.

■ **HANDICAP ACCESSIBLE** Wheelchair accessible.

■ **PARKING** Valet parking at dinner, $15. Validated parking is $9.50 for two to 12 hours in the lot at 1620 Chancellor St.

Buddakan

The sleek Stephen Starr hotspot in Old City has a giant golden Buddha and top-notch Asian fusion cuisine.

amu Amida Butsu ... Namu Amida Butsu ... " My friend, John the Scholar, intoned this chant of Buddha's name. It was, he assured me, a Japanese invocation "to allow even the most simple practitioners to attain salvation."

I can say for certain that John was the only member of our table devoting more consideration to the svelte slope of Buddha's golden belly than to the plump chicken dumplings before us. We were most simple practitioners, indeed, but the appetizers were disappearing quickly.

His fascination was understandable, though. Despite the beautiful and rich young throngs of diners who gathered in Buddha's aura —

EXCELLENT

325 Chestnut St.
Philadelphia
(215) 574-9440

NEIGHBORHOOD
Old City

CUISINE
Asian Fusion

clustered over the glowing runway slab of Buddakan's onyx community table; scoping each other with the hippest glances Old City could muster — the Deity remained a 10-foot tower of seated serenity, bathed in the radiance of a blood-red light.

It says a lot that Buddakan owner Stephen Starr could pull this off, given that the nightlife visionary has a relationship with the Buddha that is about as profound as Ally McBeal's hallucinations of a dancing baby: dubious, yet deep.

"The Buddha just popped into my head," said Starr. "People, no matter what their religion, get a warm feeling when they see the Buddha."

The Zen of spontaneous instinct has obviously paid off for Starr. His first restaurant, the Continental, showed a knack for blending style with substance in the smaller confines of a converted diner turned martini bar. But it was Buddakan that truly marked his emergence from a former music promoter/nightclub owner into the city's hottest, hippest, most ambitious restaurateur. The empire now includes eight restaurants and counting. But Buddakan easily remains his most popular draw, churning more than 500 diners on a Saturday night through the magnificently transformed giant box that used to be a post office.

Behind the heavy wood front doors, with stacked circle handles recalling the reels of a movie projector, a fantasy of cinematic dimensions unfolds. The quiet rush of a falling water wall marks your entrance to this new world, opening onto a soaring room wrapped in twinkling gauzy fabric. Extremely tall hostesses take your coat and hand you off to servers clad in white pajamas, who move among furniture and tables that seem to have their own auras. No doubt drowned in the roar of one of the city's loudest dining rooms.

Like many of Starr's other fine chefs, Scott Swiderski, formerly of China Grill in Miami, works quietly in the shadow of the impresario and this showy ambience. But it is his contemporary Asian menu that offers the best reason for Buddakan's longevity, since it is far better than might be expected from your typical trend emporium.

Swiderski has left enough elements of familiar Asian cooking to ease unadventurous customers along. The cigar-shaped crispy spring rolls, filled with shrimp and scallops, were delicious with mustard and plum sauce dips. Nicely stuffed ginger chicken dumplings were ideal over a pool of soy, rice wine vinegar, and sesame. And "eel dice," Buddakan's version of barbecued eel over avocado and rice, was as fine as any sushi bar might produce.

Ginger-cured salmon, curled like a rose on the plate, was cleverly presented with a delicious wasabi-spiked Bavarian cream, a sweetened green horseradish spread that became addictive over inventively fried sheets of nori seaweed. Mashed potatoes also get a Japanese jolt of wasabi in a side order worth requesting.

There were some dishes at a recent meal that could have been better. The hot and sour soup tasted oddly like an Asian minestrone. The appetizer prawns were wrapped too tightly in shredded phyllo, and came with a tomato salsa that was too chunky for dipping. And while the grilled shrimp entree was tasty, the portion was skimpy for $25.

Buddakan, to be sure, is not for those

Or Try These

Here are three other Asian-influenced Stephen Starr restaurants.

Morimoto

723 Chestnut St., Philadelphia
(215) 413-9070

Superstar chef Masaharu Morimoto brings cutting-edge Japanese cuisine to the undulating bamboo dining room of Stephen Starr's hip restaurant.

Pod

3636 Sansom St., Philadelphia
(215) 387-1803

Conveyor-belt sushi and light-changing booths are part of the gimmick at this cool, futuristic dining room, but good Japanese fusion fare is one of the better reasons to return.

The Continental

138 Market St., Philadelphia
(215) 923-6069

This Old City diner-turned-martini-bar is where Stephen Starr first found his restaurant mojo, serving global tapas to an endless supply of buff swingers in black.

Diners at Budakkan eat in the glow of a giant Buddha.

on monastic budgets. However, the sumo-size portions intended for sharing (save for the shrimp) bolster a sense of fair value, and I saw more than a few tables happily diving into those $65, three-pound lobsters, decadently splayed atop a basket made of deep-fried shredded noodles.

The restaurant's family-style service doesn't facilitate a well-paced meal — the good-looking but somewhat distracted young staff deliver dishes haphazardly whenever they're ready. This can be a fun way to eat, of course, if you're with a group of friends, although it might be awkward for a business meal. Some of the dishes I tasted on my recent visits were so good, though, I didn't really want to share them at all.

The wasabi tuna pizza was memorable, a grilled flatbread scattered with wasabi then covered with sheets of pristine tuna sashimi. The unusual edamame ravioli brought dumplings filled with a surprisingly light puree of fresh soybeans, their mashed-potato texture enriched with truffle in the surrounding sweet wine and shallot broth.

A green cake made from the same stuffing came alongside a recent lunch entree of sake-marinated Chilean sea bass. The fish had a similar sweet flavor to the restaurant's signature miso-marinated black cod. Too bad the cake was burnt.

There were no such flaws with the lusciously meaty five-spice duck, which came with a creamy custard of scallion spoon bread. The large mound of pad Thai was perfect, tangy and moist. The sublimely tender Asian pork barbecue was absolutely impossible to stop eating, the sweet and spicy medallions of tenderloin sparked with an herby streak of scallion oil.

The desserts here are almost as fun as the rest of the meal. Freshly fried doughnut holes dusted in cinnamon sugar spill out of a Chinese take-out box, ready for a dip in chocolate sauce, jam or ginger crème fraiche. The chocolate pagoda brings a pyramid of chocolate ganache towering atop what appears to be a brownie layered with mousse.

It is a stunning finale, but just what should be expected. For Buddakan has always struck that rare balance between those seeking fine dining and those in search of a scene, where Zen masters and "simple practitioners" alike can feast in the golden glow of a giant Buddha's belly. Even if they don't find salvation . . . *Namu Amida Butsu* . . . they can at least savor a tasty meal.

■ **MENU HIGHLIGHTS** Chicken and ginger dumplings; crispy spring rolls; hot eel dice; ginger-cured salmon with nori chips; edamame ravioli; wasabi tuna pizza; five-spice duck; black cod with miso glaze; sizzling fish; Asian barbecue pork; chocolate pagoda; fresh doughnuts.

■ **WINE LIST** The concise list is well-chosen, with some affordable bottles. There are plenty of refreshing crisp whites, and an intriguing collection of good sake rice wine. Otokoyama (Male Mountain) was our favorite by the glass.

■ **IF YOU GO** Lunch served Monday-Friday, 11:30 a.m.-2 p.m. Dinner, Sunday-Thursday 5- 11 p.m.; Friday-Saturday 5 p.m.-midnight. Dinner entrees, $15-$65.

■ **RESERVATIONS** Strongly recommended.

■ **CREDIT CARDS** All major cards but Discover.

■ **SMOKING** There is a nonsmoking section.

■ **HANDICAP ACCESSIBLE** Yes.

■ **PARKING** Valet parking for $11.

Cafe Spice

The hip Indian bistro has contemporary decor, but classic dishes prepared with quality ingredients and sharp flavors.

O ld City was in a meltdown. I'd just paid $14 for the privilege of being yelled at by a surly Allright Parking attendant. A waiter had dumped a tray of beer and glasses down my back. And as the cool Taj Mahal soaked into my shirt (a fine amber beer with a hint of banana), I was gaining new, firsthand appreciation for the kind of growing pains that tax our restaurant scene.

At the epicenter of this trembly thought was Cafe Spice, the stylish Indian restaurant on Second Street that puts cool into curry. While the menu is largely as traditional as some of the more humble Indian eateries in West Philadelphia, it certainly has given an appealing modern image to what an Indian restaurant can look like.

VERY GOOD

35 S. Second St.
Philadelphia
(215) 627-6273

NEIGHBORHOOD
Old City

CUISINE
Indian

With its cafe windows open to the street, the long rectangular room recedes into the hues of a spice box — saffron gold, chile red, and cilantro chutney green. Fabric lightshades dangle like bloomers. Box-shaped alcoves give the polished Old City crowd a shallow refuge from the tiled room's bistro din (although the deeper four-seaters were claustrophobic).

Cafe Spice has the ambience to become a presence in the mainstream dining market, but I doubt the New York owners had counted on the sparse pickings left for trained service in town. At a recent lunch, though, almost two years later, the service situation seemed to be straightening out, from the pleasant hostess to the lovely (and sure-handed) server who was not only enthusiastic about the masalas, masaledars and sambar chutneys, she could tell us what they were.

And they were surprisingly classic. Despite its high-style contemporary looks, don't expect this small chain to offer many new ideas about Indian cuisine — at least not in the way that other Asian flavors have been absorbed into fusion cooking. The menu at Cafe Spice is rooted entirely in standard Indian dishes, including skewered tandoori-oven meats and fish, puffy breads, and spicy curried stews.

There were moments when it seemed the kitchen was trying too hard to tone down the spices for the mainstream clientele. The chick-

Cafe Spice's cooking is full of sharp, fresh flavors and quality ingredients.

pea curry (channa masala) and chicken in creamy tomato sauce (murg tikka lababdar) were boringly bland.

But more often than not, the cooking was full of sharp, fresh flavors and quality ingredients. That dishes did not always burn the tongue was sometimes an advantage, all the more easy to taste the complex alliances of swirling spice. Cumin. Coriander. Cinnamon. Cardamom. Fresh cilantro. Tangy homemade yogurt. Rich coconut milk. And yes, the occasional tingle of hot pepper.

While some of the chicken dishes tended to be overcooked (chicken tandoori), the grilled cubes of yogurt-tenderized chicken (noorie malai tikka) and chicken stewed with fenugreek and fresh spinach curry (hare masala ka murg) were memorably moist and flavorful.

The kitchen, though, was particularly talented with lamb. I loved the ground lamb kebab (raunaq-e-seekh), wrapped in the handkerchief-thin sheet of roomali bread, its gingery meat sparking against fresh chopped onions and minted chutney. Oniony minced lamb infused with clove and cardamom was my favorite filling for dosa, Southern Indian rice pancakes that had perfect crisp exteriors.

Cubes of grilled lamb kebabs (boti kebab) made an awesome appetizer — the meat softened by a ginger-garlic marinade of yogurt. Lamb cubes were equally great in the Punjabi stew (khaday masala ka gosht), a fragrant tomato-based sauce in which they had been slowly simmered. The similar but more fiery lamb vindaloo was strangely tough, and its heat delivered an odd metallic flavor to the sauce. But the lamb chops (barrah) were pleasingly tender, wearing their garlicky curry paste to charred-edge advantage.

With entree prices ranging from $14 to $22, Cafe Spice is definitely more expensive than most other Indian restaurants, but in line with other midrange restaurants in the neighborhood considering the quality of their ingredients. And all the entrees are accompanied by filling scoops of fragrant basmati rice, bowls of hearty lentil dal stew, and cooling raita yogurt.

Some of the tasty appetizers were mini-meals themselves, the zesty shrimp glazed in ginger-fused tomato sauce (jingha masaledar) set over a nest of deep fried cilantro and the surprisingly moist cubes of tandoori-baked salmon tikka (saloni machi.)

Among the most satisfiying tastes at Cafe Spice were the vegetarian offerings. Deep-fried vegetarian samosa dumplings were far more flavorful and moist than their lamb and chicken counterparts. And many of the entrees were the best examples of what subtle Indian stew cooking can be — a delicate interplay between textures and complex spices.

Deep-fried vegetarian dumplings (kofta nazakat) floated in a full-flavored spinach puree. Their egg-shaped crust did not enclose the usual mush, but aromatic crumbles of potato, peas, cheese and carrots. Whole florets of cauliflower in pudina gobhi were cooked just right in minted water, still firm enough to unfold on the fork like a bouquet in coriander-ginger gravy. And the Goa vegetable curry was a variation on lamb vindaloo that was far superior in flavor to the meat dish, adding the southern accent of coconut milk to vindaloo's vinegar twist and hot chile kick.

Or Try These

Here are three other Indian restaurants.

Khajuraho

Ardmore Plaza, 12 Greenfield Ave., Ardmore, Pa.
(610) 896-7200

Top-notch traditional Indian cooking on the Main Line.

Samosa

1214 Walnut St., Philadelphia
(215) 545-7776

This sunny, bare-bones vegetarian buffet can't be beat for incredibly cheap and satisfying country cooking that stays fresh thanks to steady steam-table turnover.

Darbar Grill

319 Market St., Philadelphia
(215) 923-2410

This new Old City entry into the all-u-can-eat Indian buffet sweepstakes has a wide variety of freshly prepapred classics, from tandoori chicken to cauliflower pakora, that seems slightly fresher than its University City counterparts.

When you finally do get the burn, sweet dessert is the ultimate solution — perhaps a cooling wedge of dense kulfi ice cream infused with saffron and pistachio, so rich you can practically chew it.

The pureed phirni rice pudding was too much like mush, and overpowered with potent cardamom. I was also disappointed that one of my usual favorites, gulab jamun — fried cheese balls in syrup — was reheated in the microwave.

But Cafe Spice also delivered some great finales. Ice cream steeped with fresh mango puree. Cool yogurt shakes called lassis. And a most unusually rich homemade yogurt pudding called shrikhand. Tinted with saffron and cardamom, it was so tangy, yet refreshingly sweet, it could quench any lingering spice — especially on a night when it seemed the rest of Old City was about to overheat.

■ **MENU HIGHLIGHTS** Boti lamb kebab; jingha masaledar shrimp; palak papri chaat spinach crisps; lamb dosa; raunaq-e-seekh lamb roomali roll; noorie malai tikka chicken kebab; barrah lamb chops; khaday masala ka gosht lamb; kofta nazakat vegetable dumplings; Goa vegetable curry; pudina gobhi cauliflower; onion naan; kulfi ice cream; mango delight; shrikhand.

■ **WINE LIST** There is a small but affordable list of very drinkable wines that are appropriate for well-spiced foods, from crisp pinot grigio and tingly gewurtztraminer to richer full-bodied reds such as zinfandel and shiraz. There is also an excellent liquor selection. Still, I prefer the refreshing Indian Taj Mahal beer for my meal.

■ **IF YOU GO** Lunch served Monday-Friday 11:30 a.m.-3 p.m. Dinner served Sunday-Thursday 5-10:30 p.m., Friday-Saturday 5-11:30 p.m. Latenight menu served Wednesday-Thursday 10:30 p.m. -1:30 a.m., Friday-Saturday 11:30 p.m.- 1:30 a.m. Brunch served Saturday-Sunday 11:30 a.m.-4 p.m. Dinner entrees, $14 to $22.

■ **RESERVATIONS** Suggested, especially weekends.

■ **CREDIT CARDS** All major cards except Discover.

■ **SMOKING** There is a nonsmoking section.

■ **HANDICAP ACCESSIBLE** Yes.

■ **PARKING** Street parking only.

The Capital Grille

The out-of-town steak-house chain gets it right, from the consistently cooked chops to the outgoing service.

I f I told you the Capital Grille was a posh, wood-paneled restaurant filled with mounted animal heads, private wine lockers, and gilt-framed portraits, that would be only half the story.

The manly clubhouse decor is the uniform of expense-account steak-house chains. And though handsomely designed — the large space is carved into five dining rooms, creating a sense of warmth and intimacy — the restaurant looks like a dozen others I can think of. Even the menu is pure steak-house widget, from the shrimp cocktail and the hearts of palm salad to the creamed spinach and the cheesecake for dessert.

No, this Providence, R.I.-based chain is not about reinventing the chophouse. But its success in refining the concept makes the Capital Grille stand out in a city with a broilerful of red-meat competitors.

EXCELLENT

1338 Chestnut St.
Philadelphia
(215) 545-9588

NEIGHBORHOOD
Avenue of the Arts

CUISINE
Steak House

Almost everything is right. The dry-aged steaks are succulent and consistently cooked to perfect doneness — which, believe me, is a major challenge these days. The dining rooms, for all their cliches, are extremely comfortable and are usually lively without being overly noisy.

And the massive, 350-bottle-plus wine list is filled with excellent picks — in particular, the California cabernets — priced from the high $30s to hundreds of dollars for some of the biggest names from Napa and Bordeaux.

You may need a magnifying glass to read the list's microscopic print, but the restaurant's young staff are so well-prepared that their guidance is worth seeking out. During my visits, two of my servers seemed to know everything about the wines, from basic recommendations and the history of unfiltered wines to the subtle differences among California's wine regions.

One server even had the good instincts to call on another waiter when he couldn't answer a question. And the moment I veered from his advice, I was disappointed.

In fact, the service may be the most impressive thing about this restaurant. It isn't hard to memorize a spiel about such a basic menu.

But such confidence and enthusiasm are refreshing in a city beset by a shortage of good staff, especially in steak houses, which are notorious for favoring regulars and corporate VIPs. Even the reservationists were a pleasure to speak with on the phone.

The credit goes to managing partner Ed Doherty, who came with chef Steve Annable from the Devon Seafood Grill and has developed into one of Philadelphia's best front-of-the-house managers, moving amiably from table to table greeting diners (and memorizing faces).

The 5-year-old at Table 23 ordered a hot dog? Somebody's running to Wawa to get it. Want something from the dinner menu at lunch? No problem.

Much of Doherty's career was spent as a chef, so, not surprisingly, the food is top-notch. And as most local steak houses go, the meat entrees are fairly priced, around $30 or less.

The restaurant has a dry-aging room on-site that turns out tender beef cuts with complex flavors that don't get too funky. The sirloin steak was outstanding, whether served plain or encrusted with just the right amount of cracked peppercorns. The 24-ounce porterhouse was infused with extra flavor from the bone. But my favorite cut by far was a Delmonico rib steak with flavor as rich as fine butter.

The nonbeef chops were also superb, including an amazingly tender veal T-bone and a generous, meaty rack of well-trimmed lamb.

My only problem with the meat entrees was the sauces, which were vaguely sweet and flabby with butter.

Seafood lovers also have plenty to choose from. Except for the lobster entree — too ordinary at $20 a pound — everything was delicious. The sushi-grade tuna was seared ruby rare, and the mild, flaky swordfish, though cooked well-done, was still moist.

Or Try These

Here are three other steak houses.

The Prime Rib

1701 Locust St. (in the Radisson Plaza Warwick Hotel), Philadelphia (215) 772-1701

An old-fashioned supper-club steak house that serves a prime rib that is the region's single best slice of beef.

Davio's

111 S. 17th St., Philadelphia (215) 563-4810

This small Boston-based Italian chain has a sleek second-floor perch in a former Chestnut Street bank building, and excels with classic steaks.

The Saloon

750 S. Seventh St., Philadelphia (215) 627-1811

This manly, wood-clad South Philadelphia power-dining spot serves expensive Italian cuisine but is rightly best-known for its awesome garlic-infused chops.

If you're craving lobster, head for the appetizers. The whole steamed one-pound chick, served cold with house-made mayo, is a great bargain. Tiny lobster claws add panache to moist, lumpy crab cakes. The classic clam chowder is nicely cooked, with fresh clam flavor, firm cubes of potato, and a smoky undertone of bacon.

Raw oysters are cold, firm and perfectly shucked. The calamari are tempura-fried and then sauteed with hot peppers in garlic butter, giving the crust an addictive, spicy tang.

The desserts are fine, but the selection so standard — creme brulee, cheesecake, white-chocolate mousse — that they're hardly worth mentioning, except for my disappointment at seeing mass-produced Haagen-Dazs on a fine-dining menu.

When denizens of the steak circuit compare chophouses, the discussion inevitably comes down to the side dishes. Capital Grille's steamed asparagus resembles a raft of verdant stalks towing a boat of frothy hollandaise that I do recommend tipping. The side of mushrooms is a satisfying mix of oysters, portobellos and shiitake caps roasted in herbed garlic oil. And the creamed spinach, which improved between visits, is a lush puree enriched with nutmeg-scented bechamel sauce.

But the true test of a steak house is its potatoes. At the Capital Grille, they are hand-mashed into a creamy cloud tinged with garlic butter; roasted into crisp-skinned lyonnaise wedges sweetened with caramelized onions; or fried cottage-style and topped with a haystack of onions.

Or baked, quite simply, as is, transforming a one-pound Idaho monster into an airy wonder, a heroic spud to crown a meal that shows how good meat and potatoes can be.

■ **MENU HIGHLIGHTS** Lobster and crab cakes; cold baby lobster appetizer; fried calamari with hot peppers; Delmonico steak; sirloin steak au poivre; porterhouse; lamb chops; veal chop; grilled tuna; all potato side dishes; creamed spinach; roasted mushrooms; white chocolate mousse.

■ **WINE LIST** Our servers knew their stuff, helping us navigate a 350-bottle selection that is strong on domestic cabernets. There are some good values under $40, but the better bottles start around $50.

■ **IF YOU GO** Lunch served Monday-Friday 11:30 a.m.-3 p.m. Dinner served Monday-Thursday 5-10 p.m., Friday-Saturday 5-11 p.m., Sunday 4-9 p.m. Lunch entrees: High teens to lower 20s for steaks, $4-7 range for sandwiches and salads. Dinner entrees, $14-$30.

■ **RESERVATIONS** Recommended.

■ **CREDIT CARDS** All major cards accepted.

■ **SMOKING** Smoking in the bar only.

■ **HANDICAP ACCESSIBLE** Wheelchair accessible.

■ **PARKING** Valet parking at dinner costs $14.

Carambola

The strip-mall find in the northern suburbs has a fun atmosphere and surprisingly sophisticated eclectic fare.

 et these babies cool," I warn as a plate of shrimp Carambola lands before me, fresh from the fryer and deceptively hot.

But my fingers are magnetized to these curious creations, these long and crispy cocoons of shredded phyllo dough with shrimp tails poking out the ends. My fingers gently prune the wildly wound nests to more edible proportions, and then they get a hot and sticky dunk in the sweetened spice of homemade marmalade and Dijon mustard. I bite into this brittle tangle and it shatters in a phyllo explosion, falling to the plate, sticking to my lips, flying in every direction.

VERY GOOD

1650 Limekiln Pike
Dresher, Pa.
(215) 542-0900

NEIGHBORHOOD
Northern Suburbs

CUISINE
New American

Forget the mess. Crunch with abandon. This mouthful of circus leaves me giddy as my incisors speed through the crispy coils to discover a tender core of moist, sweet jumbo shrimp.

That is what I love about this restaurant, Carambola. Its heart exceeds its packaging in nearly every way. From one glance, it is a casual BYOB family restaurant in a suburban strip mall. From another, it is an exciting dinner destination. Its menu suggests pizza-pasta Italian, but the kitchen goes much further, grilling meats, exotic fowl and fish with creative flair and a cosmopolitan sophistication.

Its obscure location only feeds the enigma. The restaurant is wedged behind a McDonald's playland in a bland retail strip, marked by a busy little sign so inscrutable, you're likely to drive all the way through Dresher on the Limekiln Pike before you think to turn around.

But behind this facade is a dining room bursting with energy and sound. High-tech cones of colored Italian halogens dangle below exposed air ducts from a funky trapeze of track lighting, casting their beams onto the polished suburban crowd. A clutch of R-2 commuters, who've traded their briefcases in for a baby carrier, crack open a bottle of chilled wine. A well-coiffed table of hairstylists throws a send-

Daniel Nejberger serves free-form pizzas seared cracker-crisp over a 600-degree grill.

off for their departing salon-mate. Well-jeweled couples cap their dinner with a bottle of designer vodka. Meanwhile, the kids behind them play xylophone on the glasses, and bend their Happy Meal action figures to speak into toy cell phones.

Amid the tables of contented, feeding masses strides co-owner Daniel Nejberger, clad in his starched chef's whites, pumping hands in the dining room while his son and partner, Jason, maneuvers a wood-fired grill in the open kitchen that perfumes the dining room with the scent of mesquite.

Free-form pizzas, seared cracker-crisp over the 600-degree grill, come spread with micro-thin toppings — a smoky blend of cheeses swirled with zesty homemade marinara, or fancy slices of duck breast, sparked with tart dried cranberries and slivered scallion flakes. And just when you're tempted to go for one of the restaurant's gargantuan bowls of homemade pasta — say, the spinach fettuccine tossed with smoked salmon in dill cream — you spy the rack of lamb wandering by dressed in rosemary demiglace.

With food like this, the service has often seemed to lag behind, both in ambition and professional polish. A recent visit, though, proved Carambola has been working hard in this respect. Our server was informative, attentive, and especially patient with my own brood of kids. Still, judging from the number of unbussed empty tables that piled up on this busy Sunday night, it's clear that the service staff is easily overwhelmed.

This wasn't the restaurant's only weakness. The stylishly whimsical decor, with its tiled floor and terra-cotta-painted walls and flashy lighting, makes no allowance for buffering sound. Occasionally, the roar of the crowd made it simply hard to speak.

Or Try These

Here are three other restaurants in the northern suburbs.

Inn on Blueberry Hill

1715 S. Easton Rd., Doylestown, Pa. (215) 491-1777

An ambitious Bucks County inn whose talented chef, Bill Kim, formerly of Susanna Foo, is creating memorable contemporary cuisine.

Blue Sage

772 Second Street Pike, Southampton, Pa.
(215) 942-8888

A casual strip-mall bistro serving creative vegetarian cuisine that goes far beyond the cliches of twig-and-sprout cuisine.

Trax Cafe

27 W. Butler St., Ambler, Pa. (215) 591-9777

This bright little dining room has the charm of a small-town junction converted into a pleasant cafe, with trackside outdoor eating and an ambitious menu that ranges from house-smoked ribs to porcini-dusted salmon.

But who needs conversation? Great food is still the reason to visit Carambola. And the Nejbergers, formerly of Il Pastaio and Piccolo's, have put together a menu worthy of your full attention.

Fueled by homemade preparations, quality seasonal products, and consistently good cooking, they have produced very few things I didn't enjoy. And this kitchen has been remarkably consistent. When I returned last summer for the first time in four years, all of the menu's standards tasted exactly as I remembered. The shrimp Carambola was as wildly wound as ever. The grilled pizzas had heat-crisped, free-form crusts and that zippy tomato sauce.

Half a duckling was smoked for hours over cherry wood, then glazed crisp with raspberry Chambord liqueur. Its shiny skin was like fine parchment, with meat that melted in the mouth. Nejberger's homemade pastas were in equally fine form, from the springy spinach fettuccine that clung to a fine layer of cream and nuggets of salmon, to the wild mushroom-stuffed ravioli, which was napped in a delightful, tawny cream sauce sweetened gently with apple schnapps and studded with toasted walnuts.

Carambola's Caesar is a flavor heavyweight, eschewing the typical goopy, faux-ranch Caesar dressing in favor of the real thing. It pulled a solid right hook with its garlic, then landed an anchovy jab that kept me alert for the rest of the meal.

Good thing, because some tasty new spring additions showed off the range of the kitchen's culinary palette. Three skewers of tender chicken turned vibrant pink from their Indian tandoori marinade came over cold shredded lettuce and potato salad. A massive slice of pristine, perfectly seared halibut was perched over a seasonal salad of fingerling potatoes and green beans then crowned with a refreshingly cool mango salsa.

The selections on Carambola's dessert tray, most of which are brought in, were less satisfying than on previous visits. A banana cream tart was all cream and no banana. And the Oreo cookie mousse suffered from an impenetrably thick tart shell. Better to stick with the house-burned creme brulee or the moist bread pudding. Or one of the excellent house-churned gelati.

Yes, they would have made a fine finish to such a satisfying meal. I guess I'll just have to go back to Carambola soon to try them. I know I won't wait another four years to return again.

■ **MENU HIGHLIGHTS** Shrimp Carambola; homemade ravioli; chicken tandoori skewers; Caesar salad; grilled pizzas; two-salmon fettuccine; rack of lamb; Chambord duck; crab cakes; halibut with mango salsa; bread pudding; gelati.

■ **WINE LIST** BYOB.

■ **IF YOU GO** Lunch served Monday-Friday 11:30 a.m.- 2:30 p.m. Dinner, Sunday-Thursday 4-9:30 p.m., Friday-Saturday 4-10:30 p.m. Dinner entrees, $9.95-$26.95.

■ **RESERVATIONS** Not accepted.

■ **CREDIT CARDS** Visa and MasterCard only.

■ **SMOKING** Entire restaurant is nonsmoking.

■ **HANDICAP ACCESSIBLE** Yes.

■ **PARKING** Free lot.

Carmine's

The funky New Orleans-style neighborhood joint in Delaware County defies easy categorization.

This was a first. A dinner reservation with a warning label: "I want you to know it's a dive."

There was a measure of pride in chef John Mims' voice as he confirmed my party's table over the phone — but with a defensive edge. It seems Carmine's, his modest Creole cafe, had won such a reputation on the Main Line for foie gras and duck that the fur-coat crowd had started showing up. More than a few people, Mims told me, promptly did an about-face after opening the restaurant's stained-glass door.

There's blues legend Koko Taylor belting "Wang Dang Doodle" on the stereo. Checkerboard floors. Black formica tables. Fans whirling from the drop ceiling. A glass deli case with funky stainless-steel veneer. The powerful aroma of garlic. And there's John Mims himself — all muscle, packed into a black T and Elvis 'do — waiting to greet you at the door.

VERY GOOD

5 Brookline Blvd.
Havertown, Pa.
(610) 789-7255

NEIGHBORHOOD
Delaware County

CUISINE
Cajun/Creole

Excuse me. This is a dive?

Come with me for a moment to New Orleans. Stroll down decrepit Baronne Street to Uglesich's for some of the Big Easy's best oysters (but watch out for the stray cats), or behind the Magazine Street bus shelter to Franky & Johnny's for boiled crawfish. Let's eat red beans and rice under the rusty awning at Vaughan's Lounge in Bywater. Or a bowl of chicken gizzard gumbo beside the levee in the Marigny. Then you'll have seen a dive.

Not that there's anything wrong with that. In fact, New Orleanians cherish their dives as bastions of pure home cooking and no-frills repositories of the living culinary tradition — fried, stewed and tingling with deeply steeped spices.

It's the big-money, big-production slickies they mistrust. A giant golden Buddha wouldn't go far in New Orleans except on a Mardi Gras float. (And then, just for a few miles.)

Carmine's is too clean, frankly, to be a dive. Its young waitresses are too suburban-sweet, even with their funky spandex and piercings. The place is even nicer after a face-lift last summer, which erased all traces of its former life as a deli. So technically, Carmine's is a "joint." A subtle distinction perhaps, but a definite notch upward in niceness.

It's silly to be technical about Carmine's, though, because the restaurant defies easy categorization. When Mims, a New Orleans native and Manayunk restaurant veteran, opened nearly four years ago, this was a Creole deli turning out muffulettas and gumbos to go.

Slowly, it evolved into an affordable BYO sit-down adventure, gravitating from old-time New Orleans classics such as redfish courtbouillon and beef daube to the more contemporary nightly specials that now account for 60 percent of the orders. There's even a telephone "specials hotline." And virtually all entrees are less than $20.

It wasn't long before Mims was searing foie gras, truffling mashed potatoes, and drizzling balsamic glaze around the plates. Enter the fur coats. And some of that upscale business remains, judging from the classy bottles of wine I've spotted around the dining room.

I can see why. While many of Mims' dishes may not seem prototypically New Orleanian, he "Creolizes" them all, lending the unmistakable touch of a New Orleans-bred hand, two-fisted seasoning, and a passion for richness that makes most East Coast cooking seem pallid by comparison.

His foie gras is seared to a manly char, crusted with the soft burn of cracked black pepper and topped with a frizzled nest of Vidalia onions. Asian-style shiitake mushrooms fill homemade dumplings that encircle a pile of oysters poached in a crawfish-sake broth. An intriguing gravy of smoked portobellos covers deliciously crisped duck du jour, playing off the sweetness of creamy corn spoonbread on the side.

The ever-modest Mims makes no claims of kitchen greatness. But he has worked to improve a few dishes since my first review visits. At a recent meal, his once mushy crawfish spring rolls were crispy and full of snappy crawfish tails. The jambalaya was no longer touristy Creole red, but a proper Cajun brown, and filled with slices of smoky, spicy andouille sausage. The crab cakes had a better sauce than before, a reddish Tabasco butter that sparkled with heat. But the cakes themselves were bready. Succulent medallions of veal tender-

Or Try These

Here are three other restaurants with New Orleans-inspired cuisine.

Melange Cafe
1601 Chapel Ave., Cherry Hill, N.J. (856) 663-7339
In a lively dining room decked with colorful prints and garden lattice, chef Joe Brown draws inspiration from Louisianian and Italian cooking for bountiful portions of hearty food.

High Street Caffe
322 S. High St., West Chester (610) 696-7435
This funky purple BYOB has ceiling lights fringed with Mardi Gras beads and a Cajun menu that indulges the full-octane flavors of Louisiana. The smoky andouille gumbo tastes authentic, but the voodoo crawfish will burn a hole in your mouth with habanero heat, ranking it among the spiciest double-dare dishes around.

New Orleans Cafe
1 W. State St., Media, Pa. (610) 627-4393
Cajun and Creole cooking is served in a converted bank building.

loin made for a nice addition to the menu (definitely for the fur coat crowd), sauced in a deeply flavored demiglace that stopped just shy of motor- oil thick.

Mims usually keeps the gusto in check, doling out just enough oomph to keep things interesting without losing control. True New Orleans cooking is more about seasoning than scorching heat.

At a previous meal, his blackened grouper special was delightfully restrained, with a side of sweet creamed corn to put on the brakes before the spice spun into a free burn. That same measured tingle simmered under the surface of his rich crab bisques — creamed with sherry or bolstered with tomato and sweet crab fat. A brilliant-green scallion-and-shallot coulis added zip to a delicious savory cheese cake filled with crab and smoked gouda.

Seasoned flour gave the scallop special a perfect micro-crisp, sealing in natural juices that contrasted with the dark streaks of reduced balsamic vinegar and currant jelly that splattered the plate. Rich pecan butter sauce raised a simple chicken breast and mashed sweet potatoes to the next level.

Pecans are underutilized in Northern kitchens, but Mims does the Southern nuts proud, especially in desserts. Good old pecan pie was ably done and spiked with bourbon. Crisp pecan cookies were tucked between scoops of white chocolate mousse, which in turn had their own addictive choco-bit crunch.

And while the bread pudding would have been better warm, I will not quibble with its virtues. Most versions in these parts tend to be dry and spongy. But Mims' lovely loaves were soaked with custard like a true New Orleanian, pressed and nearly liquefied, quivering with each slice of the spoon, more like pudding than soggy bread. Glazed in a light, creamy caramel sheen, it's a homey confection that can make even the diviest joint start looking pretty.

■ **MENU HIGHLIGHTS** Crab bisque; pepper-seared foie gras; crab-and-smoked-Gouda tart; chicken with pecan butter; blackened grouper special; veal tenderloin; roast duck du jour; rack of lamb; bread pudding; white-chocolate praline mousse.

■ **WINE LIST** BYOB.

■ **IF YOU GO** Dinner served Tuesday-Wednesday 5-9 p.m., Thursday-Saturday 5-10 p.m., Sunday 5-8 p.m. Entrees, $12.50 to $20.

■ **RESERVATIONS** Reservations strongly suggested, especially on weekends.

■ **CREDIT CARDS** Cash or check only.

■ **SMOKING** Nonsmoking.

■ **HANDICAP ACCESSIBLE** Not accessible.

■ **PARKING** Street parking free after 7 p.m.

Chlöe

The homey Old City BYOB bistro has
an international take on comfort food.

I t wasn't exactly instant romance behind the saute station.
When Dan Grimes returned from vacation to his sous-chef job
at the Latest Dish on South Fourth Street, his former boss and
good buddy was gone. Suddenly, a woman named Mary Ann
Ferrie was in charge of the kitchen, and she wasn't about to
be run over by someone else's recipes. Namely his.

"We butted heads for a couple weeks," she said. "Oh, yeah.
We hated each other."

That was in 1997. Now the two are married and Ferrie is quick to
concede: "He's right about recipes nine out of 10 times. In fact, I married him for his cheesecake."

Our server at Chlöe, the tiny restaurant that Grimes and Ferrie
opened in Old City, was also quick to mention the romantic cheesecake, which is exceptionally light and coyly undersweetened.

VERY GOOD

232 Arch St.
Philadelphia
(215) 629-2337

NEIGHBORHOOD
Old City

CUISINE
New American

But it was already more than obvious that
this cozy little gem of a bistro was the product of a love fest. Ferrie's bridal bouquet, for
heaven's sake, is mounted on the wall, not far
from the wedding invitation.

The earth-tone decor has a homemade New
Age touch that says "potpourri": thistle
brooms, votive lights wrapped in handmade
paper cones, tables lacquered with herbs and
twigs, knickknacks on floating mantels. Even
the purple velvet wall hangings had been made by our server, who
spoke of the food with such reverence and detail that you had to wonder whether she'd also cooked it herself. (She hadn't.)

It's quite a change from the trendy Latest Dish, where a boisterous bar crowd is the main event and the cooking merely an interesting distraction.

This tiny BYO can get pretty loud, too. With hardwood floors and
only 30-some seats, all it takes is one yappy table, just as it did when
the space was Marco's restaurant. Even so, Grimes and Ferrie's food
is worth braving the noise, an ideal example of good value (all entrees
are under $20) and clever cooking that doesn't take shortcuts.

Seldom does a menu draw on so many diverse international flavors with such natural ease. This duo can borrow from Morocco, the
Caribbean, Asia, or the American South without a hitch. It's simply

Owners/chefs/spouses Mary Ann Ferrie and Dan Grimes can borrow from Morocco, the Caribbean, Asia, or the American South without a hitch.

good contemporary cooking that relies on fine ingredients and smart ideas rather than pretense, resulting in dishes that are creative but don't forget how to taste good.

A bundle of asparagus spears and garlicky Boursin cheese is wrapped in a crisp quiver of smoky bacon. A free-form grilled pizza teases between salty and sweet with smears of fig jam, crunchy nuggets of pancetta, and molten streams of Gorgonzola cheese. Homemade country pate has that perfect balance of coarse rustic chunks and liverlike spreadability, perfect for the accompanying crusty bread and grainy mustard.

Much of the menu is American comfort food at heart, whether it's an excellent pork chop stuffed with corn, bacon and dressing over port-braised collards, a heap of tender, meaty ribs glazed in bourbony barbecue sauce, or delicate cod encrusted with crisp bread crumbs that hint of coriander.

But Chlöe also has an abiding affection for more assertive, exotic spicing. Before they are grilled, skewered lamb cubes served over minted couscous are marinated in yogurt and Moroccan spices, a blend of coriander, ginger, cumin, cardamom, cloves and fenugreek that tenderizes the meat.

Moist chicken breast gets a tropical tan from its dry rub of curry, garlic and paprika, a swelling heat that contrasts with its garnish of grilled bananas soused in rum and molasses. A lively Indonesian coconut curry gives perfectly grilled shrimp exotic appeal, but it's the bed of corn-studded pancakes that makes the dish.

There were less-inspired moments. The braised fennel appetizer was a nice idea, but an awkward and surprisingly bland take on veggie Parmesan. The mussels had a tasty broth piqued with Dijon mustard, but the New Zealand mollusks were too big and chewy.

The beet salad was too crunchy, and parboiling the bulb before roasting seemed to have blanched out the sweetness. I loved the homemade asparagus ravioli in sage brown butter; they would have been perfect had the cheese filling been less runny.

But far more often than not, Chlöe's menu scored. And in light of the moderate prices, I was impressed by the quality of the ingredients. Everybody these days claims to use "sushi-grade" tuna, but the rare grilled fillet over jasmine rice and seaweed salad was such a gorgeous ruby color inside that it was like eating some exquisite melon from the sea. Likewise, the rib-eye steak was not simply tender, perfectly moist and surprisingly lean; it had a wonderful beefy flavor, no doubt enhanced by Grimes' homemade Worcestershire sauce.

In fact, if I were Ferrie, I would have married Grimes for his Worcestershire, not his cheesecake, which was a little too light for me. Why shortchange indulgence when it comes to that important genre of cakery? Even a cute candied kumquat on the side couldn't completely compensate.

On the other hand, a gentle touch is what raises many of these familiar desserts above home-cook status. The tiramisu was as light as a cloud over the cyclone of chocolate lines squiggling the plate. Grimes' deep-dish apple pie was classically tasty, but most notable for its flaky double crust.

But my favorite dessert was the banana bread pudding, yieldingly moist and fragrant with fruit. Actually, it happens to be the only

Or Try These

Here are three other neighborhood bistros run by husband-wife teams.

Django

526 S. Fourth St., Philadelphia (215) 922-7151

The neighborhood BYOB reaches new heights of sophistication at this European-inspired bistro.

Citrus

8136 Germantown Ave., Philadelphia. (215) 247-8188

This tiny restaurant offers modern seafood and vegetarian dishes with a light Asian touch and a heavy-handed dose of animal- rights activism

L'Angolo

1415 W. Porter St., Philadelphia (215) 389-4252

Authentic Italian antipasti, veal with mushrooms and almond-crusted cheesecake are among the highlights at this lovely South Philadelphia corner grotto.

dessert that Ferrie claims as her own. But if Grimes' recipes are indeed right nine times out of 10, Ferrie's 10th guarantees a dinner worth savoring from start to finish.

■ **MENU HIGHLIGHTS** Chloë salad; spicy prawns; grilled pizza; country pate; tuna; West Indies chicken; rib-eye steak with homemade Worcestershire sauce; grilled ribs; Moroccan spiced lamb; Southern stuffed pork chop; bread pudding; tiramisu.

■ **WINE LIST** BYOB.

■ **IF YOU GO** Dinner served Tuesday-Saturday 5-9:45 p.m. Entrees, $15.50-$20.

■ **RESERVATIONS** No reservations.

■ **CREDIT CARDS** All major cards accepted but Discover and Diners Club.

■ **SMOKING** Nonsmoking.

■ **HANDICAP ACCESSIBLE** There is a small step at the entrance; rest rooms are not wheelchair accessible.

■ **PARKING** Street parking only.

Citrus

Chestnut Hill's underachieving dining scene needed another interesting restaurant, no matter how small.

Little restaurants have been big news lately as a parade of one-room wonders led me to some memorable meals.

From upscale Vetri and Gilmore's to ambitious neighborhood spots such as Django, Chlöe, Blue Sage and Pif, I've been more impressed than ever by the virtues of dining with the under-40 set (under 40 seats, that is).

Of course, I love their intimacy and personal attention, as well as the good value they often provide, especially the BYOs. I also like that so many are husband-wife ventures, a throwback that epitomizes the phrase "labor of love."

Even more important is what a great little restaurant says about eating out. It shows that real cooking talent is flowing into our nooks and crannies, that good food awaits us every day, not just when we celebrate milestones in our lives. No neighborhood is complete without one.

VERY GOOD

8136 Germantown Ave.
Philadelphia
(215) 247-8188

NEIGHBORHOOD
Chestnut Hill

CUISINE
New American
Seafood/Vegetarian

Tiny Citrus in Chestnut Hill is one of the smallest yet. That there are only 18 seats in this slender room, cheerily painted avocado green and lemon-chiffon yellow, heightened my surprise at finding such sophisticated dishes arriving at our table.

Alongside slices of crusty homemade bread at lunch, for example, were several addictive gougères — hot baked puffs of airy dough with crusts embedded with salty nuggets of capers and cracked black pepper.

Then came a warm mushroom salad with whole fans of crunchy sauteed maitake mushrooms that exuded buttery white-wine juices onto a bed of baby spinach. Tender, gingery shrimp dumplings came with a sweet and spicy coconut milk dip.

Chef Chris Daher impressed with the entrees, too. I devoured a pair of excellent crab cakes, almost creamy with homemade mayonnaise inside, served with al dente angel-hair pasta tossed with buttery tomato sauce.

Daher's tasty soba noodle-crusted salmon was one of the most unusual dishes I've seen. It looked like a brick of Ramen Pride with a fish stuck in the middle. But the salmon was moist and delicate and seasoned with scallion and pickled ginger.

That pleasant ginger-scallion motif, which returned often during our meals, was one of many Asian notes on a menu that pays homage to the string of Japanese restaurants that previously occupied this space. One of those was Chiyo, which was owned by the mother of Daher's wife and partner, Margaret Welsh.

Welsh's mom still owns the building, which helps explain how the couple — he, a Culinary Institute of America-trained cook; she, a self-taught pastry chef — landed in such a diminutive storefront on quaintly cobbled Germantown Avenue.

The rent was right. And Chestnut Hill's underachieving dining scene needed another interesting restaurant, no matter how small.

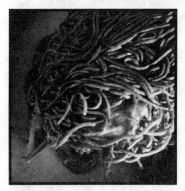

A salmon filet peeks out of a blanket of noodles.

Cooking in such tiny quarters has its drawbacks. Citrus doesn't take reservations, and the wait for dinner one recent Wednesday was downright painful.

The restaurant wasn't even terribly busy, but a table for four hadn't opened up. So my party was left waiting in the glassed-off foyer for 40 minutes, browsing the animal-rights propaganda posted in the front and sending subliminal "Leave!" messages to a quartet of ladies who lingered endlessly after paying their check. I was tempted to scribble another rule on the "No Smoking, No Furs" sign in the front window: No Loitering.

Then again, Citrus' serious, soft-spoken servers deserve credit for not pushing anyone out the door. When we were finally seated, I was happy to take my own time with Daher's food, which, in turn, takes no shortcuts.

The menu, with entrees topping out around $15, is limited to seafood and vegetarian dishes. Yet Daher doesn't shy away from using an occasional dab of dairy to lend just the right touch of indulgence.

Goat cheese gives the homemade ravioli appetizer a creaminess that contrasts with the garlicky tomato and Swiss chard sauce. A flaky puff pastry tart filled with mushrooms and spinach oozes the richness of Gorgonzola cheese.

There are plenty of butter sauces with the entrees, too, but they are skillfully light, accenting deftly cooked porcini-powdered scallops, austerely poached sesame-dusted shrimp, and meaty pan-seared tuna steaks.

There are a few nondairy/vegetarian options for vegans, including a pureed sweet-potato soup topped with spicy sweet-potato chips and a strangely bland udon noodle soup. Both needed salt. And given the artful platings during most of our meals, I was unimpressed by the orange blob of cheesy mashed roots billed as the vegetarian shepherd's pie.

Some of Welsh's desserts were also mildly disappointing. They are all homemade and handsomely displayed in a glass case along one wall. But with a few exceptions — a glazed fruit tart, a snappy lemon meringue, and a rich wedge of pecan molasses pie — most seemed to be missing a finishing touch.

The creme brulee was runny both times I tried it. A chocolate cake was too dense. And numerous variations on dry sponge cake topped with lightly flavored chantilly creams, whether tinted with green tea or with chestnut cream and rum, lacked the potent, decadent stroke that creates a satisfying finale.

But such slips seemed minor considering the overall achievement of this tiny spot. Citrus does far more with its modest space than many large restaurants even attempt.

■ **MENU HIGHLIGHTS** Caper gougères; warm mushroom salad; spinach, mushroom and Gorgonzola tart; goat cheese ravioli; noodle-crusted salmon; crab cakes; seared tuna; porcini-dusted scallops; fruit tart; lemon meringue.

■ **WINE LIST** BYOB.

■ **IF YOU GO** No longer open for lunch. Dinner: Tuesday-Thursday 5-9:30, Friday-Saturday 5-10:30, Sunday 5-9. Closed Monday. Entrees $7-$14.

■ **RESERVATIONS** No reservations.

■ **CREDIT CARDS** Visa and MasterCard only.

■ **SMOKING** No smoking.

■ **HANDICAP ACCESSIBLE** Not wheelchair accessible. There is one step up to the entrance, and rest rooms are downstairs.

■ **PARKING** Street parking only.

Or Try These

Here are three other restaurants in Chestnut Hill.

Roller's

8705 Germantown Ave., Philadelphia (215) 242-1771

Paul Roller's glassed-in strip-mall cafe is a Restaurant Renaissance survivor that still serves a reliable eclectic menu of updated comfort foods, as well as an affordable wine list.

H & J McNally's Tavern

8634 Germantown Ave., Philadelphia (215) 247-9736

Everything is made from scratch at this dark little tavern, from the lunch meat to the soups and desserts, but the Schmitter, a salami-cheesesteak fantasy on a kaiser roll, is what makes it worth the trip.

CinCin

7838 Germantown Ave., Philadelphia (215) 242-8800

This sunny little sibling of Bryn Mawr's Yangming offers thoughtfullly upscaled Chinese food with good ingredients and French accented wine-infused sauces.

Country Club Restaurant

The region's best diner maintains its excellent
Jewish and American comfort food while updating
the kitchen with a new chef.

 'm sorry, but Mr. Perloff isn't selling any more apricot
tortes today. He says they're dry."

The server's stunning bit of news was delivered with
a certain regal pride, as if it were an edict handed down
from finicky Georges Perrier or from Masaharu
Morimoto, who once refused to sell me a delicacy called
monkfish liver because it "wasn't fatty enough."

But this was a diner — the Northeast's landmark
Country Club Restaurant & Pastry Shop — home of fluffy matzo balls
and crispy blintzes, the bustling domain of grandmotherly servers
named Millie, Carole and Maryann.

Since opening in 1956, though, the Country Club has aspired to be
much more than an average diner. Owner
Noel Perloff's father, Jack, even planted
"restaurant" in the name when, in 1968, the
old stainless-steel Kullman diner cars were
carted away and replaced with the stuccoed
Spanish arches of the much-larger present
building.

EXCELLENT

1717 Cottman Ave.,
Philadelphia
(215) 722-0500

NEIGHBORHOOD
Northeast Philadelphia

CUISINE
Jewish-American Diner

It arrived from North Jersey in 20 pieces
and technically was still, by virtue of its prefab pedigree, a diner. But the senior Perloff
could brook no anti-diner snobbery. His
establishment would be regarded with the
respect of a legitimate restaurant.

Who could have known then that diners — bastions of honest,
home-style food and unpretentious atmosphere — would be supplant-
ed by fast-food chains on the one hand and trendy upscale restaurants
on the other? That diners would become the stuff of longing and nostalgia?

It's a fact, evidenced by the many new diners sprouting up along
roadsides, flashing their faux-deco veneers of stainless steel festooned with neon lights. But few have the flavor of authenticity. And
our stock of venerable old diners is dwindling, both in quality and
quantity.

Yet the Country Club seems to be getting even better, evolving
without abandoning its traditions. Noel Perloff is comfortable with

his inner-diner and determined to keep it fresh. ("I don't want to wake up and realize that all my customers moved to Florida and I'm serving 1960s food in 2010," he says.) He still serves mashed potatoes with the meat loaf, of course, but now they're redskins and Yukon golds.

The sprawling pink-and-green dining rooms won't win any design awards. But Perloff has yet to turn back the clock and sheathe his stucco in steel, even though he has fond memories of the old diner look.

The diner's Jewish and American comfort food, however, remains a constant labor of love, built on family recipes and fresh, high-quality ingredients.

Perloff even hired a well-known consultant to update the food a decade ago, but the recent surprise hiring of executive chef Marco Carrozza represents a potentially seismic shift.

Carrozza, brought in to replace retiring longtime chef William Love, made his name at the now-closed Marco's, a stylish Old City spot about as far from Northeast diner culture as you can get. The Italian- and Southern-inspired Carrozza had never made a matzo ball in his life, but he now seems a smart fit.

So far, he has added a few specials, a shrimp-pesto pasta here, a pecan-crusted chicken with Dijon cream there. But mostly he has been mastering the basics.

The closest Carrozza gets to vertical food these

Blintzes filled with cherries, blueberries and sour cream from the Country Club Restaurant.

days are the chicken croquettes, two crisp cones that tower over the plate as if molded in a '50s brassiere. I've come to dread croquettes elsewhere because they're usually just pasty stuffing flavored with bouillon. But inside these golden-crusted beauties, I found mashed-chicken heaven, the meat bound with a buttery, oniony veloute sauce.

With the new guy surrounded by kitchen veterans like William Green, the blintz master for 35 years, the Country Club's justly famous classics seem secure. The matzo balls, an ideal balance of mouth-filling fluff and resilient chew, are buoyant in homemade chicken soup stocked with carrots and celery.

The dairy platter is a study in Jewish soul food: amazing cheese blintzes of handmade crepes rolled in buttery crumbs, noodle kugel bound with raisin-studded custard, simple but satisfying potato pancakes, and the best knish I've ever eaten, its flaky crust filled with airy, oniony potatoes.

The Friday night proccas are the archetype of stuffed cabbage. The ground-meat-and-rice filling is comfortingly soft but not mushy, and the sweet-and-sour tomato-raisin sauce is endearing.

Carrozza's potpie arrived in a puff-pastry package so huge that it could have been delivered by UPS, with richly sauced chicken, peas and carrots brimming over the edge.

No restaurant is flawless, especially one with such a large menu, and I found a few duds here. The roast turkey was dry and the Western omelet ordinary. And a side dish of "escalloped apples," which looked like gooey canned pie filling, was the only item that appeared less than homemade.

But Carrozza seems to be curing the Country Club of a malady that afflicts even the best diners: overcooking seafood. His Friday night flounder francaise was perfect, its moist white flesh sealed in a browned egg-wash crust. And a broiled shad special was so deftly cooked that I could taste the fish's distinctively dusky, salty tang.

Or Try These

Here are three other landmark diners.

Mustache Bill's Diner

Eighth and Broadway, Barnegat Light, N.J. (609) 494-0155

Summer on Long Beach Island wouldn't be complete without a visit to this beautiful deco diner where the seafood omelets and creamed chipped beef are first-rate.

Mayfair Diner

7373 Frankford Ave. Philadelphia (215) 624-8886

This stainless-steel classic rimmed with green neon still draws a devoted Northeast crowd for homey '50s-era fare.

Melrose Diner

1501 Snyder Ave., Philadelphia (215) 467-6644

This 24-hour South Philly standby with the coffee-cup clock and horseshoe booths has been beautifully restored, but the menu could be spruced up next.

When it comes to dessert, some of us usually head for the soda fountain. I for the sublime chocolate shakes that go down like clouds of frothy cocoa ice and my 3-year-old daughter, Alice, for the clown sundae, a delightful ice-cream rube with cherries for eyes, cookies for ears, and a cone perched atop his chocolate-sauce hair.

By our fifth meal, though, Alice was ready for a guided tour of the pastry case: sugar-crisped wedges of cinnamon-laced Jewish apple cake, creamy rounds of cheesecake, chocolate-iced eclairs, key lime pies crowned with citrus, butter cookies with rainbow sprinkles, and golden shortcake tiered between ripe strawberries and poufs of whipped cream.

Her eyes widened, and so did mine. There were no apricot tortes, of course, not today. But the pride in Mr. Perloff's pastries, and in the region's finest diner, was still on magnificent display.

■ **MENU HIGHLIGHTS** Matzo ball soup; blintzes; potato pancakes; noodle kugel; potato knishes; chicken croquettes; meat loaf; proccas (stuffed cabbage); deviled crab cake; chicken potpie; pecan-crusted chicken; flounder francaise; broiled fish du jour (especially in-season shad); Jewish apple cake; chocolate-chip cheesecake; clown sundae.

■ **WINE LIST** The small, inexpensive wine list takes a back seat to the smooth manhattans, frosty cloudlike chocolate shakes, and classic egg creams.

■ **IF YOU GO** Breakfast is served Monday-Saturday 7-11 a.m.; Sunday 7 a.m.-noon. Lunch: Monday-Friday 12 a.m.-2p.m. Dinner: daily, 5:30-9:30 p.m. (early-bird menu till 5). Entrees: breakfast, $3.69-$6.95; lunch, $6.95-$7.95; dinner, $8.95-$14.95.

■ **RESERVATIONS** Accepted, and highly recommended on weekends.

■ **CREDIT CARDS** All major cards accepted.

■ **SMOKING** Smoking in the front room only.

■ **HANDICAP ACCESSIBLE** Yes.

■ **PARKING** Free lot available.

Deux Cheminees

One of the city's big-occasion classics is priceless
in part for the forgotten dishes it perpetuates.

There are fallback plans. And then there are fallback plans.

"If the restaurant doesn't work out in a year," Fritz Blank would say, "I can always go back to saving lives and stomping out disease."

That was 23 years ago, when Blank decided to leave his post as chief of the microbiology lab at Crozer-Chester Medical Center and Burn Unit, and open a restaurant called Deux Cheminees.

He was a talented home cook who had learned at the knee of Oma, his grandmother Mary Wild Blank. But consider that the highlights of Blank's professional experience in the food business before Deux Cheminees included stints as a herdsman for 1,600 cows and a soda jerk at the Crescent Pharmacy in Pennsauken. The decision to launch a fancy French restaurant suddenly would begin to look like a risky one indeed.

EXCELLENT

1221 Locust St.,
Philadelphia
(215) 790-0200

NEIGHBORHOOD
Washington Square

CUISINE
Classic French

Philadelphia's eclectic Restaurant Renaissance was slowing down. Le Bec-Fin had already become the city's benchmark for elegant continental cooking.

"But we thought another French restaurant would work," he said. "We'd charge no more than $10 for anything."

It is almost comical to think of Deux Cheminees' ruefully rich crab soup Marguerite laced with Johnny Walker Red for $1.50 a bowl. Or its hauntingly good rack of lamb crusted with herbs and served with truffle sauce for $8.50.

You can't even sit down after 6 p.m. at Deux Cheminees these days for less than $85. (Early birds pay $65). And that is just for the passenger-class four-course meal. If you want an upgrade to sample the crab soup, foie gras, or an appetizer instead of a salad, it will cost you — an annoyingly nickel-and-dime feature — $5 extra a pop. Just make it $90, I say, and throw in crab soup for the masses.

I love Deux Cheminees despite its inflated prices, because Blank is one of those rare individuals who does many things well. And Deux Cheminees (which means "two fireplaces") has remained one of the city's big-occasion classics under his tutelage, surviving a fire and settling into its spectacular second location, a Locust Street townhouse designed by Frank Furness in the 1880s.

Chef Fritz Blank has become one of Philadelphia's preeminent food historians.

Its sumptuously appointed dining rooms are warmed by six blazing fireplaces, an elegant montage of Victorian art, and 15 antique clocks.

Bolstered by an obsessive thirst for books, with a cookbook collection that exceeds 10,000, Blank has become one of Philadelphia's preeminent food historians and teaching chefs. Nearly 200 apprentices have passed through his kitchen, constantly bringing him soups and sauces dabbed on a plate for his tasting scrutiny.

And they will return until it's perfect.

Few chefs, to my mind, could provide lessons in cookery as valuable as Blank's. Though his food is rarely about innovation, it is technically pristine: largely creamy, stock-infused French dishes, inflected with the occasional German spaetzle or liver dumpling.

His mastery of focusing flavors is evident in every rich bite, beginning with an unforgettable soup course. From the moment that frothy crab soup touches the tongue, its bechamel edged by an alcoholic splash of Scotch, nerve endings will tingle down to the end of your toes. His amber dark consomme Celestin is so crystal pure, the ribbons of toasty crepe and snappy fresh peas lend its broth real dynamic. One recent mushroom soup brought a menagerie of fungi in rich dark broth, each mushroom coarsely cut to highlight its earthy crunch.

Institutions such as Deux Cheminees are priceless in part for the forgotten dishes they perpetuate, the kind that are numerous on this menu. Super-thin slices of calves' liver are crisp, yet medium-rare, anointed in raspberry vinegar that is a touch sweet. Tender escargots doused with garlicky Pernod butter come with a warm brioche bun on the side.

At a recent meal, the roasted duckling was practically falling off the bone, its skin crackling with the dark glaze of tangy griot cherry sauce. Perfectly medium rare medallions of venison came with a red wine gravy that highlighted a gibety undertone, then mingled with those wonderful, springy driblets of spaetzle dumplings.

The silky texture of real bearnaise sauce transformed an already wonderful New York strip steak into a paragon of meat. Lean and tender frog's legs were infused with the tang of white-wine verjus and herbaceous juniper berries.

The kitchen is quite a hike, nestled into the basement at the end of a long corridor lined with copper pots where a brass plaque reads in French, like a scientist's species label: "Kitchen, the heart of the restaurant."

Deux Cheminees' distinguished black-tie servers don't exactly seem the jogging types, which might explain the exceedingly pokey pace of dinner. There was a certain Old World grace in their unobtrusive manner that I do appreciate. Although in the translation of serving, the unobtrusiveness can feel somewhat stuffy. Or maybe it is just the weighty quietude here that always makes me feel like I need to whisper.

Such quibbles, though, will have long melted away once desserts arrive — classic, like the savory menu, and just as flawlessly performed. A banana tarte layered between oval, fluted rounds of puff pastry set onto an intense caramel.

Or Try These

Here are three other restaurants with old-world black-tie service:

Monte Carlo Living Room

150 South St., Philadelphia
(215) 925-2220

This classic Northern Italian has a tradition of exquisite continental cuisine and expert service that has remained special. The kitschy decore was recently updated, but whether it will thrive despite the recent departure of its longtime culinary genius, Nunzio Patruno, remains to be seen.

La Buca

711 Locust St. Philadelphia, PA, (215) 928-0556

This downstairs grotto off Washington Square is an oft forgetten haven of black tie service, and specialties such as whole fish, grilled langostinos, pasta fagiole and other Italian classics executed with perfect simplicity.

La Famiglia

8 S. Front St., Philadelphia
(215) 922-2803

This posh Old City institution for upscale Neopolitan cooking may no longer be our very best Italian eatery, but it still has the region's finest (and most expensive) Italian wine cellar, with nearly 13,000 bottles on display behind cages downstairs.

Creme caramel in rum sauce that is a perfect antidote to everyone else's mediocre creme brulee. A silky souffle of frozen meringue liquefies from the inside out when pierced by a stream of warm Grand Marnier liqueur. Or you can indulge a generous cheese plate laden with a thick, satisfying wedge of salty Roquefort and other, more esoteric curds.

The evening, though, would not be complete without a schmooze from Chef Blank himself, who makes a habit of roaming the dining room. Jolly and rotunde in his boxy British chef's cap, he is as entertainingly erudite as company could be.

There aren't too many chefs in the world who are steady subscribers to the Morbidity and Mortality Weekly Report, a trade journal in which culinary trends can be rather grim. But in this fickle restaurant business, it doesn't hurt — even after 20 years — to have a solid fallback plan.

■ **MENU HIGHLIGHTS** Soup course; crab soup Marguerite; beef carpaccio; escargot; frog's legs; sweetbreads; calves' liver; duckling with griot cherries; venison with spaetzle; steak with bearnaise; rack of lamb; banana tarte; creme caramel; cheese platter.

■ **WINE LIST** A medium-size list of prestige American and French bottles with very few real values. The wine-by-the-glass selection is shockingly poor.

■ **IF YOU GO** Dinner served Tuesday-Saturday 5:30-9 p.m. Closed Sunday-Monday. There is a four-course $85 fixed-price menu for dinner. The menu costs $65 if ordered before 6 p.m.

■ **RESERVATIONS** Strongly suggested.

■ **CREDIT CARDS** All major cards but Discover.

■ **SMOKING** Entire restaurant is nonsmoking.

■ **HANDICAP ACCESSIBLE** The restaurant is not accessible. There is a large staircase at the entrance and bathrooms are located in the basement.

■ **PARKING** Street parking only.

Dilworthtown Inn

The historic country inn has excellent updated continental cuisine, veteran service, and fine wines.

The blood-curdling battle cry boomed out from one of the dining rooms in back.

"*Bleep* the French!!"

It was 10 p.m. and a blur of blue blazers and silver hair could be seen scooting in a patrician fluster toward the exit of the Dilworthtown Inn. The screams became more raucous.

"*Bleeeeeep* the French!!!"

Your intrepid dining reporter, meanwhile, gingerly tip-toed closer to the room in question. This historic inn survived the destruction wrought by redcoats after the Battle of Brandywine in 1777. It rose from the ashes of a devastating fire in 1992. Perhaps this yowling demon was an apparition of its storied Colonial past come to wreak havoc on the inn's dainty, candle-lit ambience?

EXCELLENT

1390 Old Wilmington Pike,
Village of Dilworthtown,
West Chester, Pa.
(610) 399-1390

NEIGHBORHOOD
West Chester

CUISINE
Continental/
New American

I peek around the corner, only to see co-owner Jim Barnes hustling red-faced out of the private dining room in his tuxedo. These were no ghosts, he said, but the staff of Philadelphia's Four Seasons Hotel kitchen, coming to the rowdy and quite inebriated end of a daylong "in service" meeting. The hotel's French and American coworkers, it seems, were exchanging pleasantries.

I admit some surprise at the shenanigans of such an esteemed hotel staff. (Just try behaving like that at the Four Seasons.) Then again, the Dilworthtown possesses one of the very few cellars in the region that could whet such discriminating tastes, whether it's a vertical sampling of Chateau Cheval Blanc or the sweet bottle of 1976 Hungarian Tokaji Essencia they had polished off.

But a fine cellar with more than 900 selections is only one reason the inn has thrived nearly 30 years as a destination for fine dining without going as stale as the fieldstones that ballast its walls. Dilworthtown has always set the country "inn" standard as the complete package.

Beneath the starry skies and crisp fall air of the Chester County countryside, the old building emits the inviting yellow glow of candlelight through paned windows. Inside each of its 15 dining rooms,

The Dilworthtown Inn, viewed from a porch across the street, has 15 dining rooms, but a cozy, romantic scale.

many filled with brick hearths and Colonial-style tables hand-crafted on the premises, there is an intimacy that lends this big restaurant a cozy, romantic scale. (As long as you don't sit in the terribly noisy front room.)

But how many old country inns would take the ambience and run, leaving the kitchen to crank out prime rib and baked potatoes?

Yawn.

There are plenty of old classics on Dilworthtown's menu, to be sure, a Chateaubriand for two, broiled lobster tail blooming out of its shell, and sublimely creamy mushroom soup. But the kitchen here also brings some contemporary ideas to the table, adding an occasional Asian overtone to a repertoire of straight-ahead good cooking.

A delicious appetizer of lobster tail, for example, is encased in crisp tempura batter, served with a tingly ginger dip of honey, apricot and chiles. Gingered mustard spices up the crab cake.

The menu has changed little over the last few years. But some of the more modern dishes at a recent dinner seemed a smidgen less sharp under young chef Jason Barrowcliff than they did under his predecessor, sometimes lacking an extra focus of flavor.

The porcini-dusted cod had a whisper of the mushroom's musky oomph, but was surprisingly understated. A side of truffled spaetzle was a great idea, but those humble dumplings could have used a more generous touch of the truffle's luxury.

Perhaps I nitpick. But only because the talent here is obvious. The kitchen had its greatest success when it was less self-conscious and trendy, focusing instead on the satisfaction of good ingredients prepared with care.

Escargots are sauteed with garlicky button and porcini mushrooms then sauced with lobster-champagne sauce. A house-made galantine of ground veal and pistachios is flashed on the grill, the crisscross char marks highlighting the crumbly pate's meaty savor.

The selection of classic chops was as good as ever. The champagne garlic mustard-crusted rack of lamb was juicy and tender. Long, rose-colored strips of beautifully seared duck breast were served with an earthy garnish of caramelized cauliflower. And a beautiful T-bone of venison was absolutely luscious, richer than beef, almost berrylike in flavor, basted in its natural juices.

The Chilean sea bass was also just as I remember, perfectly seared with a lobster sauce and tarragon cream.

I have always enjoyed the desserts here, especially the homemade ice creams, frozen chocolate mousse cake, cheesecakes, and fruit confections. But they still lack the imagination and sophistication of the rest of the meal.

My favorite dish at the Dilworthtown Inn, though, isn't produced by the kitchen at all. It is the Caesar salad prepared tableside by the restaurant's veteran dining room staff. And if there is a better Caesar salad master anywhere than Monte Wiradilaga, I haven't found him yet.

"Today's my first day," deadpans the server, smiling slyly as he sidles up to our table with his trusty wooden bowl. The absolute elegance and charm with which he undertakes the forgotten art of tableside service belies his 27 years on the job. A dash of this, a splash of that, a gentle grind of pepper. Wiradilaga uses no measures, but an instinctual nose for the perfect dressing, mashing away with fork in hand until his masterpiece is nearly done. He signals the finale with the dramatic flip of a linen napkin, releasing

Or Try These

Here are three other country "inn" restaurants.

Inn on Blueberry Hill

1715 S. Easton Rd., Doylestown, Pa. (215) 491-1777

An ambitious Bucks County inn whose talented chef, Bill Kim, formerly of Susanna Foo, is creating memorable contemporary cuisine.

Mainland Inn

17 Main St. (Sumneytown Pike), Mainland, Pa. (215) 256-8500

A pleasant Montco inn with classy service and seasonal New American cooking.

Rat's

16 Fairgrounds Rd., Hamilton, N.J. (609) 584-7800

J. Seward Johnson's gourmet restaurant and sculpture park materializes outside Trenton like a hybrid of Giverny and the Twilight Zone, a picturesque setting for ambitious (and occasionally inconsistent) French cuisine and a first-class wine cellar.

a confetti of marvelously crisp romaine lettuce that floats into the bowl.

It is one of the best things I've eaten in a while, electrically tangy, teasingly pungent, and addictively zippy. Romaine in its moment of glory. One taste and you realize why this salad had become a classic to begin with.

But it is a sensation that repeats itself throughout the meal virtually every time I return here. No wonder the Dilworthtown Inn has survived so long and continues to thrive — come redcoat or rowdy guest chef — near the top of its game.

■ **MENU HIGHLIGHTS** Ginger crisp lobster; cream of mushroom soup; Caesar salad; galantine of veal; filet of beef au poivre; rack of lamb; duck; venison T-bone; homemade ice cream; cheesecake.

■ **WINE LIST** One of the finest and deepest wine lists in the region runs 28 pages long, with vertical selections of numerous big-name Bordeaux and Napa cabernets, plus some less common gems, including a rich and spicy zinfandel from the Lamborn family and a rarity such as a Hungarian Tokaji Essencia sweet wine from the mid-1970s.

■ **IF YOU GO** Dinner served Monday-Friday 5:30- 9:30 p.m., Saturday 5-9:30 p.m., Sunday 3-9 p.m. Entrees, $18.95-$32.95.

■ **RESERVATIONS** Highly recommended.

■ **CREDIT CARDS** All major cards.

■ **SMOKING** All dining rooms are nonsmoking.

■ **HANDICAP ACCESSIBLE** Yes.

■ **PARKING** Free lot.

Django

The neighborhood BYOB reaches new heights of sophistication at this European-inspired bistro.

I f Aimee Olexy had followed her first impulse, Django would be a lunch truck instead of one of my favorite new restaurants. Then again, had she followed her second impulse, Olexy would have been knocking on doors with a suitcase full of smelly cheeses, a sort of cheesemonger who makes house calls.

Now that's a foodie career crisis if there ever was one. But I understand. Olexy spent years rising through the world of corporate restaurant management, first for the Kimpton Group in Colorado and then for mega-restaurateur Stephen Starr, helping to open Blue Angel, Tangerine and Pod.

But the more responsibility she earned, the more she lost touch with her ground-floor passion for restaurants: the basic pleasures of

EXCELLENT

526 S. Fourth St.
Philadelphia
(215) 922-7151

NEIGHBORHOOD
South Street

CUISINE
New American

being around food. The handiwork of cooking and serving and knowing customers that attracted her to the industry in the first place, when she worked at the Spring Mill Cafe in Conshohocken 17 years ago.

I'm sure I would have liked what Olexy and her husband, chef Bryan Sikora, cooked up in their lunch truck. Sikora, trained at the Culinary Institute of America, was previously the sous chef at Tangerine. But I'm thrilled they opted instead for Olexy's third impulse — a little bistro — because Django is already setting a new standard for what a neighborhood restaurant can be, from the creative amuse-bouches that start each meal (we had thimble-size ravioli filled with ratatouille one night) to the grand finale of Olexy's extraordinary cheese plate.

It's ironic that two people used to opening multimillion-dollar eating extravaganzas for other restaurateurs had little more than a pair of mountain bikes to offer as collateral on the small government loan that launched their own business.

But simplicity by necessity is part of the beauty of this cozy yellow restaurant, which sits snugly amid the Fourth Street storefronts north of South Street. Its homey walls are covered with vintage movie posters, a few antique plates, and a couple of dangling stained-glass lamps.

Like the soft, open weave of the burlap-textured linens that give

Chef Bryan Sikora and Aimee Olexy's Django is already setting a new standard for what a neighborhood restaurant can be.

the tables a rustic charm, there is an honest plainness to this place that puts basic qualities in full relief. There are wonderful seasonal ingredients from local farms, attentive service led by Olexy (who preps food during the day), and a regional European menu quite sophisticated for under $20 an entree. It is no wonder Django has become one of the hardest reservations in town to wrangle.

Homemade bread blooms out of terra-cotta flowerpots, and it is spongy, vaguely sweet, and still fragrant with yeast. Hand-cranked ribbons of pasta twirl around veal cheek carbonara, a creamy mash of fork-shredded meat sprinkled with lemony gremolata. In another summer-themed carbonara, the noodles entwined with tender nuggets of lobster in a Pernod-scented bisque.

The bustling room still has the character of a neighborhood haunt, with its mismatched chairs, noisy crowds from Society Hill and Queen Village, and cute tattooed servers deftly opening bottles of wines. (The restaurant is BYOB.)

But Olexy and Sikora bring a polish and ambition more typical of a grander restaurant. Sikora's cooking, in particular, doesn't cut corners. Each dish is thoughtfully conceived with layers of flavor and texture.

The eggplant soup is marvelous, a creamy puree perfumed with ginger and coriander and ringed with a streak of pistachio oil. At the center of the bowl, homemade tortellini filled with tangy local goat cheese bob onto your spoon. A few large shrimp wrapped in crisp bands of prosciutto play against the surprising sweetness of cool, soft melon.

A Spanish mackerel entree brings slender fillets, sealed in a nearly translucent polenta crust, set over a complex piperade sauce that swirls with sweet, spicy roasted peppers, piquant olives, cuminy chorizo, and three kinds of stock (lobster, fish and veal).

If anything, Sikora risks overworking his plates to hit every taste-bud. An elaborate squash ravioli entree, for example, never quite came together. But rarely did nimble technique overshadow the kitchen's desire to showcase its good organic ingredients.

Or Try These

Here are three other ambitious BYOBs.

Pif

1009 S. Eighth St., Philadelphia
(215) 625-2923

A charming little bistro serving French fare inspired by the chef's daily shopping visits to the nearby Italian Market.

Chlöe

232 Arch St., Philadelphia
(215) 629-2337

A homey Old City BYOB with an international take on comfort food.

Rx

4443 Spruce St., Philadelphia
(215) 222-9590

This old apothecary-turned-contemporary-corner-spot offers creative and affordable updates on bistro food that is just what the doctor ordered for gentrifying West Philly.

Homemade crepes are folded over an oozy filling of warm Brie and shiitake mushrooms coarsely cut to highlight their woodsy flavor. A salad of heirloom tomatoes is luscious enough, but with the addition of milky sweet chunks of buffalo mozzarella, I have a memory of late summer's ripeness to carry me through winter.

Tuscan ribollita soup, its broth made from smoked Lancaster County ham, is filled with creamy white beans and a satisfying medley of fall vegetables.

The best entrees also captured seasonal flavors in a vibrant tableau. In August, pan-seared duck breast was served with plump blackberries over soft pillows of homemade gnocchi. Medallions of veal scallopini came topped with rounds of tender fingerling potatoes, oyster mushrooms, and sweet baby onions that mingled with soft nuggets of sweetbreads.

Fillets of meaty tilefish were perched over fluffy whipped potatoes and saffron-braised artichoke hearts.

The dessert list is small but satisfying. A dense chocolate terrine layered with almond praline is topped with a scoop of homemade almond ice cream and crumbled caramel praline, cleverly salted to enhance the confections.

The creme brulee, reconstructed into three crunchy custard tiers between caramelized phyllo dough, was an interesting twist on an overdone classic. And the baked peach crumble topped with white chocolate ice cream was a wholesome ode to the orchard, undersweetened a bit to let the ripe peaches speak for themselves.

Even with such temptations, I'd be hard-pressed not to choose Olexy's sublime cheese plate, a remarkable value at $9. Not only does it bring small tastes of about 10 different cheeses, several types of pears, two kinds of honey, fig jam, and toasted nuts; it is like everything else at Django, a cut above in quality.

These were world-class powerhouse cheeses, including mountain Taleggio, ethereal Epoisses, and wine-soaked Umbriaco. Olexy ages as many as 30 varieties in-house until they are perfect, quivering and creamy, ready to sing on the plate.

It is almost moving to watch her bring them to the table and lovingly describe each one. The passion of her own handiwork once again twinkles in her eye.

■ MENU HIGHLIGHTS Sweet eggplant soup; ribollita soup; veal cheek carbonara; shrimp with prosciutto and melon; Brie and mushroom crepe; polenta-crusted mackerel; tilefish with artichoke barigoule; duck breast; block steak; cheese plate; chocolate-almond terrine.

■ WINE LIST BYOB.

■ IF YOU GO Dinner served Tuesday-Saturday 5:30-10:30 p.m.; Sunday 5:30-9:30 p.m. Entrees, $15-$23.

■ RESERVATIONS Strongly recommended.

■ CREDIT CARDS All major credit cards but Discover and Diners Club accepted.

■ SMOKING No smoking.

■ HANDICAP ACCESSIBLE Handicapped access: There is a small step at the entrance; rest room is wheelchair accessible.

■ PARKING Street parking only.

Dmitri's

The wildly popular eateries' appeal is the clarity of the menu — Greek seafood done as simply and as affordably as possible.

Somewhere in the afterlife, there will be an irate octopus waiting for Dmitri Chimes. The middle-age restaurateur jokes uneasily about this, but there has to be some kind of catch, right?

"I often wonder about how I'm going to have to pay in the future," he muses, "for all this octopus I've sold."

It is an unlikely scenario for conservative Philadelphia: Former rock guitarist for '70s groups like the Broad Street Dirt Band and the Burning Dogs turns tiny neighborhood restaurant into a local phenomenon; menu includes basic Greek seafood specialties, including boatloads of grilled octopus.

VERY GOOD

Third and Catharine Streets, (215) 625-0556; 23d and Pine Streets, (215) 985-3680 Philadelphia

NEIGHBORHOOD
Queen Village/Fitler Square

CUISINE
Greek Seafood

The 35-seat corner nook at Third and Catharine Streets in Queen Village is so small, it didn't seem plausible even to Chimes and his wife, Sheila, when they began looking for their own restaurant. But more than a decade later, the octopus hath spoken. Blushing pink and touched by char, splashed with just the right amount of olive oil, herbs, and a squeeze of lemon, those pale meaty tubes of chewy goodness became a star. I liken it to chicken salad with a Mediterranean swagger.

Chimes' crack crew of efficient Hmong chefs regularly churns 175 customers through "Old Original" Dmitri's on a weekend night. And evidently it isn't fast enough. I once waited nearly two hours for a shot at one of the supremely plain grilled whole pompanos, participating in a Philadelphia dining ritual — the Dmitri's wait — that has gathered a mystique almost impossible to sustain. The pompano was good, but it wasn't *that* good.

The decision three years ago to clone the mother-raft, converting his other waning projects at Stix and Pamplona to the original stripped-down Dmitri's model, must have annoyed the Queen Village faithful. All those years spent refining The Wait and now everyone can get a table?

Nothing deflates a mystique more than accessibility, and the duplication is fraught with danger for the sainted Dmitri's name, as evidenced by the eventual closing of the former-Pamplona-turned-Dmitri's at 12th and Locust Streets. (It has since become Sukhothai.) The kitchen has fared better at the Fitler Square space formerly known as Stix, where original Dmitri's chef Chong "Hua" Xiong cheerfully navigates its open kitchen.

But I know Queen Village-loyalists who will never cede that this one is equal. "The grill is different," sniffs one. On a recent taste comparison, though, Fitler Square's grilled bluefish was easily superior, bursting with a moist and savory twang where Queen Village's was dry and fishy.

All this niggling may be a blessing in disguise. Stripped of some of its aura, this new Dmitri's on Fitler Square can avoid some of the downsides of impossible scenedom and still prove itself to be a very good affordable neighborhood seafood restaurant. Which is what the concept was intended to be all along. After all, the Dmitri's appeal is the clarity of its menu — Greek seafood done as simply and as affordably as possible, splashed with garlicky oil and lemon, and rarely more than $18 a plate.

My whole grilled pompano looked as if it had barely been touched by the chef. The snub-nosed fish sat on the plate in its silver-skinned birthday suit with only a couple of grill marks to tell me otherwise. Inside was pure moist fish, so naturally flavored that its luxurious white flesh gushed the mild juice of freshness. Grilled scallops on a skewer were seared brown with the heat of flame but still tender and ivory inside, the perfect contrast to bundles of garlicky escarole that come with every dish. (Queen Village's escarole has little, if any, garlic.)

The narrow room looks out through light-edged windows onto quaint Fitler Square and, with its clay-pot-colored walls scrawled with Greek motifs, has a modest spaciousness the original Dmitri's doesn't have. The room still gets deafeningly loud. But the westside Dimitri's takes credit cards (Queen Village takes only cash), and it also has a cute little list of very affordable international wines around $30. (Queen Village is BYOB.)

Or Try These

Here are three other affordable seafood restaurants.

Little Fish

600 Catharine St., Philadelphia (215) 413-3464

This Queen Village BYOB is one of the smallest nooks in town, but the daily changing seafood menu has wide-ranging flavors and great desserts.

Anastasi Seafood

1101 S. Ninth St., Philadelphia (215) 462-0550

The restaurant inside this South Philly fish market serves up fresh, fairly priced seafood with a neighborhood Italian flair.

Emerald Fish

65 Barclay Farms Shopping Center, Rte. 70, E. Cherry Hill, N.J. (856) 616-9192

This colorful strip-mall BYOB has an internationally inspired kitchen, with great specials like Chilean sea bass topped with miso-sweetened eggplant pate.

Jennifer Brodsky threads her way through tables at Dmitri's, very good and affordable in two locations.

Dmitri's $12 platter of Mediterranean nibbles is one of the best excuses I know to work my way through a plateful of grill-charred pita bread wedges — a musky puree of chickpea hummus; the smoke-tinged fruity mush of eggplant baba ghannouj; the walnut snap and raw garlic burn of bread-thickened skordalia dip; refreshing cucumber and yogurt tzatziki; the salty orange cream of pureed carp roe tarama salada; the sweet crimson chunks of roasted beets (these, I'll give you, are crisper and tarter in Queen Village). The creamy feta spinach pie wrapped in layers of a crisp phyllo was an addictive delight.

Comfort food desserts like creme caramel, cinnamon-dusted rice pudding, and a firm wedge of orange almond cake make for simple but satisfying sweets.

The menu's most complicated creation, in fact, turns out to be a salad, a montage of creamy avocado, toasty slivered almonds, spritzy citrus wedges, and refreshing romaine lettuce that is an amazing combination if you can manage to get every element on the same fork.

Dmitri's undeniable forte, though, is straightforward seafood preparations. A broiled fillet of dewy fresh tilapia was so pristine in its wine and lemon glaze, a speckling of black pepper gave it interesting flavor twists. Greaseless tubes of fried calamari were fresh and nicely tender, sparked higher by a squeeze of lemon. Perfectly panfried flounder was sealed beneath a delicate breadcrumb crust.

The assertive flavor of the large, nicely fried smelts is for fish fanatics only; I liked them despite their crunchy spines. Chimes, however, recommends filleting them with your teeth.

The true test, of course, would be the octopus. I liked it enough. But for purposes of authentification, I'd also brought along my very own Queen Village snob, who complained that the octopus "didn't have enough parsley." And, in fact, it never has quite attained that Queen Village tenderness and char.

Perhaps this is the payback of trading on mystique. If the octopus doesn't get Dmitri first, his zealous customers certainly will.

■ **MENU HIGHLIGHTS** Mediterranean plate; beets; grilled octopus; spinach pie; grilled whole fish; sauteed shrimp ; grilled bluefish; panfried breaded flounder; grilled scallops; grilled lamb; creme caramel.

■ **WINE LIST** Queen Village is BYOB, but Fitler Square has a decent list of affordable wines.

■ **IF YOU GO** Queen Village: Tuesday-Saturday, 5:30-11 p.m.; Sunday, 5-10 p.m.; Monday, 5:30-10 p.m. Fitler Square: Sunday-Thursday, 5:30-10 p.m.; Friday-Saturday, 5:30-11 p.m. Entrees, $8.50-$18.

■ **RESERVATIONS** Not accepted.

■ **CREDIT CARDS** Queen Village accepts cash only. Fitler Square accepts Visa and MasterCard.

■ **SMOKING** There is a nonsmoking section in Fitler Square, with smoking at the bar. Queen Village is entirely nonsmoking.

■ **HANDICAP ACCESSIBLE** There are two steps at the entrance of Fitler Square, but the bathrooms are accessible. Queen Village is not handicapped equipped.

■ **PARKING** Street parking only.

Effie's

The neighborhood restaurant, owned by a mother and daughter, has an unmistakeably Greek flair.

Come in through Effie's front door. Pass by the crush of hungry patrons waiting beside the narrow open kitchen, where skewers of lamb souvlaki, whole red snappers, and yeasty pita wedges sizzle on the charcoal grill, and slip out the back door.

Across the flagstone patio that is still unused in the chill of winter, a charming cottage dining room is warmed by the wood-fire heat of an iron stove. It is just like the stoves Paul Bouikidis knew in Northern Greece before he came to Philadelphia, where he has owned Pine Street Pizza for the last 23 years.

In contrast to his pizzeria across the street, this restaurant, owned by his wife and daughter, Loula and Effie Bouikidis, has an unmis-takeably Greek flair. The stucco walls and white-washed beams of the 16-seat back cottage, in particular, leave little doubt at all.

VERY GOOD

1127 Pine St.
Philadelphia
(215) 592-8333

NEIGHBORHOOD
Washington Square West

CUISINE
Greek

"Grandmom's dining room," as Effie likes to call it.

I couldn't think of a more appropriate setting for Effie's, a cozy gem of a neighborhood restaurant that serves the kind of old-fashioned satisfaction Grandmom herself might have offered.

Loula Bouikidis was too shy, Effie says, to let the restaurant be named in her honor. But Loula is, with the help of son-in-law Jorge Jimenez, the lively kitchen spirit who has translated this menu of Greek home-cooking so nicely to a restaurant setting.

Whether whisking her chicken rice soup into a lemony egg custard for just the right consistency or rolling her own phyllo dough into papery sheets with a broom handle so the fabulous spinach pie will have a true Macedonian crackle, the touch of a caring cook is evident here.

This cozy BYOB is rewardingly affordable. And the preparations have a straightforward simplicity that can make rustic Greek cooking so satisfying when the ingredients are fresh,

Delicate tubes of calamari, dredged simply in flour then flash fried, need only tenderness and a squeeze of lemon to disappear from the plate. Skewered cubes of grilled lamb souvlaki (which means "stick" in Greek) are irresistibly fragrant, helped along by a refreshing side of tzaziki cucumber salad cloaked in deliciously thick, homemade yogurt. A mountain of shaved gyros meat, a seasoned combination of ground lamb and beef, fared equally well.

Feta cheese, imported from the northern region of Iperos, is served in plain thick wedges with salty kalamata olives and good yellow Greek olive oil. A full hunk of it in the mouth conjures the fruity creaminess of wild sheep's milk in a way that feta never does when it's crumbled, as usual, in a supporting role over salads.

Loula Bouikidis is such a stickler for purity, she won't mix oregano and bayleaf in her tomato sauces for fear that one might cancel the other out. Her plum tomato sauce is indeed rather plain. But it is more of an accent than a centerpiece flavor, glazing hearty casseroles of eggplant moussaka and wonderful pastitsio with color and piquancy, a perfect contrast to the creamy layers of bechamel that top them.

The casseroles are big as paving stones and just about as filling. The moussaka takes one step toward lightening the classic, grilling instead of frying the eggplant slices before layering them in with potatoes, ground beef and bechamel.

Used as a braising liquid for tender leg of lamb, the tomato sauce absorbs wonderful gamy flavors, and each bite pops with the bright sparks of peppercorns gone soft over three hours of cooking.

For a small restaurant, Effie's kitchen seems to thrive on the crowds that jam its doors, undeterred by the frequent waits of a no-reservation policy. So much so, however, that it seemed to lose its adrenaline on a quiet and Loula-less evening. The spinach pie lost a hint of crispness in its crunch. And on one recent visit, the phyllo wasn't homemade. A panfried fillet of flounder was humdrum compared to the usually flavorful whole fish off the grill. A faintly fishy taste of iodine crept through the tomato sauce of shrimp Santorini. And the char-happy cooks let bread and tender

Or Try These

Here are three other Greek restaurants.

South Street Souvlaki

509 South St., Philadelphia
(215) 925-3026
This venerable South Street taverna still serves up a respectable selection of the classics, from massive moussaka to yogurt-laced souvlaki sandwiches.

Dmitri's

Third and Catharine Streets
(215) 625-0556; 23d and Pine Streets (215) 985-3680, Philadelphia
Wildly popular bistros serving affordable and delicious Greek seafood specialties including legendary grilled octopus.

Zorba's Taverna

2230 Fairmount Ave., Philadelphia (215) 978-5990
A Fairmount neighborhood standby with a steam table stocked full of steady Hellenic favorites like braised lamb shank.

octopus acquire too much burn from the grill.

The servers, however, were consistently pleasant, informative and hardworking. And while they were attentive at a respectable level for a casual restaurant like Effie's, it would be a big improvement if they took the small extra effort to replace used silverware between courses instead of leaving it directly on the bare table.

Effie's baklava, on the other hand, could not be improved at all. How many times has a lesser restaurant cheated, layering nuts and honey like a simple sandwich between thick stacks of wadded brown phyllo? The impostors slip and slide and shatter artlessly between the teeth.

I could not count the layers of Loula's baklava. There simply were too many of those fine translucent sheets, each one carefully brushed with melted butter then dusted with nuts and cinnamon. Once baked, yet still hot from the oven, the pastry is drenched in a syrupy elixir infused with cinnamon, honey and lemon. After a minimum of six hours' soaking, the phyllo leaves seem to hover invisibly in an ambrosia that only time and love could create.

Like the wonderful rice pudding, the phyllo dough tubes filled with semolina custard, and the shredded-wheat plugs wrapped around walnuts and cinnamon, the flavor of a real baklava is a triumph of authentic "grandmom cuisine."

And so is Effie's.

■ **MENU HIGHLIGHTS** Spinach pie; Northern Greek feta with olives; Thessaloniki platter; calamari; lemon rice soup special; souvlaki; gyros; braised lamb; pastitsio; moussaka; baklava; Greek coffee.

■ **WINE LIST** BYOB.

■ **IF YOU GO** Dinner served Sunday-Thursday 5-10 p.m., Friday-Saturday 5-11 p.m. Dinner entrees, $8 to $15.

■ **RESERVATIONS** Not accepted.

■ **CREDIT CARDS** Not accepted.

■ **SMOKING** No smoking.

■ **HANDICAP ACCESSIBLE** Back dining is accessible, but the bathrooms are not.

■ **PARKING** Street parking only.

Liquid Philly

If all this food is making you thirsty, here is my essential guide to the pleasures of Liquid Philly.

Beer

Monk's Cafe, 264 S. 16th St., has an awesome selection of Belgian trappist ales. **Standard Tap,** 901 N. Second St., is an advocate for fresh local beers on draught. **Ludwig's Garten**, 1315 Sansom St., makes up for its overly heavy fare with outstanding German lagers and wheat beers. These Irish bars offer my favorite pints of Guinness (in this order): **Black Sheep**, 247 S. 17th St.; **Plough & the Stars,** 123 Chestnut St.; **Bards,** 2013 Walnut St.; **Fado**, 1500 Locust St.; and **Tir Na Nog**, The Phoenix, 1600 Arch St.

The **Foodery Market**, 324 S. 10th St., has one of the largest, most diverse selections of beers-by-the-bottle in the area.

Tequila

Los Catrines Restaurant, 1602 Locust St., has the region's most extensive selection, followed by **Zocalo,** 3600 Lancaster Ave.

Whiskey

The Dark Horse, 421 S. Second St., inherited an immense, world-class collection of single-malt Scotches when it took over the Dickens Inn, including several vintage bottles of cask-strength brew that are no longer distilled. The **Black Sheep** has an excellent selection of fine Irish whiskeys. **Jack's Firehouse**, 2130 Fairmount Ave., pays homage to owner Jack McDavid's Southern heritage with its array of single-batch bourbons.

Vodka

Sonoma, 4411 Main St., has every variation of vodka known to Manayunk.

Rum

The Nuevo Latino menu at **Cuba Libre**, 10 S. Second St., tastes even better with fine rums from Nicaragua to Martinique. **Alma de Cuba**, 1623 Walnut St., **Cafe Habana**, 102 S. 21st St., **London Grill**, 2301 Fairmount Ave., and **¡Pasion!**, 211 S. 15th St., are other good rum venues.

Grappas

La Famiglia, 8 S. Front St., **Vetri**, 1312 Spruce St., **Avenue B**, 260 S. Broad St.

Sake

Morimoto, 723 Chestnut St., **Genji**, 1720 Sansom St., **Anjou**, 206 Market St., and **Margaret Kuo's Peking**, Granite Run Mall, 1067 W. Baltimore Pike, Media, Pa.

The bar at the Wooden Iron

Martinis

Martini culture has spread virtually everywhere by now, but it found its nexus in Old City at **The Continenal**, 138 Market St.

General Excellence

Here are a few other notable watering holes: **Wooden Iron**, 118 N. Wayne Ave., Wayne, Pa., **Twenty21**, 2005 Market St., **Brasserie Perrier**, 1619 Walnut St., **Swann Lounge**, 1 Logan Square; **Trust**, 121-127 S. 13th St.; **333 Belrose**, 333 Belrose Lane, Radnor, Pa.

Cocktails

I'm not much of a cocktail drinker; I prefer my spirits straight. But here are a few mixed drinks that I'd happily indulge:

■ The champagne sangria at **Mallorca**, 119 South St.

■ The Fez Fizz, champagne with pomegranate syrup, at **Tangerine**, 232 Market St.

■ The calvados sidecar at **London Grill**, 2301 Fairmount Ave.

■ The passion fruit caiprinha at **¡Pasion!**, 211 S. 15th St.

■ The alma colada at **Alma de Cuba**, 1623 Walnut St.

■ The Cuban Manhattan at **Cuba Libre**, 10 S. Second St.

■ The **Happy Rooster's** (118 S. 16th St.) special Valentine's Day Rose-hattan, which replaces the Manhattan's cherry with a candied rose petal.

Wine

Despite state liquor laws that offer a major challenge to our wine scene, hampering both variety and value, several restaurants have managed to build tremendous wine lists. Here are some of the best:

French-Based Lists

Dilworthtown Inn
Fountain Restaurant
Le Bec-Fin

Le Mas Perrier
Deux Cheminees
Blue Bell Inn

LaCroix at the Rittenhouse
Bistro St. Tropez
Rat's

Italian-Based Lists

La Famiglia
Vetri

Avenue B
Davio's

Monte Carlo
Living Room

Eclectic Cellars With a Strong American Component

Savona
Strawberry Hill
Opus 251
Fork
Jake's

Buddakan
Tangerine
Happy Rooster
Inn on Blueberry Hill
Sullivan's Steakhouse

Capital Grille
Twenty21
London Grill
White Dog Cafe
Restaurant 821

Latin-Centric Cellars

¡Pasion!

Alma de Cuba

Lists That Smartly Break the Mold

Striped Bass, 1500 Walnut St., proves definitively with its powerhouse list that fish doesn't always pair best with whites. **Susanna Foo's** (1512 Walnut St.) prestige wine collection has defied the stereotypes for Asian cuisine.

Bargain Lists

■ **Friday Saturday Sunday**, 261 S. 21st St., has an iconoclastic $10 mark-up over cost on all its bottles.

■ **Prime Rib**, 1701 Locust St., has plenty of big-ticket steak-house cabernets, but also a selection of 30 wines under $40.

■ **Ernesto's 1521 Cafe**, 1521 Spruce St., has a great selection for an Italian trattoria, with most of its all-Italian list at $30 or less, and more expensive bottles capped at a $20 mark-up over cost.

■ **Blue Angel** (706 Chestnut St.) has a fine French bistro wine list is marked down to half-price every Sunday night.

■ **N. 3rd**, 801 N. Third St., is exploring the joys of finding inexpensive wines that actually taste good, with an extensive list of wines at $25 or less.

Wines by the Glass

Restaurants from **Le Bec-Fin** to **Fork** have begun to take wines by the glass seriously, but **Ristorante Panorama**, 14 N. Front St., is the undisputed paradise for the glass-sipper, with more than 120 wines available in flights from its special state-of-the-art storage system. The new **Penne**, 3611 Walnut St., has an impressive start on a similar program, offering three-shot flights on its 30-plus Italian wines by the glass.

Hot Chocolate

Miel Patisserie, 1990 Route 70 East, Marlton, N.J., serves up a thick demitasse of hot chocolate that will transport you to Paris.

Coffee

An espresso sipped at the counter of **La Colombe Torrefaction's** Center City cafe, at 130 S. 19th St., still has no rival as the region's ultimate short shot of caffeine.

Ray's Cafe & Tea House, 141 N. Ninth St., serves what is undoubtedly the region's most expensive cup of coffee from its elaborate vacuum rig of beekers and bunson burners, but an $8 cup of Jamaican Blue Mountain (and others that sell for less) is among the finest brews I've ever tasted. Other fine coffees to be found locally are **Old City Coffee**, at 221 Church St., and at the Reading Terminal Market, and **Torreo** (which sold its cafe, and now roasts only for retail).

Tea

The House of Tea, 720 S. Fourth St., is a first-class purveyor of loose teas, from classic fancy oolongs to toasted Ecuadorian yerba mate. **Great Tea International** offers traditional Asian tea ceremonies in its basement storefront, below the Joseph Fox Bookstore at 1724 Sansom St. Trendy Asian bubble teas filled with chewy tapioca pearls can be found at **Bubble House**, 3404 Sansom St., **Zen Tea House**, 225 N. 11th St., or **Le Cyclo**, at Sixth and Washington, which also serves freshly squeezed sugar cane juice. Afternoon tea is served with class at upscale hotels such as the **Four Seasons**, the **Cassatt Tea Lounge** at the **Rittenhouse**, and the **Ritz-Carlton**.

Other Exotic Drinks

The Mango lassi shakes from **Samosa**, 1214 Walnut St. The avocado shake from **Pho Xe Lua**, 907 Race St., in Chinatown. The watermelon smoothie at **Pagoda Noodle House** in Old City.

Ernesto's 1521 Cafe

The pleasant trattoria is one of the best affordable pre-theater options near the Avenue of the Arts.

Friends still call him Ernie, the guy who grew up near Rittenhouse Square.

It was only last September, after all, that Ernest Salandria grafted that "o" onto the end of his name and transformed 1521 Cafe Gallery into Ernesto's 1521 Cafe.

But our lovely server Dianne referred to him as Ernesto with convincing flair, even though she started working at the restaurant four years before the "o" made its debut. And as I sipped a cold little glass of his mother's homemade limoncello, a potent alcoholic rendition of lemonade, I was more than happy to cede to Salandria any moniker he wanted.

Because there is far more than artifice to the evolution of this little restaurant.

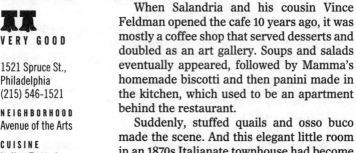

VERY GOOD

1521 Spruce St.,
Philadelphia
(215) 546-1521

NEIGHBORHOOD
Avenue of the Arts

CUISINE
Italian Trattoria

When Salandria and his cousin Vince Feldman opened the cafe 10 years ago, it was mostly a coffee shop that served desserts and doubled as an art gallery. Soups and salads eventually appeared, followed by Mamma's homemade biscotti and then panini made in the kitchen, which used to be an apartment behind the restaurant.

Suddenly, stuffed quails and osso buco made the scene. And this elegant little room in an 1870s Italianate townhouse had become a full-blown neighborhood trattoria that is one of the best affordable pre-theater options near the Avenue of the Arts.

The cafe no longer mounts gallery exhibitions (and Salandria's cousin is no longer a partner). But the minimalist off-white walls and the ornate white arch that bends over the center of the room serve as a perfect frame for the smartly dressed, urban crowd.

An even better vantage point is a seat at one of the tree-shaded cafe tables outside. From here, the view of the Kimmel Center's towering glass barrel pans right to the grand apartment facades of the brassy Drake and, across the street, the ornately canopied Touraine.

Colorful rows of flowers filling the sidewalk outside the shop next door send their ambrosial fragrance on a gentle breeze wafting across the tables. Philadelphia passes by with the grace of a European city. I even saw a Vespa motor past, ridden by Marc Vetri, coming from the direction of his eponymous restaurant across Broad Street.

Ricotta-filled ravioli with arugula cream sauce.

Ernesto's simple but tasty food, deftly rendered by chef Lewis Rice Jr., is often just as moving.

Large squares of homemade ravioli are stuffed with mashed butternut squash and glazed with sage-infused brown butter. Ricotta-cheese-plumped ravioli bask in a cream sauce green with pureed arugula.

Springy red and yellow ribbons of fettuccine tinted with tomato or saffron are tossed with garlicky broccoli rabe and shrimp. A compact brick of lasagna sauced with bright marinara conceals a piquant blend of cheeses between its layers of noodles.

Ernesto's menu relies more on clever tweaks to familiar dishes than on grand creative gestures. The superb fried calamari are one notable exception. The tender squid are drizzled with intriguing sour pomegranate molasses and served with a mango chutney dip for sweet balance. A juicy grilled pork tenderloin sided with fresh-plum compote was another surprising plate.

Yet other dishes lacked the finesse to make their good ideas work. I loved the notion of a sirloin steak topped with sauteed arugula and shaved Parmesan, but the meat was sorely overcooked. The vegetable napoleon, which uses lentil-studded polenta to mortar roasted peppers and zucchini into a tower, is a welcome overture to vegetarians.

But the fried eggplant rounds tucked in between were dry as toast. And while Ernesto's admirably prices most entrees under $18, the $15 lobster fra diavolo offered an example of why cheap seafood should be regarded with suspicion. The mealy morsels of slippertail lobster meat on top were a poor substitute for the more expensive, more familiar species of lobster.

But during my visits, the kitchen's successes far outnumbered its mistakes. The lentil soup was a bowl of hearty goodness, fragrant with bay and tangy with Worcestershire. The salads were bountiful and fresh, especially the peppery tangle of watercress and arugula topped with goat cheese and toasted walnuts.

Chef Rice also proved his mettle with some classic dishes that are often botched. His osso buco was as tender as it was massive, the slowly braised veal falling, at the tug of a fork, from the bone into vibrant yellow risotto Milanese.

The crabby crab cake had a marvelous crispness that gave way to a filling of sweet meat that seemed bound by little more than a fistful of chives.

Rice's rendition of the cioppino perfected by Salandria's mother, Livia Corman, was one of the best fish stews I've tasted in a while. Perfectly cooked seafood and a trio of grilled croutons were piled into a bowl brimming with lusty, spicy tomato broth.

Speaking of Mamma, she has a talent for homey sweets. The tiramisu has a bitter crown of espresso-soaked ladyfingers that harbor a sweet heart of cool mascarpone. The zuppa inglese is a mammoth wedge of rum-moistened cake and cream. The panna cotta offers a simple vanilla custard with a fresh fruit sauce.

The ricotta cheesecake may have been a bit dry for my taste and the chocolate torte a little dense. But these quibbles were quickly assuaged by that bracing shot of limoncello, which gives grain alcohol a sugary, lemon-zest zap.

This homemade brew isn't on the menu. It appears only when Salandria is feeling generous, though that is often. Few restaurateurs seem to take as much wide-eyed pleasure as Salandria does when he mills around the tables chatting with guests about the fine points of his excellent, affordable wine list.

His all-Italian collection is clearly a passionate pursuit, evidenced by some lesser-known but good-value

Or Try These

Here are three other Italian trattorias convenient for pre-theater dining.

Girasole

1305 Locust St., Philadelphia
(215) 985-4659

This darling of the Academy of Music crowd is a fine destination for standards such as carpaccio and homemade pasta. But its best dish may be the thin-crusted wood-oven pizza.

Ristorante Valentino

1328 Pine St., Philadelphia
(215) 545-6265

A charmingly decorated Italian BYOB with distressed walls and cherubs has been slightly inconsistent, but try the gnocchi and simple grilled fish.

Pompeii

121 S. Broad St., Philadelphia
(215) 735-8400

Don't let the high-toned Roman decor and uptown address fool you. Pompeii serves South Philly-style red-gravy fare, but at Broad Street prices that usually strike me as high. Special deal meals, though, make it worth a try, especially the three-course pre-theater menu for $25.

bottles such as a rustic Ramitello from Molise and a white Lacryma Christi from Campania.

Some customers bristled a year and a half ago when Salandria got his liquor license, completing Ernesto's evolution from coffee shop to bargain BYOB to full-service restaurant. But diners would be hard-pressed to find many more fairly priced and interesting lists that, like Ernesto's, cap mark-ups on even expensive bottles at $20. (A still-better deal: Friday Saturday Sunday, on 21st between Locust and Spruce, marks up its wines only $10.)

Scouting new additions to the list has Salandria smitten with a renewed interest in his Italian heritage. He's learning to speak the language. He just returned, in fact, from a trip to Montalcino. And someday, he muses, he may even move to Italy.

With a name like Ernie, he'll fit right in.

■ **MENU HIGHLIGHTS** Calamari; spinach-lentil soup; arugula salad; squash ravioli; ravioli with arugula cream; lasagna; fettuccine with broccoli rabe and shrimp; osso buco; pork tenderloin; crab cake; cioppino; tiramisu; zuppa inglese.

■ **WINE LIST** The excellent cellar is all Italian and fairly priced, with most wines under $30 and none — even the more expensive Barolos and Amarones — marked up more than $20. Some great values include the white Est! Est!! Est!!! ($26) and a rustic red Ramitello ($28).

■ **IF YOU GO** Lunch is served Tuesday-Friday, 11:30 a.m.-2:30 p.m.; dinner, Tuesday-Saturday, 5-11 p.m.; Saturday and Sunday brunch, 11 a.m.-3 p.m. Entrees: lunch, $6.50-$10.95; dinner, $12-$24.

■ **RESERVATIONS** Recommended.

■ **CREDIT CARDS** Visa, MasterCard accepted.

■ **SMOKING** No.

■ **HANDICAP ACCESSIBLE** No.

■ **PARKING** Street parking only.

Felicia's

One of South Philly's best "post-red-gravy" standbys remains rock-steady despite the travails of a seemingly endless renovation.

Nicholas Miglino doesn't like going out of the neighborhood much anymore. Somebody might bring up the Endless Renovations.

That would be the saga of the restaurateur's 14-year quest to expand Felicia's. It's a tale of a South Philly Sisyphus: Instead of pushing a heavy stone uphill over and over, he visited city zoning boards again and again, only to fall — splat! — back into figurative red gravy.

And when the bureaucracy isn't standing in Miglino's way, the heavens open up and shoot lightning bolts down to set his building ablaze. It could have been the end of Miglino's dream on that rainy night last summer when a vicious storm ignited the electrical fire that closed the restaurant for months.

VERY GOOD

1148 S. 11th St.
Philadelphia
(215) 755-9656

NEIGHBORHOOD
South Philadelphia

CUISINE
Italian Trattoria

But Miglino is fed up with obstacles. The end of his toil is in sight, he says, perhaps as soon as the new year, when the homey, barn-shaped dining room at the southwest corner of 11th and Ellsworth Streets will be overshadowed by the newly refurbished grandeur of the building's other rooms. The hand-blown antique chandeliers and French limestone floors. The murals and the 35-foot cathedral ceiling.

All of which remain out of view. The fine silver and china, too, remain packed away. And a wine collection that holds far more than the modest list of Italian table wines that Felicia's currently pours will soon, Miglino brags, come "oozing out of the rafters."

"I feel foolish when I try to explain it to people" after all these years, he says. "They look at me and start laughing. But it's going to be shocking."

Imagine, then, the angst-filled cries that Miglino issued over the phone when I told him that I had eaten several dinners there and was writing a review. Wait! So near the end of his baby's transformation? Not yet! It's unfair!

Actually, during my visits I was unaware of the renovations. And one year and one nearly disastrous fire later, they are still incomplete.

But given the quality of our meals, I'm even more compelled to memorialize the old Felicia's before it emerges — if ever — as the newer, shocking one. It's already a place worth remembering.

It wasn't long ago that Felicia's was establishing its first identity. When it began in 1987, it was in the vanguard of the "post-red-gravy" restaurants in South Philadelphia, places that took home cooking up a notch from the canned tomato paste gravies and mushy pasta of

yore. Instead, they'd steep fresh tomatoes (Felicia's still ripens them in basement baskets), splash extra-virgin olive oil, balsamic vinegar, and veal stock with abandon, and replace the flavorless iceberg lettuce with mounds of vibrant arugula, radicchio and endive.

Make no mistake. Felicia's retains in every way the down-home essence of a proto-South Philly joint, from the cheery valet in jeans and tank top who takes your car (for free) at the door, to the personable young waiter in the chest-hugging muscle shirt, to the old-time regulars with

The sausage special is one of the highlighted dishes at Felicia's.

slick silver hair and wide lapels who pontificate from the bar.

The restaurant is named for Miglino's father, Felix, as well as his daughter, Felicia, a tribute to family that also is evident in flavors that emerge from the kitchen, traditional Italian home cooking updated with high-quality ingredients, a few creative twists, and a consistent hand.

The ricotta gnocchi are sublime, puffed little cylinders cooked so gently they still harbor liquid cheese at the center. The mozzarella is homemade and has that telltale texture of freshness, a soft spring between the teeth that exudes milky sweetness. It's ideal for a laced tomato salad, or the gargantuan antipasto that rises from the plate like an impossibly tall Mount Romaine, a lettuce hill sloped with roasted red peppers and pink sliced meats.

Most of the pastas were excellent and fairly priced, with half-portions for under $10 that could easily be entrees. Fettuccine Alfredo was a classic: ribbons of pasta twirled in a rich ivory froth of cheesy cream. The penne alla Felicia was redolent with slow-cooked onions and salty prosciutto bits. The ziti all'arrabbiata is not for the timid. The fire-breathing red sauce tasted of toasted whole peppers, not simply shaken chile flakes. Bitter broccoli rabe, creamy ricotta, and crumbles of sausage gave corkscrewed gemelli an irresistible gusto. And the capellini alla marinara was satisfying simplicity — snappy strands of angel hair in a vibrant red gravy full of real tomato.

Only the dry bolognese was lacking. A special farfalle with blush tomato sauce and crab was good, but could have used more crabmeat.

Felicia's kitchen, meanwhile, has a few other holes in its repertoire to shore up. The dessert selection is tiny and unremarkable. And some of the ambitious entrees (most are under $20, but can hit $25) could have used more finesse — a terribly dry stuffed pork chop, a wild striped bass lost beneath too many ingredients, and a hefty porterhouse steak that didn't need the extra fistful of clumsily chopped garlic to knock the diner out.

Usually, though, Miglino's kitchen had its moves down pat. The fried calamari were crisp and tender, while a salad of grilled calamari brought the contrast of fresh greens to the soft, char-kissed white tubes.

Sauteed mushrooms were among my favorite appetizers, a medley of mushrooms in wine-scented gravy sparked by nuggets of prosciutto. Roasted peppers stuffed with ground veal is a Miglino family recipe that revealed a few surprises, a twang of anchovy, the peppery root sweetness of parsnips, and a hint of crushed nuts.

Most of the entrees, especially those with veal, were excellent, from the perfectly cooked thick chop (with just the right touch of garlic), to the grilled veal sausages splayed over a mound of broccoli rabe, to the saltimbocca, whose medallions are rolled into a tube instead of flattened and then filled with sage, prosciutto and Asiago cheese that seeps into the marsala wine sauce as you slice it.

Or Try These

Here are three other "post-red-gravy" restaurants in South Philadelphia.

Kristian's

1100 Federal St., Philadelphia
(215) 468-0104

This renovated butcher shop has matured into South Philadelphia's finest upscale Italian eatery, although the service doesn't match the finesse of young chef Kristian Leuzzi.

Tre Scalini

1533 S. 11th St., Philadelphia
(215) 551-3870

Authentic central Italian home cooking, from fresh pasta to grilled polenta and veal with mushrooms, in a bi-level BYOB.

Mezza Luna

763 S. 8th St., Philadelphia
(215) 627-4705

This crisp, contemporary space serves airy ricotta gnocchi, rabbit stew, and fine seafood that is worth the trip.

It is just the kind of dish, a classic rethought and deftly turned, that made Felicia's a standard bearer for the post-red-gravy generation in the first place. I only hope the restaurant as a whole can reemerge as successfully when it, too, is reintroduced, finally, as a classic new and improved.

■ **MENU HIGHLIGHTS** Antipasti; mozzarella alla caprese; fried calamari; funghi e prosciutto; stuffed pepper special; house gnocchi; fettuccine alfredo; spaghetti alla puttanesca; penne alla felicia; grilled veal chop; veal saltimbocca; grilled veal sausage special.

■ **WINE LIST** The restaurant's basic wine list is small, stocked mostly with affordable Italian table wines. There is a bigger reserve list with a greater depth of quality Italian bottles, but it isn't always available.

■ **IF YOU GO** Lunch served Tuesday-Friday 11:30 a.m.- 2:30 p.m. Dinner served Tuesday-Saturday 5-10:30 p.m., Sunday 4-9:30 p.m. Lunch entrees, $5.95-$10.50. Dinner entrees, $13.95-$24.95.

■ **RESERVATIONS** Suggested, especially weekends.

■ **CREDIT CARDS** All major cards accepted.

■ **SMOKING** Smoking only at the bar, although smoke can drift into the front dining room.

■ **HANDICAP ACCESSIBLE** Room is handicapped accessible, but the bathrooms are not yet.

■ **PARKING** Free valet parking for Saturday dinner only.

Fork

The definitive Old City bistro offers the ideal balance of style, good value, and thoughtfully prepared modern cooking.

Old City's red-hot dining scene owes its soul to stylish bistros. These artfully rehabbed spaces, with their cool bar crowds and seasonal menus, prove that substance can be dished out with attitude and value.

No bistro captures this spirit more completely than Fork, the Market Street storefront that Ellen Yin transformed with partners Roberto Sella and Anne-Marie Lasher in 1997.

To my tastes, the dining room is one of the best spaces that interior designer Marguerite Rodgers has ever created. The former socks store, vacant for years, glows with understated warmth, from the bustling perch of the square front bar — my favorite spot for a quick lunch and a view of the crowds — to the tall, quilted banquettes in the comfortable rear dining room adjoining the open kitchen.

VERY GOOD

306 Market St.
Philadelphia
(215) 625-9425

NEIGHBORHOOD
Old City

CUISINE
New American

Swagged with velvet curtains, dotted with palms, lighted with hand-painted fabric lamps, and punctuated by old cast-iron columns, it is a small room with many moods.

And a loyal following. With its excellent, affordable wine list and extremely capable, experienced servers, I can understand why. It simply feels good to be here.

As for the food, it has been consistently good — simple dishes garnished with seasonal flavors and clever comfort twists (a little sorrel for the pureed soup or a pat of bacon butter for the tilapia and buttermilk-mashed potatoes). But also, it has almost always landed shy of great. Always nice touches at a nice price, but the kitchen has seemed almost by design to stop short of grander culinary ambition. Accessibility and affordability were key, and there's nothing wrong with that.

But Old City's dining scene has matured considerably over the last five years, so why not Fork, too?

The restaurant has struggled a bit with that challenge over the last two years since Lasher's departure, tending more or less to maintain the status quo. A couple of recent meals under the latest chef, however, the Vietnam-born, Paris-trained Thien Ngo, showed a few sparks of promise that this kitchen was finally waking up to its full potential.

The richness of two beautifully seared scallops brought the bracingly tart contrast of pureed ginger, cilantro and lime. A lively salsa verde of tangy tomatillos highlighted the impressive sweetness of perfectly panfried lump crab cakes bound with scallop mousse.

Fork's repertoire of wide ranging flavors was put on display with the banana-leaf-wrapped salmon. Tied inside the leaf like a parcel, then cooked on the grill, the fish was perhaps a shade overdone, but still amazingly moist with its gingery peanut sauce. Delicious shiitake mushrooms and coconut rice anchored the plate. At the other end of the spectrum, morsels of leg of lamb were grilled to a Mediterranean theme, skewered on local rosemary twigs, then placed over a light Israeli couscous fragrant with preserved lemons, raisins, and an herby brush of minty pesto. The meat was superbly tender, but also completely infused with the vibrance of its garlic and herb marinade. Balanced with its lively, light-handed garnish, these were exactly the kind of bright, confident flavors that I've sought — but rarely received — from Fork all along.

There is still room for improvement under the current kitchen regime. At a recent lunch, an otherwise delicious creamed vegetable soup was full of broccoli stem fibers that should have been strained out. The Asian soy dressing for the usually sure-handed soba noodle salad was achingly salty and oversoured.

The lunch crew, though, made amends with a pork chop entree that came topped with a rustic compote of stewed tomatoes and onions, and a lovely, eggy wedge of mushroom bread pudding. It was a substantial dish and a bonafide deal at $10. Then again, the strong value always seems to tip my meals in Fork's favor, even if it isn't always perfect. The dinner entrees rarely top $20.

The dessert course, likewise, seems to be in an unexciting transition, ranging from gelatos, sorbets, cookies and simple fruit presentations (a whole papaya, or port-poached pear) to dry bread pudding and a lemon-lime cheesecake that was so tangy, the citrus seemed

Or Try These

Here are three other Old City restaurants.

Novelty

15 S. Third St., Philadelphia
(215) 627-7885

The dark and handsome younger sibling of Jake's in Manayunk has been one of the neighborhood's finest, more sophisticated spots even though its kitchen seems in constant flux.

Chlöe

232 Arch St., Philadelphia
(215) 629-2337

A homey Old City BYOB bistro with an international take on comfort food.

Cafe Spice

35 S. Second St., Philadelphia
(215) 627-6273

This hip Indian bistro has contemporary decor, but classic dishes prepared with quality ingredients and sharp flavors.

to negate the flavor of its chocolate crust.

But who needs dessert? Because the best thing Fork has done in the last year has been to cultivate one of the outstanding cheese courses in the city. At one recent meal, we chose five from a list of 17 excellent cheeses, including some that were rare (raw sheep's milk Ossau from Italy) and several that were perfectly, pungently ripe, including a particularly stinky Pont l'Eveque (yum!) and the earthy ooze of Robiola Stagionata. Garnished with sliced ripe peaches and a bundle of grapes, the plate was a sheer delight, and a perfect example of the pleasing little touches this restaurant has always achieved outside the realm of its chefs' talents.

Sella's wine list is one of the other great attractions, offering one of the area's more interesting selections of wines by the glass (an excellent $7 tempranillo from Spain's Castejon, for example) and numerous well-chosen, less common bottles for under $40. There is also an unusually large selection of madeiras.

Much of the credit for Fork's constant effort to make that next leap forward certainly goes to the ever-present Yin. She has become more involved in the menu over the years, and it has paid dividends as she defines her vision. But it is in the dining room that Yin is most valuable, lending an air of professionalism and personality to the staff that is far too rare around here. Even if the rest of Old City has spent much of the last five years trying to emulate Fork's success, that polish is one elusive trait that still lends this high-style bistro some extra substance.

■ **MENU HIGHLIGHTS** Walnut-crusted goat cheese salad; scallops with ginger sauce; crab cakes with salsa verde; grilled lamb on rosemary skewers; banana-leaf-wrapped salmon; cheese course.

■ **WINE LIST** An ideal bistro list filled with French, Italian and American bottles is skillfully chosen for quality and value, then sprinkled with more expensive reserve wines. Less common wines require guidance from servers.

■ **IF YOU GO** Lunch served Monday-Friday 11:30 a.m.- 2:30 p.m.; dinner served Monday-Thursday 5:30 -10:30 p.m., Friday 5:30-11:30 p.m., Saturday 5 -11:30 p.m., Sunday 5-10:30 p.m. Sunday brunch served 11 a.m.-2:30 p.m. Entrees: lunch, $9-$12; dinner, $15-$24.

■ **RESERVATIONS** Highly recommended. Accepted up to two months in advance.

■ **CREDIT CARDS** All major cards.

■ **SMOKING** There is a nonsmoking section.

■ **HANDICAP ACCESSIBLE** Yes.

■ **PARKING** Street parking only.

Fountain Restaurant

The city's most reliable palace of posh redefines, through its creative, top-notch kitchen, what hotel dining can be.

She suddenly appeared out of the palms, seemingly materialized from the trickling fountain and gracious couches that fill the lobby of the Four Seasons Hotel: an angel bearing Chardonnay on a silver tray.

"Would you like some chilled wine while you wait for your guest?"

A mere look at that frosted bottle was enough to revive me. We had yet to set foot inside the Fountain Restaurant. Worse, we were late. What had we done to deserve such unsolicited kindness?

Our late guest arrived with the dark cloud of her day trailing behind her. This dinner was the only thing, she griped, that could stand between her and a final leap off the balcony of her employer.

SUPERIOR

Four Seasons Hotel,
1 Logan Square
Philadelphia
(215) 963-1500

NEIGHBORHOOD
Logan Square

CUISINE
New American

So we stepped through the mirrored vault of the Fountain's vestibule, past brimming baskets of fruit and spectacular flowers, where the hostess greeted us. "Your table is waiting," she said with the sweep of a hand, leading us through a sea of softly lit tables to a wide, white round, where a window view of the bubbling Swann Fountain would mark the beginning of our transformation. One for which we would open our wallets wide enough to pay at least $150 a person — and like it.

The white-bearded chef who made the Four Seasons' reputation has moved on, quite surprisingly, to another local hotel. But Jean-Marie Lacroix, the man whom cooks here came to know as "Papa," left the house (and the executive chef's toque) in the most capable of hands.

Martin Hamann came to the hotel as an apprentice months after it opened in 1983, and over the years has been very much a part of establishing its Fountain Restaurant as one of the finest hotel dining rooms in America, as well as one of the best restaurants, period, in Philadelphia.

So it should come as no surprise that eating here feels much like it did during the Lacroix era when Hamann (now in charge of the hotel's entire food program) ran the Fountain's dinner service and current dinner chef David Jansen was preoccupied with lunch.

To enter its dining rooms is still to walk into the city's undisputed grand palace of posh, and the staff has always made a point of treating everyone like royalty.

"We don't skimp on the cheese here," said Jim Miller, our waiter, slicing off more hunks than he'd promised. Such acts of competent service, from the intricate orchestration of our silver to his unpretentious guidance with our wine, had earned Miller my tardy guest's ultimate admiration: "He's nicer than my father." But it was hardly a fluke. The Four Seasons never fails to charm and pamper its charges.

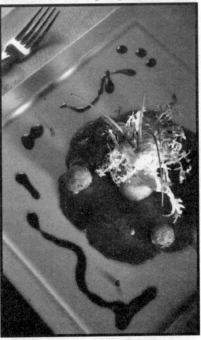

The best of its veteran servers function on telepathic anticipation, yet maintain a certain distance that distinguishes them from the chattier servers at its closest haute-rival, Le Bec-Fin. The result often seems less personal, but preferable if you like to be left alone.

The cooking here is a different species, too. The founding father may have been French and implanted classical techniques into the kitchen's DNA. But the Fountain's palette is far too international to bear that label exclusively.

Its chefs have a prolific creativity and a penchant for largesse that exude a freewheeling American feel. In a way, this costs the Fountain the benefit of a

Venison carpaccio comes scattered with deep-fried grapes that burst with the scent of juniper.

distinct culinary identity, a set repertoire that is easy to describe. But the payoff is consistent excellence no matter what the kitchen serves, with menus that weave the finest seasonal ingredients into dishes that are at once inventive and harmonious.

And what gorgeous presentations. Even the house salad comes looking like a Louis XIV topiary. The element of surprise is also used to the cook's advantage at every turn. A dumpling filled with truffled osso bucco meat bobs up from the darkness of a double-strength veal consomme. A carpaccio of venison comes scattered with deep-fried grapes that burst with the scent of juniper. A perfectly seared scallop arrives over tender fingerling potatoes and a mound of tart, crunchy Alsatian choucroute.

The Fountain's soups have a habit of pushing creamy richness to the limit. It isn't necessary, given the intensely pure flavors they steep — a puree of cabbage and parsnip was a root cellar fantasy, a velvety potato soup was warmed by the sweetness of roasted garlic.

But rarely does the kitchen opt for simplicity. An appetizer, "study of duck," brought a quartet of preparations. The highlight was a sublime Muscovy breast tartare that was the silky embodiment of a fine, peppery Bordeaux. It was immense for an appetizer, but at $25 it ought to be.

The Fountain's $40-plus entrees are even larger, but I'd rather spend less for smaller portions. The broad white spaces of the restaurant's fancy new plates can tempt the kitchen into run-on cooking and an occasionally ill-advised creative gamble.

A veal tenderloin that seesawed with a half-pound lobster ravioli on a long, narrow plate portended similar discord until I sliced the dumpling. Sweet citrus/lobster butter poured out, bathing the tender veal. The Fountain's fillet of grouper also proved that red wine and fish don't necessarily clash — its rich red wine salmis sauce perfectly accented the grouper's hearty texture.

Big spenders might want to opt for the ever-changing "Spontaneous Taste" menu, a six-course feast that balloons from $110 to $195 if you choose the flight of five superb wines by the glass from the hotel's magnificent, albeit very expensive cellar. But it's more food than I can handle.

Or Try These

Here are three other luxury-hotel restaurants.

Lacroix at the Rittenhouse

210 W. Rittenhouse Square, Philadelphia
(215) 790-2533

Former Four Seasons guru Jean-Marie Lacroix has already transformed the cuisine at the old TreeTops in the Rittenhouse Hotel, but a lavish decor revamp and a name change this fall have finally made it his own.

The Grill

10 S. Broad St., Philadelphia
(215) 735-7700

This clubby New American grill in the Ritz-Carlton delivers consistently fine cuisine and excellent service.

Hotel DuPont

11th and Market Streets, Wilmington
(302) 594-3100

The soaring, oak-clad Green Room and the Wyeth-hung Brandywine make for dining rooms of unmatched classical grandeur. The kitchens are better than average, but rarely magical.

I can barely make it past the runny Epoisses on the cheese cart, let alone indulge the elegant, although noticeably less inventive, desserts. Still, I can always make room for the Fountain's souffle, a vision of gravity-defying chocolate, whose sugar- powdered crust hovers like magic over a heart of molten cocoa.

Just as we hit souffle bottom, another angel appears at our table, showering us with diamond-shaped truffles and long-stemmed strawberries as big as melons. They glisten with the sweet ambrosia of vanilla-scented Grand Marnier.

We had not asked for these pleasures. We were even late for our reservation. But the remarkable transformation that occurs over the course of a meal here is this: The Fountain makes every guest feel as if such kindness is well-deserved.

■ MENU HIGHLIGHTS Asparagus souffle with truffle puree; venison carpaccio; creamy orzo with smoked salmon; scallop with choucroute; veal consomme with osso bucco raviolettes; study of duck; grouper with salmis sauce; veal medallion with lobster ravioli; filet mignon with chestnut-pumpkin pudding; chocolate souffle; almond financier.

■ WINE LIST The large cellar is brimming with luxury bottles from Burgundy (a delicious '95 Savigny les Beaunes) and Bordeaux, but has little consideration for quality bottles under $50. The best option for more economical drinking may be the interesting wines by the glass.

■ IF YOU GO Breakfast served Monday-Friday 6:30-11:30 a.m., Sunday 7-11 a.m. Sunday brunch served 11:30 a.m.- 2:30 p.m. Lunch served Monday-Saturday 11:30 a.m.-2:30 p.m. Dinner served every day 6-10:30 p.m. Breakfast entrees, $5-$32.50. Five-course fixed-price brunch, $46-$55. Lunch entrees, $21-$29. Three-course fixed-price lunch, $35.50. Dinner entrees, $38.50-$46. Six-course fixed-price dinner, $110, or $195 with flight of wines.

■ RESERVATIONS Required.

■ CREDIT CARDS All major cards.

■ SMOKING Dining room is entirely nonsmoking.

■ HANDICAP ACCESSIBLE Yes.

■ PARKING Valet costs $15, with a $5 discount at lunchtime only, Monday- Friday. Self-parking at 2 Logan Square costs $7.50 after 4 p.m.

Friday Saturday Sunday

The romantic "restaurant renaissance" classic has remained vital with an eclectic menu and great wine values.

I n the dizzy days of the restaurant renaissance, funky corner restaurants such as Friday Saturday Sunday laid the groundwork for a city with gourmet aspirations.

Not that great restaurant towns are necessarily built on mismatched china, blackboard menus, and cream of mushroom soup. But in the 1970s, the idea that quality dining could exist outside the stuffy confines of a private club, that good food could become the province of interested amateurs as well as the great chefs, liberated the city to new possibilities for the neighborhood restaurant.

The birth story of Friday Saturday Sunday — seven friends with virtually no experience throwing $2,000 into a hat on a dare to "take turns running it" — has the quaint ring of nostalgia in today's high-gloss restaurant atmosphere.

VERY GOOD

261 S. 21st St.
Philadelphia
(215) 546-4232

NEIGHBORHOOD
Rittenhouse Square

CUISINE
New American

By comparison, the mere survival of this cozy corner restaurant, squeezed into rowhouse romance by mirrored walls and a streak of indigo neon that rings the room, seems a fluke of naivete. Yet numerous satisfying meals over the last few years at the old haunt have given me several good reasons to explain why Friday Saturday Sunday is not only still around, but also still one of the better neighborhood eateries in town. Consistently solid cooking with quality fresh products. An intimate retro ambience mellowed by the tunes of Johnny Hartman, John Coltrane and Billie Holliday. And fair value, especially with its value-minded wine-pricing policy.

Friday Saturday Sunday adds only $10 to the cost of its wines, a big improvement over the double- and triple-cost markup that is typical in the industry. Owner Weaver Lilley, who long ago bought out his partners, didn't make made many new friends with his ad campaign comparing his wine prices to those of competitors. Oh, well. I'll happily drink to a $47 Kistler chardonnay, or an entire list, for that matter, that delivers quality bottles for less than $50, with most between $20 and $30.

I'd like to see the list push the envelope more, with some truly fine wines marked up only $10. But considering the uncomplicated style of cooking, a cellar meant more for drinking than collecting also seems appropriate.

There is a certain cheesecake nostalgia to the eclectic menu here. It blends basic French with American stalwarts from the '70s, with occasional Asian flair, and daily specials ranging from Creole to Southwestern. The result is an easy hodgepodge of gently updated comfort food, always fresh and deftly prepared by executive chef Brad Jones, who has taken the baton seamlessly from Chakapope Sirirathasuk, the longtime chef who left two years ago to open Sukhothai with his brothers across town.

Restaurant scenes may not be built on mushroom soup, but I can understand why it has anchored this menu since the beginning. Coarsely pureed and slowly steeped with cognac into a creamy, earthy essence, every bite gives the satisfaction of milky richness and texture. Other retro classics — tender breaded chicken breasts napped in mustard cream, dark-fleshed Cornish hen stuffed with sausage and walnuts — were just as nicely done.

Though this menu can seem somewhat dated at times, its appeal remains in the uncomplicated quality of the ingredients. Super fresh salads employ simple but strong combinations — tender spinach leaves topped with creamy blue cheese dressing, walnuts and tart green apples; crisp spears of poached asparagus topped with a chunky tomato dressing. A cool summer soup made of pureed yellow melons and finely chopped mint was so quenchingly delicious, it was almost impossible to stop eating.

The restaurant's longtime affinity for Asian flavors has also remained. The sashimi-grade tuna is seared with a sesame-seed crust before it is sliced and chilled, its ruby raw center perked with a sheen of spicy wasabi vinaigrette.

The pork chop was one notable recent disappointment, the impressively thick cut cooked dry as a bone.

Other traditionally prepared entrees were ideal. Delicate fillets of flounder wrapped like a bulging sandwich around an interesting stuffing — crabmeat, mixed with the tangy richness of brie cheese. Lightly breaded tilapia had the soft spark of fresh horseradish in its crust.

A meaty rack of lamb crusted in garlic and herbs was simply perfect — once my waiter took it back to the kitchen to be cooked a little more. He was quite friendly and accommodating about it, at least compared with our next visit, when the staff seemed panicked and brusque.

It was a busy night, but considering that most of this staff has been around for a decade or more, one might expect them to navigate the tiny room (and deal with unfamiliar customers) more effortlessly.

That is not to say things always get easier with experience. The restaurant's entire menu, in fact, used to be written on the fluorescent chalkboard in the center of the room. But that, says manager Joni Popowcer, was before the restaurant's aging clientele (and owner, for that matter) decided printed menus would be easier to read.

Diners will still have to squint at the board if they want to see what's for dessert, but it will be worth the eyestrain. A thick wedge of creamy coconut pie clad in a crumb crust of vanilla wafers tastes just like the one my grandma used to make (actually, better). And a tall soft wedge of luscious cheesecake, not too sweet and just a hint tangy, is unstoppably good over a refreshing pool of freshly pureed berries. Chocolate mousse pie is light and airy over its chocolate cookie crust. And blueberry pie is filled with mounds of luscious, seasonally sweet fruit.

It is a dessert list straight from the bake sales of yore, a satisfying blast from the past as much as anything here. It's also a reminder of a more innocent time, when homey cakes and pies were the ultimate seduction at dinner's end, and when a bunch of clueless friends could launch a restaurant on a dare. Who could have known that it would have endured this handsomely for nearly three decades?

Or Try These

Here are three other restaurants with romantic ambience.

Inn at Phillip's Mill
2590 River Rd., New Hope, Pa.
(215) 862-9919

The straightforward country French cuisine tastes all the better in the candlelit flicker of this historic Bucks County farmhouse.

Roselena's Coffee Bar
1623 E. Passyunk Ave.,
Philadelphia
(215) 755-9697

This quirky Victorian coffee parlor offers multicourse dinners upstairs, but the main draws are the after-dinner desserts by lamplight in the Victorian parlor downstairs.

Inn Philadelphia
251 S. Camac St., Philadelphia
(215) 732-2339

The New American menu and service have sagged of late, but this hidden inn, tucked away in a historic enclave, has roaring fireplaces and a piano bar that offer the feeling of country romance in the city.

■ **MENU HIGHLIGHTS** Cream of mushroom soup; spinach salad with blue cheese dressing; chilled sesame tuna; asparagus with tomato vinaigrette; chicken Dijon; horseradish-crusted tilapia; crab and brie stuffed flounder; roasted rack of lamb; cheesecake with berry sauce; carrot cake; coconut cream pie; blueberry pie.

■ **WINE LIST** The fairest wine-pricing policy in town makes this modest French and American cellar apealing, with a $10 markup on all bottles, whereas other restaurants typically double or triple their costs. The list has a few marquee names such as Kistler chardonnay, but could use more special bottles to truly fulfill its bargain splurge potential.

■ **IF YOU GO** Lunch served Tuesday-Friday 11:30 a.m.-2:15 p.m. Dinner served Monday-Saturday, 5:30-10:30 p.m., Sunday 5-10 p.m.

■ **RESERVATIONS** Recommended during the week, required on weekends.

■ **CREDIT CARDS** All major cards but Discover.

■ **SMOKING** There is no nonsmoking section.

■ **HANDICAP ACCESSIBLE** Not wheelchair accessible.

■ **PARKING** Street parking only.

Fuji Japanese Restaurant

A brilliant unsung chef creatively prepares some of the region's most memorable meals in an unlikely Cinnaminson hideaway.

"We would be happy, frankly, if no one ever found out about Fuji."

Such a little place. Their special secret. Tucked away on a gritty South Jersey highway, just where no one would ever look — the restaurant and its brilliant, unsung chef. My source and his sake-swilling pals would gladly keep him to themselves, thank you.

And yet, there was a deliberate tone of temptation in my source's voice, so many superlatives, that I had to find out for myself. How is it possible that a chef of such talent could cook at the same place for 20 years and remain in relative obscurity? And what exactly is it that Masaharu "Matt" Ito can do?

EXCELLENT

404 Route 130 North,
Cinnaminson, N.J.
(856) 829-5211

NEIGHBORHOOD
South Jersey

CUISINE
Japanese

Sushi and much, much more. Japanese food is more than raw fish, you know. Try the seven-course "kaiseki" tastings, and Ito will never cook you the same thing twice.

Seared tuna wrapped around foie gras. Crispy squab spiced with curry and anise-scented sanshou pepper. Teriyaki sauce as dark as night. Tempura so light, you see through it like a veil. Lamb that sizzles on a hot rock at your table. And, on rare occasions, Ito will steep his guests' sake with the fins of tiger blow fish — fugu — very dangerous, if you don't know what you're doing.

"Just go," my source advised, "and tell him to make you dinner."

I descend from the mist of the Betsy Ross Bridge and turn north on a rain-slicked Route 130. A neon blur of strip malls and highway overpasses keep me scouting for a sign — any sign — of gastronomic life.

Cinnaminson welcomes me.

If you head to New Jersey for sushi, it is usually assumed you are going the other way down Route 130 to Sagami, the august Collingswood institution with the strangely dark interior and wonderful, pristine fish.

If you are headed for somewhere called Fuji, it is usually assumed you are going to any number of the other well-placed, well-marked Fujis and Fuji Mountains.

But if you are heading to the independent Fuji Japanese Restaurant that Ito began 23 years ago after a stint as sushi chef at Sagami, just look for the Relax Motel.

Heart-shaped jacuzzis! Cut rates! Mirrored ceilings!

I veer right into the motel parking lot and there it is: a low-slung hut of a brick building. Inside, its 46 seats (including six at the sushi bar) are wrapped in an intimate space recently redone, with woody accents of woven pine and cedar. The walls are decorated with typical Japanese prints. The servers are sweet once you know them, but overwhelmed by a crowd. They are not particularly adept at explaining exotic dishes. And food can arrive in fits and starts. But when it does, I consistently encounter some of the most memorable meals I've eaten in the Philadelphia region.

The eight-course kaiseki is a relative bargain at $65, considering the quality and creativity it entails, unfolding in wave after wave of gorgeously presented little dishes.

One recent kaiseki began with a mince of toro tuna tartare dolloped with caviar then ringed by a spicy wasabi broth. A jewel box of other delicacies followed: black bean jellies, tiny lamb chops barbecued with a smoky miso glaze, and butterflied shrimp encrusted

Chilean sea bass coated in pebble-shaped puffed rice explodes with garlicky sauce.

with red and green roe. A leek consomme was filled with a daintily peeled turnip stuffed with foie gras. Seared foie gras came topped with candied kumquats. Beautifully sliced sashimi then made way for an exquisite roulade of cooked sea bass rolled around shiitake mushrooms, Cornish hen stuffed with sweet cherry rice, and then a spiced kabocha pumpkin tart for dessert.

Past kaisekis have introduced me to similar wonders. Thin strips of seared tuna wrapped around foie gras into maki rolls, then set over minty shiso leaves. A tropical roll filled with ripe mango and sweet lump crab. Cold squares of sweetened egg topped with chips of sharp cheddar cheese and a spoonful of salty caviar. Sheer little bundles of sea bream sashimi, wrapped around slivered scallions and rich monkfish liver, the "foie gras of the sea."

Some dishes are so spontaneous that, in one case, a server had never seen it in her 15 years working at Fuji — a tempura-fried spinach-leaf package, inside of which a small lobster tail was dabbed with cheese.

Flaccid oysters represented some of my only disappointments at Fuji. And an elaborate sukiyaki hot pot was less than superb — its soy and mirin broth too sweet.

There was nothing wrong with the delicious ginger and red bean ice creams. But desserts here have always seemed too understated for the otherwise spectacular meals, from the sublimely sweet sea urchin to the strips of sake-marinated lamb we seared ourselves on a 550-degree ishiyaki rock.

There is also a regular menu at Fuji, of course, and the kitchen does it well. The beef and chicken teriyakis are outstanding, offering a midnight glaze steeped from days of simmering beef bones. The tempura is so light, its crisp jacket looks like fallen snow flakes suspended in crust.

There are crunchy seaweed salads such as hijiki, dark filament threads dressed in sweet vinaigrette. And steamed edamame, green soy beans that slip out of their salty pods, are the perfect munchie to start the meal. I also loved the sliced pork loin, tenderly slicked with ginger teriyaki.

Nightly specials, especially good on weekends when there is no kaiseki, keep new options alive. Chilean sea bass coated in pebble-shaped puffed rice exploded with garlicky sauce. A firm fillet of broiled pompano slipped into soy-tinged flakes on the tongue, then washed down with a sour burst of grapefruit segments.

After so much great food, I could almost have rented a room just for an hour next door to digest.

I could also understand my tipster's conflicted message — to keep

Or Try These

Here are three other Japanese restaurants.

Morimoto

723 Chestnut St., Philadelphia
(215) 413-9070

Superstar chef Masaharu Morimoto brings cutting-edge Japanese cuisine to the undulating bamboo dining room of Stephen Starr's hip restaurant.

Sagami

37 W. Crescent Blvd.,
Collingswood, N.J.
(856) 854-9773

One of the area's first and finest sushi haunts, this dark, wood-paneled restaurant keeps strictly to tradition, resisting trendy maki rolls in favor of pristine fish served in classic ways.

Mikado

2370 Route 70 West, Cherry Hill, N.J. (856) 665-4411

This Route 70 newcomer is giving classic Sagami a run for the South Jersey sushi crowd, especially those who crave Mikado's wildly busy maki rolls.

the secret under wraps and tell the world at the same time. Fuji is an unexpected find that any food adventurer would jealously guard. But then, on the other hand, Matt Ito's kaiseki magic is an experience too good not to share and praise.

■ **MENU HIGHLIGHTS** Yakitori; shrimp tempura; beef teriyaki; ginger pork; crispy rice sea bass; spiced squab with foie gras; lamb in miso san-shou pepper sauce. Sushi: eel box, Fuji roll, tropical roll, sturgeon and caviar; raw shrimp; egg and cheddar. Kaiseki specials: sea bass stuffed with mushrooms in mushroom sauce; tuna and foie gras maki; bonito flake tower; spinach-wrapped lobster tempura; sea-bream-wrapped monkfish liver; ishiyaki-rock-seared lamb; turnip soup with duck; foie gras with candied kumquat; cornish hen stuffed with sweet rice.

■ **WINE LIST** BYO (Sake)

■ **IF YOU GO** Lunch served Tuesday-Friday 11:30 a.m.-2 p.m. Dinner served Tuesday-Thursday 5-9:30 p.m., Friday-Saturday 5-10 p.m., Sunday 4-8:30 pm. Closed Monday. Eight-course kaiseki, $65; entrees, $17-$24.

■ **RESERVATIONS** Always recommended, and required one week in advance for kaiseki-tasting dinners, which are available only on weekdays.

■ **CREDIT CARDS** All major cards.

■ **SMOKING** Entire restaurant is nonsmoking.

■ **HANDICAP ACCESSIBLE** Restaurant is accessible but bathrooms are not.

■ **PARKING** Free lot.

Happy Rooster

The quirky hideaway bar-restaurant serves
a sophisticated blackboard menu.

I n the Technicolor glow of stained-glass poultry, Rose Parrotta is stomping her feet to Johnny Cash, reliving her wilder days in the apple orchards of New York and filling her Happy Rooster with an infectious energy boost.

She welcomes friends to her little restaurant in a playful headlock, leading them around the thick brass bar pole. Even diners unknown to this diamond-studded dynamo get a blast of her charisma. She preens like Vanna White beside her ambitious chalkboard menu, discoursing on everything from her hand-scribbled boutique wine list ("people want forward fruit, but I won't give it to them!") to her tireless search for the perfect chocolate cake ("finally, I went to the source.")

If it seems as if she is gushing, Rose can be forgiven. After all, the first time she came to the Happy Rooster, in the mid-80s, then-owner "Doc" Ulitsky wouldn't even let her order a drink until her escort came. It was a policy that perfectly captured the old-world chauvinism of this burnished hideaway, a manly corner nook with quilted burgundy booths, famous menus on the wall, and a reputation for caviar and top-shelf liquor.

EXCELLENT

118 S. 16th St.
(at Sansom),
Philadelphia
(215) 963-9311

NEIGHBORHOOD
Rittenhouse Square

CUISINE
New American

Parrotta pestered an uninterested Doc for years, while she did front-of-the-house time at Buddakan, Tony Clark's and Apropos, among others. Now that she has finally purchased it for her own, she has a swagger when she says: "I'm the new [rooster] in town."

But it is more than practiced coq-iness and a collection of porcelain birds dressed with Christmas lights that has made Rose's Rooster a success. There is a fine list of fairly priced wines to be had once you get over the makeshift spiral notebook. And, most important, there has always been a chef in the basement to be reckoned with, sending up surprisingly sophisticated delights.

The latest in Parrotta's string of culinary finds is Steve Latona, who has worked at Avenue B, Striped Bass, and the defunct BLT's Cobblefish, not to mention a valuable turn in Manhattan at the Union Square Cafe.

Latona owes his spaghetti bolognese to Michael Romano at the

Union Square Cafe, and since his arrival in September, it has become one of the best additions to the blackboard menu. Its buttery tomato gravy clings to the noodles, and it is hearty with milk-steeped crumbles of veal and pork and prosciutto that lend it a lingering savor. Grilled pork tenderloins are also memorable, drawing on a two-day garlic-herb marinade for a powerful flavor and succulence that finds a perfect contrast with fresh fig relish. And Latona maintains the Rooster's tradition of serving one of the best steaks in town; the superbly tender strip comes with a classic dark Bordelaise and a crisped polenta cake sweetened with caramelized onions.

This is not exactly the kind of cooking you'd expect from the corner bar, and neither are entree prices in the high $20s. But the quality ingredients are obvious on the plate.

Parrotta recently annexed the building next door for an additional 30 seats, and the room is nonsmoking. It too has gradually acquired that Rooster look of bird tchotchkes and Christmas lights. But I'd much rather endure the smoke in the busy bar, not to mention the time-beaten booths rimmed with brass cage dividers. We need more places like this — quirky unexpected hideaways that are ripe with edgy character and food of real epicurean ambition. Where else you can nibble on fabulously crispy calamari with tea-smoked tomato remoulade and watch

Poultry in stained glass and bird knickknacks adorn the Happy Rooster.

some pinstriped Market Street mover at the bar woo his high-fashion date while a dreadlocked skateboarder behind him downs one of Parrotta's "rose-hattans," a Manhattan garnished with a candied rose petal instead of the cherry.

This restaurant isn't perfect. The room can be deafeningly loud. And the service sometimes plays favorites, dragging its feet on nights when Parrotta's not in, forgetting which diner gets which dish, and basically not paying close enough attention.

In addition, Latona has not been quite as interesting a chef as his predecessors, who played with everything from homemade salts to spinach spaetzles and red-eye gravy. His more straightforward Italian-driven cuisine, though, is still tasty enough to be worth the hassle.

Mushroom-filled raviolis come slicked with garlic-infused cream ribboned with sundried tomatoes. Vibrantly crisp Caesar salad is crisscrossed with gently salted fresh white anchovies. Beautifully browned scallops with roasted vegetable couscous get only a drizzle of basil oil, a minimalist sauce that adds just a whisper of herb to the pristine sea juices of the ivory meat.

Latona's crisp tofu-veggie samosas with carrot ginger sauce were downright flavorful for a macrobiotic dish. But they were too sloppily done and falling apart to charge $20. And his spice-crusted tuna would have been completely ordinary had it not been for the deliciously rich garnish of risotto filled with a snappy succotash of corn and green beans.

One fine tradition this kitchen has maintained nicely, however, is that deliciously sloppy curiosity called poached mozzarella, a.k.a. "pizza in a bowl." The melted balls of fresh white cheese reside at the bottom of a bowl filled with bright tomato sauce and an herby dollop of pesto, all to be scooped up by long croutons in one gooey, drippy, scoop of crunchy gusto.

Latona is no pastry chef, but he has taken the right tack, adding clever twists to homey confections. Peach and blueberry crisp captured the essence of late summer's ripe fruit. A massive bowl of rice pudding was filled with puffy risotto grains, its warm custard filled with rum-plumped raisins.

The Rooster's true dessert ringer, though, speaks more to Parrotta's good industry contacts than any pastry epiphany downstairs. Finding the recipe for Parrotta's beloved homestyle chocolate cake ("I wanted one just like Duncan Hines, but better") was a task that drove her kitchen to distraction.

When all appeared lost, former Le Bec-Fin pastry master Robert

Or Try These

Here are three other gourmet hideaways with great food.

Le Bar Lyonnais

1523 Walnut St., Philadelphia
(215) 567-1000

The no-reservation downstairs bar at Le Bec-Fin is still one of the city's best deals, where the a la carte menu — from steak-frites to cheese plate — more than compensates for the claustrophobic room.

Opus 251

The Philadelphia Art Alliance, 251 S. 18th St., Philadelphia
(215) 735-6787

Sophisticated New American cuisine is served in a Rittenhouse Square mansion with a secret garden.

Jolly's Bar and Grill

135 S. 17th St., Philadelphia
(215) 563-8200

This casual offshoot of the Prime Rib sits just below the Walnut Street sidewalk, offering a black-lacquer piano lounge for fine American fare at affordable prices.

Bennett (now owner of Miel Patisserie in Marlton) kindly gifted the Rooster with cake. And it is a recipe that seems to defy the boundaries of darkness, stuffing its glorious sheets of ebony sponge with a pale cloud of silky chocolate mousse frost. No wonder Parrotta is stomping to Johnny Cash over by the bar. She finally got the bittersweet cake she wanted. And we're eating it up.

■ **MENU HIGHLIGHTS** (Note: Entire menu changes daily.) Lobster with smoked tomato remoulade; mushroom ravioli; poached mozzarella; spaghetti bolognese; sirloin steak; scallops; burger; chocolate cake; rice pudding.

■ **WINE LIST** Don't let the scribbled notebook fool you; owner Rose Parrotta's list is carefully chosen, stocked with boutique wines from France and California that, for the quality, are fairly priced, with depth at the top and bottom of the list.

■ **IF YOU GO** Lunch Monday-Friday 11:30 a.m.-2:30 p.m. Dinner Monday-Thursday 5:30-10:30 p.m., Friday-Saturday 5:30-11 p.m. Caviar menu served Monday-Friday 11:30 a.m.-1 a.m. Dinner entrees, $18-$31.

■ **RESERVATIONS** Highly recommended.

■ **CREDIT CARDS** All major cards but Discover and Diners Club.

■ **SMOKING** A recently added dining room is nonsmoking. But the Rooster's front dining area/bar is not recommended for those bothered by smoke.

■ **HANDICAP ACCESSIBLE** No.

■ **PARKING** Street parking only.

Horizons Cafe

Creative vegan cooking brings sizzling seitan
to this casual strip-mall bistro.

U nless you've seen a flock of seitan birds lately, these barbecued "wings" never did much flying. But nearly everything else about these grilled wheat-gluten strips at Horizons Cafe in Willow Grove is a convincing facsimile of the original.

Slicked with a barbecue glaze that shines with a hint of Jamaican spice (there's a chili version, too), they are curled and caramelized around the edges from the charring heat of the grill. So I close my eyes and take a bite.

The chew is just right, resilient and snappy; the flavor, smoky and sweet. It has the consistency of dark-meat chicken more than a wing, everything but the lingering natural juices and inimitably fine texture of meat fibers. One of them even has fake bones!

VERY GOOD

101 E. Moreland Ave.
(Routes 63 and 611).
Willow Grove, Pa.
(215) 657-2100

NEIGHBORHOOD
Northern Suburbs

CUISINE
New American Vegetarian

Oops, it's just a skewer.

I know plenty of people who limit their diet to such alternative foods for health or ethical reasons, and many of them do it happily. But no matter how convincing and clever, the culture of fake meat is one that some people will never embrace.

I can sympathize after more than a few brushes with bad tofu, which can be worse than bland. It can paralyze the taste buds, freeze them numb and render them powerless under the suffocating jiggle of a soybean curd.

Poorly handled, tofu is partly responsible for much of the flavorless glop that too often passes for vegetarian cooking. The memory alone is enough for the sign in front of Horizons Cafe that reads "Food of the Future" to produce an apocalyptic shudder.

But what you'll discover inside this casual and friendly storefront restaurant — which moved not long ago to a colorful new space just up the strip mall — is something quite different: an entire vegan menu (meatless and dairy-free) of prime soy and seitan cuts that does not sacrifice good flavor or creative cooking. Peppercorn-crusted "tofu" scallops? Seitan "steak" and potatoes? It's better than it sounds — which, of course, is part of the problem.

Chef Rich Landau does not do his kitchen justice by insisting on these mock titles — tofu will never taste like crab or scallops, and seitan can never measure up to meat. "Horizonizing," as he calls it, is a

Chef Rich Landau, who gave up meat for ethical reasons, still cooks like a meat-lover.

concept built on unfavorable comparisons.

But I've been to the dark side of the soy pantry and back, and for what it is, Horizons' food is a breath of fresh air — organic, of course, filtered through reverse osmosis (like the seltzer) and steam-cleaned (like the turbinado sugar).

Landau, who abandoned meat-eating for ethical reasons, still cooks like a meat-lover, focusing his dishes on well-seasoned hunks of wheat or soy protein rather than on pure vegetarian cooking, drawing on Asian, Latin and tropical flavors to give them interest and color.

One of my favorites is the enchilada stuffed with an earthy filling of smoked tofu and mushrooms, a crispy tube candy-striped with vibrant green and red pepper salsas. The Yucatan tofu, topped with crumbled blue tortillas, salsa, then set over a satisfying blob of guacamole, is a satisfying meal of textures and spice. Artichoke bottoms are mounded New Orleans-style with a Creole stuffing of bread crumbs and faux sausage, then set over an orange puree of sherried bell pepper bisque. A bracing green cilantro chimichurri sauce, sweet plantain rounds, and corn give a hunk of tofu some mambo, mingling with the powdery texture of crushed Brazil nuts on top.

Landau has a tendency to mix his ethnic metaphors. The "Moroccan" seitan could just as easily have been called "Thai," considering that the chile-spiced grilled gluten came over a bowl of noodles in coconut-milk sauce.

The similarly sauced Thai wild-mushroom bouillabaisse had nothing in common with the Provencale seafood classic, except that they both use broth. It was tasty, but I was disappointed in the pedestrian mushroom assortment — buttons, shiitakes and portobellos are hardly wild, and barely "exotic" anymore.

I'd think a vegetarian restaurant with an ode to mushrooms would go out of its way for some interesting fungus — lobsters, chanterelles, hen of the woods perhaps. Of course, that would be hard to do for $12, which is near the top of this restaurant's reasonable entree price range. But it is also a sign of the kitchen's greatest weakness — its focus on refining true vegetable cookery takes second place to its fondness for fake meat.

That is not to say some of the vegetarian selections don't appeal. Horizons' salads, for example, are bolstered by some truly excellent dressings — a rosy-colored smoked onion and horseradish, a gingery carrot puree spiked with sesame and garlic, and a green Asian vinaigrette that tingles with wasabi and rice vinegar. Horizons' soups tend to be brothy, and slightly undersalted, but full of good flavors: milled mushrooms tinted with cilantro; Polynesian rice soup sweetened with curried coconut and banana.

Landau's cooking may be at its best, however, in dishes that have no ethnic bent, but that simply convey his enthusiasm for hearty plates and satisfying flavors. His pecan- and sage-baked seitan is a triumph for gluten, with meaty seitan filets layered between a dark mushroom duxelles and an unctuous smear of Dijon mustard cream dusted with crushed pecans.

Tender chunks of fresh hazelnuts transform one of his fall specials into a gem, highlighting an herby Madeira sauce that moistens mushrooms and tofu "scallops." No, they don't taste like seafood, but the nicely browned cylinders (at least U-12s), with their crackly crust of crushed peppercorns and salt, are about as tasty as tofu gets.

Or Try These

Here are three other vegetarian-friendly restaurants.

Blue Sage

772 Second Street Pike, Southampton, Pa.
(215) 942-8888

A casual strip-mall bistro serving creative vegetarian cuisine that eschews fake meat, but also goes far beyond the cliches of twig-and-sprout cuisine.

Citrus

8136 Germantown Ave., Philadelphia (215) 247-8188

This tiny bistro-bakery offers modern seafood and vegetarian dishes with a light Asian touch, as well as a heavy dose of animal-rights activism.

Cherry Street Vegetarian

1010 Cherry St., Philadelphia (215) 923-3663

One of Chinatown's best mock-meat vegetarians, Cherry Street doesn't skimp on flavor, with dishes like Dynasty mock shrimp and emerald soup and salt-baked oyster mushrooms.

When it comes to desserts, Horizon has made some strides. Their early attempts at dairy-free chocolate desserts always had the off-flavor of carob. A recent taste of their chocolate raspberry tarte, though, was as smooth as cocoa silk.

It was a fine finale to justify my server's genuine enthusiasm for the possibilities of "horizonizing." And it was infectious. So much so that it would seem, for the first time in their unnatural lives, seitan wings had learned to fly.

■ **MENU HIGHLIGHTS** Stuffed artichoke bottoms; smoked tofu and mushroom enchilada; quesadilla; seitan wings; nori salad; pecan- and sage-baked seitan; hazelnut tofu scallops; Yucatan roasted tofu; sopa de tortilla; Brazil nut crusted tofu; chocolate raspberry tart.

■ **WINE LIST** BYOB.

■ **IF YOU GO** Lunch served Tuesday-Friday 11:30 a.m.-2:30 p.m. Limited menu available Tuesday-Friday 2:30-4:30 p.m. Dinner served Tuesday-Thursday 4:30-9 p.m., Friday-Saturday 4:30-10 p.m. Closed Sunday-Monday. Lunch entrees, $5.25-$8.50. Dinner entrees, $10.50-$13.50.

■ **RESERVATIONS** Recommended but not required.

■ **CREDIT CARDS** All major cards but Discover and American Express.

■ **SMOKING** Entire restaurant is nonsmoking.

■ **HANDICAP ACCESSIBLE** Yes.

■ **PARKING** Free lot.

The Inn on Blueberry Hill

The ambitious Bucks County inn has a talented chef, formerly of Susanna Foo, who is serving memorable contemporary cuisine.

We live in a mushroom mecca, but you wouldn't know it from eating in many local restaurants. A mix of domestic button and shiitake mushrooms is still too often called "exotic," and somehow the "wild" ones always end up in soup. Rarely do mushrooms sauteed whole transcend the anonymity of garlicky brown blobs.

To understand how exciting wild mushrooms can truly be, chefs and diners alike might travel up Broad Street and follow Route 611 as it wends its way into central Bucks County. There, at a country inn oasis surrounded by Doylestown's commercial sprawl, chef Bill Kim's mushroom ragout basks in a bowl of crystalline broth.

EXCELLENT

1715 S. Easton Rd.
Doylestown, Pa.
(215) 491-1777

NEIGHBORHOOD
Central Bucks County

CUISINE
Asian Fusion

Coarsely cut and still firm, these mushrooms — like virtually all of the fine ingredients used at the Inn on Blueberry Hill — seem to exist in a heightened state. Crinkled black trumpets twist into their twiny stems. Chunky hedgehogs have a solid, snappy crunch. Spongy oysters sop in the buttery, herby juice to which golden chanterelles also lend their nutty forest sweetness. Vibrant green petals of brussels sprout scattered atop lend each mushroom a faintly bitter contrast.

It would be enough for Kim to master mushrooms, but how about elevating something less obvious, such as chubs? Considering that the Korea-born Kim has an affinity for Asian fusion, his fondness for Brooklyn smoked whitefish is surprising. But his rendition is sublime, separating the meat into nuggets, then tossing them with pencil-thin green beans and a tart cucumber yogurt sauce that cuts straight through the smoky, oily fish. Matchstick shreds of Gala apple bundled on top add a fruity, crunchy finish.

This is serious cooking, in fact, some of the most exquisite food in the region. But, what's that, you haven't heard of Bill Kim?

Perhaps you've heard of a few of his previous superstar employers: Charlie Trotter's in Chicago, Bouley Bakery in Manhattan, and our own Susanna Foo, for whom he was executive chef when I first rated that restaurant four bells in 1998.

It was at Susanna Foo that Kim met Mark Dombkoski, who left his job there as general manager in 1999 to take over The Inn on Blueberry Hill, which resides in a converted Victorian house that, along with a barn and steepled carriage house, is all that's left of a 300-acre, 18th-century farm.

Under Dombkoski's watch, Blueberry Hill has become pretty enough, with a glassed-in porch, a parlor and — my preferred spot — a large stone-walled room to choose from. And yet there is still a generic quality to the ambience, a sort of corporate palette of bland earth tones that could use a more personal touch, a quirkiness to match the warmth of the thoughtful and outgoing service. Perhaps if Dombkoski ever realizes his dream of purchasing this complex and converting the outbuildings into a bakery, B&B and banquet hall, Blueberry Hill will become the major dining destination it clearly has the potential to be.

It already took the most important step in finding Kim. When he joined the

Chef Bill Kim's mushroom ragout basks in a bowl of crystalline broth.

restaurant in 2000, it was an opportunity for the longtime protege to finally run his own show. Unlike so many former sidekicks, though, the 33-year-old chef does more than simply mimic his mentors. He is evolving a style of his own, Asian-inflected but thoroughly American, rooted in fresh local ingredients but still exotic, with dishes that reveal layers of flavor without ever seeming heavy or convoluted.

A fan of thyme-scented duck breast is sparked with the bittersweet marmalade of kumquats candied with anise. A pureed corn soup is enriched with coconut milk and a salty twinge of fish sauce, then dolloped with steamed milk and a frond of "popcorn shoots," tiny green blades that taste like just-picked sweet summer corn.

The corn shoots are just some of the unusual and exceptional greens that Kim has found at Blue Moon Acres, one of many Bucks County purveyors that are oddly better known in Manhattan than in Philadelphia. Baby red amaranth adds a sharp, peppery bite to the whitefish salad. Grassy tangles of micro-cilantro decorate tamarind-streaked tempura shrimp made with a chardonnay-based crust. A tuft of tiny celery greens garnishes Kim's excellent crab cake, a creamy puck of jumbo lumps that is perfumed subtly with lemon zest.

And you've got to love a top-notch chef who still makes room for his mother's recipes. The Pennsylvania-raised ostrich fillet tingles with the caramelized soy char of the Kim family's ginger-scallion barbecue marinade.

Even the Dombkoski family gets a nod from Kim's kitchen, with a succulent pork chop sided with rounds of Northeast Philadelphia kielbasa and a tangy mound of caraway-infused homemade sauerkraut. An equally hearty loin of lamb seared in garlic oil played against tender nuggets of stewed lamb shank over lentils and glazed root vegetables, studded with a delicate green surprise of fresh fava beans.

There were a few less-inspired dishes. The swordfish was moist, but its seasoning too busy, hiding any recognizable swordfish flavor. The pristine diver scallops were overwhelmed by a crunchy couscous crust. And aside from the meringue-enrobed baked Alaska brownie, a tart goat cheese cheesecake, and a startlingly refreshing blood orange granita, the desserts were on the whole less intriguing than the savory courses.

Otherwise, my meals here were superb. A thick fillet of flounder, baked in a steamy parchment envelope with sweet cloves of oil-poached garlic, fingerling potatoes, and baby bok choy was one of the finest fish entrees I'd eaten in months.

As the server snipped open the balloon-taut bag and napped the fillet with a buttery tomato caper sauce, the steam wafted away, leaving a clear view of an otherwise empty restaurant.

Where, I wondered, were the crowds on this Friday night? Perhaps

Or Try These

Here are three other restaurants to be found heading north on Route 611 out of Philadelphia:

Marco Polo

8080 Old York Rd., Elkins Park, Pa. (215) 782-1950

Ignore the old fern bar decor and strip-mall location. The China-born chef is a surprisingly gifted Italian cook specializing in fresh whole fish.

Horizons Cafe

101 E. Moreland Ave., Willow Grove, Pa. (215) 657-2100

A creative mock-meat vegan chef brings sizzling seitan and pepper-seared tofu to a casual strip-mall bistro.

Otto's Brauhaus

233 Easton Rd., Horsham, Pa. (215) 675-1864

Don your liederhausen at this German outpost for schnitzel, brats and snapper soup, where the big beer garden hops during Oktoberfest.

they've simply yet to be told about a chef named Bill Kim, whom everyone should know. Consider it done.

■ MENU HIGHLIGHTS Wild mushroom ragout; smoked whitefish; crab cake; chardonnay-battered shrimp; ostrich; parchment-baked flounder; wild striped bass; duck breast with kumquat sauce; pork chop with cabbage; baked Alaska; blood orange granita; three-cheese cheesecake.

■ WINE LIST The 140-bottle cellar has a well-chosen selection of mostly California vintages that is particularly rich in chardonnays (try the excellent Hendry, $52), eclectic whites, and versatile pinot noirs.

■ IF YOU GO Dinner served Tuesday-Thursday 5-9 p.m., Friday-Saturday 5-10 p.m., Sunday 4-8 p.m. Entrees, $20-$35.

■ RESERVATIONS Suggested but not required.

■ CREDIT CARDS All major cards accepted.

■ SMOKING Entire restaurant is nonsmoking.

■ HANDICAP ACCESSIBLE Accessible through the side entrance.

■ PARKING Free lot.

Jake's

The innovative restaurant, after 15 years, is still Manayunk's best.

My friends have three young girls, and they don't get out much. But when they do, they like to brag.

So what would they say about our dinner at Jake's in Manayunk?

"We go to Jake's," boasted the girls' mother in her best Ivana Trump imitation, "... for the mashed potatoes."

Before you jump to the conclusion that these friends really don't get out enough, let me illuminate our potato nirvana. For starters, we spooned into silky Yukon golds, mashed with Lancaster County buttermilk and niblets of roasted corn, a veritable country cloud beneath a crisp breast of moist chicken.

And then came the lobster mashed, a fluffy pedestal for medallions

EXCELLENT

4365 Main St.
Philadelphia
(215) 483-0444

NEIGHBORHOOD
Manayunk

CUISINE
New American

of tender veal, ringed with the brilliant green of pureed chive. Trendy? Yes. But this satiny pink puree infused every taste bud with the richness of cream slow-steeped with lobster shells. Then, like a vision fulfilled, a long tail of white meat unfurled from the potatoes on the end of my fork, lobster sweet and tender.

It's no shock that more than a few customers at Jake's refer to this dish as "sex on a plate." And it's hardly much of an exaggeration when something so mundane is elevated to the sublime.

But in the fickle world of fine dining, you need more than mashed potatoes for longevity. And Jake's owner and chef, Bruce Cooper, who helped pioneer Manayunk's fine-dining scene, has discovered some of the most elusive ingredients — a stylish culinary vision, a fix on top-quality products, and a kitchen as consistent as a Swiss watch.

After more than 15 years, Jake's has obviously struck an enduring chord with an eclectic menu that runs the gamut from homey comfort (grilled calves' liver) to Asian sleek (seared tuna with gingered sushi rice). Whereas Novelty, Cooper's second restaurant, has struggled to find its true niche in Old City, Jake's still displays a remarkable command of Main Street. It remains, judging from an impressive recent lunch, without competition as Manayunk's finest restaurant.

The 65-seat dining room, with its undulating-backed banquettes and low vaulted ceiling of acoustical metal mesh, has a vibrant ener-

The 65-seat dining room, with its undulating-backed banquettes and low vaulted ceiling of acoustical metal mesh, has a vibrant energy about it.

gy about it, accentuated by walls striped with panels of pulsing yellow. There is a stylish clientele to match, wearing designer eyewear and good tans, slinky dresses, and the required cell-phone accessories.

One can sink a tad too low in the banquettes for dining comfort. But it didn't seem to bother one courting couple, who, in the throes of passionate mauling on the side banquette, only reluctantly took a hint from their server, who placed the entree on the opposite side of the table before the gentleman's unoccupied chair.

I used to find the service a bit cool here. But not at lunch this summer. Our server took care of the table with the kind of grace and attention only a longtime veteran can achieve, surprising us with an apology when it seemed that our lunch's smart pacing had begun to lag. No apology was necessary. A meal at Jake's is hardly one I'd want to rush.

While this is, by most standards, an innovative restaurant, I was surprised by how much of the menu hadn't changed in the last four years. But many of these dishes are so good, the restaurant's regulars forbid them to be removed.

There were still many of the refined renditions of comfort-food favorites that give this sophisticated place a smidgen of folksy appeal, with crisp roast chicken, grilled veal meat loaf, and calves' liver that seemed to disappear from every ordered plate.

And several of the kitchen's Asian-inspired standards remained, from the fine veal dumplings to the spring rolls bundled like a package with string of chive. Filled with duck confit, they were perfectly crisp and ringed by Technicolor dots of blackberry, mustard and mandarin orange sauces. The veal with lobster mashed potatoes, as well as the barbecued salmon marinated in tangy teriyaki, were also untouched staples.

But Jake's, I learned, is much more than a restaurant running on automatic. Numerous new offerings gave plenty of evidence that this kitchen is still vital.

A gorgeous plate of tuna carpaccio is topped with refreshing crab and avocado salad, the pristine fish slicked with the sparkling sweetness of a pickled ginger vinaigrette. A cool summer soup of the pureed red and yellow watermelons bloomed like a two-toned starburst in the bowl.

I owe Jake's a great debt for feeding me in mid-June the first ripe local tomato of the year, an absolutely luscious beefsteak that dripped red juices into milky rounds of sweet mozzarella. There was also a lovely, panfried soft-shell crab perched over diced red and yellow watermelons — the melons and crab each delivering their own juicy countercrunch. And three big grilled shrimp entwined in an elegant knot over a refreshing gazpacho sauce filled with bits of cucumber.

The kitchen's most impressive move, though, was an impromptu dish whipped together for a vegetarian guest. It was a napoleon extraordinaire — a crisply paneed tomato topped with sauteed shiitakes, melted mozzarella, and a nest of homemade spinach fettuccine tossed in a zesty tomato vinaigrette.

Pastry chef Debbie Tonsey didn't quite reach such heights with her creative but ultimately flat Roquefort gougere. But the raspberry port ice cream that came with it was excellent, as was the perfect blueberry cobbler, the warm chocolate cake, and the classic of all Jake's standbys: the cookie taco, a deep-fried, cinnamon sugarcoated flour tortilla filled with ice cream, fresh berries, and curls of white chocolate. When a taco was taken to our now-necking neighbors on the side banquette — a special-occasion candle burning in

Or Try These

Here are three other restaurants in Manayunk.

Kansas City Prime

4417 Main St., Philadelphia
(215) 482-3700

This chic local chophouse from Derek Davis is satisfying as long as you stick with the excellent steaks; the rest is inconsistent and overpriced.

Il Tartufo

4341 Main St., Philadelphia
(215) 482-1999

Alberto Delbello's "Roman-Jewish" trattoria is tight inside, but has a lovely sidewalk cafe from which to watch Main Street pass by while you nibble awesome fried artichokes, homemade mozzarella, and truffle-sauced scallopini.

Le Bus

4266 Main St., Philadelphia
(215) 487-2663

The eclectic fare at this bakery-cafe is a lunchtime favorite for many, although for a family-friendly place, the service has often been snippy.

this colorful confection like a ticking tortilla time bomb — we all ducked for fear they might explode.

With customers like that, who needs "sex on a plate"?

Well, me for one. And I get out enough to know that ethereal mashed potatoes — and a restaurant with the rare consistency of Jake's — make for first-rate bragging material.

■ **MENU HIGHLIGHTS** Beet and goat-cheese timbale; tuna carpaccio; soft-shell crabs with melon; spring rolls; grilled foie gras; veal dumplings; pink peppercorn-seared tuna; goat-cheese gnocchi with oyster mushrooms; grilled tuna with sticky rice; barbecued salmon; veal with lobster-mashed potatoes; cookie taco; chocolate pot de creme; homemade ice cream.

■ **WINE LIST** An excellent French-California cellar, with plenty under $50. Good wines by the glass are a bonus, as is the great list of premium after-dinner spirits.

■ **IF YOU GO** Lunch served Monday-Friday 11:30 a.m.-2:30 p.m., Saturday 11:30 a.m.-2 p.m.; Sunday brunch served 10:30 a.m.-2:30 p.m. Dinner served Monday-Friday 5:30-9:30 p.m., Saturday 5-10:30 p.m., Sunday 5-9 p.m. Dinner entrees, $22.50-$33.95. Four-course $35 prix-fixe menu available Sunday-Thursday.

■ **RESERVATIONS** Recommended.

■ **CREDIT CARDS** All major cards but Discover.

■ **SMOKING** Entire dining room is nonsmoking.

■ **HANDICAP ACCESSIBLE** One small step at the entrance and another step into the dining room.

■ **PARKING** Valet parking available after 5 p.m. for $5.

John's Roast Pork

The city's best pork sandwich and cheesesteaks
are served at a gritty South Philly luncheonette.

I n the waning months of John Bucci's life, he pulled John Jr.
aside for a serious talk.

"Whatever you do," he told his son, "I don't care how drunk
you are, I don't care how in love you are, never give this recipe
away. This is my family's name. This is what's important to
me."

Bucci, who died more than a decade ago, was speaking of
his roast pork sandwich, of course. The Bucci family has
served them from its modest luncheonette on Snyder Avenue and
Weccacoe Street in South Philadelphia since 1932, two years after
John Sr.'s father, Domenico, engineered this flavor explosion in a
garage across town.

I happened into John's Roast Pork a few years ago, wrapped my

EXCELLENT

Snyder Avenue
and Weccacoe Street,
Philadelphia
(215) 463-1951

NEIGHBORHOOD
South Philadelphia

CUISINE
Steak and Pork
Sandwiches

hands around a crusty, sesame-seeded roll
stuffed with meat, and took a bite. I looked up
from my seat at one of the picnic tables outside, from which one has a spectacular view
of the Center City skyline and the Walt
Whitman. And as the juices dripped down my
chin, I suddenly knew how a pork sandwich
could become a legacy.

Flavor filled my mouth like a cascade. The
layers of finely shaved meat snapped between
my teeth with tenderness, unlocking from
beneath each layer the nuances of rosemary
and bay. Intoxicating juices swirled like a
whirlpool with each bite, washing across the

farthest-flung taste buds with the essence of garlic and something
more elusive. A hovering shade of clove was flowing through this river
on a bun.

The humble pork sandwich is a South Philly survivor if there ever
was one, stuck in the shadow of the cheesesteak. And yet, in the tra-
dition-steeped neighborhoods of Italian Philadelphia, the roast pork
sandwich always lurked, the old wedding banquet standby simmering in a pan of gravy next to the shiny chop-chop griddles.

"When people think of Philadelphia, they think cheesesteaks," says
Anthony Lucidonio Jr., a.k.a. Tony Luke Jr. "But locals, they think cut-
lets and pork."

At the Tony Luke restaurants, including the original neon-

John Bucci Jr. and his mother, Vonda, serve up succulent steak and pork sandwiches at John's Roast Pork in South Philadelphia.

awninged outpost on Oregon Avenue nearby, roast pork is the number-one seller.

"It's more comfort food than anything else," he says. "It was a very big part of my growing up. Holidays. Christmas banquets. Birthdays. Confirmations. Baptisms. Roast pork was always there."

Tony Luke's pork, a nice, clean-flavored sandwich, has garnered more than its share of notoriety, and been featured in national magazines and shipped to movie sets. It is even better now that the Oregon Avenue restaurant is baking its own crusty rolls.

But it doesn't quite measure up to John's, where the volume on the flavo-meter gets turned up to 11. John's pork sandwich is so good, in fact, that it took more than two years for me to order anything else here. Somehow, I wasn't surprised to learn that John Jr. also makes what may very well be the best cheesesteak in town, whether it's beef or chicken. There is a fabulous roast beef sauced with deep, dark, meaty gravy and also hearty Italian wedding soup. For his steaks, Bucci caramelizes each batch of onions to order on the hot griddle, seasoning his meat and searing it brown and tasty around the edges. Then he blends in just the perfect amount of real cheese. Ask for Cheez Whiz on your steak and you will get a cold stare and a "No" as sharp as the provolone. The atty-tude here is authentic tough love. But it's rooted in pride of product.

The only things to avoid are the deep-fried crab and fish cakes, which tasted more like doughy knishes than anything from the sea. You should also come fairly early if you want your sandwich on one of those seeded rolls. These couple of details, though, are excusable. It seems a triumph that John's has managed to endure this long at all, marking time from its wedge of earth as Philadelphia and the industrial zone around it changed. Snyder was a dirt road when the Buccis opened shop.

"My in-laws started in a little wooden shack," says Vonda Bucci, John Sr.'s wife, who, after 42 years there still works the register. "Now we have a cinder-block shack."

The old alcohol distillery that once anchored the blue-collar neighborhood is gone, replaced by the strip mall across the street. But the chemical factory next door still towers over the low-slung, clay-colored luncheonette, its chimneys puffing smoke. And when the CSX trains rumble past the other side, customers sitting at the counter inside still have a tendency to tremble.

And John Jr. still follows the two-day pork ritual his father and grandfather passed down to him: boning

Or Try These

Here are three other restaurants serving roast pork sandwiches.

Tony Luke's

39 Oregon Ave., Philadelphia
(215) 551-5725

The homemade rolls elevate the broccoli rabe-topped steak, Italian and pork sandwich at this Oregon Avenue picnic-table stand, making this branch the best of the big-crowd famous steak emporiums.

Shank's and Evelyn's Roast Beef

932 S. 10th St., Philadelphia
(215) 629-1093

The all-woman crew at this tiny luncheonette dishes out counter-side sass with the big flavors of cutlet sandwiches topped with hot roast peppers, everything-omelets, and excellent roast beef and pork.

Porky's Point

3824 N. Fifth St., Philadelphia
(215) 221-6243

This take-out stand in North Philadelphia is the Latino equivalent of Tony Luke's, where cars triple-park and the line grows long into the night with people hungry for homemade blood sausage, red beans and rice with chopped pig ears, and — my favorite — what is undoubtedly one of the very best, most tender pork sandwiches in town.

the fresh hams, seasoning the meat, slow-roasting, cooling, skimming the gravy, straining the bones, shaving it down, heating it up, and serving it forth with lightning speed in a blur of spoon and juice. The pork sandwiches here come three ways: dry, wet and "overboard."

These are sandwiches you can't take home with you.

There are days when the luncheonette is too small for the big tempers behind the counter, when John Jr. screams "Mother!" from the grill, and Vonda will tell you the tale of how they all "got stuck" in this place.

John Sr. got stuck helping his folks. She got stuck helping him. John Jr. got stuck, too, when his father was diagnosed with cancer, leaving his third year at St. Joseph's to keep the luncheonette alive.

But the satisfaction of a third-generation business quickly overwhelms the complaints.

And the memory of John Jr.'s father is everywhere, from the way he manages the hot spots on his grill to the way he, too, puts his leg up on the counter. He can even see himself as a little boy keeping his father company in the back room while he boned the hams, pestering his father with an endless litany of questions.

How much salt, Dad? How much garlic, Dad? How many sandwiches do you sell, Dad?

"Shut up!" his father would finally say, sending his son — even decades later — into peals of laughter. Could John Sr. have known the significance of their ham-bound heart-to-hearts? How a secret recipe could become so much more than a delicious sandwich?

"Roast pork has meant everything to me and my family," John Jr. says. "It has been our whole life."

■ **MENU HIGHLIGHTS** Roast pork sandwich with greens and provolone; cheesesteak; chicken cheesesteak; roast beef.

■ **WINE LIST** Alcoholic beverages are not allowed.

■ **IF YOU GO** Open Monday through Friday, 6:45 a.m.-3 p.m., but cheesesteak grill closes at 2:30 p.m.

■ **RESERVATIONS** Not accepted, although sandwiches can be ordered ahead for take-out.

■ **CREDIT CARDS** Cash only.

■ **SMOKING** Permitted at picnic tables only.

■ **HANDICAP ACCESSIBLE** Luncheonette is accessible, but bathrooms are not.

■ **PARKING** Street parking available.

Judy's Cafe

The affable Queen Village fixture with updated comfort food has a devoted and diverse clientele.

In the fickle and ever-changing world of restaurants, 27 years is a long time to remain up and running, a life span that some restaurateurs might find impossible to attain with any vibrance.

But at Judy's Cafe in Queen Village, there is a warmth to the ambience — still palpable even after a recent makeover — that has cured over the years like a well-seasoned cast-iron pan. Its moody lights and hardwood floors cast a comfy patina over the neon-traced bar dining room that is appealingly down to earth and durable, like the fabulous meat loaf and mashed potatoes that anchor the restaurant's eclectic comfort food menu.

Over the years, Judy's devoted clientele has grown into one of the area's most diverse, including, but hardly limited to, those drawn by its reputation as a gay-friendly destination. One segment is the "coupon" crowd, the near-fanatical followers of this restaurant's ever-morphing two-for-one coupon deals, which help to make the already reasonably priced menu a bargain.

VERY GOOD

627 S. Third St.,
Philadelphia
(215) 928-1968

NEIGHBORHOOD
Queen Village

CUISINE
Comfort Food

And then, of course, there are the "public humiliation" birthdays that some guests relish, when celebrants don wigs and stiletto heels for a birthday strut to the tacky tune du jour. A 94-year-old former judge did it in a floor-length blond number. So did the father of a previous chef, a former Air Force sergeant who didn't shrink when the staff fitted him with the same 6-foot-long wig. With Tom Jones piping up "She's a Lady" or "What's New Pussycat," who could dare to sit still?

A sense of humor, obviously, has been one of the key ingredients of this restaurant's longevity. But all of it would be simple novelty without a legitimate kitchen.

The menu has grown considerably more eclectic since the early days, when Eileen Plato (now sole owner) launched Judy's with Judy Galfand as a 24-hour cold-food and omelet-to-order shop on Leithgow Street. At its current location, behind the hot pink neon sign and mint-green masonry at Third and Bainbridge Streets where it has been for nearly three decades, it has a menu that changes significantly from night to night.

Chef Anders Divack, a former coffee roaster who took over the kitchen since my initial review, has guarded many of Judy's standards well, but also brought a noticeable polish to the food, adding a notch of sophistication to fare that was always known for its homey comfort.

At a recent visit, a number of menu classics were in good form. The chicken breasts coated with pulverized cheddar sticks might sound like a cast-off from the back of a snack box (Goldfish, in fact, are occasionally used as an emergency substitute), but ours were wonderfully moist and flavorful, sided with fluffy horseradish-mashed potatoes. Horseradish sauce also came in handy for the nut-crusted

trout, panfried to perfection.

The pate was not only an ideal, coarsely ground rendition of the French country classic, it was served with triangle-shaped toasts that were perfect for spreading, plump raisins, and a tasty chutney of figs and nuts. Bowtie pastas came tossed in a fresh tomato sauce piqued with the saltiness of olives and shaved ricotta salata. One of the kitchen's patented hearty salads came topped with a warm puck of breaded goat cheese streaked with balsamic vinegar and tomato coulis.

Judy's famous meat loaf, actually Italian polpettone, a mixture of beef, veal and pork seasoned with cheese and spices, remains the prototype of the souped-up home food this restaurant does well. Sided with a mound of the superb, hand-whipped red bliss mashed potatoes, then topped with a flavorful saute of mushrooms and gravy, this is the kind of dish regulars are built on.

After tasting a few of the chef's recent nightly specials, though, I can imagine Divack is winning over some new fans with deft interpretations of some more modern, eclectic dishes. His five-spice roasted duck was pristine; the exotic anise and gingery seasonings of the marinade and sauce were clear but didn't mask the bird's natural flavors. A silky mash of sweet potatoes completed the dish. Divack's curried shrimp were equally intriguing, with succulent crustaceans ringed by a saffron-curried cream with the vibrance of a Van Gogh yellow. In the middle of the plate, a tomato compote stewed with cardamom and mustard seeds added marvelous new layers of flavor, a whiff of tradewind spice and a spark of acid that elevated the entire dish into something special.

The veteran waitstaff was still in fine form, thoroughly pleasant and outgoing, and well-informed on the menu. And the homey desserts prepared by Plato were as steady and satisfying as always. Flaky crust gave peach pie a wholesome country goodness. Peanut butter cheesecake was wonderfully dense and rich, its nuttiness edged by a great dark chocolate pastry crust. Pecan pie was moistened with the added lubrication of melted chocolate chips.

Divack's savory kitchen may be making a few welcome strides to update its act, but these desserts remain hopelessly, endearingly old-fashioned. But when you've been around as long as Judy's, it pays to stick with at least a few sweet comforts.

■ MENU HIGHLIGHTS Wild mushroom soup; five-spice duck; shrimp with saffron-curried cream; country pate; pear and gorgonzola salad; antipasto plate; cheddar-floured chicken; meat loaf; panfried nut-crusted trout; key lime pie; maple-date cheesecake; peach pie.

■ WINE LIST Two pages of mostly California vintages are well-chosen and fairly priced, with most under $40.

■ IF YOU GO Dinner served Monday-Saturday 5:30- 11 p.m., Sunday 5:30-10 p.m.; Sunday brunch served 10:30 a.m.- 5:30 p.m. Dinner entrees, $11-$19.

■ RESERVATIONS Accepted for parties of four or more.

■ CREDIT CARDS All major cards but Discover.

■ SMOKING There is a nonsmoking section.

■ HANDICAP ACCESSIBLE There are steps at the entrance, and the bathroom is not handicapped accessible.

■ PARKING Street parking only.

Or Try These

Here are three other restaurants serving updated comfort food.

Morning Glory Diner

735 S. 10th St., Philadelphia
(215) 413-3999

Indulgent macaroni and other homemade diner favorites are served in this hip, flower-decked Bella Vista eatery.

Rx

4443 Spruce St., Philadelphia
(215) 222-9590

This old apothecary-turned-casual contemporary corner spot offers creative and affordable updates on bistro comfort food that is just what the doctor ordered for gentrifying West Philly.

Jones

700 Chestnut St., Philadelphia
(215) 223-5663

Stephen Starr's latest venture reenvisions classics like fried chicken and waffles, turkey pot pie, and grilled cheese with tomato soup in a sunny, retro '70s room that also throbs with noise.

Khajuraho

Top-notch cooking sets the Main Line restaurant
apart from other traditional Indian establishments.

Who knew that ancient stone could be as sensuous as this? These voluptuous maidens, whose chiseled curves are frozen in mid-gyration above us, stand in alcoves around the dining room at Khajuraho silhouetted against the light. They look down at our table with blissful indifference, as if daring us to quit the inhibitions of our meal and imagine them come to life.

The heavenly Aspara maidens of Khajuraho — the little town in central India where ancient Hindu temples festooned with erotic sculpture have been the focus of sensuality for 1,000 years — have a rightful place in this Main Line restaurant of the same name. Owner Bharat Luthra has placed 18 of these celebrations of love around the dining room to evoke the equally ancient and sensual pleasures of Indian cuisine.

VERY GOOD

Ardmore Plaza,
12 Greenfield Ave.
Ardmore, Pa.
(610) 896-7200

NEIGHBORHOOD
Main Line

CUISINE
Indian

Considering that this culture also brought us the steamy Kamasutra, the ultimate lovemaking manual, is it any wonder that even the mildest of India's mysterious curries can leave a tingling kiss of heat on the tongue?

In deference to the mores of his clientele, Luthra has deemed two of his replica sculptures a bit too spicy for the Ardmore crowd and left them out of the dining room. Likewise, Khajuraho's kitchen has largely kept its peppery flavors in check for American taste buds. This notwithstanding the fried mirchi hot peppers stuffed with mango powder that left me sweating and lightheaded — although Luthra assures me the real thing would be much worse. Good thing the fire station is conveniently located across the street.

The soft lighting, intriguing art, and beautiful copper pots in which food is served add a polished ambience to this BYOB that most Indian restaurants in our region do not possess.

The largely northern Indian menu offers few surprises, with the usual lineup of tandoori, biryani, curries and fried appetizers. But what really sets Khajuraho above the rest is a matter of execution, thanks to a kitchen that derives subtleties in texture and flavor from quality ingredients and a pantry of spices that are ground freshly every day at the height of their essence.

How many times have I encountered a sad medley of canned vegetables in gloppy cream passed off as navratan korma, the royally rich vegetarian delicacy in which no fewer than nine fresh garden vegetables should be found? Khajuraho's was one of the best I've ever had, a vegetarian triumph of surprisingly spiced, blushing cream in which grooved rounds of carrot, flat green beans, minced cherries, peas, cashews and ethereal cardamom pods snapped with freshness in a chorus of dynamic flavors.

Fresh ginger and garlic sing in the tomatoey gravy that cloaks the earthy chickpeas of chana masala. An amazing tomato curry touched with cream complimented the malai kofta, balls of ground vegetables and homemade cheese that confirmed Khajuraho's mastery of vegetarian cuisine.

Khajuraho did produce a few mild disappointments: a dry chicken tikka, a dull mixed appetizer of overcooked meats, and tomatoey sweet rice pots that never quite lived up to the complexity of the best biryani. Service also leaves something to be desired. The understaffed crew was simply overwhelmed by the crowds that uncomfortably crammed its two dining rooms on our weekend visit, leaving a room full of dirty, unbussed tables until the evening was nearly done. Too many tables for not enough waiters. Even on a quiet night recently, there did not seem to be enough help.

But the delights of Khajuraho's kitchen far outweigh its deficits, with several dishes that left lasting memories of excellence.

The deep-fried puri was the finest of the homemade breads, puffed with hot steam like a buttery crepe balloon. The vegetarian pakora fritters, sweet onion bhaji, and vegetarian samosa dumplings, each leavened with fruity mango powder and an alluring blend of spices, were the best of the restaurant's greaseless fried appetizers.

Or Try These

Here are three other Indian restaurants.

Cafe Spice

35 S. Second St., Philadelphia
(215) 627-6273

This hip Indian bistro has contemporary decor, but classic dishes prepared with quality ingredients and sharp flavors.

Sitar India

60 S. 38th St., Philadelphia
(215) 662-0818

The best of the University City buffets keeps the bargain steam-table fresh and cheap.

Minar Palace

1605 Sansom St., Philadelphia
(215) 564-9443

It may not have the best food (although the vegetarian eggplant curry is good), but Minar Palace is so inexpensive and so impossibly quick, it has become one of Center City's most dependable delivery standbys.

Spinach curry called saagwala, vibrant with an exotic whiff of cilantro and thickened with cornmeal, was also delicious, even if the sea flavors of shrimp did not pair as well as chicken or homemade paneer cheese might have.

Chicken tikka masala, unlike most typical renditions, had a wonderful sauce that was not dominated by sweet cream, infused instead with zesty tomato, nuts and coriander. It also boasted a marvelous pureed texture that sat with silkiness on the tongue. The gravy for rogan josh was equally amazing, cast with a tan hue from a puree of onions, nuts, and the juices of lamb cubes so tender they dissolved in the mouth. The lamb vindaloo was also tender, but its devilish tomato curry left no illusions of soft cream; the fiery chile heat swelled on a sour edge of coconut vinegar and lingered on my lips for half an hour after the meal.

Such titillating spice stokes a thirst for intense sweetness as a balm, and Khajuraho ably obliges with traditional desserts that go heavy on the milk and honey.

Fried dough balls made from powdered milk called gulab jamun float in a comforting pool of warm sweet syrup. Milky kheer rice pudding exudes the irresistible eucalyptus breath of steeped cardamom pods, rose water and almonds. And homemade kulfi ice cream flavored with cardamom and pistachio slips off the spoon with icy crystals. They may have soothed the palate, but they could not snuff out the lingering sparks of a dinner so voluptuous. Its flavors made the chiseled curves of ancient stone come alive.

■ **MENU HIGHLIGHTS** Vegetable pakora; michi pakoa; vegetable samosa; chicken tikka masala; lamb vindaloo; lamb rogan josh; navratan korma; malai kofta; chana masala; chicken saagwala; kheer; kulfi.

■ **WINE LIST** BYOB.

■ **IF YOU GO** Lunch served Monday-Friday 11:30 a.m.-2:30 p.m., Saturday-Sunday 11:30 a.m.-3 p.m. Dinner served Sunday-Thursday 5-9 p.m., Friday-Saturday 5-10 p.m. Weekday lunch buffet, $7.50. Dinner entrees, $7.95-$15.95.

■ **RESERVATIONS** Recommended for weekends.

■ **CREDIT CARDS** All major cards.

■ **SMOKING** There is a nonsmoking section.

■ **HANDICAP ACCESSIBLE** Yes.

■ **PARKING** Free lot.

Kristian's

The renovated butcher shop has matured into
South Philadelphia's finest upscale Italian eatery.

"I'm going to kidnap you and take you to Florida!"

There was an odd hint of seriousness to this ominous threat, even if it did come from the seemingly sweet personage of Jean DiCicco, proud mama of City Councilman Frankie DiCicco.

Then again, the handsome chef was standing before her. The swarthy young man, Kristian Leuzzi, had given her crab cakes from heaven — and she was moved. We thought she might burst into tears of happiness. Instead, she turned to us and cursed her adopted home.

"They don't know how to cook in Florida," she lamented, ruefully shaking her head. "I haven't had a good meal in two years!"

There is nothing like time away from South Philly to stoke an appetite for the flavors of familiar cooking. But there has been an extra excitement growing here around Kristian's Ristorante, the little gem that opened four years ago at 11th and Federal Streets. It is the flutter of something new for the old neighborhood.

VERY GOOD

1100 Federal St.
Philadelphia
(215) 468-0104

NEIGHBORHOOD
South Philadelphia

CUISINE
Upscale Italian

Sure, Leuzzi is the local boy who grew up right next door, at 1102 Federal St. His brother, Dominick "Sonny" Leuzzi, is the friendly and firm-gripped maitre d' sending guests into the cozy restaurant where everyone, it seems, knows his neighbors.

But when Leuzzi's father, Dominick, finished eight years of renovations on Angelo's old butcher shop, this pretty corner building and its slender 50-seat dining room had an upscale polish uncommon downtown. From the striped canopies and ornate cornicework outside to the white, corral-tiled walls, crisply pleated curtains, and high-tech halogen track lights inside, there is an "audaciousness" about this place, one neighborhood friend observed, that has attracted a sleek local power crowd that counts DiCicco's son a regular.

And the food has followed suit, with the talented Leuzzi now turing out what is unquestionably South Philly's most sophisticated Italian cuisine. Leuzzi pays homage to his mother's home cooking with appetizers such as delicious red peppers filled with sausage and bread-crumb stuffing. But he gives it an ingenious twist, setting them

A renovated butcher's shop turns out South Philly's most sophisticated Italian cuisine.

over a bed of lettuce shredded into crunchy fresh "noodles" that twirl through a lusty, meaty ragout.

But there's no typical downtown red gravy on this menu. No bargain-priced eggplant parmigiana. Leuzzi honed his knives for nine years at DiLullo Centro on Locust Street, and the spirit of his kitchen is pure uptown sophistication, melding expert risottos, balsamic reductions, and stock-infused sauces with superb technique and an artful hand.

Having sampled one of Leuzzi's risotto specials, recently, I can say Jean DiCicco's enthusiasm those few years ago was well-placed. Leuzzi's cuisine has become even more enchanting. The buttery, toothsome rice was studded with sweet lumps of crab and little bursts of refreshing grape tomatoes, the entire mound crisscrossed with slender stalks of char-grilled scallion. A boneless rainbow trout was panfried whole, it's moist flesh sandwiching a crisp ribbon prosciutto inside that scented the whole pristine fish with a hint of bacony smoke.

There are still moments when the youth of this restaurant is apparent. Namely in the service staff, which, despite their stylish burgundy uniforms, can have a rough, frustratingly disinterested demeanor. Our most recent server knew his menu well, but once we ordered, was nowhere to be found. And that's some trick in a restaurant this small (and with these prices).

The kitchen also had a couple of slips. The usually impressive pork loin with cranberries was dry and dull. And while the dessert selection has made some strides, with excellent confections such as the delicate hazelnut mousse chocolate cake, some other creative ideas have yet to fully gel. The deep fried ricotta zeppoli had a nice crisp and puffy center, but were slightly undersweetened.

So many important things are done well here, though, remedying these details would simply add icing to the cake.

It is no small thing to perfect risotto, a dish that requires love and attention rarely found in restaurants. But Leuzzi has it down, drawing pure flavors and natural creaminess from arborio rice. Topped with ivory curls of tender shrimp, the richness found its perfect foils — a saute of bitter radicchio and a sour-sweet drizzle of reduced balsamic vinegar. Ordered in a half-portion (as the pastas are also available), it was a substantial appetizer.

Tinged yellow with saffron, risotto plays a supporting role to the remarkable osso buco, properly pink and moist from hours of cooking, and falling off the bone.

I also loved my recent bowl of pappardelle, the fresh pasta ribbons snapped in a lightly creamed veal sauce filled with great wild mushrooms. On previous visits, I've savored hollow perciatelle spaghetti as a perfect match for the bold pepper-crusted tuna and its piquant tomato sauce of olives and capers. And a bowl of littleneck clams, yawning in a pool of garlicky broth, gained earthiness from a shower of toasted orzo and smoky pancetta.

Leuzzi's excellent meat and fish entrees have always struck memorable chords. The ripieni was wonderful, a chicken breast stuffed plump with spinach then tinged with a balsamic sauce. Regular mashed potatoes, spiked with roasted garlic and a handful of wild mushrooms, became irresistible next to a thick grilled veal chop.

A braised whole red snapper was worth all the effort of maneuvering its bones. Topped with a crunchy fine mince of onions, parsley and capers, its moist white flesh was infused with wonderful stock.

Or Try These

Here are three other fine Italian restaurants in South Philadelphia.

Felicia's
1148 S. 11th St., Philadelphia
(215) 755-9656
One of South Philly's best "post-red-gravy" standbys remains as steady as its great ricotta gnocchi despite the travails of a seemingly endless renovation and a recent fire.

Tre Scalini
1533 S. 11th St., Philadelphia
(215) 551-3870
Authentic central Italian home cooking, from fresh pasta to grilled polenta and veal with mushrooms, in a bi-level BYOB.

L'Angolo
1415 W. Porter St., Philadelphia
(215) 389-4252
Authentic Italian antipasti, grilled veal, and almond-crusted cheesecake are among the highlights at this lovely South Philadelphia corner grotto.

The filet of beef marsala, despite a faint livery shadow, was expertly prepared and happily devoured. And the meaty rack of lamb, radiating rosemary and garlic, was another perfect companion for risotto, this one sparked with sundried cherries.

It is not hard to see, as we cleaned our plates, how dinner here might make a South Philly expatriate long to return. Yes, I understand. But there will be no kidnappings at the ristorante tonight, Mrs. DiCicco. We're going to keep young Kristian around.

■ **MENU HIGHLIGHTS** Stuffed pepper; shrimp risotto; crab and tomato risotto special; pappardelle with mushrooms; whole trout with prosciutto; perciatelle with seared tuna; osso buco; rack of lamb; beef marsala; spinach-stuffed chicken; braised red snapper; hazelnut mousse chocolate cake.

■ **WINE LIST** The modest list pairs affordable Italian vintages with a handful of "cellar selections," mostly high-quality, expensive Italian reds.

■ **IF YOU GO** Dinner served Monday, Wednesday-Thursday, 5-10 p.m.; Friday-Saturday, 5-11 p.m.; Sunday, 3:30-8 p.m. Closed Tuesday. Entrees, $15-$25.

■ **RESERVATIONS** Accepted only for settings before 8 p.m.

■ **CREDIT CARDS** All major cards but Discover.

■ **SMOKING** No smoking in entire restaurant.

■ **HANDICAP ACCESSIBLE** Yes.

■ **PARKING** Free valet parking.

La Encina

The pleasant BYOB offers a menu steeped
in a classic vision of regional Spanish cooking.

To say that Javier Cuesta's first impression of the Philadelphia area came as a shock would be an understatement.

The young Spaniard had flown halfway around the world from Seville to join his girlfriend, Jessica Cottrell, a move that promised some adjustments. But nothing had prepared the hot-blooded Mediterranean chef for the Blizzard of the Century, which greeted Cuesta on Jan. 7, 1996, just days after his plane touched down.

He peered warily out of Cottrell's West Chester apartment at a frigid landscape buried under more than two feet of snow — a record for the region. He wasn't in the South of Spain anymore.

"What the hell am I doing here?" he asked himself.

VERY GOOD

2 Waterview Rd.,
East Goshen, Pa.
(610) 918-9715

NEIGHBORHOOD
West Chester

CUISINE
Spanish

But Cuesta, it turns out, quickly warmed to his new life. He married Cottrell a year later and settled into the local dining scene, working at Alberto's in Newtown Square before moving on to the old Ritz-Carlton Hotel on 17th Street.

Now, at his year-old La Encina, Cuesta has given Chester County a taste of home, creating some of the most authentic, elegant Spanish flavors I've sampled outside the Iberian peninsula. Great tapas in tiny East Goshen Township? Sounds about as likely as a blizzard in Seville. Fine Spanish food has been rare in the Philadelphia region, with just a handful of Portuguese eateries and one Spaniard on South Street coming close. But Cuesta has transformed this pleasant room into a 65-seat saffron-colored haven for the Serrano-seekers among us.

He not only serves salty pink slices of that famed Spanish ham, but also has gone to pains to import numerous other products that give his food the look and taste of the real thing, from the little earthenware crocks called cazuelas that hold his tapas to many of the cuisine's key ingredients.

Scarlet piquillo peppers have a tangy, roasted flavor that pairs perfectly with their stuffing of whipped salt cod. A midnight-black streak of rich squid ink adds yet another vivid contrast. Thin coins of tender Galician octopus are served on a platter beneath a sheen of peppery Spanish olive oil and a dusting of earthy paprika. Plump white anchovies called boquerones come laced across slices of dark olive bread smeared with salmorejo, a thick Cordoban gazpacho.

And platters laden with wedges of oozy tetilla sheep's-milk cheese, arbequina olives, and cuminy chorizo sausage made me wish I had remembered to bring my well-chilled bottle of Lustau fino sherry. (La Encina is BYOB.) But my bottle of 1996 reserva Marques de Murrieta Ygay did just fine.

Cuesta began his formal culinary education at the age of 11, and his menu is steeped in a classic vision of regional Spanish cooking. There is an occasional contemporary flight of fancy such as the wonderful olive oil sorbet, a dessert that starts sweet and fruity, then finishes with a peppery bite. But Cuesta focuses mostly on honing traditional dishes to their best.

His gazpacho may be one of the finest I've tasted, a cone-shaped wooden bowl brimming with chilled pink broth vibrant with ripe tomatoes and sweet peppers, tart with a flamenco snap of aged sherry vinegar. The individual-size paella was also a delight. Its moist saffron rice was festooned with perfectly cooked mussels and clams, hunks of sausage and chicken, green peas, red peppers, and a whole langostino draped atop the pan.

Cuesta misfired a few times during my visits. The cold garlic and almond soup was intriguing at first, but the raw garlic breathed such fire that it could have made Antonio Banderas fear halitosis. The roulade of flounder stuffed with smoked salmon was overcooked and unpleasantly fishy. I loved the goat cheese melted over the grilled rib-eye steak, but the meat itself was undistinguished.

Or Try These

Here are three other restaurants serving cuisine inspired by the Iberian peninsula.

Berlenga's Island

4926 N. Fifth St., Philadelphia
(215) 324-3240

This obscure grotto bar and restaurant is a survivor from when the neighborhood was known as Little Lisbon, offering flaming sausage, grilled quail, and clam and pork stew.

Mallorca

119 South St., Philadelphia
(215) 351-6652

An upscale Spanish restaurant with great tapas, champagne sangria, and old-world service, but the expensive entrees were disappointing.

Caffe Monticello

236 Market St., Philadelphia
(215) 627-0588

The menu at this stylish Old City bistro speaks mostly Italian, but with a Portuguese accent, evident in the caldo verde potato-kale soup and lemony steamed clams.

Cuesta also overcooked one of his specialties, a whole fish baked beneath a pound of sea salt. Yet on my second try, the two-pound striped bass that emerged from the chef's tableside salt-mound excavation was incredibly moist and pristine. A squeeze of lemon was all it needed to sing.

Most of my meals had been leading up to this excellence, starting with a fabulous assortment of tapas. Cuesta's croquetta del dia brought crisp fried plugs of creamy bechamel flavored with bits of ham. Empanadilla pastries were filled with ground beef scented with Spain's Moorish influence — piquant olives, sweet raisins, and an exotic whiff of cinnamon and cumin. Cumin also elevated a little dish of beef stew above the ordinary.

Fat, snappy curls of shrimp arrived in a crock of garlicky olive oil still bubbling from the broiler, a seething elixir I sopped up with airy Portuguese bread. Another time, broiled shrimp were tossed with ham and mushrooms in a white wine sauce.

Cuesta showed an occasional elegant touch with some softer-flavored dishes, saucing an awesome gratin of scallops and shrimp with champagne butter and using fish stock to add complexity to a fine white veloute sauce that graced a delicious saute of clams and fava beans, as well as the grouper and white asparagus.

And he displayed competence, if not inspiration, in decent versions of standard desserts such as the tocino de cielo, a rich dairy-free caramel custard, and a gooey almond tort.

But when I sliced into his amazingly tender pork chop Castellana, it was clear that Cuesta's heart is in producing flavors with the full gusto of his homeland. The potent dark sauce was rife with rosemary and the tang of slivered ham that added a double pork punch.

"I love the pork, of course," concedes Cuesta, "because I am Spanish."

So, give the man his Serrano, and settle in for a feast. Cuesta has made himself at home.

■ MENU HIGHLIGHTS Tapas: Assorted Spanish meats, olives and cheeses; olive bread with salmorejo and marinated anchovies; empanadillas; ham croquettes; shrimp with garlic; shrimp with mushrooms and ham in white wine sauce; beef ragout. Main menu: Galician octopus with paprika and olive oil; clams and fava beans; gratin of scallops and shrimp in champagne sauce; pork chop a la Castellana; sauteed grouper with asparagus and clams; olive oil sorbet; almond torte.

■ WINE LIST BYOB

■ IF YOU GO Dinner is served Tuesday- Saturday 5-10 p.m. Entrees, $18-$28.

■ RESERVATIONS Recommended, especially on weekends.

■ CREDIT CARDS All major cards but Diners Club and Discover.

■ SMOKING Permitted on patio only.

■ HANDICAP ACCESSIBLE Yes.

■ PARKING Free lot.

Lakeside Chinese Deli

The modest Chinatown nook serves great made-to-order dim sum and other fine Cantonese classics.

I must admit it was a clever stratagem to grouse in print a year ago that there was no great dim sum in Philadelphia.

Of course, plenty of decent dim sum carts roll around the big banquet-hall restaurants in Chinatown such as Ocean City, H.K. Golden Phoenix, and Imperial Inn. But none I'd call great — consistently fresh, conscientiously grease-free, and displaying the endless variety seen in the dim sum palaces of New York, such as the Golden Unicorn, or at San Francisco's posh Yank Sing, where I have nibbled lettuce cups filled with minced chicken salad, airy Peking duck bun sandwiches, and curried cream cheese wontons.

Sure enough, after my complaint I began getting promising tips in the mail, including several about a restaurant I'd never heard of.

VERY GOOD

207 N. Ninth St.
Philadelphia
(215) 925-3288

NEIGHBORHOOD
Chinatown

CUISINE
Chinese

"Excellent dim sum . . ." one reader wrote in blue pen at the top of a take-out menu, " . . . not a bit elegant."

The restaurant was called Lakeside Chinese Deli, and as hard as I imagined the stretch of North Ninth Street between Ray's Cafe and Sang Kee, I couldn't picture where it was. There was no lake to sidle up to, as I recalled. Furthermore, I didn't know the Chinese had delis (though a nice hot pastrami dumpling would intrigue me).

So I ventured to Chinatown to investigate, and sure enough, there's a little storefront called Lakeside at 207 N. Ninth St. But holes were smashed into the sign in two places. And if it weren't for the "Open" sign perched in the door, I might have walked right by.

Not a bit elegant . . .

Score one point for accuracy for my anonymous tipster.

Lakeside is indeed the anti-elegant Chinatown nook, a 60-seat shoe box with yellow tile walls. Hand-scribbled on construction paper taped to a room-length mirror are some house specialties (conch with snow peas, snails in black bean sauce). The large, round tables and utilitarian metal chairs are usually filled with a mostly Asian crowd.

As for the dim sum, this very modest 12-year-old restaurant owned by Brenda Leung and her brother, chef Eric Ng, eschews the roving steam carts some larger halls favor. Instead, the bite-size dumplings, buns and appetizers are prepared to order in the kitchen, a practice I grew fond of as the dishes arrived, delicately steamed or crisply fried, fresh from the wok to our table. And, unlike the dim sum at most other places, where the same gristly pork/shrimp stuffing is simply repackaged into different shapes, each had clean flavors and distinct textures.

There were chiu chow shrimp rolls, with tender shrimp and crunchy water chestnuts wrapped in a delicate square of crisply fried bean curd sheets. And steamed vegetable dumplings stuffed with Chinese chives so fresh that they shone vibrant green beneath the rice-dough skins.

Cakes of springy shrimp paste played off the sweet snap of roasted bell pepper and the smooth pulp of slender stuffed eggplant. Steamed buns puffy and white as clouds concealed a dark heart of tangy barbecued pork. No gristle anywhere.

I didn't love every dish. The griddle-fried turnip cake was pasty. The pork

Dumplings are prepared to order in the kitchen.

sui mei dumplings were a little too firm. The conch with snow peas was a bit crunchy for my taste. And the stir-fried lamb hot pot was too gamy.

But usually the kitchen showed a zeal for quality ingredients and careful cooking, and it extended far beyond its fine dim sum.

The Hong Kong-style wonton soup was excellent, brimming with thin-skinned dumplings stuffed with chopped shrimp. The chicken-corn soup (my daughter's favorite) was silky with egg-drop broth. The simple pork and watercress soup was pristine, the flavor green with the still-crunchy watercress stems curled inside the bowl.

Lakeside's wok-fried greens were also great, especially the tiny knots of pleasantly bitter baby bok choy that arrived heaped on a plate fragrant with roasted garlic and homemade oyster sauce.

The noodle dishes were notable for their clarity of flavor. The house chow fun brought delicate, wide rice noodles tossed with a brown sauce that magnified the flavor of every ingredient it covered — strips of chicken, big shrimp, and Chinese broccoli stems. A stir-fried lo mein with pork found a perfect foil in accompanying ribbons of spicy pickled cabbage. Cold sesame noodles were splashed with an invigorating dark vinegar that perfumed the pasta without making it sticky.

One caveat: Lakeside is the sort of unglamorous insider find that seems a logical stop for Chinese take-out. But when I ordered out, our food just didn't taste the same. Even more vexing, some of the restaurant's best dishes are deep-fried, so the wilting steam in the carry-out containers is their nemesis.

What a shame it would be to ruin the General Tso's chicken, each morsel encased in an airy puff of batter, then glazed in a spicy black bean sauce that has a mysterious sweetness on the finish. On the way home, it turns into a soggy blob.

And what of Lakeside's fried seafood and its tempura-light crust tinged with salt and spice? The crackle of its soft-shell crabs? The succulent scallops, flash-fried with asparagus tips and rings of hot pepper? And the strips of tender squid so light and crisp as they twist like sea coral?

They provide all the elegance I need to make this journey again and again.

■ **MENU HIGHLIGHTS** Dim sum: chiu chow shrimp rolls, meat-and-peanut dumplings, crispy vegetable rolls, steamed barbecued pork buns. Spicy satay beef appetizer; sweet-and-sour pork appetizer; cold sesame noodles; Hong Kong shrimp wonton soup; sauteed baby bok choy; General Tso's chicken; crispy fried squid; crispy fried soft-shell crabs.

■ **WINE LIST** BYOB.

■ **IF YOU GO** Open Friday-Wednesday 11 a.m.- 8 p.m. Closed Thursday. Entrees $5.50-$15

■ **RESERVATIONS** Suggested.

■ **CREDIT CARDS** No credit cards or checks accepted.

■ **SMOKING** No smoking (though it is not strictly enforced).

■ **HANDICAP ACCESSIBLE** There is one step at the entrance, but rest rooms are wheelchair accessible.

■ **PARKING** Street parking only.

Or Try These

Here are three other Chinatown destinations for dim sum.

Ocean City

234 N. Ninth St., Philadelphia
(215) 829-0688

The newest of the big dim sum palaces has become popular for banquets and multi-dumpling feasts from lunch until 3 a.m.

H.K. Golden Phoenix

911 Race St., Philadelphia
(215) 629-4988

One of the first Hong Kong-style dim sum houses in Chinatown isn't quite as good as it used to be, but is still a good bet for a big assortment of competently done flavors.

Joy Tsin Lau

1026 Race St., Philadelphia
(215) 592-7228

This classic is still decent for standard dim sum, but the worn dragon red dining room could use a sprucing-up.

Shopping Center City

The Reading Terminal Market and the Italian Market are wonderful places to shop for foodstuffs, and both would be worth chapters on their own. But here are a few other staples that help make eating in Center City a joy:

Bakeries

Metropolitan Bakery (1136 Arch St.; 262 S. 19th St.; 1114 Pine St.; 126 Market St.; 1036 Marlborough St.; 8607 Germantown Ave.) is the finest of our local artisan bread bakers (although **Le Bus** comes a close second), whether it is a crusty round of sourdough "miche," those addictive chocolate-espresso rolls, or the divine little canneles pastries with crunchy caramelized shells and the rummy, pudding-like centers.

Cheese

DiBruno's

Any cheese-aholic would be thrilled with a trip to one of our two finest cheese purveyors — **DiBruno Bros. House of Cheese**, 930 S. Ninth St. in the Italian Market and 109 S. 18th St., and **Downtown Cheese** in the Reading Terminal Market, 12th and Arch Streets. Both are excellent. Downtown tends to find more of the rarer, artisan cheeses, but DiBruno's also has a wide array of superb olive oils, olives and vinegars.

Prepared Foods

Prepared-foods markets have helped to take the load off busy urban life, offering restaurant-quality food designed to take home. There are several excellent venues, from **Wolf's Market** at 1500 Locust St. to venerable **Chef's Market**, 231 South St., in Queen Village (home to classic smoked whitefish salad) to DiBruno's Italian-flared **Pronto**, 103 S. 18th St. to **Carlino's**, 2616 E. County Line Rd. in Ardmore. My favorite, however, remains **Bacchus Catering**, 2300 Spruce St., a tiny corner shop near Fitler Square that offers just the right combination of homey cooking with a sophisticated touch. Fabulous soups, excellent fish, indulgent sides, and irresistible bake-sale-styled desserts add up to a satisfying dinner.

Las Cazuelas

The bright little BYOB offers authentic Mexican home cooking in a festive atmosphere.

Who is this cheery man in a green sweater following the minstrel's every step through Las Cazuelas? Vincente Castaneda, the mustachioed guitarist, doesn't seem to mind. Every verse of the Mexican love ballad he croons is followed by an enthusiastic chorus from the man in the green sweater.

"Oh, that's my father," our waitress, Teresa, tells us. "Give him a tequila and he'll sing all night."

He'll have to bring his own bottle, of course, since this restaurant has no liquor license. But since Armando Aguilar's son Alfredo owns this charming little eatery, he has plenty to sing about, even without the extra spirits.

Here on the northern frontier of Northern Liberties, in the brightly painted, tile-floored confines of this affable corner restaurant, which sits fringed by banners in the shadow of the St. John Neumann shrine, the Aguilars are serving rustic Mexican cooking with a sincerity that is hard to find. You won't find those tired Tex-Mex cliches here, the gloppy beans and cheese-gooed nachos. Neither will you find a Frenchified pastiche of upscaled Latino flavors that is working its way into the mainstream of fine dining.

VERY GOOD

426-28 W. Girard Ave.
Philadelphia
(215) 351-9144

NEIGHBORHOOD
Northern Liberties

CUISINE
Mexican

This is pure home fare, from a family repertoire with roots in the Azteca cooking of Puebla, south of Mexico City. There are refried beans, but they are fresh, beguilingly light in a pinkish mist of mashed bean gravy. There is Mexican rice, infused with chicken broth and studded with little dice of fresh-cut veggies. There are soft corn tortilla tacos, topped with soft sweet slivers of beef tongue, onion, and cilantro.

And there is the intriguingly dark mole poblano sauce, rich with an edge of chocolate, cinnamon and almonds, that tingles with spice and just a fruity hint of banana. It shadows tender chicken two ways, a solo breast (slightly overcooked but still tasty), or wrapped inside soft enchilada tubes of corn tortilla. An equally intriguing chicken with green mole made of pumpkin seeds comes alongside a fabulous tamale ribboned with black beans that has been steamed with an avocado leaf that lends it a slightly minty flavor.

Vincente Castaneda plays to the patrons of Las Cazuelas.

Alfredo's mother, Teresa, keeps a close watch over her son as the mole pot simmers, making sure that both the sauce and his temper don't boil.

"When you're in a bad mood she won't let you cook; she says it affects the food."

With precious few exceptions (the sour glass of gazpacholike tomato juice that doubled as "shrimp cocktail" being one), it was obvious that good humor rules Las Cazuelas' kitchen. With modest ingredients used to best advantage for dishes that are both skillfuly crafted and affordable — entrees top out at $15 — it would be hard to leave here grumpy, or hungry.

A surprisingly diverse range of chiles are used with authority, tuned to different shades of heat that highlight various dishes without rising above a controlled burn. Deep red guajillos add their sweet spark to the earthy broth of mole de olla beef stew, or play off the musky marinade of the achiote and orange juice that gives the tender pork chop its tang. Smoky chipotles lend their woody fire to grilled shrimp, then elevate a modest cut of beef medallions into something special, gutsy and addictive.

A large poblano chile stuffed with cheese almost had the mildness of a roasted sweet pepper — quite a contrast to the tuna-stuffed jalapenos, the only dish that turned up the volume on the burn-o-meter. Streaked with a frothy green cilantro cream, I nearly passed out from the peppers' capsicum voltage, which tugged at my ears like invisible sweaty fingers, pulling from behind. It was thrilling.

It is always a bonus, amid such robust cooking, to find softer-flavored dishes to buffer the meal. I particularly loved the tacos dorados, tightly rolled tubes of tortilla-wrapped chicken breast, crisply fried then streaked with a saucy Mexican flag of green, red and white. A chicken breast stuffed with cheese highlighted the bright tanginess of its mild green tomatillo salsa. The thin strip of broiled beef flank — tender and not overcooked as thin cuts often are — sprang with the coriander vibrance of its herby chimichurri marinade.

The puffy tortillas called sopes were also ideal for tamer flavors, a comforting little hotcake topped with refried beans, mildly spiced tomatoes, and onion.

My complete respite from peppers, though, was gratefully only brief. A wonderful soup special, filled with pureed fresh corn and crushed epazote weed, shimmered with a measured pique of jalapeno. Even the big, refreshing salad came with a splash of heat, brushing a demure cilantro dressing with a little cha-cha-cha. A bowl of melted Oaxaca cheese was swimming in the orange oil of crumbled chorizo, but the combination of resilient salty cheese and spicy sausage made it impossible for us to stop eating.

You will find nothing but sweetness when it comes to dessert, but this limited selection was more ordinary — and less consistent — than the savory menu. Sometimes the rice pudding was sticky; at other times it was creamy and bursting with plump raisins. Sometimes the flan was firm and rubbery; other times it was soft and rich.

Even the classic dairy-soaked cake called tres leches had some drier nights than others. But I prefer to dwell on its finer moment, when a cream-heavy morsel of sponge cake disappeared from my fork

Or Try These

Here are three other authentic home-style Mexican restaurants.

La Lupe

1201 S. Ninth St., Philadelphia
(215) 551-9920

The latest in a wave of authentic new taquerias serving South Philly's growing Mexican population brings great tacos with homemade tortillas to the heart of cheesesteak country.

Xochimilco

6560 Market St., Upper Darby, Pa. (610) 352-2833

Upper Darby has a charming BYOB in this colorful Mexican, where the tortilla soup is tangy and the ebullient singing owner will serenade your meal.

Mexico Lindo

3521 Federal St., Camden
(856) 365-9004

Try the saucy beef tacos on homemade tortillas and succulent roast chickens on the weekends at this humble but tasty bungalow on the outskirts of Camden.

like a cool liquid cloud.

I looked up from the plate just in time to bid farewell to Vincente and Armando. "Gracias!" I call out as their act meanders into the next room. Vincente stops at the doorway with a dramatic sweep of the hand, as if to say this food was more than worth the tune: "Buen provecho."

■ **MENU HIGHLIGHTS** Melted Oaxaca cheese with chorizo; jalapenos rellenos; tacos dorados; sopes; mole poblano; mole verde; enchiladas de mole; beef medallions in chipotle sauce; grilled pork chop; tres leches; cafe de olla.

■ **WINE LIST** BYOB

■ **IF YOU GO** Entire menu is served Monday-Thursday 11 a.m.-9 p.m., Friday-Saturday 11-10 p.m., Sunday 3-9 p.m. Sunday brunch is served 11 a.m-3 p.m. Entrees $10-$15.

■ **RESERVATIONS** Recommended for parties of four or more.

■ **CREDIT CARDS** Visa or Mastercard.

■ **SMOKING** Entire restaurant is nonsmoking.

■ **HANDICAP ACCESSIBLE** Wheelchair accessible.

■ **PARKING** Street parking only.

Le Bec-Fin

Georges Perrier's pricey haute-French gem remains the city's finest gastronomic experience.

My last supper at the old Le Bec-Fin was hardly a feast of nostalgia.

Chef-owner Georges Perrier didn't mope around the padded pink room that June night, just weeks before its demolition and subsequent makeover. The faux-Versailles decor that had witnessed so many extraordinary meals at this temple of French gastronomy evoked from him not a soupçon of sentimentality.

Instead, with an extra bounce to the chef's rooster strut and unmistakable glee in his voice, he announced to the table beside us: "Everything you see here is about to be RIPPED out!" With a grand sweep of his arm, he dismissed the old finery like a bored emperor ready to freshen up the palace.

SUPERIOR

1523 Walnut St.
Philadelphia
(215) 567-1000

NEIGHBORHOOD
Rittenhouse Square

CUISINE
Modern French

"I've also hired a new American chef," he crowed. "And this time, I'm done with Frenchmen!"

For dining room theatrics, Philadelphia's most famous Frenchman is still unsurpassed. And the drama has spiraled to greater heights as Perrier has scrambled to try to recoup the cherished fifth star he lost in the Mobil Travel Guide in 2000. He finally regained it this fall, but not before instigating some major tumult.

Last year he replaced two of his longtime local chefs with Frederic Côte, a Lyon native then working at Daniel in New York. Côte lasted barely 15 months, though he was a fine cook.

Perrier then named Cherry Hill native Daniel Stern, 32, as chef de cuisine. And in August, he closed the restaurant for a four-week, $500,000-plus renovation by DAS Architects and Designers.

Redoing the 20-year-old dining room would be Perrier's boldest gesture. Even the restaurant's platoon of waiters — normally attired in black tie — got in on the act, ripping down moldings and doors in the dining room.

At one point, one server said, the staff could see from the front door to the back alley. Walls were removed, opening the small front and rear mezzanine rooms onto the larger central dining space.

The tired, salmon-colored Louis XVI decor has been replaced by a 19th-century-style Parisian salon replete with gilt molding, woven

The newly redone dining room is a 19th-century-style Parisian salon.

gold silk panels, and antique mirrors that lend the room the luster of a treasure chest.

Despite the extent of its dismantling, I'm struck by how familiar the new room feels. There have been myriad detail changes in lighting, crystal, wine storage and furniture. Most were improvements except for the comfy leather chairs, which take up so much space that diners are squeezed by traffic jams of tuxes and dessert carts.

But the transformation is less dramatic than, say, the recent luxury makeover of the Rittenhouse Hotel's TreeTops restaurant into Lacroix at the Rittenhouse. Was Perrier's investment a colossal waste of money or a triumph in the subtle evolution of a classic?

I side with the wisdom of subtle change. The emperor has donned a new robe rather than slipping into an entirely new groove. Le Bec-Fin's regulars should be pleased — and pleased, too, that the six-course dinner is still $120 (lunch has crept up to $45, from $40 before the redo).

But I'm even more impressed with the progress in the kitchen, where Stern is tackling the challenge of both maintaining a legendary tradition and moving it forward.

There are still fine renditions of mainstays such as the galette de crabe and a magnificent Dover sole for two. But Stern is already showing a talent for honing flavors to a powerful new depth and focus, melding cutting-edge technique with old-fashioned gusto.

He brings along plenty of tricks from the elite kitchens where he earned his stripes, mostly in Manhattan (at L'Espinasse, Daniel, and Jean-George Vongerichten's Mercer Kitchen).

There are several examples of "water cookery," in which he steeps the liquid essence from pureed vegetables into vibrant-colored broths that add potent flavor without the weight of a traditional sauce.

A sashimi of scallops and yellowtail is splashed with a fennel and celery broth and crushed fenugreek seeds. Cucumber water adds a fresh tang to a creamy avocado emulsion served alongside the meltingly rare Arctic char.

Or Try These

Here are three other French fine-dining restaurants.

Savona
100 Old Gulph Rd., Gulph Mills, Pa. (610) 520-1200
Exquisite seafood inspired by the French Riviera, with fine service and top-notch wines.

Deux Cheminees
1221 Locust St., Philadelphia (215) 790-0200
Classic French dining from jovial chef Fritz Blank in an elegant 19th-century townhouse.

The Restaurant at Doneckers
333 N. State St., Ephrata, Pa. (717) 738-9501
Former Le Bec-Fin-chef Greg Gable blends French haute cuisine with regional flavors at this upscale Lancaster County shopping complex. The dinners are considerably more interesting than the shopper-friendly lunches.

The art of slowly poaching seafood in an olive oil or butter bath is put to good use in the subtle rouget trio and in a succulent lobster tail with a vividly sweet pea puree.

Yet many other dishes demonstrate why Perrier calls Stern a traditionalist, but with a modern touch. Leek soup, already smoky with lardon bacon and a crispy crown of quail, gets nutty backbone from the New Age addition of wheatberries.

The guinea hen, brined with black tea and fennel before being roasted and smoked, may be the best fowl I've ever eaten. Each tender bite gushed gamy juices onto slices of tart heirloom tomatoes and chunks of pickled onion that gave the dish a rustic savor.

At a midsummer meal, white asparagus soup brought a cool ivory froth that tasted like liquid candy from the garden, scattered with spears of tempura-fried wild asparagus. Gently curried carrot soup tasted so profoundly of carrots that it was as if we were channeling the earth through every spoonful. And an amazing duck breast was stuffed with a ribbon of sweet apples that gave it the perfume of an orchard.

While the large new chairs make the dining room feel overcrowded, the servers maintain their appealing, unpretentious enthusiasm (though some talk *too* much).

New sommelier Gregory Castells has plumped the restaurant's boutique cellar of 150 selections into a more substantial 500. He also has added some intriguing wines by the glass, among them a fine

Chambolle-Musigny and an unusual superb Slovenian white Movia.

A new pre-dessert dessert course, which has experimented with fruit soups and other composed savory sweets, borders on excessive. At this stage of the feast, I missed the concise pleasure of the wondrous sorbets they replaced.

I was not, however, bothered by the smaller dessert carts now rolling around. There were only about 20 confections to choose from, instead of the usual 40. But the old multitiered carnival of all-you-can-eat babas au rhum, floating islands, and chocolate-ribboned fantasies had slipped from perfection since its longtime caretaker, Robert Bennett, left two years ago to open his own patisserie in Cherry Hill.

This new abridged edition seems just right, more precisely crafted and with a few charming additions (spiced creme brulee with chocolate mousse; cake laced with strawberry-basil cream) among the pecan coffee cake and other old standards.

Most restaurants, of course, would kill to have just five of these exquisite pastries. But Le Bec-Fin is still in a class of its own. And for an institution striding into the heady flamboyance of its gilded middle age, this is brevity at its most welcome and sublime.

■ **MENU HIGHLIGHTS** White asparagus soup; galette de crabe; snails in chartreuse butter; oxtail terrine; poached lobster tail with sweet pea sauce; arctic char with avocado emulsion; Dover sole; tea-scented guinea hen; apple-stuffed duck; veal chop with morels and sweetbreads; potatoes brulees; pear and apricot sorbets; cheese cart; dessert cart.

■ **WINE LIST** The wine cellar has ballooned from 150 boutique selections to a more substantial 500, with verticals of some of Bordeaux's most prestigious names. There are also several excellent wine by the glass selections.

■ **IF YOU GO** Lunch is served Monday-Friday 11:30 a.m.-1:30 p.m. Dinner seatings: Monday-Thursday 6 and 9 p.m.; Friday-Saturday 6 and 9:30 p.m. Three-course lunch, $45. Six-course dinner, $120.

■ **RESERVATIONS** Required.

■ **CREDIT CARDS** All major cards accepted.

■ **SMOKING** No smoking in dining rooms.

■ **HANDICAP ACCESSIBLE** Yes.

■ **PARKING** Valet parking for dinner only costs $16.

Le Castagne

The sleek, contemporary Northern Italian from the owners of La Famiglia offers more than a few pleasant surprises.

ho could have known before 9/11 that eating out in a fancy new place would suddenly feel so different, so extracurricular, after the terrorists attacked and the economy plunged?

Certainly not Giuseppe Sena. Nearly a year earlier, Sena, owner of Old City's La Famiglia, was busy planning Le Castagne with his chef-elect, Stefano Savino, who in turn was scouring his native Northern Italy for Botticino marble floors, Venetian leather chairs, sculptured Florentine light fixtures, and inlaid cherry veneer from Brescia, where it was being cut to span an entire wall in this chic new Philadelphia restaurant.

VERY GOOD

1920 Chestnut St.
Philadelphia
(215) 751-9913

NEIGHBORHOOD
Rittenhouse Square

CUISINE
Upscale Italian

But amid the funk that hung over the country last fall, I didn't find myself craving the polish of high-design restaurants. Instead, I was taking comfort in the cozy bistros that began sprouting across the city with ambitious food scaled to more modest budgets and warm little neighborhood spaces.

So it was mildly jarring to approach the lavishly rehabbed Chestnut Street building where Le Castagne awaited, glass doors gliding open to bid diners into a room of deliberate sleekness softened only by a few white curtains.

Though Chestnut Street lies just beyond Restaurant Row's luxury-dining frontier, there is more than enough money around Rittenhouse Square to support a restaurant like this, with entrees in the mid-$20s. And there were a few patrons who fit the mold one recent evening — a man in an orange leather coat with matching purse, and several women with hair-sprayed helmet coiffures and earrings the size of belt buckles. Otherwise, despite a growing lunch crowd, Le Castagne has been nearly empty every time I ate there.

No, with its Milanese decor and upscale menu, Le Castagne is not a restaurant crafted for troubled times. But the Sena family has a long history of offering quality dining, both at fussy, formal La Famiglia and at its neighboring wine-by-the-glass haven, Ristorante Panorama.

It would be a shame if this ambitious new venue fell victim to unfortunate timing.

The most exciting aspect was the debut of Savino, an old friend of Sena's who came from Brescia to cook here. A year later, Savino had unfortunately returned to Italy — although not before passing on some of his best secrets to his sous-chef and successor, Brian Wilson. A recent post-Savino lunch showed a few mild changes, but proved to be faithful to the taste and spirit of the old chef's concept, especially with the extraordinary homemade pastas.

Savino wasn't the only chef in Philadelphia preparing sophisticated Northern Italian food, as Sena was apt to boast. But the 36-year-old veteran brought original touches to a menu that has more than a few surprises.

The Parmesan mousse appetizer was among the most striking, a dense little cheesecake whose rich, savory custard is stuffed with chunks of walnut and pear, then dolloped with a sweet-tart garnish of green tomato marmalade. Celery is seldom a vegetable placed in the spotlight, but the tortino — an airy puree of celery and fennel that is whipped with mascarpone cheese and then baked — opened my eyes to its virtues. The tart has the comforting flavor of cream of celery soup, accented with black olives and a bright tomato-and-basil sauce.

An appetizer of warm chicken medallions layered beneath a gratin of smoked mozzarella and olive puree is an excellent holdover from Savino's repertoire. More important, though, most of Savino's superb semolina-flour pastas remain menu fixtures.

Thick strands of spaghetti made from chestnut flour are napped in a delicate walnut cream that is dusted with cocoa, an accent that deepens the flavor more than it sweetens. Toothsome ribbons of tagliatelle twirl with sweet strands of colorful peppers into a nest that is lightly glazed with melted ricotta cheese. Squiggly trofie pasta comes with a mild garlic and olive sauce that captures the mild essence of its julienned squid and bitter broc-

Or Try These

Here are three other contemporary Italian restaurants.

Vetri

1312 Spruce St., Philadelphia
215-732-3478

A sublimely sophisticated homage to rustic Italian cuisine in the tiny dining room of a legendary townhouse.

Vivo Enoteca

110 N. Wayne Ave., Wayne, Pa.
(610) 964-8486

Stylish Old City meets the Main Line at this modern Italian hot spot, which has undergone a stunning transformation from its days as upscale Fourchette 110. Now, Fellini films are projected in the sleek downstairs lounge, while friendly servers in black leather boots serve Christopher Todd's small-plate Italian fare on the second floor.

DiPalma

114 Market St., Philadelphia
(215) 733-0545

This sleek Old City Italian has been a showcase for ever-inventive Salvatore DiPalma, who produces enough gems to counter the occasional creative miss.

The striking Parmesan mousse appetizer has a rich, savory custard stuffed with chunks of walnut and pear.

coli rabe.

Wide, curved tubes of grooved maccheroni are tossed with a delicious combination of rich carbonara and basil pesto. And large gnocchi-like dumplings made of bread crumbs are scented with a smoky whiff of the cured meat called speck, then sauced with an irresistible mushroom tomato gravy. An appetizer of ravioli stuffed with pungent robiola cheese, then glazed with brown butter, was absolutely sublime.

Like that of any newcomer trying to size up a new audience, Savino's cooking occasionally seemed timid. It took its least inspired turns in some of the expensive entrees and desserts. The chocolate and strawberry mousses and the hazelnut spumoni — tasty, but conservative — were the only notable finales. At my recent meal, the desserts showed a little more pizzazz.

A fillet of perfectly seared striped bass napped with a delicate citrus sauce also proved that Wilson was getting a handle on the kitchen's problems with overcooking. The addition of more veal dishes and filet mignon also hint that the new kitchen is hedging away from some of Savino's more unusual creations — such as the surprisingly good tuna steak with orange cream — in favor of some more conservative ideas.

Of course, I can't help but be disappointed to see this promising new chef leave so soon. But perhaps, for now, leaning back onto some of these more familiar flavors will bring to one of the city's sleekest restaurants some of the warmth and attention it deserves.

■ **MENU HIGHLIGHTS** Fennel and celery cake; warm chicken with smoked mozzarella appetizer; chestnut tortelloni; robiola-stuffed ravioli; maccheroni carbonara e pesto; veal medallions with truffle essence; veal roast; striped bass; tuna steak with orange sauce; chocolate mousse; strawberry mousse.

■ **WINE LIST** A medium-size cellar of mostly Italian wines offers several excellent midprice bottles, including two very appealing, versatile reds — a ripe Moletto Colmello and a drier, more rustic Terre di Galatrona — for $35.

■ **IF YOU GO** Lunch is served Monday-Friday noon-2 p.m. Dinner Monday-Thursday 5:30-9:30 p.m., Friday-Saturday 5:30-10 p.m. Entrees: lunch, $12-$20; dinner, $18-$28.

■ **RESERVATIONS** Recommended.

■ **CREDIT CARDS** All major cards but Discover.

■ **SMOKING** Smoking at the bar only.

■ **HANDICAP ACCESSIBLE** Yes.

■ **PARKING** Street parking only.

Lee How Fook

The reliable Chinatown standby masters
an encyclopedic menu of Cantonese classics.

f you eat often in Chinatown, you have seen the All-Knowing Menu. That list of 300-plus items offering everything from chicken feet to chow fun appears virtually everywhere, an encyclopedia of Cantonese flavors with an occasional tingle of Hunan, Szechuan and Mandarin.

Of course, precious few restaurants can deliver all the dishes with equal skill. So the real trick to navigating the pleasures of Chinatown hinges on discovering which place best cooks which part of the All-Knowing Menu. Peking duck and noodles from Sang Kee. Salt-baked seafood, wok-fried greens and steamed dumplings from Shiao Lan Kung. Pungent, hearty soups from the Nice Chinese Noodle House. Creative mock meats from Cherry Street Chinese Vegetarian and Charles Plaza. Great made-to-order dim sum from Lakeside Chinese Deli.

VERY GOOD

219 N. 11th St.,
Philadelphia
(215) 925-7266

NEIGHBORHOOD
Chinatown

CUISINE
Chinese

But when I crave the comfort of a great hot pot, I set a course for Lee How Fook. Here the half-glazed earthenware pots arrive at the table radiating heat from the range, still tightly covered as if the kitchen has trapped every vapor inside until a waitress can remove the lid right under your nose. A billow of fragrant steam buffets your face and then disappears, revealing a vessel of bubbling, dark stew with strands of steamed cilantro tracing lines of vibrant green on top.

There are several hot pots to choose from, and I've never been disappointed. Each delivers that perfect balance of heartiness without overthickening, of intense flavors that harmonize rather than compete.

There is the chicken with mushrooms, its tender white meat playing against the woodsy flavor and mouth-filling resilience of shiitake caps bathed in gingery gravy. Another chicken hot pot, this one with crisp asparagus spears, is strikingly different. Its dark sauce seems to have captured the fruity essence of black peppercorns without more than a prickle of sneezy heat.

The beef hot pot came with a warning from our pleasant, efficient server: It is filled more with suety tendon than brisket flesh. But it's worth it just to spoon the gravy over rice, the meaty puree punctuated by crunchy stems of bok choy and an exotic undercurrent of anise and clove.

No such warnings are needed for the excellent fish hot pot. The largely boneless chunks of fried fish in a tangy oyster sauce melt on the tongue. The Buddha's Delight hot pot isn't on the menu, but it's easy to request and is executed with a master's respect for ingredients. A clear, vibrant sauce shows off tiny ears of corn, springy cubes of bean curd, snappy broccoli, and crunchy sheets of Chinese mushrooms.

While the hot pots are a highlight, this little restaurant run by chef Shing Chung and his wife, Doris, has a better grasp of the All-Knowing Menu than most. And that consistency accounts for the longevity of the modest, 40-seat dining room, which also has a banquet room in back. Despite its unglamorous decor — brown linoleum, a mirrored ceiling, plastic plates — Lee How Fook has remained a reliable Chinatown mainstay for two decades.

There were some less-inspired dishes during a few of my visits — gristly beef in black bean sauce and squishy kung pao scallops.

But most of the offerings are easily a cut above those of your standard Chinatown joint. The soups are positively rejuvenating and the wontons among the best I've tasted, seasoned and stuffed to order in thin skins of dough and floating like plump comets through the golden broth. The Szechuan turnip and pork soup is spicy, clear and pristine.

The duck and abalone soup brims with roasted duck flavor but is more a study of textures: delicate meat, chewy abalone and snappy green slivers of snow pea. The crab and winter melon soup is another winning bowl, strikingly subtle in flavor but all comfort in the spoon, the soft cubes of mashed, unsweetened melon flecked with the sea-pink fibers of crumbled crab. But the hot-and-sour soup has a mean streak of sourness with only a flicker of fire.

Lee How Fook's dumplings are a little bland and the spring roll a tad greasy. But the wonderful Buddha's Delight roll is a magnet of deep-fried magic: two long, flat vegetarian dumplings wrapped in a

Or Try These

Here are three other small Chinatown restaurants.

Shiao Lan Kung
930 Race St., Philadelphia
(215) 928-0282
Don't expect anything fancy at my Chinatown favorite, a tiny, crowded room where the kitchen turns out some of the brightest, most consistent renditions of standard Chinatown cooking around.

Lakeside Chinese Deli
207 N. Ninth St., Philadelphia
(215) 925-3288
This gritty Ninth Street nook serves great made-to-order dim sum and other fine Cantonese classics.

Sang Kee
238 N. Ninth St., Philadelphia
(215) 925-7532
Long a favorite for Peking duck and noodles, this humble institution underwent an ambitious renovation three years ago.

crust of bean-curd skin.

The kitchen's vegetable side dishes also are excellent, from the heat-blistered green beans in smoky brown sauce to the garlicky mountains of wok-fried Asian greens. The snow pea leaves are a pillow of pure, soft chlorophyll. The watercress has a peppery bite. The broad white stems of baby bok choy burst with refreshing juice, and the tender stems of Chinese broccoli crunch with pale-green sweetness.

All of our noodle dishes were delicious, from the threads of a rice-stick stir-fry moistened with soy sauce and chicken broth to the crisp-bottomed beds of deep-fried lo mein that softened under a juicy saute of vegetables and pork.

Even more impressive are the whole fish and roasted duck. The steamed striped bass brought to our table was expertly deboned and then spooned with an amber sauce so redolent of ginger and scallions that I could taste it long after the luxurious white fish disappeared. More than a bargain at $9.50, the roasted half duck was the quintessential bird, its moist meat wrapped in a wafer of crisp, honeyed skin. We gnawed the bones clean.

Other restaurants could easily stake their entire reputation on either specialty. But at Lee How Fook, those dishes are simply more proof that most of the All-Knowing Menu is indeed within its reach.

Of course, there is no dessert beyond orange wedges and fortune cookies. This is one Chinatown restaurant that knows when enough is enough.

■ **MENU HIGHLIGHTS** Wonton soup; crab and winter melon soup; Szechuan turnip and shredded pork soup; Buddha's Delight roll; hot pots (chicken and mushroom, chicken with asparagus and black pepper sauce, fish, Buddha's Delight); steamed whole striped bass with ginger and scallions; roast duck; Chinese broccoli; green beans.

■ **WINE LIST** BYOB.

■ **IF YOU GO** Open 11:30 a.m.-10 p.m. daily. Entrees (all day), $6.50-$18.

■ **RESERVATIONS** Recommended, especially on weekends.

■ **CREDIT CARDS** Visa and MasterCard only.

■ **SMOKING** No smoking.

■ **HANDICAP ACCESSIBLE** Not wheelchair accessible.

■ **PARKING** Street parking only.

London Grill

The Fairmount institution strikes the ideal balance between neighborhood pub and ambitious fine dining.

The distance between great bar food and fine dining gets a little shorter each time I visit the London Grill.

In one hand, I see an English muffin squeezing what may be the best burger in town — a charred organic patty of ground Lancaster beef smothered in sauteed onions and herby Boursin cheese.

In the other, I wield a crackly crisp spring roll stuffed with meltingly soft ginger duck. A tart cabbage slaw and a hoisin peanut streak completes the plate — a deftly rendered icon of contemporary Asian-fusion cooking.

This venerable Fairmount standby has made a career of the split personality. One former chef recalls London's former life as "a good place for a beer and a brawl."

VERY GOOD

2301 Fairmount Ave.
Philadelphia
(215) 978-4545

NEIGHBORHOOD
Fairmount/Art Museum

CUISINE
New American Pub

But since Terry and Michael McNally purchased the taproom and restaurant in 1991, they have crafted what may be the ideal balance between the neighborhood pub and a destination for ambitious fine dining.

Where else could you find then-presidential candidate Bill Bradley pow-wowing with the police union in one room, seniors from the Philadelphian apartment house sawing into grilled calves' liver in another, and people in their 20s riding Calvados sidecars and buffalo wings in the bustling bar to the tunes of a live small band?

I have friends who have eaten at London for years but never ventured beyond the lively tin-roofed bar, where beefy, cornbread-topped chili; buffalo wings; and crisply battered fish and chips are as good as they can be.

But it is in the red warmth of the adjacent split-level dining rooms that Michael McNally really stretches his culinary creativity. Some of the cleverest notions — like tater tots laced with truffle oil, sweet corn bread pudding, and creamy black bean succotash — blip on and off the daily menus as the fidgety chef modifies his pantry. But if the hearty and eclectic fare ranges wide from season to season, it is reliable for solid, thoughtful cooking and quality products.

At a recent meal, porcini-dusted halibut came crisped over a mar-

Since Terry and Michael McNally purchased the restaurant in 1991, they have crafted what may be the ideal balance between the neighborhood pub and a destination for ambitious fine dining.

velous summer clam chowder, a lightly creamed broth filled with new potatoes, green beans, zucchini and the smoky kiss of bacon. A gingery, jerk-spiced grouper fillet was accompanied by a wonderful take on Jamaican rice and peas soaked with rich coconut milk.

This kitchen has a charming way of upscaling some down-home ideas. Fried green tomatoes are an occasional feature here, and were most recently topped with pulled smoked turkey. At Sunday brunch, there is also homemade scrapple and watermelon juice, which I find intriguing. But I especially loved the meaty little quail at dinner that came sealed beneath a perfect country-fried crust and a tan, peppery glaze of red-eye gravy. At a recent lunch, I also happily spooned my way through a nouveau rendition of Pennsylvania chicken and dumplings, the chicken breast freshly seared, levitating over a light broth filled with parsnips and brussels sprouts and dumplings with the texture of fluffy matzo balls. (Speaking of which, London's annual Passover seder is among the few interesting events oriented to the Jewish holidays in local restaurants.)

Terry is Michael's counterpart in the dining room, and her enthusiasm is particularly notable in the drinks, from the bar's creative cocktails and rum collection to the excellent, affordable and diverse wine selection and list of local beers. Most of her staff embodies the ideal of casual fine dining — attentive servers dressed in casual black who know the menu and at least something about the wines. At times, though, certain waiters were far too casual for a restaurant that wants to be taken seriously.

Over the years, I've encountered one server who showed up in droopy jeans and a T-shirt with the meal check jammed into the rear of his visible waistband — unappetizing no matter how good the meal was. Another young man recently kept trying to clear our plates — while we were still eating. And still another server, meanwhile, ran us through an amusing drill in passive-aggressive ordering.

We could have our chile-rubbed pork loin cooked any way we liked, he said, as long as it was well done. So . . . how would we like our pork?

Or Try These

Here are three other restaurants in the Fairmount area.

Illuminare

2321 Fairmount Ave., Philadelphia
(215) 765-0202

A gorgeously appointed dining room and patio features Italian cuisine with a special forte for brick-oven pizzas.

Rembrandt's

741 N. 23d St., Philadelphia
(215) 763-2228

This Fairmount bar and restaurant serves one of the better burgers in town, as well as weekly psychic readings.

Bridgid's

726 N. 24th St., Philadelphia
(215) 232-3232

A surprising menu of eclectic comfort food and a great beer selection make this an appealing neighborhood destination.

It's a long story. But we thankfully graduated to our food, which has almost always proved more than worth the semantics.

Fried oysters were crisply done. Tender pappardelle noodles made up for their unappealing brown look with surprisingly light flavors, a medley of ricotta cheese, roasted tomatoes and olives. A savory panna cotta custard made of goat cheese came with thick slices of roasted beets.

Rich porter beer thinned a hearty cheese soup made from Lancaster cheddar that had a mildly smoky flavor. Tortillas thickened a Mexican flavored tomato soup. Another summer soup, recently, brought a cool puree of corn and squash topped with a saute of mushrooms.

A delicious grilled New York strip had a marvelous homemade steak sauce that was both tangy and exotic, with everything from tamarind paste and coconut milk to ketchup in the mix. Butter-soft medallions of veal paired with seared scallops in a worthy revamp of "surf and turf."

And yes, our awesome chile-rubbed pork was even still blushing by the time it came to our table. Beneath the fiery glaze tomatillo salsa, I detected the faintest rosy hue.

A beef brisket Rueben sandwich was one of the few disappointments I've encountered lately. Although the desserts — mostly homey confections like pound cake and panna cotta and chocolate tart — also have room for improvement before they catch up to the imagination of the savory meals.

Then again, I quibble. Because you can't get this kind of cooking in most neighborhood restaurants, and the London Grill continues to pull it off with a blend of laid-back ambience and quality food that sits just right.

■ **MENU HIGHLIGHTS** Duck spring rolls; hamburger; chili Elizabeth Taylor; fish and chips; country fried quail with red-eye gravy; porcini-dusted halibut; jerk-spiced grouper; fried oysters; strip steak with Michael's sauce; panna cotta; chocolate pecan pie.

■ **WINE LIST** The one-page wine list offers several excellent, well-chosen, and fairly priced bottles under $50, including a deliciously lush Adelsheim pinot noir ($38), and a rustic but refreshing vin gris de cigare from Bonny Doon ($23) as well as a handful of big-ticket bottles. The beer list is great, but front-of-the-house partner Terry McNally is also a mixologist extraordinaire, with a flair for creative cocktails and a special passion for rum.

■ **IF YOU GO** Lunch served Monday-Friday 11:30 a.m.-3 p.m. Dinner served Monday-Saturday 5:30-10:30 p.m, Sunday 4-9 p.m. Sunday brunch served 11 a.m.-2:30 p.m. Cafe bar menu served Monday-Thursday 3-11 p.m., Friday-Saturday 3-midnight.

■ **RESERVATIONS** Recommended, especially weekends.

■ **CREDIT CARDS** All major cards.

■ **SMOKING** The dining rooms are mostly nonsmoking.

■ **HANDICAP ACCESSIBLE** There are two steps to a side entrance, and the bathrooms are not accessible.

■ **PARKING** Restaurant validates for adjacent parking lot.

Los Catrines Restaurant & Tequila's Bar

The upscale Mexican offers a beautiful art-filled decor to complement its authentic cuisine and top-notch tequila list.

'Our heroine, the tortilla, faithful friend of the Mexican, has been present since the beginning of time . . ."

No, this isn't the prologue to a sultry Latin novel. But there are a few passages on the menu at Los Catrines Restaurant & Tequila's Bar in which the descriptions begin to glow with magical realism.

The cactus leaves and tamarind sauce invite chipotle chiles to witness the "lynching" of a filet mignon. Mediterranean olives and capers are "seduced" by the pre-Columbian tomato. Boiled chicken with mole is "exalted from the past," while the good old nacho is "drawn toward its destiny yet does not embrace it."

VERY GOOD

1602 Locust St.
Philadelphia
(215) 546-0181

NEIGHBORHOOD
Rittenhouse Square

CUISINE
Mexican

I can imagine being conflicted over my destiny, too, if it meant tangling with refried beans beneath a blanket of melted Chihuahua cheese. But one gets the sense that nothing — not even a good version of the most banal dish in the Mexican-American repertoire — is less than a drama worth embellishing for David Suro-Piñera, who last year moved his 14-year-old Mexican restaurant into lavish new quarters across Locust Street.

It turns out, the menu descriptions were even longer at his former location at 15th and Locust. But now that Suro-Piñera has expanded the restaurant's name (it had been Tequila's, which he considered too generic) and moved into the big, storied space once occupied by La Panetiere and the Magnolia Cafe, there is more than enough ambience to take up the slack.

The incredible chandelier and the ornate ceiling moldings alone — beautifully restored to their original warm wood finish — would merit a toast with one of Los Catrines' exquisite sipping tequilas. A Porfidio Blanco or Herradura Reposado would do just fine.

But it is the collection of Mexican art that really brings new life to these rooms, beginning with the foyer's whimsical mural of los catrines, the family of skeletons dressed like dandies whose image became a symbol of the 1910 Mexican Revolution's victory over the country's aristocratic dictatorship.

Dozens of other beautiful artworks fill the dark, candlelit dining rooms with romantic intrigue: prints of women with bunches of garlic and bananas on their heads, a wall of photos, and a mural by José Clemente Orozco-Farias (grandson of the famed Jalisco artist) depicting Suro-Piñera's children in the agave fields, along with Zapatista Sub-Comandante Marcos. Even the hammered copper plates and water pitchers add a shimmer to the rooms.

A diner enjoys her meal under a mural in the back dining room.

But it is los catrines that lend the restaurant its new name and best symbolize its spirit — at once serious and irreverent and fiercely patriotic, with a menu rooted in some of the Delaware Valley's most authentic Mexican flavors.

Suro-Piñera's goal has always been to bring to Philadelphia the universe of Mexican cooking beyond Tex-Mex chimichangas and fajitas. And for the most part, he does it well. Few local restaurants, for example, indulge diners with huitlacoche, the coveted corn mushroom that grows into swollen black pouches of earthy ambrosia.

It tastes vaguely like a cross between corn and truffle and, pureed into an inky-dark sauce, was sublime beneath crab-stuffed zucchini blossoms. A floral-yellow puree of the blossoms themselves added another layer of contrast. But another huitlacoche dish was dull, made with chicken breasts too mundane to do the royal fungus justice.

There were other frustrating moments like this, when it seemed as if the kitchen, poised to strut with the dandies in all their plumage, refused to step up to the next level along with the decor. There was a hint of too much sweetness in the mole sauce. The signature red snapper, with a wonderful Veracruz salsa of tomatoes, capers and olives, was slightly overcooked. And in a couple of dishes (pork tinga, chorizo-sauced filet mignon), the flavor was surprisingly muted when the menu's prose had me expecting a mariachi band in my mouth.

Still, even before we drained our pitcher of marvelous margaritas, it was clear that the kitchen, led by chef Carlos Molina, has most of its moves down pat. The tortilla soup was a soulful gem, its rust-colored broth ribboned with noodles made of sliced tortilla. The empanada was also exceptional, its pillowy corn dough stuffed with ground meat moistened with tart tomatillos.

The tomatillo-sauced flautas — corn tortillas rolled into tubes and filled with chicken — were soggy in the center from sitting too long before being served. But their half-size cousins, the taquitos — essentially the same dish but covered with mild red salsa — were ideally crisp and tasty.

A tostada carefully mounded with crab, tomato and avocado was fresh and crunchy. The ceviche of flounder and plump shrimp was so satisfyingly straightforward — marinated in citrus juice, cilantro and serrano peppers — that it was a classic antidote to some of the overwrought nuevo follies I've tasted lately.

And fabulous crepes covered with warm cajeta caramel, made with goat's milk, made up for the otherwise lackluster dessert list (I really hadn't come here to eat cheesecake).

Or Try These

Here are three other ambitious Mexican restaurants.

Las Cazuelas

426 W. Girard Ave., Philadelphia
(215) 351-9144

This colorful little eatery isn't fancy, but the homespun specialties from mole-loving Puebla are an irresistible attraction.

Paloma

6516 Castor Ave., Philadelphia,
(215) 533-0356

Chef Adan Saavedra's French-influenced "haute Mexican" has evolved into one of the more intriguing menus around, but slow and inattentive service still holds the restaurant back.

Zocalo

3600 Lancaster Ave.,
Philadelphia (215) 895-0139

Jackie Pestka's kitchen offers house-made tortillas and a contemporary take on authentic Mexican flavors that remain a draw to Powelton Village.

I've heard complaints that Los Catrines is more expensive than most Mexican restaurants, with entrees ranging from the high teens to the low $20s. But Molina seems committed to using good ingredients that justify the prices. Served in most nonethnic upscale Center City restaurants, some of the dishes would be a pretty good bargain, from the jumbo shrimp in garlic butter spiked with tequila ($18.75) to the numerous variations on filet mignon ($21.95) that are among the restaurant's most interesting offerings.

For example, the carne aguacate was glazed with a vibrant green avocado and cilantro cream that lightened the meat's rich epazote-scented mushroom stuffing.

And the filete grito had a dark, tart tamarind sauce and a bed of cactus leaves to give it gusto. But it had something even more scintillating: The meat had been shot through with whole serrano chiles that riddled the filet with little explosions of heat.

It was an execution by hot pepper rather than the "lynching" the menu had promised. But truth, in this case, proved to be more sultry than fiction.

■ **MENU HIGHLIGHTS** Nachos; taquitos de pollo; empanadas; sopa de tortilla; ceviche; crab tostada special; pollo entortillado; camarones con salsa Tequila's; filete grito; carne aguacate; caramel crepes.

■ **WINE LIST** There is a small list of affordable South American, California and Spanish table wines. But the restaurant's 50-plus tequila list is stocked with top-shelf sipping spirits, from Herradura to Porfidio to El Tesoro de Don Felipe. The margaritas are also dangerously quaffable.

■ **IF YOU GO** Lunch is served Monday-Friday 11:30 a.m.-2 p.m. Dinner Monday-Thursday 5-10 p.m., Friday-Saturday 5-11 p.m. Appetizer menu Monday-Friday 2-5 p.m.The bar is open Monday-Saturday 11:30 a.m.-1 a.m. Lunch entrees, $8.95-$22.95. Dinner entrees, $14.50-$28.95.

■ **RESERVATIONS** Not accepted.

■ **CREDIT CARDS** All major cards accepted.

■ **SMOKING** Smoking in the bar only.

■ **HANDICAP ACCESSIBLE** There is one step at the entrance, but the rest of the restaurant is wheelchair accessible.

■ **PARKING** Valet parking, available at night only, costs $12.

Margaret Kuo's Peking

The surprisingly elegant restaurant serves
top-notch Chinese and Japanese in a mall.

The rumored existence of a secret "insider" menu at Chinese restaurants has always intrigued me. What's written in English may be fine, but I've had my fill of moo shu pork and kung pao chicken.

What I really want to order is probably scrawled in Chinese characters on the kitchen wall or guarded jealously inside my waiter's brain. But — given my dubious grasp of Mandarin — where could I enter this mysterious, exclusive eating club and taste the wonders of authentic Chinese cooking?

The Granite Run Mall in Media, of course.

"The mall?" my Center City guests sniffed as they piled into my car and we headed to the far reaches of Delaware County. Yes, indeed, I told them. And we will aim for a parking space right between Sears and J.C. Penney, where the glowing red sign of Margaret Kuo's Peking beckons like an exotic port.

EXCELLENT

Granite Run Mall,
1067 W. Baltimore Pike
Media, Pa.
(610) 566-4110

NEIGHBORHOOD
Delaware County

CUISINE
Chinese

The ubiquitous Kuo has opened a smaller version of Peking in downtown Media, owns Margaret Kuo's Mandarin in Malvern, and is building a fourth restaurant, slated to open this fall in Wayne. But Kuo got her start 28 years ago at Granite Run. And the former chemist has been determined to introduce authentic Chinese cooking to the masses ever since, offering shark's fin soup, alongside the traditional wonton, and more than a few rare provincial specialties.

She has since added a superb sushi and sake bar for extra trendy appeal. And the restaurant's space (her second location in the mall) has been polished to an impressive elegance, with a sleek granite foyer and well-padded booths in a dining room decorated with carved wooden screens, massive Ming-style vases, and a working gong.

GOONNNNNGGGGGG!!!!!!!

Every restaurant should sound a gong, I think, to announce the arrival of another Peking duck in the dining room. Every restaurant should have a venerable duck chef like Zhang Ho, who effortlessly carved the bird tableside for us in his white hat and black tennis shoes.

The cooking here is as regal as the ceremony. The duck was roasted tender and lean, then wrapped with scallions and pieces of honey-crisped skin inside supple envelopes of particularly fine homemade pancakes.

Peking has a secret Chinese menu, too, with interesting goodies such as duck palms and slippery sea cucumbers that are available if you know to ask. The fried bean curd and scallop balls called zhu sen tofu, which come napped with a velvet crab sauce and gauzy strips of bamboo fungus, are definitely worth seeking out.

But Peking also offers far more authentic specialties on the English menu than most.

All you need to do is stumble across an extraordinary waiter like David Yu to give you a guided tour. Yu's eyes widened when he sensed a table of diners eager for culinary adventure. Before we knew it, we were sipping delicate silver needle tea, savoring juicy steamed pork buns splashed with gingery black vinegar, and crunching on the tail fin of a fried whole red snapper glazed with tangy Hunan gravy.

I've also had less exciting service here from an inexperienced waiter, but even that couldn't dim the kitchen's delights.

Duck Chef Zhang Ho carves "Royal Peking Duck."

The Shanghai braised pork shoulder is one of the best dishes I've sampled in the last year. The massive, osso buco-like hunk of pork was so tender from a six-hour turn in the oven that, at the touch of a fork, it fell off the bone into an intensely reduced gravy scented with anise. A brilliant green corona of fresh Shanghai cabbage (similar to baby bok choy) ringed the pork.

The Peking-style shrimp was another highlight that showed the restaurant's commitment to fine ingredients and subtle cooking. The large, succulent shrimp basked in a clear sauce that was delicate despite fistfuls of chopped garlic. The quality of the filet mignon was also impressive, the meat sliced into thin lily pads paired with smaller rounds of shiitake mushrooms in a peppery sauce.

Among the appetizer specials printed on a blackboard menu, we loved the baked Chinese leek buns and the open-ended dumplings, half-moon-shaped pouches with holes that allowed the oil to cook the filling directly, tenderizing the gingered pork.

For more conservative diners, Peking offers fine examples of more familiar dishes. The General Tso chicken is tender and perfectly fried, its dark sauce the perfect balance of sweetness and spice. Tiny dried chiles give a potent dry heat to the kung pao shrimp.

The kitchen also offers a few worthwhile upgrades to standard soups. The wonton, a house specialty, is a golden broth filled with thin-skinned shrimp-and-pork dumplings. The exceptional hot-and-sour seafood soup is less hot and sour than most, but is spiked with white pepper instead of chile oil so the seafood flavor shines through with a full, sherry-splashed richness.

It would be hard not to love this food no matter who served it. But a waiter like Yu completes the Peking experience. Not only does he pace the meal and tend the table with aplomb, but he interprets the menu's flavors and philosophy more adeptly than most servers I've known.

Yu even made the Japanese half of the menu feel like a natural addition to the Chinese kitchen. It helps that this sushi bar is one of the best around, both in the quality of its standard fare and for the rarer delicacies that occasionally appear. There was monkfish liver one night and Japanese sea urchin — considerably sweeter and more custardlike than its common California cousin — on another. (Also try the sea urchin deep-fried into oozy tempura nuggets.)

The sushi bar, presided over by Tony Chen, also offers some excellent composed dishes: tuna nuta, pristine sashimi sauced with sweet miso; naluto, which holds a trio of salmon, tuna and whitefish inside a tube of refreshing shaved cucumber; and an awesome angel roll, which wraps fish and matchsticks of sweet apple inside delicate sheets of white seaweed blanched and tenderized with vinegar.

Or Try These

Here are three other suburban Chinese restaurants.

Chez Elena Wu

910 Haddonfield-Berlin Rd., Voorhees, N.J. (856) 566-3222
This upscale Chinese restaurant brings a French influence to a largely Cantonese menu, with separate chefs for the wonton soup and the escargots.

FuziOn

2960 Skippack Pike., Worcester, Pa., (610) 584-6958
The team behind the now-closed Ly Michaels in Overbrook Park has brought its ambitious Asian-fusion cuisine farther west to a pretty little BYOB near Skippack Village.

Hunan

47 E. Lancaster Ave., Ardmore, Pa. (610) 642-3050
This cozy Main Line standby may be run by Susanna Foo's in-laws, but the cooking is strictly traditional, featuring excellent hot-and-sour soup and scallion pancakes.

But leave it to Yu to put his own spin on the sushi. He presented a plate of usuzukuri — gossamer slices of raw striped bass fanned around a pool of citrusy soy ponzu sauce — then deftly rolled each ribbon of fish into a tiny bundle around a sliver of shaved lime.

Cushioned by a layer of sweet fish and enlivened by the puckery ponzu, the usually bitter citrus rind found new life inside this package, washing across my palate with an intense burst of zest that I didn't expect.

How could I have, though? It wasn't on the menu.

■ **MENU HIGHLIGHTS** Steamed pork buns; open-ended dumplings; seafood hot-and-sour soup; house special wonton soup; Peking duck; filet mignon with shiitake mushrooms; Peking shrimp; zhu sen tofu. Sushi menu: angel roll; tuna nuta; raw Japanese uni (sea urchin); uni tempura; usuzukuri; naluto cucumber roll.

■ **WINE LIST** There is a very fine selection of sakes and creative sake cocktails.

■ **IF YOU GO** Lunch is served Monday-Saturday 11:30 a.m.-3 p.m. Dinner: Monday-Thursday 3-10 p.m., Friday-Saturday 3-11 p.m.; Sunday noon-10 p.m.

■ **RESERVATIONS** Suggested.

■ **CREDIT CARDS** All major cards.

■ **SMOKING** Smoking in the bar area only.

■ **HANDICAP ACCESSIBLE** Yes.

■ **PARKING** Free mall lot.

Max's

The quaint brick house is South Jersey's best new destination for contemporary fine dining.

Even owner Robert Recchiuti sees the apparent illogic of opening an upscale restaurant on this tired stretch of South Jersey's Route 130.

"Let's face it," he says, "some of it isn't pretty."

Low-rent motels and vacant strip malls with vast empty parking lots line the highway from the Betsy Ross Bridge north through Cinnaminson. No wonder a superb restaurant like Matt Ito's Fuji has operated here for more than two decades, yet remains virtually unknown.

But with the emergence of Recchiuti's new Max's, just a few doors up from Fuji, this unlikely restaurant-row-in-the-making (including the Friendly's across the street) is now home to two of the best South Jersey dining spots I've found in the last four years.

EXCELLENT

602 Route 130 North
Cinnaminson, N.J.
(856) 663-6297

NEIGHBORHOOD
South Jersey

CUISINE
Upscale
Italian/French

Originally a Friends meetinghouse built in 1850, the handsomely refurbished brick building, with its pale blue shutters and candlelit windows, looks like a country inn plopped onto a landscape of suburban sprawl. But Max's, named for Recchiuti's yellow Labrador retriever, may not be as poorly placed as it seems. It is undeniably convenient, within easy reach of affluent Moorestown, Mount Laurel and Cherry Hill, and just a 20-minute drive from Center City.

And Cinnaminson Township itself, after years of redevelopment pipe dreams, also took steps last summer to rejuvenate Route 130. Township Committeeman Anthony V. Minniti promises big changes within a year and is already hailing Max's as a pioneer in that renaissance.

It's no small role for a restaurant, but Max's has the makings of a legitimate head-turner.

Recchiuti built it in the space previously occupied by his now-folded advertising agency, Chase Kettering, and for a first-time restaurateur, he has shown remarkable good taste. The rooms are classic but sophisticated, with hardwood floors and French doors, evocative oil paintings, and a 700-bottle, climate-controlled cabinet where regulars can store their wine.

This serious approach to wine — despite the fact that Max's is a BYOB — is a reflection of the entire dining experience here: thought-

Originally a Friends meetinghouse built in 1850, the handsomely refurbished brick building looks like a country inn plopped onto a landscape of suburban sprawl.

ful and polished, down to the embroidered logo on the servers' shirts.

If those young servers are impressively poised, the kitchen, run by 28-year-old Alex Capasso, is downright stellar. Capasso and his sous-chef, Anthony DiPascale, are both Brasserie Perrier alums, and it shows in the style of their simple contemporary plates, which use Italian and French flavors to highlight good ingredients.

Two diver scallops as big as doorstops arrive seared rare and juicy atop thick slices of yellow tomatoes warmed in olive oil. Another substantial seafood appetizer perches the succulent meat of half a lobster over a nest of homemade linguine tossed with pulpy tomato compote.

The handmade gnocchi are memorable. I had them at lunch, glazed with an earthy porcini cream topped with chives and sauteed mushrooms, and, one night at dinner, tossed with a buttery tomato sauce filled with morsels of melting mozzarella cheese.

Capasso's kitchen wastes few opportunities to impress. A soup du jour brought a butternut squash froth that was stunningly rich, but not so creamy that I couldn't taste the vegetable. Even the complimentary predinner hors d'oeuvres were sharp — a tiny crock filled with vibrant yellow tomato-basil gazpacho one night and, on another, a divine Provencal chicken salad with moist meat piquant with olives and rosemary.

There were a few mild disappointments. The homemade linguine with clams and spinach lacked the needed punch of seasoning and garlic needed to give it zip. A giant crab and shrimp galette was reminiscent of the popular Georges Perrier dish, but was filled with so much shrimp mousse instead of lump crabmeat that it tasted more like a seafood burger.

Or Try These

Here are three other restaurants in South Jersey.

Fuji Japanese Restaurant

404 N. Burlington Pike , Cinnaminson, N.J. (856) 829-5211

Creative Japanese kaiseki-tasting meals from one of the region's best unsung chefs in an unlikely Cinnaminson hideaway.

The Red Hen Cafe

560 Stokes Rd., Medford, N.J. (609) 953-2655

Traditional Eastern European specialties are updated gently with good ingredients and careful cooking at this warm strip-mall bistro, where a husband-wife team is creating new respect for the pleasures of borscht.

Ritz Seafood

910 Haddonfield-Berlin Rd., Voorhees, N.J. (856) 566-6650

This diminutive restaurant wraps diners in a natural ambience of waterfalls and swimming koi, a tranquil and homey setting for chef Daniel Hover's creative pan-Asian seafood menu.

The chef also made a poor choice when he presliced the dry-aged sirloin steak into a fan across the plate. That showy presentation would dry out the juices of even the finest piece of meat.

Yet other meat dishes were superb. The double-cut rack of lamb was incredibly meaty, served over potatoes whipped to an herby green with basil pesto. A roasted veal chop arrived over truffled Parmesan risotto lightened with a little whipped cream. The classic duck confit was tender and gently salted.

Capasso's special talent, however, is for fish.

At lunch, a thick grouper fillet was seared to a perfect crisp and ringed with an ivory seafood froth scented with sweet roasted garlic. On the late-summer dinner menu, porcini-dusted striped bass was paired with delicate fingerling potatoes. And pan-roasted halibut came with lobster-studded mashed potatoes and a red wine lobster sauce whose dark intensity contrasted with the downy flakiness of the white fish.

Capasso, who also worked at the eclectic Krazy Kats near Wilmington, isn't afraid to put a few well-placed non-European flavors on the menu. A coriander and Sichuan pepper crust, for example, gave a pristine slice of yellowfin tuna a deft Asian turn. Sliced into gorgeous rounds that revealed the tuna's ruby center, then stacked with grilled scallions over a pedestal of sticky rice, it was a stunning plate complemented with a tangy ginger butter sauce that had only one flaw: I wish there had been more.

Few new restaurants can afford to hire a pastry chef, and that luxury might help Max's become a more complete package. Meanwhile, sous-chef DiPascale has done a nice enough job turning out fine variations on the basics.

Strong coffee gives a jolt to the exceptionally silky custard in the creme brulee. An individual tart shell filled with almond cream is topped with sliced pears that caramelize in the oven, melding with the buttery, flaky pastry.

The most impressive dessert is the luxurious chocolate caramel tart, a pastry round filled with shiny black chocolate ganache, hazelnut brittle, and a creamy caramel heart. Decadent and intense, each forkful trails sweet strings of caramel from the plate, melting with the bitter chocolate in the mouth like a high-class candy bar.

Classy enough to give this down-on-its-luck old highway some new respect? Civic rebirth should only start with something so sweet.

■ **MENU HIGHLIGHTS** Gnocchi; roasted lobster appetizer; scallop appetizer; roasted halibut with lobster-mashed potatoes; rack of lamb with pesto potato puree; pepper-crusted tuna; chocolate-caramel tart; pear tart.

■ **WINE LIST** BYOB. The restaurant has a large, climate-controlled wine cabinet where customers can store wine.

■ **IF YOU GO** Lunch is served Tuesday-Friday, 11:30 a.m.-2:30 p.m. Dinner: Tuesday-Saturday, 5:30-10 p.m.; Sunday, 5-9:30 p.m. Entrees: lunch, $9-$18; dinner, $15-$32.

■ **RESERVATIONS** Suggested.

■ **CREDIT CARDS** All major cards but Discover.

■ **SMOKING** No smoking.

■ **HANDICAP ACCESSIBLE** Yes.

■ **PARKING** Free lot.

Moonlight

Exciting New American cuisine is served in an arty, moon-white dining room.

n another, far less elegant scenario, New Hope's most exciting new restaurant could have been called White Goop.

It's kind of poetic. And though the words may not make you salivate for Matthew Levin's excellent New American menu, "white goop" does say a lot about this unusual and intriguing restaurant. After all, nearly 1,000 gallons of the stuff — joint compound, primer, and textured latex paint — were sprayed over every surface of the rambling dining rooms once occupied by the Hacienda Inn.

Each of the 21 still lifes that artist Robert Rabinowitz copied in 3-D from the masters has been sealed under an eerie white cast, as if unearthed from a dig at Pompeii. Or caught in the glow of Moonlight, which, in the end, I suppose, is a more tasteful name.

EXCELLENT

36 W. Mechanic St.
New Hope, Pa.
(215) 862-3100

NEIGHBORHOOD
New Hope

CUISINE
New American

There is Picasso's jigsawed guitar. Van Gogh's sunflowers. Cezannne's fruit. White. White. White. The bookshelf filled with 700 psychology books left by a previous owner? Gooped. Even the barren bushes out front were once painted white until the spring, when they got a cheery coat of green.

The white motif offers a housekeeping bonus. Instead of dusting the sculptures, says owner Andrew Abruzzese, who also owns the Pineville Tavern in Bucks County but is a painter by trade, he simply sprays white over the grime. But, of course, a serious statement also is being made in the deliberately stark moonscape conjured in part by Lambertville restaurateur Jim Hamilton. As Abruzzese puts it:

The restaurant is but a canvas. The food and customers are the color.

The idea would be little more than pretentious goop if it didn't work. But at Moonlight, which opened in December 2000, it really does, giving New Hope's flagging restaurant scene a bolt of sophisticated dining to compete with Lambertville, flourishing across the river.

The black-clad waitstaff had improved noticeably on a recent visit from my earlier meals — our servers were warm, outgoing and well-prepared — adding some extra polish to this surprising spot. But no doubt, the real key to Moonlight's success has been chef Matthew

Chef Matthew Levin, one of the region's rising stars, in front of an all-white dining-room still life.

Levin, whose lively imagination and stunning presentations have made him one of the region's most exciting rising stars.

The Philadelphia native and Culinary Institute of America grad has worked in many of the area's top kitchens — Susanna Foo, Striped Bass, Le Bec-Fin, Brasserie Perrier, and the Ryland Inn in North Jersey. And it shows in his cooking, a polished distillation of the now-pervasive New American style — French technique touched with Asian accents — plated in artsy towers over streaks and foams and droplets of sauce. But what separates Levin from most other young chefs is his knack for using the best local ingredients and intelligent combinations that never lose their focus or clarity of flavor.

A thick lobe of seared foie gras is posed alone on one side of a large plate, a monument to sheer indulgence, waiting for the diner to swab each morsel through clove-scented cherry sauce and a sprinkling of pistachio dust on the other side. A tall cylinder of diced tuna tartare is bound with an irresistibly spicy miso dressing, then dolloped with the salty bursts of tiny ossetra caviar.

A few missteps reminded that Levin is still learning, but at least his mistakes were bold. A recent soup du jour was completely infused with porcini mushroom, but too much acid in the mix erased the mushrooms' richness. At a previous meal, an appetizer of boar's loin over a bed of maitake mushrooms held promise but, seared sushi-rare, was impossible to chew.

But Levin's ambitious dishes usually were within easy reach. Even an outlandish concoction such as one recent special — tempura fried lobster tail "lollipops" speckled with pink candy pop rocks and sauced with blue cheese cream — turned out to be a stroke of minor genius. The tangy, mouth-fizzling candy added a surprisingly subtle textural surprise. A beautifully moist and delicate saddle of rabbit was stuffed with vibrant leaves of sage, then scattered with sublimely sweet oven-dried tomatoes and little chanterelles. A gorgeous filet of halibut was moist and luscious beneath its crispy envelope of basel-lined brik pastry crust, the fish's mildness played against sweet cloves of braised garlic and nuggets of lump crab.

The menu isn't cheap, with entrees in the upper $20s, but the quality and portions merited the prices. I've rarely seen a veal chop as immense as the one I had here for $30, three inches thick on the bone and meltingly tender over a tomato sauce splashed with Madeira and ribboned with prosciutto. (Levin said later that he had chosen the calf himself at a local purveyor's farm.)

The tuna entree seemed nearly as large, a brick of fish sliced on the bias to reveal rings of color that ran the gamut of doneness, from the seared five-spice crust to the sweetly rare ruby heart.

Or Try These

Here are three other restaurants in the New Hope/Lambertville area.

Frenchtown Inn

7 Bridge St., Frenchtown, N.J.
(908) 996-3300

This historic inn along the Delaware River has a long tradition of sophisticated dining, with a menu rooted in seasonal French cooking, fine wines, and cozy fireplace dining rooms.

Sergeantsville Inn

601 Rosemont-Ringoes Rd., Sergeantsville, N.J.
(609) 397-3700

This cozy inn (circa 1734) has ambitious young owners and an adventurous fine dining menu that ranges from lobster risotto to a fondness for exotic meats.

Inn at Phillip's Mill

2590 River Rd., New Hope, Pa.
(215) 862-9919

The straightforward country French cuisine tastes all the better in the candlelit flicker of this charming Bucks County farmhouse just north of New Hope.

A hefty slice of wild striped bass was seared to a crisp but amazingly moist inside, its luxurious, downy flesh slipping into lentils bathed in a red wine lobster stock. Smoked bacon permeated the crust of crispy sweetbreads. Juniper berries perfumed a mahogany sauce beneath a meaty duck breast paired with red cabbage and figs plumped with vanilla. A tower of red and golden beets was layered with creamy goat cheese that tempered their earthy sweetness — a dish that, on the recent summer menu, presented the goat cheese as ice cream.

The savory side may playfully imitate desserts, but the desserts themselves are less imaginative than the rest of the menu. They were good nonetheless — a warm chocolate cake sided with excellent banana chocolate chip ice cream, a sweet cheese tart crowned with a mountain of ripe blueberries, and a vanilla-speckled creme brulee learned from ex-Le Bec-Fin pastry maestro Robert Bennett.

Those specks of vanilla bean are tiny, of course. But against the lunar whiteness of Moonlight's world, they are unmistakable, swirling across the bottom of the custard dish like a galaxy of stars.

■ **MENU HIGHLIGHTS** Tuna tartare; foie gras with cherries; beet and goat cheese salad; lobster and pop rocks "lollipops"; wild striped bass; scallops; tuna entree; veal chop; crispy halibut brik; stuffed saddle of rabbit; banana chocolate chip ice cream; blueberry cheese tarte; creme brulee.

■ **WINE LIST** A midsize list of French, American and Italian bottles offers an excellent selection of uncommon wines for various budgets, including several around $40 or less.

■ **IF YOU GO** Lunch served daily 11 a.m.-3 p.m. Dinner served daily 5-11 p.m. Entrees: lunch, $8-$15; dinner, $23-$32. Three-course "neighborhood" menu is $24.

■ **RESERVATIONS** Required on weekends.

■ **CREDIT CARDS** All major cards but Discover and Diners Club.

■ **SMOKING** Smoking permitted in the bar dining room.

■ **HANDICAP ACCESSIBLE** Not wheelchair accessible.

■ **PARKING** Free parking behind the New Hope Inn with validation.

Morimoto

Superstar chef Masaharu Morimoto brings cutting-edge Japanese cuisine to Stephen Starr's futuristic dining room.

This is better than TV.

I've watched this "Iron Chef" many times on the Food Network. While my wife dozed on the couch, I'd be riveted as Masaharu Morimoto battled in the cooking show's "Kitchen Stadium," whipping up wonders with giant eel and fermented soybeans, and titillating the giggly Japanese starlets judging the contest, who always seemed to say, "I do not think this is Japanese . . . but I like it!"

Yet in person, five feet away across the sushi counter at the Chestnut Street restaurant that bears his name, Morimoto is far more real than I'd imagined. And, with the inimitable largesse of his benefactor Stephen Starr, the two have produced Philadelphia's most exciting new restaurant since Vetri and ¡Pasion! opened three-and-a-half years ago.

EXCELLENT

723 Chestnut St.
Philadelphia
(215) 413-9070

NEIGHBORHOOD
Washington Square

CUISINE
Japanese

Morimoto has shed the silvery robes he wore as an Iron Chef, in favor of everyday working whites. He has grown his crew cut into a ponytail and replaced his game-show scowl with an easy, magnetic smile. But from the moment he unzips his case of long, shiny blades, there is no doubting his mastery.

Morimoto launches into my $100 omakase multicourse tasting with the precision, finesse and power of a world-class athlete. He is drowning live shrimp in sake, dispatching scallops from shells the size of Frisbees, grating gnarled wasabi roots with a sharkskin-covered paddle, squeezing soy sauce droplet by droplet from a brush, dicing, slicing, deboning tiny fish in a blur of knife-work so deft that some of the most crucial moves are imperceptible.

And the food is wondrous. Toro tartare is a tall plug of minced buttery-sweet tuna belly filled with garlic and crunchy fried shallots. Set in a pool of soy broth and crowned with caviar, it sets off bells in every corner of my mouth. Fresh wasabi on the side adds heat and a touch of fruitiness without the bitterness of the usual reconstituted powder.

A sashimi of half-cooked lobster tail comes showered with black truffle and splashed with boiling olive oil mixed with lemony soy.

The Iron Chef, Masaharu Morimoto, holds a drunken shrimp.

Thinly sliced baby abalone arrives with a blazing-hot river rock, so diners can sear the shellfish at the table. The papery white sheets turn slightly crunchy but remain delicate, with a faint aftertaste of oyster.

A thin slice of kobe beef packs a potent, savory punch that doesn't need the extra indulgence of the accompanying foie gras. But, oh well . . .

All I need is a palate refresher of wasabi sorbet, a bamboo cup of fragrant, spicy snow with the zesty sparkle of grated yuzu, a Japanese citrus fruit. Bring me more!

It's easy to get carried away at Morimoto, especially during an omakase prepared by the master himself. The bamboo carafes of sake don't hurt, either.

The intensity of eating at the bar, however, doesn't always translate to the dining room.

This is clearly Stephen Starr's best restaurant, in part because he has stepped back and let a big-name chef drive the concept. Yet what prevents Morimoto from being even better is that Starr — whom I saw circling the room maniacally in a stylish knee-length coat — has not stepped back far enough.

The high-design dining room created by Karim Rashid is stunning, with an undulating bamboo ceiling and molded walls shaped like scattered seashells. But just as at the Blue Angel, Alma de Cuba, and Starr's other restaurants, the room is unbearably loud.

The glass tabletops are too long for the otherwise diligent servers to keep clean. And all those gimmicks — the phallic electric "candles" that can't be moved out of the way, the $15,000 3-D photo of a woman in the foyer, and even the booths that glow with soothing colors — seem like childish distractions from the main event: Morimoto's food.

There were a few rough spots on the menu, too. The watch-us-make-tofu-at-your-table appetizer failed to elevate soy curd to greatness. The rib-eye steak was surprisingly tough.

Yet such slips were easily overshadowed by the successes. Morimoto can be extremely expensive, but you get what you pay for: the best sushi I've ever eaten, down to the amazing rice that is polished white from brown by a machine in the basement.

Rarities such as needlefish, monkfish liver, Japanese shad wrapped in translucent sheets of kelp, and extra-fatty o-toro tuna belly are presented like art over rice. The sashimi sampler is cut into thick cubes that set off a chain of flavor explosions, with caviar bursting over toro, for example, or cracked pepper and chives over salmon.

An appetizer of luscious king crab legs was the essence of raw-bar luxury. Sea urchin dissolved on my tongue like chantilly cream whipped with sea foam. And thin slices of live scallop slipped down my throat like disks of sea-sugar.

The cooked items were just as good. Fabulous rock-shrimp tempura was drizzled with spicy mayonnaise. The steamed drunken shrimp was notably tender, too, but I was most intrigued by the garnish: charred strips of crust skimmed from fermenting sake.

The poussin had a wonderful teriyaki sauce. The juicy lobster epice was perfumed with an exotic blend of eight spices. Ishi yaki "buri bop" was an inventive take on a Korean rice bowl.

The crispy whole fish entree includes not only fillets of flounder but the entire skeleton, which is fried three times and eaten like a cracker. It's not bad, actually; the fins had the most flavor.

There are some fine desserts — pumpkin cake, Italian-style rice cake, and a chocolate-hazelnut mousse. But none could quite match

Or Try These

Here are three more Japanese restaurants.

Fuji

404 Burlington Pike North
Cinnaminson, N.J.
(856) 829-5211

Creative Japanese kaiseki-tasting meals from one of the region's best unsung chefs in an unlikely Cinnaminson hideaway.

Genji

1720 Sansom St., Philadelphia
(215) 564-1720

It may have slipped a shade since the tragic death of its owner two years ago, but this remains Center City's most reliable venue for standard sushi.

Sushikazu

920 Dekalb Pike, Blue Bell, Pa.
(610) 272-7767

The smartly renovated little bungalow is home to a surprisingly creative sushi counter, where premium ingredients, from toro to live scallops, are sliced with great skill. Try off-the-menu specials such as the spicy tuna over crunchy rice or the Area 51 roll.

that wasabi sorbet for sheer surprise and sprightly flavor.

For all of Morimoto's virtues, there is undeniable novelty in watching an international media star who is far more substance than hype cooking in our own backyard. But relying on that star power also poses a greater risk — especially given talk of a

The sashimi sampler is cut into thick cubes that set off a chain of flavor explosions.

planned Morimoto restaurant chain — if we lose the chef, even part time, to Manhattan.

Until then, Philadelphia's real-life Iron Chef will beat the TV fantasy every time.

■ **MENU HIGHLIGHTS** Omakase tasting — toro tartare; lobster sashimi with truffles; hot rock-seared abalone. Raw bar and sushi — king crab legs; needle fish; live scallops; sea urchin; monkfish liver; Japanese shad; Morimoto sashimi. Cooked menu — rock shrimp tempura; drunken shrimp; teriyaki poussin; lobster epice; ishi yaki buri bop; wasabi sorbet; Italian rice cake; pumpkin spice cake.

■ **WINE LIST** The medium-size cellar has an excellent international selection with many bottles under $50, including a strong group of crisp, aromatic whites, such as a Spanish Albariño from Morgadio ($47), that are a good match to the cuisine. The very good house sakes are served in neat bamboo carafes.

■ **IF YOU GO** Lunch is served Monday-Friday 11:30 a.m.-2 p.m. Dinner Monday-Thursday 5-11 p.m. Friday-Saturday 5-midnight. Sunday 4-10 p.m. Entrees: lunch, $14-$28; dinner $17-$34. Omakase lunch, $40; dinner, $80-$120.

■ **RESERVATIONS** Strongly recommended.

■ **CREDIT CARDS** All major cards accepted.

■ **SMOKING** Smoking permitted in the upstairs lounge only.

■ **HANDICAP ACCESSIBLE** Wheelchair accessible.

■ **PARKING** Valet parking costs $12.

Morning Glory Diner

The hip Bella Vista eatery provides updated, homemade diner fare.

A bright noon sun beamed into the Morning Glory Diner to illuminate the grill where owner Samantha "Sam" Mickey was a short-order flurry of cookery and chatter.

"Talk, talk, talk," she clipped to a few of her pals, who gathered around the counter in debate over an exotic new beverage. "They say it tastes like a chocolate diet shake . . . not that I've ever tasted one of those."

She chuckled as the oven door opened, billowing out wafts of the world's cheesiest macaroni, baking away inside as big as a loaf, its crust toasting golden and crisp. Beside it, frittata omelets filled with roasted peppers, ham and spinach puffed and browned in their pans.

What's good for lunch, Sam?

VERY GOOD

735 S. 10th St.,
Philadelphia
(215) 413-3999

NEIGHBORHOOD
Bella Vista

CUISINE
Comfort Food

"Me," she said, scooping whipped cream onto a biscuit.

What else?

"Her," she said, pointing a spatula to the waitress with curly blond tresses.

"Get the macaroni, hon'," said the waitress. "You're going to love me."

So, I did. And I did. South Philadelphia's Morning Glory Diner was just the very thing I ordered.

When so many of our old-fashioned diners are slipping away into the microwave age of convenience, this modest, low-slung brick building at 10th and Fitzwater Streets has been breathing new life back into the genre, pouring heart and soul into comfort food that still bothers to be homemade.

Even the ketchup is made from scratch, in 12 hours of toil and trouble that bring apples, clove and ginger to the sometimes spicy tomato mix. The results are imperfect. (My daughter, the Heinz aficionado, refused to eat it.) But that is one of the charms of the Morning Glory, where Mickey, a longtime bartender and waitress who opened this spot five years ago, learned pro cooking on the job before turning the reigns over to co-chefs Joan Gigliotti and Donna Fitzgerald nearly three years ago.

The menu still bears Mickey's personality, with tried and true staples such as the macaroni, frittatas and "samwiches" remaining large-

Samantha Mickey, owner of the Morning Glory Diner.

ly unchanged. And Mickey, now the mother of two young children, still occasionally cooks on Sunday. But the arrival of Gigliotti and Fitzgerald has added a needed polish to the Glory's lunch and dinner menus. The two cooks previously shared the kitchen at Judy's Cafe, where Mickey also once worked. So it is little surprise that the recent offerings here bear some resemblance to Judy's menu, with delicious cheddar-crusted chicken (actually crusted with "cheddar" flavored goldfish) and horseradish cream, nut-crusted trout, and cheese-stuffed meat loaf — this one a comforting turkey version.

But I've had enough delicious originals here to know the Morning Glory's kitchen does more than just copycat its inspiration. A massive burrito came filled with marvelous stewed pork, the moist, tender meat infused with a tangy red Mexican gravy that tingled with poblano peppers, only to be cooled by a refreshing banana salsa. Excellent crab cakes were filled with scallions and sweet lumps of meat that paired nicely with a spicy mustard dip. A giant grilled cheese sandwich oozed gooey strings of good white cheese from inside its challah toast.

The new kitchen wasn't perfect. A fabulous bourbon barbecue sauce was wasted on two overcooked pork chops. And they have yet to improve the restaurant's doughy biscuits, which are cut from a pan rather than cooked individually.

But Morning Glory's successes easily outpace its mistakes. With quality produce, healthful salads, and good ingredients such as the breakfast meats from Godshall's and Italian sausage from Fiorella

Bros., it's hard to go wrong when you keep it this simple and affordably priced.

Morning Glory is not Philadelphia's first effort to reclaim good cooking for the diner. Jack McDavid's Down Home Diner in the Reading Terminal Market set the standard before its decline of late. Mickey, also a former Down Home employee, readily concedes it as one of her big culinary inspirations.

But the Glory has what the Down Home never will — a colorful, down-to-earth neighborhood that has embraced the eatery as a Bella Vista corner fixture. Every year, it seems an even more preposterous number of flowers burst riotously from its front flower boxes and covered back patio. And whether you are among the faithful, an odd mix of local elderly and grungy hipsters who line the sidewalk for weekend brunch, or a stranger taking refuge from a blustery midweek night over a steaming bowl of onion soup covered with molten cheese, you are bound to wish there were more diners just like it near you, cooking with the same enthusiastic determination to find just the right recipes.

Mickey and her troops have discovered many.

French toast made from challah bread has a hint of vanilla in its custard and a homemade strawberry compote that completes the dish. The macaroni and cheese, which blends Swiss, Provolone, Cheddar and Parmesan, comes out more like noodle kugel than anything creamy out of a box. But it is the dream my waitress promised. The hamburgers are a half-pound victory of char-grilled beef served on excellent Metropolitan Bakery buns.

As for Mickey's traditional pancake batter, it is so smooth it has the texture of silk. Add a heaping handful of fruit or chocolate chips, and it becomes one of the Glory's best desserts.

Or Try These

Here are three other restaurants for American comfort food.

Judy's Cafe

627 S. Third St., Philadelphia, (215) 928-1968

An affable Queen Village fixture with famous stuffed meat loaf, cheese-crusted chicken and a gay-friendly atmosphere.

Country Club Restaurant & Pastry Shop

1717 Cottman Ave., Philadelphia (215) 722-0500

The region's best diner maintains its excellent Jewish and American comfort food while updating the kitchen with a new chef.

Down Home Diner

51 N. 12th St., Philadelphia (215) 627-1955

Jack McDavid's Reading Terminal outlet for hog-jowl soup and panfried chicken could be so good if the food were more consistent.

But there were others I tasted one recent night that I've since been dreaming of, too. A peach pie brought piles of fruit beneath its lattice crust that still tasted tree-picked fresh. And the chocolate mousse pie was amazing, its densely rich custard layered over an Oreo crust then topped with a cumulus cloud of fresh whipped cream.

With the stereo oscillating between the Buena Vista Social Club, cool folkies, and souped-up Beatles, the diner's air hummed with sustainably good vibes. Three customers behind us, with the spring of music and a good meal to guide them from their booth, even moved toward the exit in a mini-samba line. Swiveling their hips in unison as the door swung open, they twisted happily from the Morning Glory Diner out into the Bella Vista night.

■ **MENU HIGHLIGHTS** Glorycake pancakes; challah French toast with strawberry sauce; potato pancakes; frittatas; turkey meat loaf; macaroni and cheese; hamburger; stewed pork burrito; crab cakes; cheddar chicken; berry biscuit; peanut butter chocolate square.

■ **WINE LIST** BYOB.

■ **IF YOU GO** Breakfast served 7 a.m.-3:30 p.m. Tuesday through Friday; brunch served 8-3 p.m. Saturday-Sunday; lunch served 11 a.m.-4:30 p.m. Tuesday-Friday. Dinner served 4:30-9 p.m. Tuesday-Friday. Closed Monday. Lunch entrees, $4.50-$7.50. Dinner entrees, $5-$15.

■ **RESERVATIONS** Not accepted, except for large parties.

■ **CREDIT CARDS** Cash only.

■ **SMOKING** Front portion of restaurant only.

■ **HANDICAP ACCESSIBLE** The side-door entrance on Fitzwater Street has a ramp. The bathrooms are large, but not officially handicapped certified.

■ **PARKING** Street parking.

The Cheesesteak Project

Eat cheesesteaks for class credit? Four high school seniors join Craig LaBan on a quest for the best example of Philadelphia's gift to world cuisine.

When Josh Brawer announced to his parents what he and three friends were planning for their senior project at Lower Merion High School, the reaction was skeptical.

"C'mon," said Josh's father, David. "You're going to go around eating cheesesteaks for a month? You've gotta be kidding me."

To David Brawer, the projects tended to divide the high school seniors into two groups. There were the kids who'd take the month off before graduation to do something socially active, such as work for a charity or a political campaign. And there were the others, who'd do nothing but hang out at the old man's office.

In other words, the do-gooders and the slackers.

Josh's cheesesteak adventure sounded — at least in the beginning — suspiciously as if he'd be joining the ranks of the latter. It sounded like a scam.

But it didn't seem silly to me when I was asked to mentor this project. Josh and his classmates Andy Shore, Jeffrey Steinberg and Tommy Conry would become my eating team.

After all, they were trying to answer one of the great culinary questions of our time: Who makes the best cheesesteak?

Talk about ambition. No food has defined our region more than this double-fisted roll of gusto. Nothing cuts across class lines, or bonds the generations with more unifying power than a steaming hot steak "wid" or "widout." (That's wid onions, if you have to ask.) The topic is an endless obsession, from gym locker rooms to the pages of the local media to Steinberg's car every time he and his buddies headed out of school for yet another lunch-period steak adventure.

From left: Andy Shore, Josh Brawer, Jeff Steinberg, Tommy Conry.

Which is the best? Settling this question (at least once, though probably not for all) is a matter of regional preoccupation and a rite of gastronomic closure for these four friends about to leave for college. But it wouldn't be easy. Before it was over, the journey would take us more than 110 miles, through two states, 23 steakeries, 65-plus sandwiches and countless hours of challenging digestion.

In four days.

"Ever since the first time my dad took me to Geno's, we have shared an incredible bond. During the car ride home, we began to argue over what really made the steak. I believed that it was the Whiz, while he claimed that the Amoroso's roll was integral. Apparently, we were both wrong."
— *Josh Brawer's cheesesteak diary*

The anatomy of a cheesesteak would appear simple enough — roll, meat, cheese and toppings. But how would we know the merely good ones from greatness?

My new students were experienced in the ravenous joy of attacking a juicy sandwich. I could see that the moment we met: Josh, the shy devotee of Classic Coke who loved to reminisce about his favorite cheesesteaks; Jeff, the loquacious sophisticate, who had honed his palate during family dinners at the Palm; Andy, who wasn't going to let the cast on his arm from a basketball mishap get between him and a sandwich; and Tommy, the meticulous note-taker and future plastics engineer.

Four wide-eyed 18-year-old cheesesteakaholics.

But they hesitated a moment when I informed them we would not be visiting a single steak shop that day, but several. Maybe even 20 if they could keep up. They were in the big leagues now. Their senior project was serious business. And it demanded a brief primer in the science of cheesesteak scrutiny.

There is the meat itself, I told them. It can range from rib-eye to top round to, yes, even beef knuckle (... gulp!?). But most important, how it is cooked? Look at the color of the meat before it hits the griddle. Is it as faded as an unripe tomato, drained of its flavorful juices? Or does it have a fresh crimson blush, marbled with the lacy white lines of fat that will baste it?

Is the griddle a glorified factory, lined with a tall berm of precooked steaming meat? Or is each sandwich cooked to order, seared to a caramelized brown around the edges and placed on a roll still dripping its natural essence? Is it shredded to a hamburger fineness (a method I always find dry), or is the thinly sliced meat left largely intact? Is the meat seasoned?

This, we decided, was key. But there was so much more. The crusty rolls versus the soft ones. Whether the onions were fried to a sweet golden brown. The girth of the sandwich (for which we were armed with a ruler) mattered. So did the quality of the cheese (was it real Cheez Whiz, or imitation?) The fire of the chiles and sauces on the condiment bar counted for extra points. As did an authentic level of atty-tude at the cashier's window.

Ultimately, we judged each restaurant on three sandwiches: a traditional steak with Whiz or American cheese, a specialty steak, and a chicken cheesesteak.

The variations we found were numbing. In fact, Josh Brawer returned home from our forays so bursting with nuances of the day's investigations that his father — awaking to our project's critical merit — soon wrote me to address the "great chasm" between him and his son.

"I come from the Secret-to-a-Great-Cheesesteak-Lies-in-the-Roll School and I have not been able to convince him of this basic truism. I wish you would work with him on this."

If only it were so simple. The truth is that a transcendent steak must exist in perfect harmony, an ethereal melding of cheese and onion and juicy meat, swirling at the height of its flavors through your roll at that very moment you take a bite. Call it the perfect storm of steaks.

Jeffrey Steinberg has his own name for this elusive trait: Good Drip.

"I placed it down and opened it a tiny bit just to glance at the onions, meat and cheese all united. I then took a large and scrumptious bite. The Whiz, oil and steak juice dripped out of the bottom. It was breathtaking."
— Jeffrey Steinberg's cheesesteak diary

Devotion to a particular cheesesteak is, for most Philadelphians, a territorial birthright.

If you are from Roxborough, for example, you will most likely consider a sandwich piled with finely chopped meat at Dalessandro's the quintessential steak. If you are from Bala Cynwyd, the cheesey pouf of shredded meat that plumps the roll at Mama's will define your preference. If you are from the Northeast, perhaps you were lucky enough to be weaned at Chink's on Torresdale Avenue, the charming old-time soda shop that, despite its un-PC name, serves one of the city's best traditional steaks. That's the only steak owners Joseph and Denise Groh will make — succulent ribeye, American cheese, soft roll and onions.

If you are a visitor, a newly minted Philadelphian, or a night owl with a 2 a.m. case of the munchies, it is more likely that you have been initiated into the rites of steakerie at the corner of South Ninth Street and Passyunk Avenue.

There's still something quintessentially Philadelphian about making a pilgrimage at least once to this particular crossroads, where rivals Geno's and Pat's King of Steaks stare at each other across the sharply angled intersection like neon battleships ready to rumble. Sandwiched between the clang of the auto body shop and the grunts of local boys playing hoops in the park, muscle cars cruise to a double-parked halt in the crosswalk. And the faithful hordes wait as long as it takes for the taste of a Whiz-slathered steak on their lips.

The tops in cheesesteak-land: John's Roast Pork

In local lore, Pat's King of Steaks has long been ceded the honor of having invented this delicacy (without cheese) in the 1930s. But if these rivals were the focus of our debate, it wouldn't last long. The tough-but-flavorful steak from Geno's was far superior in heft and drip to the skimpy, gristly sandwich from Pat's.

Neither titan, though, came close to snaring the crown. Nor did the sandwiches from two other tourist favorites — the dry hamburger-like steaks on squishy rolls at Jim's on South Street, and the bland, water-splashed skinnies at Rick's in the Terminal Market, a descendant of the Olivieri family that founded Pat's.

The best of the big-name eateries was Tony Luke's Old Philly Style Sandwiches on Oregon Avenue. Snug in the shadows of the I-95 overpass, it has all the genuine South Philly ambience one could want. The broad sidewalk awning is lit with yellow neon. The walls are covered with celebrity photos (though, as Tommy Conry observed, mostly of people who were "big back in the early '90s"). Even better, Tony Luke's has a staff that seems to relish heckling its clientele, a mix of businessmen, contractors and grandmothers, as well as police and paramilitary officers — ranking this among the best-armed lunch crowds in town.

A gunshot goes off somewhere in the distance. Not a soul in line flinches. Not with the promise of a juicy steak Italian — tender meat wrapped with broccoli rabe and aged provolone — snug inside one of the excellent house-baked rolls.

This was a true contender, but not quite the top. No, the real joy of cheesesteaks, the ultimate proof of their vitality as street food, is that the greatest sandwiches are still being cooked at some smaller places you might never have heard of.

The Schmitter, for example, was a wonderful sandwich layered between garlicky salami and tomatoes on a kaiser roll at the virtually unmarked McNally's H & J Tavern in Chestnut Hill (which also happens to make a superb chicken steak). But the Schmitter, we decided, was a fancy steak variation rather than a purely great steak. So was the kaiser steak with a mop-top of onions at Donkey's Place in Camden that was copied recently with wild success by an eatery in Manhattan.

We found our nirvana of steakdom at a take-out sandwich shack wedged between a train track and a chemical plant off Snyder Avenue near Columbus Boulevard. John's Roast Pork has been in business there since 1930, and its juice-drenched pork sandwiches are so good, it is little wonder I hadn't tried the steaks until I brought my posse here in search of a sleeper.

What we discovered was a rarity in second-generation owner John Bucci Jr.: a cook who knows what to do with a griddle, who plays the searing hot spots and cooler regions of his flat-top like a virtuoso. Frying each batch of meat and onions to order, deftly seasoning his steaks, strategically crumbling and folding his cheese into the middle, Bucci packed the marvelous seeded rolls from Carangi Baking Co. with nearly a pound of explosive flavors.

At the picnic tables outside, we took three bites and knew: John's had taken all three categories by unanimous decision. The traditional cheesesteak was a cosmic flow of meat and molten American cheese. The steak with sauteed spinach and salty aged provolone lit our palates. The chicken steak — usually the dieter's penance — was as succulent as anything we tasted, and even better with a dark streak of sausage-infused red gravy.

"Wow ..."

"This meat tastes so ..."

"I'm bringing my dad ..."

Their words kept disappearing into the sandwiches.

The catch is that John's grill is open only weekdays and

only until 2:30 p.m. Wait too long after noon, and those seeded rolls will be gone, too.

"You gotta come early, kid," John Jr.'s mother, Vonda, told me curtly from behind the register. "We're dedicated here to the working man."

"After I had eaten half I almost threw in the towel. Thank God my friends were there to save me. 'You wussy, eat the rest of your steak!' they shouted. Ten minutes later, I lay sprawled along the back seat of Jeff's car, reminiscing about the steak while falling asleep."

— *Andy Shore's cheesesteak diary*

By the end of our odyssey, my students had honed their skills to the point where, by the time we merely opened a sandwich and inhaled its aroma, they knew whether it was worthy.

"I'm not going to eat that," said Andy the moment we dropped a floppy, five-pound "belly filler" from Larry's Famous Steaks on the table.

He was right, of course; this steak was a kitchen-sink mess.

Josh Brawer, too, had refined his tastes to the point where his dad had to admit that his son had "learned a lot. ... Go figure!" David Brawer also says their conversations now incorporate the nuances of steak shop talk. "I've never really been into talking about sports," David said, "but this has kind of taken the place of it."

But for these friends, going in search of the great cheesesteak, it turns out, was always about more than the consumption of an ultimate sandwich.

"For Josh and his buddies," said David Brawer, "I think it represented freedom. To be able to pile into the car and go to places that were, if not taboo, beyond the reach of parental control."

That thrill of adventure may explain, at least in part, their frequent lunch-hour visits to unfamiliar neighborhoods in the city.

It may be no coincidence that their final steak frenzy arose in the weeks before their departure for college. Josh, Andy and Jeffrey were heading off to Penn State, while Tommy was going to the University of Michigan.

Sure, they passed their senior project. Their teachers were "impressed," Brawer said, "that we actually learned something."

But it was also as if making the summer rounds of their favorite steakeries was finally cementing their roots in place. No one expressed this better than Tommy, the only one going out of state. He wrote in his cheesesteak journal:

"I have known the true greatness of Cheez Whiz mixed with fried onions and fried-up steak, because I have Philly running through my veins (along with lots of cholesterol). ... Now that I am about to head out to the Midwest for college, only now that I am leaving the world of cheesesteaks behind, can I reflect on how lucky I was."

How They Scored

How many great cheesesteaks are there in the Philadelphia region? Far more than I and my four high-school-age eating machines could sample in four days. I'd still like to get to Leo's Steaks in Delaware County and sample the steak at Shank's & Evelyn's in South Philly. Even so, the cheesesteak-tasting team made a serious dent, putting 23 restaurants to a triple-header test, basing our rating (with 5 being the best) on samples of three styles of steaks — traditional, specialty and chicken.

5: Cheesesteak Paradise

John's Roast Pork, Snyder Avenue and Weccacoe Street, Philadelphia, 215-463-1951. Wedged between a train track and a chemical plant, this sandwich shack has existed in delicious obscurity since 1930. Aside from serving the city's best pork sandwiches, chef-owner John Bucci Jr. unanimously swept all three categories of the cheesesteak competition, serving up heavyweight portions of zestily seasoned, perfectly seared beef and chicken steaks on crusty rolls with real cheese and garlicky spinach. The picnic tables offer a great, gritty city view. It's open only weekdays through lunch; come early if you want a seeded roll.

4: Worth Busting the Diet

Tony Luke's Old Philly Style Sandwiches, 39 E. Oregon Ave., Philadelphia, 215-551-5725. Crusty house-baked rolls, bitter broccoli rabe and aged provolone give the hefty steak Italian a gutsy neighborhood flair, and the neon-lit awning lends the South Philly location an authentic ambience, from the employees in black T-shirts to the diverse and colorful clientele. The Rittenhouse Square outpost has the food, but none of the ambience.

Chink's Steaks, 6030 Torresdale Ave., Philadelphia, 215-535-9405. Step into a time warp at this marvelously preserved soda shop where chocolate egg creams and frothy shakes are the ideal pairing for what may be the most succulent traditional soft-roll American cheesesteak in town. Owner Joseph Groh's rib-eye steaks have a great, lingering beefy flavor. The restaurant's monicker is the late founder's nickname.

McNally's H & J Tavern, 8634 Germantown Ave., Philadelphia, 215-247-9736. This unmarked tavern atop the hill in Chestnut Hill produces one of the region's great specialty cheesesteaks, the Schmitter, a steak-and-salami fantasy on a kaiser roll. The marinated chicken steak was also one of the best of the poultry genre.

3: Will Satisfy the Craving

Geno's Steaks, 1219 S. Ninth St., Philadelphia, 215-389-0659. This South Philly institution easily bested rival Pat's on the day of our tasting. Not only did it seem to have been recently spruced up, but the steaks were meaty and full of juicy drip. A splash of the killer hot sauce tastes like flame on a roll.

Sonny's Famous Steaks, 216 Market St., Philadelphia, 215-629-4828. The owner of this Old City newcomer takes her traditional steak seriously, slicing the never-frozen domestic beef to order, and insisting on real Cheez Whiz. (Imagine!) The result is a superbly tender, flavorful sandwich — as long as you keep it simple. The pizza and chicken steaks were big disappointments.

Chick's Deli of Cherry Hill, 906 Township Lane, Cherry Hill, 856-429-2022. I have fond memories of savoring chicken steaks from this back-alley find off Route 70 when I worked in Jersey years ago. But it was the beef steak this time that moved me, a perfect blend of flowing cheese, sweet onions and tender meat.

White House Sub Shop, Mississippi and Arctic Avenues, Atlantic City, 609-345-8599. It's the light and crusty roll that makes the steak at this casino-city institution, but it's the sprinkling of sweet-hot pepper relish and the people-watching that give its sandwiches real panache.

Real Pizza, 100 N. Narberth Ave., Narberth, 610-664-1700. This low-key neighborhood pizzeria turned out a very respectable assortment of steaks, the most remarkable being a pizza steak, which gets excellent sauce, a blanket of real pizza cheese, and a smart turn in the oven to crisp the top of the roll.

Donkey's Place, 1223 Haddon Ave., Camden, 856-966-2616. Imitated to great acclaim by an eatery in Manhattan, Donkey's specialty is a fistful of flavor on a kaiser roll, as notable for its generous mop-top of onions as it is for its grease-dripping, salty punch.

Steve's Prince of Steaks, 2711 Comly Rd., Philadelphia, 215-677-8020. This outpost of the Northeast chain, just off Roosevelt Boulevard across from the Nabisco factory, is a stainless-steel food bar trimmed with white-and-black tile and a bulletproof glass viewing window through which you can watch them cook thick-cut pads of steak. The unchopped meat has a minimalist effect (especially with skimpy onions), but is very tasty, with a particularly oozy white American cheese.

Abner's, 38th and Chestnut Streets, Philadelphia, 215-662-0100. The Big Five sports memorabilia leaves little doubt where allegiances lie at this University City institution. The standard steak was too dry and too finely chopped, but the pizza steak was a hit, with sauce and cheese completely melding with the meat.

Grilladelphia, 2330 Aramingo Ave., Philadelphia, 215-739-3801. It gets points for turning one end of an Exxon station convenience store into a serious steakerie. The hollowed-out round rolls are unusual, but the steaks themselves are satisfying fare.

2: If You Had To

Mama's Pizzeria, 426 Belmont Ave., Bala Cynwyd, 610-664-4757. This Main Line darling has a particularly pink and frilly dining room as well as a secret blend of cheeses. Unfortunately, there was way too much of that cheese, overwhelming what would otherwise be some tasty, finely shredded steaks, including the house special, ham-wrapped Cordon Bleu.

Rick's Steaks, Reading Terminal Market, 12th and Arch Streets, Philadelphia; 215-925-4320. Jurors get a 10-percent discount at this Reading Terminal spot, which descends from the Olivieri family that founded Pat's. The quality of the unchopped meat is decent, even if it does get splashed with water and steamed on the grill. But it doesn't get seasoned, and there wasn't enough of it. The onions were pale and flabby even though we asked for them well done.

Lenny's Italian Deli, Ninth and Fayette Streets, Conshohocken, 610-825-4569. This spot was a personal favorite when it was the pork sandwich haven known as Mastrocola's. But the team was shocked and dismayed when the new owner reheated our steak from cooked meat sitting in Tupperware by the grill. We were even more shocked, though, to admit how good it tasted.

Dalessandro's, Henry Avenue and Walnut Lane, Philadelphia, 215-482-5407. The staff couldn't be nicer at this Roxborough classic, but the huge mound of steaming, mass-cooked beef on the griddle has a dryness that soaks the drip out of its generous sandwiches. The flavor just wasn't there.

Jim's Steaks, 431 N. 62d St., Philadelphia, 215-747-6615. The other branches got their black-and-white tile deco style from the original in West Philly, which is a sentimental favorite of my eating team. I'll cede this Jim's some of the best fried onions in town, but even the partisans had to admit the meat was stringy.

Jim's Steaks, 400 South St., Philadelphia, 215-928-1911. A tourist favorite and proponent of the finely chopped hamburger-style steak, this art-deco stop gives a good hot schmear of Whiz, but the meat is a little tough and the sandwich is inconsistent.

1: Save the Calories

Pat's King of Steaks, 1237 E. Passyunk Ave., 215-468-1546. The inventor of the steak is coasting on its reputation, serving up puny, gristle-laced sandwiches at a famous corner that could use a good scrub.

Campo's, 214 Market St., Philadelphia, 215-923-1000. With dried roses hanging in the bathroom, this was by far the quaintest steak shop on the tour. But this spiffy branch of the Gray's Ferry original jarred the eating team with pleasant small talk and a sweet demeanor. Unfortunately, the sandwiches were also far too polite, with parsimonious portions and sterile flavors.

Ishkabibble's Eatery, 337 South St., Philadelphia, 215-923-4337. This pink-and-black South Street take-out window is famous for its chicken steaks, but we don't know why. The precooked breasts were smashed into such dry fibers it was like eating chicken drywall.

Larry's Famous Steaks, 2459 N. 54th St., Philadelphia, 215-879-1776. The home of the five-pound "belly filler" was a bust. Not only was there too much food piled onto a single, flabby roll, but it was unseasoned and of low quality.

Ms. Tootsie's Soul Food Cafe

The pleasant South Street bistro serves soul food simply prepared, with a respect for tradition.

Dawn Staley is at the next table, doing some serious damage to the fried chicken wings. Her friends are dishing gossip, but the WNBA star and Temple women's basketball coach is quiet and focused, stripping those teeny bones clean as she would a flat-footed opponent trying to dribble the ball past her.

They don't stand a chance. Not with Ms. Tootsie's secret recipe working its moves tonight.

Where have I heard this secret-recipe fried chicken thing before? KeVen (Kuh-VON) Parker, owner of this sharp little South Street cafe, does a stellar job of protecting his mom's mystery formulas from nosy folks. Whether it is the fruity sweet tea or the rich, peppery gravy that smothers those country-fried turkey chops like a blanket, mum's the word.

VERY GOOD

1314 South St.
Philadelphia
(215) 731-9045

NEIGHBORHOOD
South Street

CUISINE
Soul Food

"Even I don't know what's in her gravies," Parker admits later, as I push for details over the phone.

Still, I suspect there is more to Joyce "Tootsie" Parker's kitchen magic than a teaspoon of this or a pinch of that. The dishes that made hers the Sunday supper table of choice for so many of KeVen's childhood friends have transcended time and landed quite nicely in this pleasant bistro.

Ms. Tootsie's Soul Food Cafe, open now for two years, stands out like a beacon on an otherwise scrappy block on South Street between Broad and 13th. On balmy nights, the windows are open beneath a crisp black awning, and the busy 45-seat dining room, clad with brushed-copper walls, wavy-backed banquettes, and dangling bundles of fabric, emits a mellow Marvin Gaye vibe to the weekend crowds that wait for tables.

Mellow unless you're there during one of the occasional spoken-word performances. The artist we saw strode around the room belting out poetry so loudly that the chairs (and a few customers) seemed to rattle.

The dining room staff is charming, but nobody's in a hurry. You may have to listen to a few verses before you get much more than sweet corn bread muffins and airy biscuits to nibble. Most of the time, however, it's worth the wait.

There has been an upsurge for soul food in Philadelphia, lately, with a few black-owned restaurants finally trying to fill the void in Center City's dining scene. Given the area's large, long-established African American community, I'm mystified it hasn't happened sooner.

But most of the efforts have been mixed. The nouveau soul concoctions at Delilah Winder's Bluezette in Old City have been less of a draw than the power networking scene at the bar; her food stand at the Reading Terminal Market is a better bet.

At the short-lived T. Rodgers, the Southern-style kitchen that replaced Fishmarket near Rittenhouse Square, two very average meals left me cold. And at Savannah at 19th and Callowhill (not black-owned, but soul food-themed), there are still Asian dumplings on the menu from when it was Martini's, and the hit-or-miss soul fusion takes a back seat to chocolate cocktails and throngs of DJ groupies.

Ms. Tootsie's stands out because it doesn't feel the need to reinvent soul food. Dishes are simply prepared with a respect for tradition, good ingredients, and a stylish setting that does them pleasant justice.

Two big fillets of fresh catfish came sealed inside a greaseless buttermilk crust, their juices perfumed with a lime-basil marinade. Fried whiting tasted equally fresh, though milder and flaky inside its simple bread-crumb crust. And the macaroni and cheese was a wonderful testament to Ms. Tootsie's special touch: a certain feel for the six blended cheeses, how thickly each should be shredded, and when each should be added to the mix for maximum effect.

Not that the restaurant is perfect. Much of the food is prepared ahead of time, overseen by Ms. Tootsie herself at her son's commissary in West Philadelphia, where he also runs Cafe 3801 and a catering business. But there are variations, depending on which of their three cooks is behind the stoves in the restaurant's open kitchen.

At one meal cooked under the watch of head chef Sheila Goslee, I was convinced that Ms. Tootsie's would become the city's new Fried

Or Try These

Here are three more traditional soul food restaurants.

Corinne's Place

1254 Haddon Ave., Camden
(856) 541-4894

This homey pink dining room comes alive at Sunday brunch with one of the best soul food buffets around, thanks in no small part to the cast-iron skillet-fried chicken.

Delilah's Southern Cafe

Reading Terminal Market, 12th and Arch Streets, Philadelphia
(215) 574-0929, and 30th Street Station, 30th and Market Streets, Philadelphia
(215) 243-2440

Before Delilah Winder attempted nouveau soul food at her stylish Bluezette in Old City, these casual food stands set decent local benchmarks for Southern classics.

Big George's Stop-N-Dine

285 S. 52d St., Philadelphia
(215) 748-8200

It's best to visit Sundays when the turnover keeps this vast steam table of soul food specialties fresh.

Chicken Hall of Fame. The chicken comes two ways: boneless strips over salad, zippy with lime and a faint honey sweetness, or classic Southern style, a crackly crisp leg and thigh sparkling with seasoning and gushing juice from inside their microcrust.

Yet on another night, the fried chicken wings were bland and the bone-in breast dry and overcooked. The ribs were tasty, but tough.

One day, the sweet potato pie was special, with a light, lively filling and memorably flaky crust. Another day, the crust was soggy and the custard under-sweetened.

Ms. Tootsie's could also rethink the menu, which, without appetizers, seems limited for a sit-down restaurant. Adding a few might make the wait for entrees seem less pokey.

But when they do arrive, I'm usually grateful for the good, down-home cooking, a blend of family recipes from Virginia jazzed with a dash of Louisiana spice.

The thick turkey chops are one of my favorite dishes, crisp around the edges beneath their rich tan gravy. The tender center-cut pork chops were also good, the gravy slightly darker and stirring with a little more pepper heat. The roasted turkey wings come irresistibly smothered, too. Though they weren't the meatiest I've seen, they were generous in herb-marinated flavor.

All go beautifully with the sides (you get a choice of two) of buttery cabbage, spicy collard greens filled with bits of smoked turkey, or the sweet balm of Ms. Tootsie's caramelized candied yams.

Making the yams is a production in itself, a two-day affair that moves from boiling pot to cast-iron pan to griddle and then steamer. And when they emerge, slick and sweet with buttery pie spice but still firm enough to the bite, they are the epitome of yummy yamdom.

"Oh, I could tell you that recipe," KeVen Parker says finally. "But you'd still never be able to make it like my mom."

■ **MENU HIGHLIGHTS** Fried chicken salad; fried chicken leg entree; fried catfish; fried whiting; smothered turkey chops; smothered pork chops; cheesy macaroni and cheese; caramelized candied yams; rice and gravy.

■ **WINE LIST** BYOB.

■ **IF YOU GO** Dinner menu served Wednesday-Thursday 5-10 p.m.; Friday- Saturday, noon-midnight; Sunday, noon-9 p.m. Entrees, $11-$18.

■ **RESERVATIONS** No reservations.

■ **CREDIT CARDS** No credit cards.

■ **SMOKING** No smoking.

■ **HANDICAP ACCESSIBLE** Wheelchair accessible (ramp available for front door).

■ **PARKING** Parking is $3 after 5 p.m. (with validation) at adjacent lot on the 1300 block of South Street.

Nan

Elegant French-Thai fusion cuisine is prepared
in the fairly priced BYOB with understated decor.

There are times when cooking for a living can seem like playing professional football. If the grueling blasts of pressure-cooker performance don't get you sooner, a litany of nagging injuries will sack you later.

Out go the knees. In gives the back. Puff go the ankles. Woe to the aching, aging chef.

To hear 60-year-old chef Kamol Phutlek speak of his days and nights at Nan, just barely making it in his two-tone sneakers up to the stoves of his delightful restaurant in University City, one gets the image of Broadway Joe Namath limping to the line of scrimmage for one last chance at Super Bowl victory. Phutlek, a veteran of Alouette, the Frog, La Terrasse and La Panetiere, even took two years off from cooking to recover from health problems before opening Nan.

EXCELLENT

4000 Chestnut St.,
Philadelphia
(215) 382-0818

NEIGHBORHOOD
University City

CUISINE
Thai-French

Now, five years later, Phutlek says his shoulder hurts, too. But his cooking remains among the most reliable in town. And to taste his wonderful food is to be reassured that the most skillful cooks, like the best quarterbacks, can overcome the physical challenge with a cunning heart and a wealth of experience.

While so many other chefs struggle to contrive a vision of international fusion cuisine, the Thailand-born Phutlek's menu floats from Asia to Europe and back with the most natural ease, sometimes blending, sometimes residing solely within the borders of one tradition.

A deceptively simple broth of chicken soup washes over the palate in waves, with the familiar warmth of chicken followed by an exotic whiff of lemongrass and kaffir lime, piqued by a lingering tingle of hot Thai pepper.

Velvety soft sweetbreads come sandwiched in layers of puff pastry, buttered with creamy leeks and a rich port wine sauce. Even Italian-style crostini are a delight, crisp rounds of garlic-rubbed toast smeared with goat cheese and then mounded with a fine dice of sweet, ruby-fleshed tomatoes.

In his modest venture, Phutlek has shown that you can put up big points without many of the frills that better-financed restaurateurs often fall back on.

Chef Kamol Phutlek is still plying his trade, and diners are the better for it.

The location, at 40th and Chestnut Streets, is hardly a magnet for the city's trend-seekers. And while the restaurant's non-decor is pleasant enough, its bare-wall and ficus tree theme is serene at best. It is a treat, then, to look up and discover those ornately painted beams that crisscross the ceiling with an essential splash of pastel.

As for the wine list, it is only as good as the bottles you bring. Nan's dining room staff, usually attentive, but also maddeningly prone to the occasional off-night in the warmth department, can usually handle the rest with aplomb.

The restaurant's modest packaging is thankfully reflected in the tariff, with most of the entrees under $20. But there is nothing second-rate about plates that emerge from Phutlek's kitchen, which find dynamic and elegant flavors in quality ingredients, excellent execution, and a unique culinary sensibility.

Phutlek was trained over three decades in Philadelphia's best kitchens, and his cooking is really more French than Thai, but exotic flavors brush the menu at every corner with a knowing touch.

Nicely seared fillets of black sea bass come over a classic butter sauce that has been nudged into the exotic with soy miso and ginger, additions that give the tangy sauce an addictively smoky richness. A generous salmon fillet is topped with a thin brown crust of lemongrass, basil and bread crumbs, a fragrant crisp that complements the lightly creamed red curry.

Seared duck breast is fanned over an irresistible dark gravy, tangy with Chinese black vinegar. Tender rack of lamb, sheared off the bone and sliced like a stack of cards, comes smeared with Dijon mustard and bread crumbs, its meat infused with herby flavor.

Nan's appetizers were equally divine. Strips of chicken sate, slicked in a tan sheen of peanut and coconut milk curry, are so tender that each morsel practically melts on the palate. A special soup of cool cucumber, thickened with a puree of jasmine rice, sour cream and dill, was just impossible to stop eating.

Or Try These

Here are three other Thai restaurants.

East of Amara
700 S. Fifth St., Philadelphia
(215) 627-4200

This bright Queen Village sister to crosstown Amara Cafe serves a mix of deft Thai classics and more unusual specialties such as snowflake soup.

Sukhothai
225 S. 12th St., Philadelphia
(215) 627-2215

A pleasant Thai-inspired eatery in the contemporary space of the former Pamplona is owned by six Hmong brothers all nicknamed Chuck.

Little Thai Singha Market
Reading Terminal Market, Philadelphia (215) 873-0231

This has become one of the best stands in the Reading Terminal Market, where lunchers line up for the fresh BBQ salmon and crab dumplings topped with crunchy garlic.

Arugula and radicchio salad looks as beautifully composed as a pile of freshly fallen leaves, studded with soft dabs of goat cheese. Thai cabbage is a crunchy shred of purple and green and carrot doused in a dressing that prickles (Tabasco), puckers (fish sauce), and teases with a nutty edge of roasted peanuts.

More authentically Thai flavors distinguish the great shrimp and eggplant appetizer, bathing luxuriously soft, slender tubes of Asian eggplant in an intriguingly dark, sour juice racing with fish sauce, lime, garlic and fresh mint.

Phutlek has an uncommon fondness for puff pastry, which makes an ideally crisp package for lemony sauteed mushrooms or tender escargot, nestled inside their pastry dome on a wonderful cushion of minced mushroom duxelles.

Puff plays a leading role in the dessert course, too, that is, if you choose not to opt for the delicious creme brulee. Puff pastry rises beneath slices of caramelized apples from a puddle of intense caramel sauce. It sandwiches rosettes of whipped cream and strawberries. It does the same for kiwi. It simply does the trick without fussing for too many frills, like most of the food at Nan.

The value of this restaurant is balanced so precariously on Phutlek's ability to render these simple elements of good cooking into satisfying and sublime flavors that one cannot help wondering how long the aching chef can carry on.

"Every day is tough, and I'm still looking [for help]," he says wistfully, wishing, perhaps, that he hadn't sent so many proteges off to start their own restaurants. "I just wanted to open something simple, where I don't have to cook. But it didn't work out that way."

It has, on the other hand, worked out quite nicely for us.

■ **MENU HIGHLIGHTS** Lemongrass soup; escargot; shrimp and eggplant appetizer; chicken sate; Thai cabbage; arugula and raddicchio salad; roasted tamarind duck; sea bass with ginger-miso sauce; lemongrass crusted salmon; sweetbreads in puff pastry; creme brulee; apple tart.

■ **WINE LIST** BYOB.

■ **IF YOU GO** Lunch served Monday-Friday 11:30 a.m.-2:30 p.m. Dinner served Monday-Thursday 5-10 p.m., Friday-Saturday 5-11 p.m. Closed Sunday. Dinner entrees, $13.95-$19.95.

■ **RESERVATIONS** Recommended.

■ **CREDIT CARDS** All major cards but Diners Club and Discover.

■ **SMOKING** Most of the restaurant is nonsmoking.

■ **HANDICAP ACCESSIBLE** Yes.

■ **PARKING** Street parking only.

New Wave Cafe

The neighborhood bar has evolved into a gastronomic surprise.

The notice was printed in big black letters and posted in the bar: "The New Wave has made a deal with Satan . . . We will be able to televise EVERY NFL game this coming season."

It was the kind of notice that might not raise eyebrows for habitues of the New Wave Cafe, a Queen Village corner bar known for its Monday night Quizzo games and pool room, its walls of autographed memorabilia, its fun-lovin' beer-chugging crowd, and, of course, its proximity to the wildly popular but very small fish place across the street. It had become most noted, in its 18 years, as an ideal waiting room for Dmitri's.

But I could read between the lines. I had sniffed a Faustian bargain all evening — although this one was in the kitchen.

VERY GOOD

784 S. Third St.
Philadelphia
(215) 922-8484

NEIGHBORHOOD
Queen Village

CUISINE
New American/Pub

Like the old philosopher who sold his soul to the devil in exchange for knowledge and power, like the crossroads bluesman who traded long life for musical immortality, this previously undistinguished eatery has been in the unlikely throes of a gourmet surge.

While more than half the bar sipped away obliviously beneath the blare of televisions broadcasting the Flyers, diners at the black Formica tables nearby were indulging visions of culinary grandeur.

Puff pastry orbs filled with escargots, levitating over Pernod-scented butter. Tenderloin of venison fanned beneath rich bordelaise sauce and earthy slices of fresh porcini. Housemade pate. Salmon tartare. Heavenly cushions of homemade gnocchi filled with basil. Roasted halibut in truffle essence. Demiglace everywhere. Chive blossoms rising from silky mashed potatoes like alien beings.

It was not Beelzebub, of course, searing away behind the New Wave's range, whipping peaked meringues and rendering duck. But a circumstance of odd serendipity had brought to the modest pub one of my favorite chefs in town. I had been chasing Ben McNamara for a couple of years, embarking on a review of his cozy little restaurant in the Northeast, Isabella's, only to see the gem close before I could make a reservation for my final meal. It was a brave attempt to bring high-end dining to less-than-haute Castor Avenue, but doomed in the end.

How long would such a skilled chef lay over at the New Wave Cafe? It was a transition period, I cynically assumed, during which McNamara would plot the reappearance of Isabella's, and New Wave owners Nate Ross, Sam and Al Lynagh — all childhood friends of McNamara's — would be given a delicious glimpse of the other side, even if it were brief. (Those Satan deals always have a catch.)

But that was two-and-a-half years ago. And McNamara shows no signs of discontent. In fact, the British-trained vet of Monte Carlo Living Room, the Garden, and Dickens Inn says he is happy to shirk the hassles of restaurant ownership and focus on food and the blessing of spare time to be with his young children.

The result is that he and his crew have turned this bar on its ear, making it easily one of the best gourmet bargains around, with virtually an entire menu of entrees transplanted from Isabella's for less than $20 each.

Puff pastry orbs filled with escargots.

Crisp roasted duck comes with a shine of rosemary demiglace kissed with cassis. Sauteed risotto cakes studded with sweet lump crab pose against a sunset of saffron butter. Perfectly seared ahi tuna is crusted with coriander then laid over frothy wasabi sauce. A generous cut of prime rib-eye steak is rubbed with homemade chipotle spice, then grilled, its earthy but evenly spiced juices tempered by the ivory richness of Gorgonzola cream.

While much has been duplicated from McNamara's previous venture, the New Wave is no Isabella's Part Two. The pleasant servers are often understaffed, but well-versed on the menu. And you may be staring at exposed midriffs and jeans instead of crisp black and white, as they dress down to the bar ambience.

At moments like these, the contrast between McNamara's sophisticated cookery and the New Wave's limitations as a pub seems downright bizarre. But more often, the coexistence is a gas, a triumph for the neighborhood joint. The chef, whose style is an inspired modern blend of classic French and Italian flavors, has even shown that his kitchen can turn out the archetypes of bar food with the best, a greater test of any real cook's mettle than searing off foie gras.

The "Arkansas" chicken wings are simply awesome, meaty and extra large, impossible to resist. Their crisp skins are mopped with a chipotle barbecue sauce that is equal parts tang, smoke and snap. A creamy side of real Gorgonzola seduced even the most reluctant wing lover in for a dip. McNamara's skillet of molten aged provolone, filled with mushrooms, sun-dried peppers and basil, with a side of garlic toasts for scooping, is a big improvement on nacho cheese and chips.

McNamara's crusty chicken cutlet sandwich, breaded in panko crumbs and romano cheese, then topped with broccoli rabe, was an authentic echo of South Philly credited to his wife, Marisa. And his hearth-warming shepherd's pie, a recipe dating to his long stint at Dickens Inn, was a superbly moist mince of tomatoey ground beef snug beneath a buttery blanket of mashed potatoes.

McNamara's desserts were pristine also, recalling the fabulous tray of confections at Isabella's, where the former baker's apprentice showed his talents.

A wedge of flourless chocolate cake melts on the tongue like rich lava. Cheesecake seems simple enough, but spreads with an uncommon richness, the languid stroll of heavy cream taking its own sweet time. Profiterole pastry puffs are crisp, delicate shells for pastry cream. And Key lime tart is a wonder, a low-rise snap of citrus custard topped with cumulus clouds of fluted meringue. Drops of caramel cling to their bending browned peaks like dew.

I don't suppose the devil could cook this sweetly if he tried. But I'm not pushing our good luck. Let's just hope this is one bargain he doesn't cash in on for a very long time.

Or Try These

Here are three other bars with great food.

Standard Tap

901 N. Second St., Philadelphia
(215) 238-0630
The hip neighborhood bar is redefined in Northern Liberties where this historic tavern serves gutsy yet sophisticated rustic fare with great seasonal ingredients and one of the best local beer selections in town.

Magazine

2029 Walnut St., Philadelphia
(215) 567-5000
Bar Noir impresario David Carroll has crafted a tiny hotspot that feels like an updated Victorian parlor with a Bohemian edge, where the tony crowd comes for Peter Dunmire's seasonal bistro fare.

Monk's Cafe

264 S. 16th St., Philadelphia
(215) 545-7005
The city's best Belgian beer bar also serves great mussels, burgers, and a surprisingly good brunch.

■ **MENU HIGHLIGHTS** Escargot with Pernod butter sauce; risotto crab cakes; Arkansas wings with Gorgonzola dip; chicken cutlet sandwich; duck breast with cassis demiglace; blackened rib-eye with Gorgonzola sauce; homemade gnocchi; venison in porcini red wine sauce special; tuna special; roasted halibut with white truffle beurre blanc special; shepherd's pie special; Key lime tart; cheesecake.

■ **WINE LIST** The list is tiny enough to fit on a table tent, but filled with excellent and interesting wines virtually all under $40, ideal for the informal spirit of this ambitious but casual cafe. A very good selection of beers may be a better bet for the wings.

■ **IF YOU GO** Dinner served Monday-Tuesday 5 p.m.-midnight, Wednesday-Saturday 5 p.m.-1 a.m., Sunday 1-11 p.m. Dinner entrees $13- $24.

■ **RESERVATIONS** Not accepted.

■ **CREDIT CARDS** All major cards but Diners Club and Discover.

■ **SMOKING** Dining room is meant to be nonsmoking, but smoke filters over from the nearby bar.

■ **HANDICAP ACCESSIBLE** No. There is one step at the entrance and the bathrooms are not handicapped-equipped.

■ **PARKING** Street parking only.

Opus 251

A Rittenhouse Square mansion and secret garden offers sophisticated contemporary cuisine.

 ou can almost see the stars when the sky is clear above Opus 251, the hideaway restaurant in the Philadelphia Art Alliance. And that's some trick in the heart of the city.

On one of those hot nights that blur the season from late summer into early fall, the tall French doors at the back of the grand Italianate mansion have swung open into the walled garden.

The dining room indoors is lovely, an olive-tinted parlor ringed by a mural of an Asian summer scene — mountains, trees and exotic birds hovering in a bronze mist near the ceiling. And the paprika-colored bar, an intimate cubby favored for trysts and afternoon martinis, is as enticing as ever.

But it is to the garden that diners have come this sultry evening.

VERY GOOD

The Philadelphia Art Alliance, 251 S. 18th St. Philadelphia (215) 735-6787

NEIGHBORHOOD
Rittenhouse Square

CUISINE
New American

Beneath broad white umbrellas, a patrician, silver-haired crowd is nibbling foie gras and stuffed quail and speaking French as the cool breeze and jazz soundtrack soften the city's edge. The tony cafes of Rittenhouse Square may be just one block north, but this tranquil garden seems miles from the brash show-and-tell of those chic boites.

Opus 251 has the air of a private eating club (which is what this space used to be, from Prohibition — when its speakeasy was known for great drinks — until shortly before Opus opened in 1997). And that cloistered quality has always been an asset to the restaurant.

An even greater asset has been its impressive streak of kitchen talent, beginning with Alfonso Contrisciani, whose famously verbose menus only began to convey the complexity of his creative cooking. Despite his departure three years ago, Contrisciani remains a partner with owners Bryan and Lydia Marton. But he is just one of the fine chefs to have run the kitchen here, a short list that includes Guy Sileo, who coincidentally was convicted of murdering his business partner at the General Wayne Inn in Lower Merion the day of my first review meal at Opus.

That might explain the distracted state of the staff that evening and the interminable wait between courses.

But newly arrived chef Anthony Bonett, a former Navy weather-

A trio of unusual sorbets: beet, cucumber-ginger, and Thai basil pepper.

man and veteran of the Four Seasons Hotel and the now-shuttered Tony Clark's, seemed more than focused on bringing excitement back to the food. His plates are less baroque than Contrisciani's creations. But he has the same commitment to high-quality ingredients and an obsession with seasonality. And these dishes have a lighter touch, a spontaneity, and a focus on natural flavors that I truly enjoyed.

On a visit last spring, I savored succulent chunks of lobster, cooled and mounded with sweet nibs of white corn and mashed avocado. Seared fillets of branzino sat atop a package of refreshing eggplant caviar wrapped in crisped eggplant sheets, then ringed by an ethereal sauce of pureed asparagus. Sweet seasonal strawberries infused the molten heart of an awesome white chocolate bread pudding.

On the late-summer menu last year, a trio of savory sorbets was startlingly pleasant: a crimson scoop of beet sorbet that tasted like wonderful frozen borscht; an icy quenelle of pureed cucumber that sparkled with ginger spice; and a pinkish scoop of bell pepper tweaked with minty Thai basil. The same cucumber ginger puree, in cool liquid form, made a delightful warm-weather soup with a surprise — raw oysters — hidden inside.

Heirloom tomatoes — unusual antique varieties cultivated for flavor rather than shelf life — were everywhere on Opus' August menus. Big reds and yellows were sliced lusciously thick and layered between mozzarella. Green and yellow tiger-striped ones were an incredibly fresh garnish alongside a perfect rib-eye steak. Pureed into gazpacho served with a single seared scallop in the center, heirlooms gave the soup a viney, high-strung vibrance.

Other than the sporadic service, which can be charming and attentive (with staff well-versed on the excellent wine list), my biggest complaint about Opus 251 is the runaway prices, which often seem $5 or $10 too high, although the three-course $21 lunch menu is a pretty fair deal.

The vegetarian entree may be delicious, but I have a hard time paying $24 for a stuffed tomato. In other cases, the kitchen simply didn't deliver.

The squab, for example, was underwhelming at $36. The sweetbread appetizer was also a letdown, the meat oversalted and chewy. Other tasty dishes, such as the bouillabaisse, seemed skimpy for the price.

But so often, Bonett's food hit the mark with pristine flavors and light but satisfying contemporary presentations. Crisp seared fillets of branzino were perfect, stacked in a wide bowl over golden beets and cockles bathed in cucumber broth, then scattered with fine ribbons of tart green sorrel. Roasted beets were used in a great hamachi appetizer in which buttery raw yellowtail, thickly sliced like sashimi, was laid against the firm chunks of sweet root, an intriguing contrast of earth and sea.

The duet of quails fared better than the squab, with one bird grilled and the other stuffed with truffled chicken mousse and whole morels. More traditional meats were also deftly rendered. The thick veal chop was excellent, encircled by red pepper puree, artichokes and baby squash. The rack of lamb was a classic done right, sided with dollops of red and yellow tomato compote.

Dessert brought a few missteps — a runny creme brulee and a muffin-like cherry cake. But there were also winners — a caramelized peach tart, a molten chocolate cake with homemade pistachio ice cream, and the signature Lantern, a cookie tube with a candle inside illuminating its heart of chocolate parfait. And that wonderful bread

Or Try These

Here are three other city restaurants with outdoor dining.

Azafran

617 S. Third St., Philadelphia
(215) 928-4019

One of the city's first to serve creative Latino cooking, this saffron-colored BYOB has a charming garden patio out back.

Jamaican Jerk Hut

1436 South St., Philadelphia
(215) 545-8644

With steel drums and tall grass hedging in from the vacant lot next door, this South Street Jamaican has a shaded back patio (and the jerk sauce) to conjure a convincing Caribbean mood.

Effie's

1127 Pine St., Philadelphia
(215) 592-8333

Classic Greek homefoods can be had in the lovely brick patio behind Effie's townhouse.

pudding.

But I was particularly fond of the fruit soup. The clear broth of pureed kiwi and melon was just thick enough to suspend a constellation of blackberries and raspberries in the bowl. Set around a scoop of coconut sorbet that slowly melted in the sultry heat, it looked like the Milky Way surrounded by some of the season's ripest stars.

■ **MENU HIGHLIGHTS** Tuna ceviche; marinated mozzarella and heirloom tomato salad; lobster salad; hamachi carpaccio; savory sorbets; cucumber ginger soup with oysters; grilled rib-eye steak; veal chop with artichokes; rack of lamb; seared branzino; white chocolate bread pudding; chilled fruit soup.

■ **WINE LIST** An excellent international selection of about 100 wines, ranging from prestige Bordeaux to lesser-known values. Some high-quality bottles for less than $50 include a balanced white Pouilly-Fuissé from Burgundy ($44), and an intriguing Rhône-style red from California's Qupé ($38). Help with wine selection was one of the staff's strong suits.

■ **IF YOU GO** Lunch served Tuesday-Friday 11:30 a.m.-2:30 p.m. Dinner served Tuesday-Thursday 5-10 p.m.; Friday-Saturday 5-11 p.m.; Sunday 5-9 p.m. Sunday brunch served 11 a.m.-2:30 p.m. Entrees: lunch, $12-$16, or three-course prix fixe for $21; dinner, $24-$36.

■ **RESERVATIONS** Recommended.

■ **CREDIT CARDS** All major cards but Discover.

■ **SMOKING** Smoking in the bar and garden only.

■ **HANDICAP ACCESSIBLE** Restaurant is wheelchair accessible through the garden.

■ **PARKING** For Art Alliance members, 10 percent parking discount at the 1728 Rittenhouse St. garage.

¡Pasion!

Tropical ambience and Chef Guillermo Pernot's ingenious ceviches are highlights of the Nuevo Latino gem.

The Sorcerer of Ceviche has been busy lately, riding his mojo magic at ¡Pasion! to well-earned accolades and new opportunities.

Among the best of these for Argentina-born Guillermo Pernot were two recent James Beard Awards naming him the region's best chef and lauding his beautiful book, ¡Ceviche! (written with Aliza Green), in which we learn how to show off at home with surf clams, Tahitian abalone, and pickled lamb's tongue.

The most disappointing, I suspect, have been Pernot's adventures as a consultant and minority partner in other restaurants. His short-lived help in launching Cuba Libre, in Old City, and his nearly-as-brief duty overseeing the food at Trust, at 13th and Sansom Streets, threatened to tarnish his peerless reputation.

SUPERIOR

211 S. 15th St.
Philadelphia
(215) 875-9895

NEIGHBORHOOD
Rittenhouse Square

CUISINE
Nuevo Latino

So what a thrill it is to discover that those distractions have had little, if any, effect on ¡Pasion! This nearly four-year-old gem has not only doubled in size with a gorgeous addition accented by ornate wooden screens, Moorish tile, and a sky-blue cathedral ceiling. It has also become one of our finest restaurants.

Much of the attention, of course, goes to Pernot, whose early explorations of pan-Latin cuisine have matured into a sophisticated mastery of the exotic flavor palette. Through the prism of his ceviches — complex jewel boxes of cured seafood that are constructed with everything from salsas to fruit and squid ink — he has shown a rare combination of virtuosic technique and boundless imagination that make him one of the region's most exciting culinary creators.

The evolution of ¡Pasion!, though, is also a credit to Pernot's partner, Michael Dombkoski (who has no stake in Trust or Cuba Libre). Dombkoski oversaw the addition, built the great Latin-focused wine cellar, and runs one of the smoothest dining rooms around.

The servers effortlessly explain the kitchen's novel cuisine and maintain the tables with grace and attention to detail without ever getting in the way. And talk about team spirit.

"I've eaten here 22 times on my off nights," one of our waiters gushed.

I can understand why. Few local chefs cook with the colorful exuberance of Pernot, who has expanded on the lessons drawn from the constraints of his tiny ceviches — the architectural challenge of building contrasts with textures and flavors — and translated them to the rest of the menu.

His camarones-and-pollo appetizer, for example, arrives in a baby coconut shell cleverly branded with the restaurant's logo and brimming with sublime large shrimp and strips of chicken glazed with a Caribbean jerk sauce that swirls with clove and ginger. Dig a little deeper to discover a surprise at the bottom: a tangy sweet pudding of rice moistened with coconut milk and studded with raisins and slivered almonds. Scrape the shell, and strips of milky coconut meat fall into the mix.

The camarones-and-pollo appetizer.

With his arepa-tasting, Pernot uses a staple of peasant cooking as the canvas for a gastronomic fantasy. Three earthy little corn cakes presented on a sleek oval plate are each topped with a startlingly different flavor: foie gras streaked with cinnamon-edged chocolate; ground chicken picadillo cloaked in cilantro cream; and salty cod stew sparkling with Peruvian rocoto peppers.

For Pernot, spice comes in myriad shades. It doesn't just burn, but teases, swells and fades, giving shape to a spectrum of other flavors that shimmy through his food. Fabulous fried squid have a cornmeal crust that bewitches with cuminy "Calypso spice," only to be quenched by a bed of salad doused with sugarcane-lime vinaigrette. The flame is reignited at the bottom of the plate by pears steeped in wine with habaneros and star anise. Powdered chipotle pepper lends a whisper of smoke to los puerquitos, an amazing Antillean pork stew layered with nutmeg, sherry and molasses. A Mexican adobo paste gives the massive grain-fed veal chop served with red beans a powerful rustic punch.

Spices also play a key role in Pernot's stunning ceviches, which have only gotten better over the years. Habanero-sparked sturgeon tangles with tiny cubes of sweet pineapple laced with ribbons of basil. Citrus-cured sea scallops bathe in a blackened tomatillo salsa whose tartness is cut by truffle oil. Butter-poached lobster tails lathered with passion fruit mojo are spiked with toothpicks of deep-fried yucca. Raw red snapper and sweet beets are topped with slivers of pickled lamb's tongue so awesomely tangy that my dining companions and I abandoned our initial squeamishness and fought over the last one.

Or Try These

Here are three other restaurants serving Nuevo Latino cuisine.

Alma de Cuba

1623 Walnut St., Philadelphia
(215) 988-1799

Douglas Rodriguez, the nation's godfather of Nuevo Latino cuisine, has paired with Stephen Starr to bring his culinary fireworks to this chic and dark Walnut Street space.

Azafran

617 S. Third St., Philadelphia
(215) 928-4019

This saffron-colored BYOB was among the city's first to serve creative Latino cooking, and has continued to improve under new chef Scott McLeod.

Cibucan

2025 Sansom St., Philadelphia.
(215) 231-9895

The tapas here are inconsistent, but this beautiful restaurant now has a liquor license and an upstairs bar worth a late-night mojito and snack.

It would be easy for a chef to sit back after a lamb's tongue like that. Instead, Pernot fires up the grill and pushes the flavors of his entrees to the limit. His hickory-smoked rib-eye steak triggers a voracious feasting reflex the moment it hits my tongue. The grilled skirt steak is equally addictive, permeated with the limey cilantro tang of chimichurri, an Argentine herb sauce. The tall crab cake is packed with meat but really got interesting when I tasted the sauce, a fiery puree of amarillo peppers and smoked fish stock that heightens the crab's sweetness.

Pernot's creativity spills over into dessert as well. The flan is wrapped a la Cristo in a billowing phyllo sheet that shatters into the creamy custard inside with the stroke of a fork. The crepes are filled with dried blueberries and caramel made from the milk of Lancaster County goats.

Empanadas are stuffed with bitter Cuban chocolate and bananas. A tower of dulce de leche mousse wrapped in a sleeve of chocolate is served alongside tiny roasted apples. The bunuelo beignets explode on first bite with molten chocolate flavored with rum and raisins.

But if there is a dessert that speaks to the chef's genius, it's la torre, a boxy caramel tuile tower filled with a lime-themed parfait — Ksey lime custard beneath Persian lime sorbet beneath a puff of whipped cream. Knock it over and crack it open. You'll discover an old-fashioned key lime pie deconstructed and reenvisioned for Pernot's nuevo world order.

■ **MENU HIGHLIGHTS** Ceviches: scallops with tomatillo truffle sauce; habanero-cured sturgeon with pineapple; red snapper with pickled lamb's tongue; lobster with passion fruit mojo. Appetizers: arepa-tasting; camarones y pollo; scallop gratin; guacamole Cubano; calypso calamar. Entrees: los puerquitos; smoked rib-eye steak; adobo-rubbed veal chop; baby goat; la torre; bunuelos; dulce de leche.

■ **WINE LIST** This wine list is among the city's most fascinating and focused. It concentrates on Latin American and Spanish bottles (with a few Californians) at reasonable prices, whether a rustic Argentine malbec from Lurton ($30), a big Spanish Rioja such as the Muga Reserva ($54), or a big-ticket bottle from the small reserve list. Also, don't miss the creative Latin cocktails, such as the passion fruit caipirinha.

■ **IF YOU GO** Dinner is served Monday-Thursday, 5-10 p.m.; Friday-Saturday, 5-11 p.m.; Sunday 5-9 p.m. Entrees: $18-$29.

■ **RESERVATIONS** Strongly recommended.

■ **CREDIT CARDS** All major cards accepted.

■ **SMOKING** Permitted at the bar only.

■ **HANDICAP ACCESSIBLE** Yes.

■ **PARKING** 20 percent discount for validated parking at the Parkway lot at 15th and Chancellor Streets (parking averages about $14.40)

Penang

The Malaysian chain from New York has the most stylish dining room in Chinatown, great service, and authentic Southeast Asian fare.

From the moment we approach the iron facade of Penang, just steps from the ornate, pagoda-crowned arch over 10th Street, it's clear we are about to enter a world unlike any other in Chinatown.

The cafe windows of this Malaysian outpost, an emissary from a budding chain of New York restaurants, frame steel-covered woks shaped into tall tables. Opened onto the street, it has a striking iron smile, welded at the seams in a postindustrial fantasy.

On this hot summer day, two young women spoon into a tall pile of icy confection shaved from a hefty solid block that whirls beside the cash register. Behind them, giant copper coils dangle from the ceiling. Brushed steel sheets weave a basket-like wall sculpture, echoing the metal awnings over the open kitchen, where a battery of chefs work away at flaming woks.

VERY GOOD

117 N. 10th St.,
Philadelphia
(215) 413-2531

NEIGHBORHOOD
Chinatown

CUISINE
Malaysian

But what emerges through the open kitchen window is what makes Penang so intriguing.

The cuisine of Malaysia, the part-peninsular, part-island nation that arcs into the South China Sea below Indochina, is a prism that binds the lights of Chinese, Indian and Thai cooking into its own vibrant beam. Fragrant coconut milk curries, chili-spiced sweet and sour sauces, exotic fruits, brimming soup casseroles, and stir-fries transform fresh products into dishes that are at once familiar and curiously exciting.

There is some of the best satay I've tasted, moist grilled skewers of curried chicken or beef topped with a tamarind peanut sauce so good I could spoon it straight from the dish. There are steamy, soft spring rolls filled with crunchy shredded jicama. And there is an endless selection of seafood swimming in the blue tanks along the wall, waiting to be steamed or fried upon demand, and then sent through the dining room in an aromatic cloud of ginger and lemongrass.

Watch as a chef whips a gauzy sheet of dough above his head, as if twirling a gossamer pizza. Two turns on the griddle, and it comes to the table as Indian roti canai, a bundled crispy veil of hot pancake, ready for dips in the dish of coconut chicken curry, a brothy elixir stewed with coriander, cinnamon and anise.

There are also, in cautionary red ink, less familiar options — fish-head casseroles, sweet and spicy treated duck web, and crispy pork intestines — that are almost too tempting not to try, although I managed to miss a few.

Even so, it seems to be adventure at minimal risk. More than once, Penang's efficient and outgoing staff stopped at our table to ask if we didn't like our dish, and whether we would prefer something else. Sometimes the dining room was so loud, I wasn't sure the server had heard our order right in the first place. But they were determined to get it right.

The crispy, lacquered calamari was one sweet and funky dish that tested my tastebuds' goodwill, although I have, over time, come to regard them as delicious, fishy candy. The chewy duck web and red onion salad was not for me. Still, such authentic flavors are part of what draws me back to Penang, where the chef doesn't dumb down his flavors for the gringos. And now they bring them directly to your Center City house, becoming one of Chinatown's first restaurants to deliver.

One only needs to sip a spoonful of prawn mee soup broth, taste its chili-streaked shrimpy edge and know you're getting the real thing. But the giant menu allows for plenty of safe bets to counter your experimental jaunts — and at prices that make this restaurant a good value.

The menu's range might be a bit too wide for its own good, as some dishes were much better than others — the aromatic steamed crab, for example, was overcooked, and the deep-fried ribs were very fatty.

But our ordering adventures ended with pleasant discovery.

The kitchen turned out a perfectly fluffy omelet full of tender little oysters bound with tapioca. Tender chunks of mango chicken, one tasty but inauthentic dish that's a ringer for adjusting Western palates, nestled with slivers of the yellow fruit in a delicately sweetened and tangy sauce.

Although not for everyone, the pungent Penang rojak fruit salad,

Or Try These

Here are three other Southeast Asian restaurants.

Indonesia
1029 Race St., Philadelphia
(215) 829-1400
The spicy peanut curries and multicourse rice table feasts of Indonesia are deftly served at this Chinatown newcomer.

Rangoon
112 N. Ninth St., Philadelphia
(215) 829-8939
Pungently delicious Burmese cuisine, from spicy crisped lentil cakes to flaky thousand-layer bread, is among the most flavorful menus in Chinatown.

New Phnom Penh
2301 S. Seventh St., Philadelphia (215) 389-2122
The hardscabble hub of South Philly's Cambodian community has this tasty corner spot as an authentic reminder of home. Try the cubed beef with lime.

which actually comes with squid mixed in and a tar-black sticky sauce, had such complexity, I could not resist trying it again and again as waves of surprising flavors surged across my mouth. A fruity burst of sweet mango. A smothering shadow of earthy soy. A salty fermented twist of dried shrimp paste. A snap of chili spice that fizzled through the next bite.

To prevent palate fatigue, I always find it a good idea to order a few blander flavors as ballast. The Malaysian version of pad Thai, chow kueh teow, was excellent for this purpose, a tumble of springy flat noodles stir-fried with soy, shrimp, sprouts and egg that is less assertive than its Thai cousin. Mee siam fried noodles were equally delicious, with a peanutty brown chili sauce full of lemongrass. Stir-fried watercress is always a wonderful vegetarian side.

Rice dishes like nasi lemak were also quite good. Its grains were sweetened with coconut milk and perfumed with screw pine leaves. Chunks of curried beef rendang, also nice with rice, were stewed soft in coconut milk that released a chorus of gentle spices with each bite.

If there is a strong point for Penang, its whole steamed fish are hard to beat. We devoured an entire striped bass whose luxurious meat was infused with lemongrass and ginger, then flattered by a garlicky hot bean sauce. And cheng-lai stingray was also a find, trapping the spicy sweetness of tamarind, five-spice and mango sauce between the long ruffles of the skate wing's flesh.

Desserts, on the other hand, were somewhat limited. The best two are a rich banana ice cream and a grilled roti pancake wrapped around a sweet butter and peanut mixture. But there were also two mountainous shaved-ice desserts to consider, both of which sport colored syrups, jellied candies and red beans in the mix.

These were anticlimactic endings, perhaps. But they could not dampen the spirit of adventure I felt. It was a sense of excitement Penang has kindled since its welded smile opened on Chinatown's streets.

■ **MENU HIGHLIGHTS** Roti canai Indian pancakes; satay chicken; baby oyster omelet; poh piah Malaysian spring roll; watercress with preserved bean curd; mee siam fried noodles; nasi lemak coconut rice; mango chicken; curried beef rendang; whole steamed striped bass in hot bean sauce; cheng-lai stingray; coconut prawns; peanut pancake.

■ **WINE LIST** A small selection of beers is available.

■ **IF YOU GO** Whole menu served every day 11:30 a.m.-1 a.m.

■ **RESERVATIONS** Accepted for parties of 5 or more.

■ **CREDIT CARDS** Cash only.

■ **SMOKING** There is a nonsmoking section.

■ **HANDICAP ACCESSIBLE** Yes.

■ **PARKING** Street parking only.

Pif

The charming little BYOB serves French bistro fare in the Italian Market.

W hat chef hasn't dreamed of opening a little place where a new menu can be created every day, inspired by a morning stroll through the local market?

Ah, to be moved to cook by an unexpected glimpse of petite turnips or a serendipitous bundle of rare dandelion greens. To hem and haw with your butcher over whether to serve venison or game birds that night. To peruse your cheesemonger's Alsatian Muensters and Reblochons for the nicest, ripest one.

The notion is just a fantasy for most chefs, who are far too busy to leave their kitchens and often are locked into set menus with only a few specials to express their moods.

VERY GOOD

1009 S. Eighth St.
Philadelphia
(215) 625-2923

NEIGHBORHOOD
Italian Market

CUISINE
French Bistro

But David Ansill is proving at his bright, new Pif that cooking in the heart of the Italian Market can translate this romance into reality. His small blackboard menu of French bistro fare changes daily depending on his shopping whims, and the food is not simply fresh and seasonal, but spontaneous and surprising.

Constrained by time from overcomplicating things, he turns out plates with just the right balance of deft technique and simplicity that puts the focus on good ingredients.

One night, beautiful chanterelle mushrooms from Michael Anastasio's produce warehouse on Christian Street infuse a rich cream sauce served over chicken breasts. Freshly roasted chestnuts, another find, add subtle sweetness to the veal and cognac stuffing inside two quail whose juices hint of smoky bacon.

Another night, a stop at Sonny D'Angelo's butcher shop on Ninth Street has provided the menu with two more gems. The first is sweet garlic sausage served with cabbage sauteed with onions and apples in bacon fat. The other is tender medallions of venison, rich and ruby red, with a giblety hint of game that Ansill massages with a marinade of sherry vinegar and juniper berries.

Opened a year ago July with the help of his French wife, Catherine Gilbert-Ansill, this plainly decorated nook has only 38 seats, a size that lends itself to a freewheeling, flexible format. But Ansill's market-bas-

David Ansill and his wife and partner, Catherine Gilbert-Ansill, can create a new menu daily, thanks to Pif's proximity to the Italian Market.

ket cuisine is also in keeping with the spirit of Pif, the name of a French comic book character and a word that is also French slang for "improvisation."

Pulling it off as well as Ansill does is harder than it looks.

To begin with, who would risk opening a French restaurant in South Philadelphia, where the restaurants are typecast as Italian? Judging from the surprising number of reservations from area code 610, it's a gamble that seems to be paying off.

Perhaps Pif only exemplifies that the Washington Avenue corridor a block away has become far more diverse than its red-gravy-and-meatballs reputation would suggest. There are Asian and Mexican kitchens thriving there now, and Pif — which replaced a Vietnamese noodle house — adds yet more spice to the neighborhood's evolving international stew.

Spur-of-the-moment menus can be so challenging that some inconsistency is inevitable. There were no complete misses, but there were a few less inspired creations. The bouillabaisse was skimpy at $23, considering that most of Pif's entrees are around $18, although lately, to my chagrin, prices have been creeping higher. The coins of poached foie gras terrine were also underwhelming for $12.50.

And while a few desserts — a rich chocolate galette and a low-rise rustic apple tarte — were worth craving, that course seemed most problematic. The creme brulee was runny. The chocolate pot de creme was lumpy. The crepes themselves were excellent, but their fillings — blueberries with honey one night, chestnut cream another — were unevenly spread throughout.

Likewise, Pif is still coming to grips with the limitations of its casual esprit. The servers often seemed slow and overwhelmed, though they more than made up for it with the sort of quirky, personable repartee that makes a neighborhood bistro a place where real personalities — and good, honest food — can transform an ordinary space into something special.

Still, we had to wait so long to place our orders that when the appetizers finally arrived, my usually dainty guest devoured the gnarled head of roasted garlic on her plate of escargots as if it were melba toast. (Though after sampling those tender snails, nestled among the sweet whole garlic cloves in Pernod and almond-scented gravy, I must admit that I'd have devoured them all, too, even if they'd been delivered promptly.)

An appetizer of crepinettes was among the most uncommon and delicious items, lightly breaded patties of veal sausage, sauteed in duck fat, that gushed ambrosial juices brushed with tarragon.

Simple salads, such as the beets with Roquefort cheese and the baby spinach with sherry vinaigrette that came piled high with morsels of duck confit, were two more straightforward hits.

Or Try These

Here are three other sophisticated bistros with French-inspired cooking.

Birchrunville Store Cafe

Hollow and Flowing Spring Roads, Birchrunville, Pa. (610) 827-9002

A bucolic country-store-turned-restaurant with seasonal French cooking.

Gilmore's

133 E. Gay St., West Chester, Pa. (610) 431-2800

A charming converted townhouse in downtown West Chester is home to the French cuisine of former Le Bec-Fin chef Peter Gilmore.

Tartine

701 S. Fourth St. (215) 592-4720

A minimalist Queen Village newcomer offers classic Gallic flavors from a veteran French chef.

Some of the best entrees reaffirmed Ansill's knack for mildly tweaking a classic to make it shine. An excellent sirloin steak came topped with a haystack of fried shoestring potatoes mingled with delicate green beans. Sauteed skate was perfectly rendered with vinegared brown butter and fried capers, its wing of feathery white fish fanned over a mound of basmati rice fragrant with precious saffron.

A thick, tender veal chop arrived on a silky puree of acorn squash. It offered a simple yet satisfying contrast in textures and flavors that

I could easily imagine coming together as Ansill made his morning rounds among the Ninth Street merchants: stop at Esposito's for veal, happen across squash at Scott and Judy's produce stand, and return to Pif around the corner to make a chef's — and diners' — dreams come true.

■ **MENU HIGHLIGHTS** Escargots with roasted garlic; spinach salad with duck confit; crepinettes; garlic sausage with cabbage; venison medallions; chestnut-stuffed quail; chicken with chanterelle cream; seared skate; apple tarte; chocolate galette.

■ **WINE LIST** BYOB

■ **IF YOU GO** Dinner is served Tuesday-Sunday, 5:30-10 p.m. Entrees, $16.50-$26.

■ **RESERVATIONS** Strongly recommended.

■ **CREDIT CARDS** All major cards accepted.

■ **SMOKING** No smoking in entire restaurant.

■ **HANDICAP ACCESSIBLE** There is one step at the entrance; rest rooms are not wheelchair accessible.

■ **PARKING** Free street parking and a free municipal lot next door, at Eighth and Kimball Streets.

Porcini

The Italian nook welcomes its patrons with open arms and indulgent flavors.

When the door opens onto Porcini's dining room, it is as if someone has pressed a replay button, and we get to watch the same scene from a favorite food movie over and over again.

Diners squeeze into this closet of a room with their bottles of wine in tow, and one of the Sansone brothers steps out from the kitchen into the middle of the room, spreads his arms impossibly wide, and shouts: "My friend! Where have you been?"

Bear hugs. Back slapping. Two-fisted hand-shaking. Even the occasional kiss.

I saw this exuberant greeting ritual so many times over the course of two dinners, I began to suspect that Steven and David Sansone had hired an extensive cast of extras to pose as friends.

VERY GOOD

2048 Sansom St.,
Philadelphia
(215) 751-1175

NEIGHBORHOOD
Rittenhouse Square

CUISINE
Italian Trattoria

But there's no fakery here. Porcini is the kind of down-to-basics Italian trattoria that everyone would like to call home. Of course, with so many competing distractions lately, I can understand why some returning customers might suddenly seem like long-lost faces. A seemingly endless wave of other no-frills Italian bistros have popped up across the city since Porcini opened in its Sansom Street nook six years ago, from La Baia near Graduate Hospital to Valentino on Pine Street just east of Broad to Hosteria da Elio in Queen Village.

But Porcini easily remains one of the best — and smallest. The low-ceilinged space is as claustrophobic as ever. That it manages to squeeze in even 35 seats is a feat of spatial engineering, although it creates a frightful din when the room is full.

Even so, there is a familial energy to the boisterous little room that is irresistible, especially when the food is this good. Porcini's menu isn't fancy, but it is stocked with affordably priced pastas and other simple entrees that excel with the careful attention to good, home-style flavors.

Self-taught executive chef Steven Sansone draws on the tastes of his childhood near Buffalo, where he grew up in an Italian family with seven kids, as well as his experiences in several restaurants. And his attention to details is keen.

Consider his wonderful bruschette. The toppings are delicious — meaty sauteed mushrooms glazed in a tangy splash of balsamic; thick pesto fragrant with sweet emerald basil; creamy Tuscan white beans; ripe tomatoes filled with herbs and a touch of garlic. But it is those char-grilled slices of olive-oiled bread that I most covet, thick and rustic, but not so crusty you can't bite through.

Char-grilled slices of olive-oiled bread make the Bruschette.

Actually, after devouring two loaves of Sansone's mozzarella alla carrozza, I've come to think of Porcini as one of the best bread restaurants in town. This special dish brings a pan-fried loaf of bread stuffed with mozzarella, then glazed with caper anchovy butter. It is the savory answer to French toast, a lightly battered tube of crusty, oozy, tangy gusto.

Porcini's kitchen let a few disappointments slip. Our veal salvia brought some less-than-tender medallions of meat. And the signature pappardelle, which came topped with porcini mushrooms in a brothy sauce, had a strange tang that overwhelmed the prized earthiness of my favorite fungus. And while the desserts were obviously homemade — domed cassata cake, ricotta-filled cannoli shells imported from Buffalo, and gelatinous flan — none really rose above ordinary.

Usually, though, Sansone's cooking was anything but.

The fritto misto brought a perfectly fried medley of fresh scallops, shrimp and calamari encased in the lightest, most ideally seasoned crust. A slice of salmon Positano was sauced with a simple white wine butter that highlighted the quality of the fish.

The chicken breast was overcooked, but the silky dark balsamic sauce that glazed the plate was so addictive — a wood-aged elixir of sweet and sour — it could have made anything taste good.

The sauces here have crisp, distinct flavors that lend real character to the food, especially Sansone's marinara, a quickly steeped, chunky gravy of plum tomatoes that conveyed the essence of freshness.

It added a sprightly, basil-inflected bounce to the pillowy homemade gnocchi. Served beside the low-rise lasagnette, it added a much-needed tang without drowning out the roasted vegetables and herb-flecked ricotta sandwiched between the noodle sheets. Mixed with a dose of crushed peppers, the marinara took on a piercingly delicious arrabbiata spice over hollow bucatini noodles. Softened with a little cream, it bloomed into an aurora sauce over the marvelous cannelloni, whose delicate handcrafted pasta tubes encased sweet ricotta ribboned with spinach.

There was a similar filling inside the ravioli, but it was the delicate snappy skin of those dumplings that made the dish, glazed with a cream sauce sparked with a touch of pecorino cheese, the southern Italian's salty answer to Parmigiano.

My favorite pasta, though, was the penne rustica, an eggless carbonara whose creamy pecorino glaze took on the added oomph of smoky pancetta. It's just the kind of dish I've come to crave from my local trattoria — a notch more involved and indulgent than I might undertake at home, but perfectly rendered here for $12.50. With a complimentary dose of the Sansones' open-armed ebullience, you can't beat the price.

■ **MENU HIGHLIGHTS** Bruschette; mozzarella alla carrozza; fritto misto; bucatini arrabbiata; cannelloni; ravioli selvatica; gnocchi; penne rustica; chicken with balsamic sauce; salmon Positano; cannoli.

■ **WINE LIST** BYOB

■ **IF YOU GO** Dinner served Monday-Thursday 5-10 p.m., Friday-Saturday 5-11 p.m. Entrees, $11-$22.

■ **RESERVATIONS** Not taken.

■ **CREDIT CARDS** All major cards but Diners Club and Discover.

■ **SMOKING** No.

■ **HANDICAP ACCESSIBLE** No.

■ **PARKING** Validated parking for $1 off at all three Elgin garages on the 2000 and 2100 blocks of Sansom Street.

Or Try These

Here are three other Italian trattorias.

Radicchio

Fourth and Wood Streets, Philadelphia
(215) 627-6850

This contemporary corner spot is one of the best in a wave of affordable new trattorias in Center City, with authentic Italian fare, from great mozzarella starters to excellent whole fish. The biggest drawbacks are the noise and the long lines.

Caffe Casta Diva

227 S. 20th St., Philadelphia
(215) 496-9677

One of the newest of Center City's storefront Italian bistros has transformed an old burrito house into a pretty and tranquil new spot, with homemade pastas (try the spinach fettucine with walnut pesto), interesting salads, and nice veal dishes that are whimsically tied to an opera theme.

L'Angolo

1415 W. Porter St., Philadelphia
(215) 389-4252

Authentic Italian antipasti, grilled veal, and almond-crusted cheesecake are among the highlights at this lovely South Philadelphia corner grotto.

Critical Mass

I am actually paid to dine on amazing food. It's the repayment plan that's the killer.

ood morning, Machine, my friend. I had a big meal last night. It was *work*. Of course. But that does not change our cruel and sweaty ritual.

Beep.

Time? Thirty minutes. I've got to suffer for my risotto.

Beep.

Weight? Punch in 200. It's always better to overestimate.

Beep.

Resistance? There is nothing like Hill Climb No. 2 the morning after. It will vaporize a rich dinner like cognac over an open flame — *fffft*!!

Beep.

The machine flashes and my feet begin to push up and down. They circle upward, over and down. Pushing. Resisting. Rolling forward. My pumping legs strain against the whirring gears and rising track — until suddenly my heart and breath land in sync, panting along in one sustainable burning groove.

Yes! My double-cut veal chop is melting away. Peking duck, be gone! Outta here, dumplings!

A Christmas tree of red lights spreads across the screen. It reveals a seemingly endless climb. A jagged flight of plateaus stepping higher, higher and higher, leaping from one table to the other for as long as I do this job.

'Is that a full-time job?'

I picked up a friend at the airport recently and on the way home her new fiance, a doctor, asked me what it was like to be a restaurant critic.

"Is that, like, a *full-time* job?" he asked incredulously. "I mean, what do you do when you're not eating dinner?"

"Well, I perform neurosurgery when I'm not on deadline."

And I work out. A lot. Gym duty is one titanic asterisk

to the world's greatest job. When I resist it, I am always reminded of the bratty girl in Willie Wonka's chocolate factory who broke the rules and rolled away inflated like a giant blueberry.

Considering that 2,000 dishes or more a year will cross my lips — from the divine (cream soup laced with Scotch and lump crab) to the disgusting (broiled brains of spring goat) — I hesitate to become a frightening footnote to the adage "You are what you eat."

And so I choose to sweat, three times a week for two hours a shot. It won't get me skinny. A pudgy equilibrium would do just fine.

Reviewing restaurants for a living is many things. It is a nightly adventure through the city's public hearths, a pursuit of sensual sociology, and a thrilling sneak peek into the temples of privilege.

It can be an ego-rattling excercise in fielding irate phone calls. (*"Maybe you were just having a bad hair day!"*) And for those of us who choose to work incognito, dinner can also become an elaborate clandestine affair of assumed identities and the requisite gear.

Perhaps I was thinking about good subsidized food when I stepped in this direction nearly a decade ago, a hungry expat in Paris hoping to find steady sustenance as a cooking-school translator.

But after a few years back in the States, wielding my fork and pen for magazines and newspapers from Boston to New Orleans to Philadelphia, I've come to learn that restaurant reviewing is anything but a free meal. As this swelling burn in my legs is beginning to remind me.

My mornings with Gravitron

My first phone message of the new year: *Mr. LaBan, this is Ms. Kelly calling. You seem to get a great joy out of trashing the city. This is a great city and I don't like your supercilious restaurant reviews. Don't dine out if you don't like it. No one's making you go to these restaurants.*

My second phone message of the new year, 13 minutes later: *Mr. LaBan, this is Ms. Kelly calling you again. I'm still furious with you and the way you treat the restaurants in Philadelphia. What the hell do you know? Why don't you go to New York? You will be chewed up and spit out in two sec-*

onds. *Philadelphia needs people who promote the city, not tear it apart. We don't need you here. Just get out.*

Dear Ms. Kelly:

It is hard to be an honest critic. My praise or chiding is never personal. What comes on the plate is what matters most. It's between me and the dish.

Sometimes we tango. And sometimes it steps on my toes.

But when I hit the gym the next morning, I'm already on to the next dance. Would you care to join me?

Meet Gravitron.

Gravitron is an imposing black tower of steel plates, a dungeon master's contraption of pulleys and platforms and bars that will wrench a few pull-ups from even the most reluctant body.

Since it sends the greatest amount of blood to my brain, the Gravitron is where I reflect on my schedule of coming meals and suitable accomplices. Scheduling may sound easy, but it can be as frustrating as a Rubik's Cube.

No dining critic can work alone. With as many as five restaurants shifting and staggering across my calendar at once and as many as 30 separate dishes to sample discreetly at each, I can definitely say that I would not want to.

The prospect of dinner, compliments of The Inquirer, has been tempting enough to attract a fine roster of dining companions — flexible eaters who will come at a moment's notice, who won't flinch at eel and banana blossom soup, who order their meat medium rare, who don't shun anchovies in the Caesar, who know that every dish is a critical morsel of information. The guests of my guests, however, have been less predictable.

There was the kosher-vegan-diabetic, a lovely, gentle man who refused to eat anything but fried eggplant sticks.

There was the woman who ordered what I'd asked her to, but then refused to share. When I reminded her that this was the *reason* she was there, she reluctantly sawed off a a sliver of fish the size of a minnow.

For a critic, keeping a low profile in the restaurant is always a priority. But how do you scold your own mother for repeatedly calling you "Craigee" in front of the waiters and maitre d'?

My mother-in-law makes the same faux pas, but with an added flourish, thrusting her arms into the air with exasperation, then saying even more loudly, "Oh no, I did it again!"

These episodes were still far less embarrassing than our dinner in another city with a former boss, whose husband drank too many Manhattans at a world-renowned restaurant, then stood up and snapped his fingers at our waiter across the room.

"Hey, Tyrone!" he bellowed. "Are there any famous people here tonight?"

My boss gave him a look. But he failed to see the problem.

"Well, that's his name, isn't it? He's wearing a name tag."

A craving for pasta and red sauce

Strangers to restaurant reviewing, it could be argued, are to be excused for not knowing the rules of the road. My most frequent dining partner, my wife, ought to know better.

Once she has wearied of our relentless schedule, Elizabeth's typical table rebellion begins with an hors d'oeuvre of public guilt: "This is your job, not mine."

Why does it seem that this occurs just when I need her most to pick up the slack for, say, the persnickety fat-phobe across the table, when I need somebody to order something interesting? She pouts and grumbles and begs: "Please, can I get pasta and red sauce and a simple green salad?"

Then she'll say to our guests, "I never get to order what I want," until they stare me down with disapproving looks. Bad husband.

It's true. No one can complain more legitimately than Elizabeth. She earned five stars from me for dangerous eating during a marathon campaign through Cajun country several years ago.

We still don't know if it was the cornbread-stuffed pork chop, the onion soup, the crawfish etouffee, the shrimp remoulade, the seafood-stuffed soft-shell crabs, the spicy boudin sausage with pepper jelly, the jambalaya-stuffed quail, the bread pudding, the coush-coush corn mush with cane syrup, or the beignets stuffed with boudin we had tasted in our first four meals of the day.

Later that evening, as the Cajun band at our restaurant du soir cut loose with the washboard and accordion in a raucous two-step tune, Elizabeth began to look as pale as the 14-foot stuffed alligator over the door.

Next thing you know, it is 2 a.m. and Elizabeth is nearly unconscious on a gurney in the emergency room of a Lafayette, La., hospital. Over and over again, she deliriously mutters the name of the nearest body of water: "Atchafalaya Basin, Atchafalaya Basin, Atchafalaya Basin."

The nurse could only nod: "Coulda been da boudin. Coulda been da soup. Coulda been da pork chop. Coulda been da bread puddin'. Who knows? But ya might wanna go a little easier on the eatin' from now on."

I could only watch quietly as she gave my wife a pill for nausea and an IV to replace the nutrients she'd lost. What had my dream job reaped?

I would make it up to her some day. She could have pasta and red sauce any time she liked.

At least for a week.

A twisted Jenny Craig voodoo chant

"Baklavaaaaaaaaarg!"

I am hanging upside down against a board, and for the first time in my morning workout, I allow myself the satisfaction of a scream. My knees and ankles are locked into two padded rails above me. And as my torso rises stiffly upward, my abs begin to burn like skewered lamb kebabs turning over a charcoal grill.

This half-hour ab workout is the final course of my ritual torture, so I fondly refer to it as Satan's Dessert Tray. It makes for a nice motivational theme as the crunches get harder. I simply replace the sit-up count with a recitation of the recent week's desserts.

"Creme brulee! . . . Kiwi gelato! . . . Chocolate soup! . . . Tiramisu! . . ."

Like some twisted Jenny Craig voodoo chant, I set out to turn each confection to low-cal dust. It is a grueling trial that endures for 180 tantalizing repetitions.

And then I retreat to wither in the sauna. The heat there restores my sense of humor and my will to go on.

Most important, my appetite returns.

The Prime Rib

The old-fashioned supper-club steak house serves a prime rib that is the region's single best slice of beef.

oaring above the leopard-print carpeting, a gargantuan prime rib made its way to our table in the clutch of a tuxedoed waiter.

Past plush banquettes crowned with urns of gorgeous silk flowers. Past the reunion of heavily hair-sprayed ladies waving forks and glittering knuckles. Past the deeply tanned fellow with a golden oak-leaf necklace dangling from his turtleneck. Past the city councilman holding court at a table near the back of the room.

The jazz combo struck up "Satin Doll" and the prime rib landed gracefully before us, so prehistorically huge, I sank a little deeper into the polished black leather chair. Just one slice of this 27-ounce

EXCELLENT

1701 Locust St.
(in the Radisson Plaza
Warwick Hotel)
Philadelphia
(215) 772-1701

NEIGHBORHOOD
Rittenhouse Square

CUISINE
Steak House

mastodon chop was enough to cover half a bread plate with a sheet of meat. It steeped in juices the faded pink hue of a fine, cellared Bordeaux, with an intoxicating flavor nearly as complex.

I've had many a steak since I first tasted this monument to meat four years ago at the Prime Rib in the Warwick Hotel (now the Radisson Plaza). But it remains the greatest slice of beef in town. Dusted with black pepper. As tender as butter. One perfectly seasoned, mouth-filling bite spreads a sense of well-being through my body like a warm and lingering blush.

The rib also seemed to stoke in my guest a ravenous hunger — an impulse that carried over to dessert as he plundered his strawberry cheesecake with the privileged abandon of someone who was King for the Day.

This, of course, is the desired effect of the supper-club steak-house experience — that old-fashioned sense of special-occasion dining, where the jazz combo effortlessly rolls out "Stardust" and the black-tied servers pad about the posh dining room like silent sentries.

There are far more inventive spots to drop $90 a person in Philadelphia. The newer Capital Grille is in many ways a more complete restaurant, as steak houses go, with better sides and a slightly more creative touch to the menu. But if you are seeking a path to pure carnivore indulgence, the Prime Rib is the finest red-meat emporium in town.

For the largely older, monied crowd that typically fills its black-lacquered dining room, it is a concept that has never really gone out of style. I wouldn't have guessed that Wall Street had just plunged to a depressing new low on the day of our recent visit. On a Tuesday night, no less, the room was packed.

For managing partner Garth Weldon, who opened the Philadelphia Prime Rib with brother Jolly (who left to open Jolly's in the Latham Hotel), and Buzz BeLer, who founded the restaurant in Baltimore in 1965, there was never any question: "There is a market for this kind of operation in every economy."

The comfy, riveted leather chairs would make any guest feel like a captain of industry. The tables are well-spaced for easy conversation. The live music from pianist Kenneth Gates is classy. And the courteous servers are eminently professional.

This is also a drinker's haven, with tall, stiff cocktails, a wonderful selection of single-malt Scotches, and a very good wine list that is pleasantly dedicated to offering real values. Along with its stash of big-ticket Napa cabernets, the Prime Rib offers 30 very good wines under $40. We sampled a fume blanc from Ferrari-Carrano that was ideal with the elegantly broiled crab cakes bound with homemade mayonnaise and a hint of mustard powder. A spicy "Seven Oaks" cabernet from J. Lohr ($39) did the meat justice.

There are few pretensions to haute cuisine here; the restaurant thrives on straightforward simplicity, from the crunchy hollowed shells of Greenberg potato skins, which are named for a customer in Baltimore, to the good flavors of its prime Angus meat.

A plateful of excellent little lamb chops were tender and lean, served already sliced over a natural jus. Escargots in mushroom caps offered a delightful texture contrast, doused in a potent bath of garlicky butter and wine.

There is nothing quite as satisfying as a proper side of silken creamed spinach, with just enough bechamel to take the roughage off the green. Except, perhaps, for a dish of sweet buttered corn sheered fresh off the cob. Or a tall wedge of chilled iceberg lettuce glazed in a creamy dressing filled with Roquefort cheese.

The Prime Rib still has a few lingering disappointments. The over-thickened lobster bisque had the unfortunate texture and look of nacho cheese dip. The clams casino topping was overly salty and overly saucy.

But this restaurant also seems to have made some significant progress over the last few years, conquering most of the consistency problems that hampered it during my initial review. Every cut of meat was cooked exactly as ordered. Each had a distinct and appealing character. The grilled rib steak was every bit as tender as the prime rib, but sealed beneath the flavorful edges of a fire-darkened crust. The sirloin was so full of complex beefiness, it didn't need the pungent Roquefort sauce on the side. The veal chop was simply extraordinary, a memorably tender T-bone that bathed in a pool of its own juices. Only the filet mignon was a mild letdown. The meat was perfectly tender, but its delicate flavor was overwhelmed by its burnt exterior.

The desserts follow a similar concept of simple, well-played classics. The mountainous wedge of cinnamon-laced apple pie comes sandwiched between a flaky double-crust. The tall chocolate mousse pie is light and airy, but still intense with chocolate

But prepare to bring out the long spoons and do battle for your hot fudge sundae. As any King for the Day knows, a sundae topped with whipped cream and a maraschino cherry is a prize that may never fall out of style. And it's one of a handful of old-fashioned indulgences at the Prime Rib that are still worth fighting for.

■ **MENU HIGHLIGHTS** Prime rib, grilled rib steak, lamb chops, veal chops, sirloin, crab cakes, swordfish steak, Greenberg potato skins, creamed spinach, apple pie, hot fudge sundae.

■ **WINE LIST** An excellent cellar of fine California and French vintages, with many available by the glass and more than 30 bottles available under $40. Selection of single-malt Scotches and after-dinner drinks is first-class.

■ **IF YOU GO** Dinner served Monday-Saturday, 5-11 p.m.

■ **RESERVATIONS** Recommended, especially for weekends.

■ **CREDIT CARDS** All major cards but Discover.

■ **SMOKING** There is a nonsmoking section.

■ **HANDICAP ACCESSIBLE** Yes.

■ **PARKING** Valet parking costs $8.

Or Try These

Here are three other extraordinary steaks.

Vetri

1312 Spruce St., Philadelphia
(215) 732-3478

The occasional rib steak special is aged several weeks in-house before Marc Vetri sears them with a crust of rock salt in his cast-iron pan.

¡Pasion!

211 S. 15th St., Philadelphia
(215) 875-9895

Guillermo Pernot's smoked rib-eye is one of the most intensely flavored and tender cuts of beef around, with a campfire taste that is for smoke lovers only.

The Blue Angel

706 Chestnut St., Philadelphia
(215) 925-6889

The hanger steak and frites defined the flavorful-yet-affordable bistro classic, and launched a half-dozen imitators around town.

The Red Hen Cafe

The pleasant South Jersey BYOB offers gently updated Eastern European cooking.

O f all the frumpy foods emerging from the shadows of archaic comfort into the trendy limelight, spaetzle seemed only a notch more likely to make the leap than gefilte fish or liverwurst.

Yet those squiggly Germanic noodles have been popping up in some surprising venues. Nestled alongside pesto-stuffed free-range chicken at Brasserie Perrier. Propping up a fillet of misoyaki-glazed butterfish at Roy's, the upscale Hawaiian-fusion restaurant where they've even been tinted green with fiery wasabi.

The spaetzle, my friends, is the dumpling du jour, the gnocchi of the new millennium. And I must admit that I love them, too, which explains why I've been on a roots mission of sorts to enjoy them in their purer forms.

VERY GOOD

560 Stokes Rd.
Medford, N.J.
(609) 953-2655

NEIGHBORHOOD
South Jersey

CUISINE
Eastern European

I've gone to Trenton and Port Richmond and Sansom Street in search of spaetzle. But my most fruitful outing brought me to an unlikely strip mall in Medford, on the fringe of New Jersey's Pinelands. There roosts the Red Hen Cafe, a haven for Eastern and Central European fare.

The Red Hen certainly has the potential to transform those old-world classics into something thoroughly modern. The small, glassed-in dining room feels like a contemporary bistro. And the young couple who own it, chef Tracey Slack and her husband, Bill Roka, who runs the front of the house, have the education (she's a Restaurant School alum; he's a New York University film school grad), the family background (she's part Croatian; he's half Hungarian), and the talent to make it happen.

But the nuevo paprikas will have to wait. Slack has opted instead to be a caretaker of traditional flavors, relying on good ingredients, careful cooking, and a penchant for modest updating rather than radical revision. And that's just fine with me.

Slack aspires to elevate culinary folk art with a wink of passion and technique, like the entrancing Marc Chagall prints that grace the walls, which are upholstered in Transylvanian-red taffeta.

Her vegetarian borscht is a perfect example. The crimson beet broth is layered with myriad shades of root vegetable oomph — spicy

A painting of a red hen overlooks the dining room.

turnip, anise celeriac, peppery parsnip — framed by a perfect balance of sweet, sour and dill.

The mushroom pelmeni, a play on the Siberian dumpling but with a woodsy mushroom stuffing, is all the more intense floating in pristine chicken consomme. A Hungarian palacsinta crepe is not the typical dozen-layer cheese pie, but a satisfying Frenchified version wrapped like a four-cornered package around a ham-filled, blintz-style custard.

As for Slack's lovely spaetzle (actually a Hungarian variation called nokedli), they make their much-awaited appearance with virtually every entree. Eggy rich and rumple-edged like doughy pipe cleaners, they have a springy chew that does wonders for the stewy soul food of Middle Europe.

And most of it is done just right.

Tender cubes of lean beef in the goulash, braised to a deep brick-red, exuded the sweet tinge of roasted peppers. The chunks of filet mignon in the stroganoff were cooked pink to order, then glazed in a wine and sour-cream sauce sparked with whole-grain mustard.

A German beef rouladen special brought pounded top round rolled around a filling of smoked bacon, caramelized onions, and a dill pickle that somehow kept its crunch after two hours of cooking.

Two hours, of course, is nothing compared with the five days it takes to cure the Red Hen's sauerbraten. But the meltingly tender pickled roast beef, sliced into thick rounds, is so infused with the perfume of clove, allspice and garlic that it's more than worth the time. Even without the traditional gingersnaps and raisins, this gravy-slathered roast was memorable.

Slack, who spent some time as a pastry chef at the Garden, goes the extra mile with the desserts, too. She stews the sour cherries that go into the homemade jam in the palacsinta crepes, whips up a luxurious classic chocolate mousse, and stretches her puff pastry thin to make apple strudel with an exceptionally buttery, flaky crunch.

A low-rise cheesecake — made from a customer's family recipe — is soft and slightly undersweetened to keep its cream cheese tang.

There were some minor slips. The stuffed cabbage was a little too meaty, lacking the balance of rice that would have given it more comforting softness. The seared fillet of Chilean sea bass was a little overcooked and overwhelmed by its tart mustard-horseradish crust.

The veal schnitzel was grease-free but less delicate than it could have been. And while I loved the winy flavor of the chicken paprikas' cream sauce, the dry breast meat did not hold up to the slow cooking as well as the leg and thigh. But these were quibbles all.

A surprising highlight was the spinach dumplings that garnish the vegetarian plate. The handful of thick plugs were dense with leafy green enriched with goat cheese, and arrived glazed with Roquefort cream.

These unabashedly zaftig little sinkers weren't quite the ethereally light spinach gnocchi I've craved from Italian kitchens.

But like I said, the limelight is shifting east. And in the land of the spaetzle eaters, this kind of frumpy comfort has never gone out of style.

Or Try These

Here are three other restaurants that serve Eastern European fare.

Syrenka Luncheonette

3173 Richmond St.,
Philadelphia
(215) 634-3954

The steam-table service can be gruff, but the Polish specialties are pure comfort, from the thick potato pancakes to the delicious breaded pork chops, hearty bigos stew, and mashed beets.

Blue Danube Restaurant

538 Adeline St., Trenton
(609) 393-6133

Rustic fabrics festoon the half-timbered dining room of this Hungarian eatery, where a shot of palinka and a plate of paprikash can make a Trenton neighborhood feel like the old country.

Warsaw Cafe

306 S. 16th St., Philadelphia
(215) 546-0204

The tiny, windowpaned bistro that sits behind the Kimmel Center is a charming old spot, but the pan-Eastern European menu has seen better days.

■ MENU HIGHLIGHTS Ham-filled palacsinta, mushroom pelmeni, vegetarian borscht, beef stroganoff, sauerbraten, goulash, chicken paprikas, rouladen special, spinach dumplings, cheese pie, dessert palacsinta, apple strudel.

■ **WINE LIST** BYOB. Hungarian wines and Alsatian and German rieslings are among the most compatible with the food.

■ **IF YOU GO** Dinner Wednesday-Sunday, 5-9 p.m. Entrees, $18-$21.99.

■ **RESERVATIONS** Recommended.

■ **CREDIT CARDS** All major cards accepted.

■ **SMOKING** No smoking.

■ **HANDICAP ACCESSIBLE** Yes.

■ **PARKING** Free lot available.

Restaurant 821

Chic contemporary cooking is practiced in the downtown Wilmington conversation piece, and decadence is all around.

our lobe will be up in a few minutes, folks."
My tablemates shudder with a mixture of fear and giggles each time our waiter updates the status of our whole foie gras, roasting in the wood-fired ovens at Restaurant 821.
"Your lobe is in the oven . . ."
Snicker, snicker.
" . . . Why don't I go check on your lobe?"
"By the way," a vegetarian guest asks me, "what is foie gras?"
"Your lobe is almost done!"
"Force-fed fattened duck liver? Oh. . . ."
"Ladies and gentlemen, your lobe!"

EXCELLENT

821 N. Market St.
Wilmington
(302) 652-8821

NEIGHBORHOOD
Wilmington

CUISINE
New American

Only in resurgent Wilmington, the tax-free empire of the credit-card Caesars, should such decadence exist. Servers clear room on our table. A wide, white basin of Roman proportions is set before us, its sloping brim ringed by a wreath of tiny greens. Inside, eight thick charred slices of oozing pink richness sit atop a proscenium of diced mango and pineapple glazed in sweet Sauternes wine and rendered fat. I place a jiggly pink slice on butter-soaked brioche toast and hum as this epic ode to indulgence melts away against the roof of my mouth. My guests, still fearful but now eating, have come to regard this as one heck of a fruit salad.

For $60, six people could eat their liver's worth out of this luxury lobe, a pre-dinner nibble on the menu section appropriately named "Conversation Starters." The restaurant now offers a romantic half-lobe for two at $45. But after several impressive meals here, I've begun to understand why this restaurant itself has become a conversation piece: Wilmington has a real winner, even if you don't do organ meats.

The three-year-old restaurant from chef Tobias Lawry and his partner Obadiah Ostergard is directly across the Market Street Mall from the Grand Opera House, a fortunate location for a team that has begun to waken the city's somnolent restaurant scene. The decor of

The decor of the comfortable 90-seat dining room has a corporate feel.

this comfortable 90-seat dining room has a corporate feel, with upside-down fabric cones glowing over a central banquette and a bland, earth-tone decor that seems to put all focus on the food.

It is a safe approach, considering the vibrance of Lawry's cooking, an inventive blend of American wood-oven roasting with Mediterranean accents. There is an obvious indulgence in high-quality luxury products here — the Sonoma foie gras and dayboat-fresh seafood, the house-made gelati and trendy little greens referred to as "infant" (which is somewhere, I suppose, between "micro" and "toddler"). And the all-American wine list could satisfy the most demanding connoisseur.

But from the moment that crusty bread and a plate of sweet roasted garlic cloves in olive oil are brought to the table, you know this food is rooted in a more primal love of lusty flavors.

Citrus and herb-marinated feta. Wood-oven-baked flatbread melded with piquant cheese, port-soaked cherries and rosemary. Tender nuggets of herby duck confit tossed with lemony endive strips, greens, and sweet pearl onions. Bread-thickened onion soup that, in one spoonful, conveys the textures and flavors of five different kinds of onion, from the sweetness of steeped shallots to the delicate crunch of freshly snipped chives.

On a recent visit, Lawry's twist on onion soup was filled with snappy green fava beans and chunks of fennel. Plump mussels basked in an addictive, rustic broth, a buttered citrus juice streaked with saffron aioli, then scattered with crunchy panzanella croutons. Amazingly soft pork tenderloin came over a mound of brussels sprouts cooked down with cream and caramelized onions. A bowl of bouillabaisse brimming with fine seafood was topped with an odd but charming touch, gnocchi that had been crisped in the pan.

Impressively, Lawry's food was as memorable as when I first came two years ago.

A spectacular fillet of skillet-roasted monkfish, paired with coins of mushroom ravioli, came over some of the best creamed spinach I've ever eaten, still springy and fresh, its milky broth flecked with pancetta and sweet onion. Those tender shards of delicious pancetta are scattered throughout the menu like flavor flakes, giving crispy gnocchi with truffle dressing a salty little edge, lending their subtle, smoky spark to seared scallops and potatoes glazed in butter sauce.

A seared foie gras appetizer was perhaps even better than the whole lobe, sandwiching a sweet-tart compote of apples and raspberry with toasted brioche. Buttermilk-dipped soft-shell crab, crisped by a dusting of risotto rice flour, teetered atop an herby green whip of basil mashed potatoes and a pool of carrot juice. A thick triangular hunk of tuna was seared with just the right amount of pepper. With the press of a fork, it fanned into blades of deliciously pink rare meat.

While this menu is a treat for those who eat on the edge, it also has the perfect selection for the conservative eater of well-done beef: "Forever braised short ribs." There aren't even any bones by the time you get this unctuous, deeply steeped pile of meat, glazed in a stock tinged with sherry vinegar and juniper berries. The slow-cooked lamb shank is a smidge on the more exotic side, but with its natural gravy and a mince of sun-dried tomatoes, it is equally recommendable.

The cheese selection is excellent, filled with some unusual Spanish and Italian cheeses worth trying for something different. But it would

Or Try These

Here are three other Wilmington-area restaurants.

Krazy Kats

Route 100 and Rockland Road, Montchanin, Del.
(302) 888-2133

A wacky animal motif somehow fits in at this beautifully refurbished inn with adventurous New American cooking.

Hotel DuPont

11th & Market Streets, Wilmington
(302) 594-3100

The soaring, oak-clad Green Room and the Wyeth-hung Brandywine make for dining rooms of unmatched classical grandeur. The kitchens are better than average, but rarely magical.

Deep Blue

111 W. 11th St., Wilmington
(302) 777-2040

This chic, contemporary restaurant features seafood with international influences and an excellent raw bar.

be hard to forgo dessert altogether. A recent apple galette was case in point, a rustic fan of apples topped with rich caramel gelato and Mickey Mouse ears of dried apple chips.

Among the highlights of my earlier meals was a rum-soaked savarin cake that unleashed a stream of warm caramel when its doughnut shape was broken, mingling with a scoop of burnt-orange pecan gelato. An excellent ice cream tingling with white pepper played in the mouth against warm raspberry syrup and crumbles of pistachio biscotti. But my favorite was an ivory-colored chocolate gelato filled with pistachios and more chocolate chunks. They called it "white chocolate decadence" — a label that fits this restaurant well.

■ **MENU HIGHLIGHTS** Schiatta, whole foie gras, mussels, fava bean soup, deep-fried ravioli, braised short ribs, pork tenderloin, bouillabaisse, savarin cake with burnt orange-pecan gelato, apple galette, cheese selection.

■ **WINE LIST** A nearly all-American list is stocked with quality bottles that blend value with prestige. There are also numerous excellent wines by the glass.

■ **IF YOU GO** Lunch served Monday-Friday 11:30 a.m.-4:30 p.m. Dinner served Monday-Thursday 5:30-10 p.m., Friday 5:30-10:30 p.m., Saturday 5-11 p.m.

■ **RESERVATIONS** Highly recommended.

■ **CREDIT CARDS** All major cards but Discover.

■ **SMOKING** Entire restaurant is nonsmoking.

■ **HANDICAP ACCESSIBLE** Yes.

■ **PARKING** Nightly valet parking costs $5.

Ritz Seafood

One of South Jersey's hottest bistros, the BYOB offers creative Asian-fusion.

Thanks to the realities of strip-mall politics — yes, there is such a thing — tiny Ritz Seafood has had more than a few wrinkles to smooth out during its meteoric rise from a simple take-out fish market to one of South Jersey's hottest bistros.

It seems monumental enough for husband-wife proprietors Gloria and Steven Cho to have transformed this anonymous shoebox of a room in Voorhees into an exotic garden, complete with koi pond, willows, and rock-sculpture fountains. Throw a few silk pillows onto the banquettes, drape streamers from the ceiling, adorn the walls with exquisite iron teapots and drawers of imported tea, and you have a 42-seat BYOB so tranquil and transporting that it's easy to forget you're sitting in a strip mall.

Even the tree stumps placed on the sidewalk out front soften patrons' view of the massive mall parking lot as they wait for tables.

VERY GOOD

Ritz Center, 910
Haddonfield-Berlin Rd.,
Voorhees, N.J.
(856) 566-6650

NEIGHBORHOOD
South Jersey

CUISINE
Asian-Fusion Seafood

But the reality for Ritz Seafood, which opened in 1998 as a retail market and quickly evolved into a full-fledged restaurant with its own brand of Asian-fusion, is that a few doors away, the much larger Chez Elena Wu wields more weight in the mall.

And if someone else appears to be competing with Chez Elena Wu's French-Chinese menu — a concept to which its lease gives it exclusive rights — that someone else's menu is going to change. Just ask Ritz chef and co-owner Dan Hover, whose lease and menu were renegotiated two years ago in response to Wu's objections. Hover even rephrased the words "dim sum" (too Chinese), "bouillabaisse" and "poached" (too French) on the menu to keep the peace.

Such exclusivity rights are not uncommon for important tenants. But it's hard not to step on toes with a menu as wide-ranging as Hover's, a pan-Asian ode to seafood that also zigs to Spain for paella and then zags to Louisiana for jambalaya.

But somehow Hover, a seasoned chef who has worked for country clubs and hotel chains and owned a restaurant in Manhattan called Truffles (now closed) before teaming up with the Chos, manages to keep most of it straight.

So do Ritz's attentive servers, charged with reciting nearly a dozen specials and advising diners on the restaurant's list of 32 teas.

Many of my favorite dishes have a distinctly Korean flavor emphasized by an earthy, almost sweet chili paste called gochu jang.

That's not surprising because the Chos, who also own the Coastal Cave Trading Co. fish market in the Reading Terminal Market, were born in Seoul. Three years ago, Gloria Cho even took Hover on a field trip to Korea, where, at a cafe in the woods near Pusan, he learned his killer calamari-scallion pancake recipe from a monk.

Back in Voorhees, Hover presents the wedges of thin pancake fanned beneath sheets of irresistible char-grilled calamari, which seem tenderized by their gochu jang marinade.

The chili paste spikes homemade mayonnaise served with crispy butterfish. We found the silvery little flat fish tasty even without eating the bones, as is the custom in Korea. Gochu jang also made a marvelous barbecue sauce for salmon, its mild heat enhancing the fish's natural flavor.

The bi bim bap, a Korean rice bowl topped with vegetables, a runny fried egg, and a spoonful of gochu jang, was an exceptionally fresh version of one of my favorite comfort foods.

There were other successes. Hover's version of a rarely imported Malaysian mackerel he calls devil fish is one of the best whole-fish dishes around. The crisp surface is glazed with a tangy, dark Thai chili-tamarind sauce. Its moist and firm flesh is deeply scored into diamond-shaped nuggets that easily slip off the bones.

The ahi tuna appetizer, a deft rendition of tuna tartare, is a parfait of minced raw tuna layered with colorful rings of flying-fish roe and a micro-thin schmear of pepper-speckled whipped cream. It's a stretch to call this roe "caviar," but the tiny tobiko eggs lend a satisfying pop to the sweet layers of fish.

Several other dishes I tried were still en route to perfection. Steamed mushroom dumplings had an intensely woodsy flavor, but the fillings needed firmer binding. The doughy lobster-shrimp sticks

Or Try These

Here are three other Asian-fusion restaurants.

Twenty Manning

261 S. 20th St., Philadelphia
(215) 731-0900

Audrey Taichman's noisy corner magnet for the urban chic blends solid Asian bistro fusion fare with a loungey decor of black leather couches and trendy people.

FuziOn

2960 Skippack Pike.,
Worcester, Pa.,
(610) 584-6958

The team behind the now-closed Ly Michaels in Overbrook Park has brought its ambitious Asian-fusion cuisine farther west to a pretty little BYOB near Skippack Village.

Roy's

124-34 S. 15th St.,
Philadelphia. (215) 988-1814

An old bank has been beautifully transformed into a branch of this upscale Hawaiian-fusion chain, but the creative fare, from wasabi spaetzle to pork chops with plum sauce, is a bit too inconsistent for these prices. Poor service makes matters worse.

lacked chunks of real meat.

Other dishes were cleverly conceived — shrimp steeped in sake-saffron broth in a teapot, for example, and seafood shepherd's pie topped with wasabi mashed potatoes — but the flavors didn't quite live up to the presentations.

The kitchen also has a heavy hand with sweetness, in the orange sauce served with the nut-crusted Chilean sea bass and in the thick coconut-panko crumb crust that dulled the delicacy of fried lobster tails and shrimp. I was much more attuned to the spicy surprise Hover unveiled in the tonkatsu fried scallops, whose stuffing revealed the fiery ka-boom of raw wasabi.

The salty-sour note in the kobe beef's teriyaki marinade also made an impression. We plucked the morsels of precious raw Japanese beef ($35 for 5 ounces) from a bowl and seared them ourselves on a 900-degree river rock delivered to our table in a flowerpot. At first, the gingery soy dominated our palates, but the savory power of the well-marbled beef surged forward with a final, lingering word: Moo.

It's amazing, with a menu of 21 regular entrees and numerous specials, that Hover sails essentially a one-cook ship. He'd do better to pare down the offerings, focusing his creativity instead of letting it overflow. But let's hope he keeps making his fine desserts, especially the moist bread puddings, which these days come ribboned with sweet Fuji apples and glazed with caramel.

The creme brulees, though, could use work — or actually, less work. Hover has a penchant for gilding this simple lily by stuffing it with strawberries, nuts or other sundry fillings. Why not jettison this overdone classic altogether?

It does sound awfully ... French. In the name of strip-mall politics, that could mean one last wrinkle smoothed out.

■ **MENU HIGHLIGHTS** Ahi tuna with caviar appetizer; Korean calamari with scallion pancake; smoked chicken and andouille spring roll; crispy butterfish appetizer; bi bim bap; devil fish; everything-crusted tilapia; rock-grilled kobe beef; Fuji apple bread pudding; dessert bento box.

■ **WINE LIST** BYOB. (A crisp New Zealand sauvignon blanc or Alsatian white would pair nicely with the Asian fare). One of the region's largest selections of loose teas, served in exquisite iron pots, is worth trying.

■ **IF YOU GO** Lunch is served Tuesday-Saturday 11:30 a.m.-2:30 p.m.; dinner, Tuesday-Sunday, 5:30-9:30 p.m. Entrees: lunch, $12-$20; dinner, $18-$27.

■ **RESERVATIONS** Recommended on weekends.

■ **CREDIT CARDS** All major cards accepted but Discover.

■ **SMOKING** No smoking.

■ **HANDICAP ACCESSIBLE** Yes.

■ **PARKING** Free lot.

Rose Tattoo Cafe

No ordinary leftover '80s fern bar, the date-destination favorite has vibrant eclectic fare.

The turreted rowhouse at 19th and Callowhill must have one of the ugliest paint jobs of any restaurant in town, its bay-windowed brick facade darkened to a forboding black and its shutters trimmed the color of antacid pink.

But the ominous look hasn't stopped the Rose Tattoo Cafe from becoming one of Philadelphia's most popular date destinations over the last 20 years. That's because the grim exterior gives way to a happy warren of lively, rambling rooms with giant bouquets of fresh flowers and the viny tendrils of nearly 300 exotic plants.

A wrought-iron arcade on the second floor encircles the bar below with a romantic balcony reminiscent of New Orleans. But there is so much chlorophyll and oxygen charging the rooms that you might as well bring a plant mister when you come.

VERY GOOD

1847 Callowhill St.
Philadelphia
(215) 569-8939

NEIGHBORHOOD
Fairmount/Art Museum

CUISINE
New American

Yet the Rose Tattoo is no ordinary leftover '80s fern bar. It's got fiddle-leaf figs, crotons, bromeliads, fishtail palms and grapevines, among other botanical specimens, all meticulously tended by owner Michael Weinberg, who bought the restaurant with his wife, Helene, in 1989.

Weinberg does his best to keep the foliage fresh, even if the rest of the dated decor could use revamping. Helene still handles the office. It's left to their son, Sean, to keep the kitchen up-to-date. And unlike many places from the same era that are basically running on Restaurant Renaissance fumes, the Rose Tattoo has eclectic fare that is still vibrant, creative and carefully cooked.

There are some tried-and-true classics, such as the cream of mushroom soup, which is steeped with intense forest flavors and filled with great, chunky morsels of shiitakes, porcinis, and the occasional black trumpet. The fried calamari are perfectly done, paired with large grilled shrimp and a tomatoey puttanesca sauce piquant with olives and anchovy.

Then there are some newer ideas. Tender shrimp dumplings, sealed inside four-cornered wontons, bask in smoky miso-ginger broth with a spicy mound of hijiki seaweed and lotus-root salad. Airy wedges of grilled Cuban flat bread come with a dollop of creamy goat

Plants adorn the balcony dining room.

cheese and delicious homemade fig jam. Wonderful agnolotti made from house-crafted pasta are filled with sweet butternut squash and crushed amaretto cookies, then served with wild mushrooms and brown butter — an indulgent ode to winter.

As one might expect, Sean Weinberg worked as a teen in his parents' restaurant. But his experiences elsewhere before becoming chef a few years ago — study at the Culinary Institute of America and travel in Italy and Mexico, as well as stints at local spots including Restaurant Taquet in Wayne and Passerelle in Radnor — have polished his wide-ranging repertoire.

An elaborate preparation involving a 24-hour Thai brine, smoked plum sauce, and a peanut butter-chile glaze produced some of the most delicious ribs I've tasted recently. The jambalaya that helps lend the restaurant a New Orleans theme, however tenuous, is one of the more credible renditions around, filled with fistfuls of fresh seafood, andouille sausage, smoky ham, and flavorful brothy rice.

Weinberg's enthusiasm for complex dishes didn't always translate into success. The veal involtini, a cutlet wrapped around a stuffing of mushrooms and cheese, had the texture of odd sausage and was overwhelmed by its intense, dark jus.

The Indian fry bread turnover, which looked like a lumpy biscuit filled with ground meat, had the off tang and half-mashed texture of about five too many ingredients, all clashing with the sweet lemon-grass cream dip. A free-form lasagna special might have worked had the shredded osso buco meat inside been more tender.

But Weinberg usually gets it right. The lobster quesadillas were delicious, each light tortilla wedge crisped around the edges and filled with lobster meat and cheese, with a chipotle-sour cream dip on the side. The sweetness of tender pork medallions served with maple-glazed yams and a reduced cider sauce found a nice contrast in a garnish of gingery black beans.

The tuna steak with mushrooms and wasabi-onion puree was beautiful — the bright ruby meat enhanced by a sesame-soy marinade. The salmon fillet was another big production, sandwiched between a pancake-like horseradish crust on top, and lentil-potato cake below. There also was a notable garnish of creamed pearl onions on this busy plate, but each flavor was clear and complementary.

Even dishes that needed tweaking had some memorable high points. The very strange addition of chorizo-filled tomato sauce — so thick it could have been sloppy joe mix — could not dull the excellent crab cakes on top, bursting with beautiful lump meat and cilantro-scented homemade mayo. The duck was overcooked, but the dried fruit sauce was excellent, a multicolored medley of sherry-plumped blueberries, currants, and gold and black raisins.

Ironically, while the Rose Tattoo has long been known for its sweets, the dessert tray dated the restaurant far more than the savory menu.

Some items needed more attention: the ice-cold pecan pie, the dry panettone bread pudding, and the creme brulee that had been caramelized too much and too far in advance. But many of the gussied-up bake-sale confections — the flourless chocolate cake filled with moist cherries, the banana-caramel cream pie, and the brownies topped with caramelized macadamias (if there ever was a trendy '80s nut, that was it) — communicated a casual, homey comfort.

Or Try These

Here are three other survivors from the Restaurant Renaissance.

Friday Saturday Sunday
261 S. 21 St., Philadelphia
(215) 546-4232
A romantic classic that has remained vital with an eclectic menu and great wine values.

Astral Plane
1708 Lombard St., Philadelphia
(215) 546-6230
Loyalists still come for the Bloody Mary brunch and the Bohemian tented ceiling decor, but the wide-ranging menu could use some inspiration.

Judy's Cafe
627 Third St., Philadelphia
(215) 928-1968
This warm Queen Village institution was one of the first great neighborhood restaurants and remains a vibrant destination for a diverse clientele, thanks to two-for-one coupons, updated comfort food, and "public humiliation" birthdays in drag.

It's an appeal that has rightfully secured the Rose Tattoo a spot in the hearts of Philadelphia diners, paint job and all.

■ **MENU HIGHLIGHTS** Rib appetizer; lobster quesadillas; shrimp dumplings in ginger-miso broth; crispy calamari; cream of mushroom soup; squash agnolotti; sesame-soy-marinated tuna; horseradish-crusted salmon; jambalaya; banana-caramel cream pie; macadamia nut brownie.

■ **WINE LIST** The selection is small but generally affordable, with several good selections under $40, including a rustic cabernet franc from Domaine Gasnier ($30) and a flavorful California chardonnay from R.H. Phillips ($38).

■ **IF YOU GO** Lunch, Monday 11-3, Tuesday-Friday 11-4. Dinner, Monday-Thursday, 5-10 p.m.; Friday-Saturday, 5-11 p.m. Entrees: lunch, $8.50-$12; dinner, $16-$31.

■ **RESERVATIONS** Recommended, especially for the balcony.

■ **CREDIT CARDS** All major cards accepted.

■ **SMOKING** No smoking in upstairs dining rooms.

■ **HANDICAP ACCESSIBLE** Front-door wheelchair ramp available on request. Rest rooms are handicapped accessible.

■ **PARKING** Free parking at night on the street or in a municipal lot across the street in the 1900 block of Callowhill.

Rouge

The high-style Rittenhouse Square cafe serves surprisingly sophisticated fare to the poodle people.

omebody's chauffeur is snoring. His head is slung back against the seat of a convertible Rolls-Royce and, on this sultry summer night — with the car wedged against the curb of Rittenhouse Square between a Jaguar and a Porsche — his mouth is stuck half-open.

Ho-hum. Just another night in the passenger-loading-zone in front of Rouge.

Meanwhile, throngs of fabulous people are bubbling through the wide-open French doors beside him, framed against the sidewalk in a Felliniesque tableaux — nipped, tucked and inflated to perfection, hands bobbing with cocktails and cell phones, breast pockets bulging with cigars, wriggly fur-ball doggies yapping at their feet.

VERY GOOD

205 S. 18th St.
(Rittenhouse Claridge)
Philadelphia
(215) 732-6622

NEIGHBORHOOD
Rittenhouse Square

CUISINE
New American Bistro

And who was that I saw one recent summer day, striding between the crowds in his brown Armani and designer shades, waving to his friends with a waggle of his pinky, shaking hands at every table as if he owns the place, which he does. His name is Neil Stein, *restaurateurus Philadelphiensis maximus*, the trend-setting genius behind this scene.

How many normal people, I wonder, would brush against such glamour and run the other way? I did for months until I sat down at one of the cushy velvet booths inside to eat. Only then did I discover that the real performance worth watching at Rouge is taking place in the kitchen, a little galley nook that has produced a surprisingly talented string of chefs.

The latest is Michael Yeamans, a Striped Bass alum whose updated bistro menu blends high-style with pristine ingredients and some new takes on comfort favorites.

In summer time, the fare has a lovely light touch. A tower of Asian-scented tuna tartare came tiered between three crispy chips that were great for scooping. A vibrant green drizzle of wasabi soy added a whiff of fire. An appetizer of fritto misto brought a handful of perfectly fried scallops, shrimp, mussels and fish, their crisp panko crusts and tangy lemon parmesan dressing an elegant step-up from your typical seashore combo platter.

When the patrons are few and the weather serene, Rouge is a lovely sidewalk balcony onto the park.

Incredibly succulent browned scallops posed over a silky sweet pea essence and the bright orange pleasure of al dente risotto cloaked in the buttery sweetness of carrot puree. Perfectly grilled salmon came atop a frothy creamed chowder filled with corn and morsels of sweet lobster. A luscious dish of baked peaches was topped with a praline crisp, and a scoop of blackberry ice cream completed an idyllic warm-weather repast.

These fresh flavors are typical of the menu at Rouge, which has always offered bright salads such as hearts of palm topped with great grilled shrimp and refreshing citrus wedges, as well as an assortment of delicate Asian-inspired dishes. The lobster spring rolls have always been a little skimpy on the crustacean. But the tuna mushroom potstickers were as satisfying as any pork dumpling in Chinatown.

Those fusion frills are fine for all the dainty folks nibbling for show-and-tell of public consumption. But I think Yeamans' talents really emerge in his renditions of heartier cold-weather comforts.

Early in the year, I savored an oversized ravioli stuffed with goat cheese and scallions that came topped with a soulful ragout of oxtail. One large braised short rib came with an unglamourous hunk of meat attached, burnished a deep mahogany brown from slow cooking. One taste, though, turned heads at my table — the meat was so tender, its deeply flavored gravy flared with an exotic Asian five-spice.

Yeaman's cassoulet was classically French, but one of the best versions I've tasted in town, its soft and herby white beans studded with rounds of garlicky sausage, then topped with salty duck confit and a juicy link of Toulouse-style sausage.

Other notable dishes included a grilled lamb tenderloin with porcini mushrooms, and a braised rabbit stew vibrant with bacon and rosemary. The wonderfully fresh herb-seared fluke came over toasted orzo filled with snappy fava beans and artichoke hearts.

The restaurant has no pastry chef, but the desserts are excellent nonetheless. I loved the delicate pear and hazelnut tart sauced with tangy cider sauce. But even more delicious was the chocolate bombe that brought a milk chocolate dome over a crunchy praline base, a decidedly retro dessert that is happily coming back into style. Even if style is something that diminutive Rouge already has in excess.

If Rouge were a dog, as one friend noted, it would most probably be a poodle. From the curling gold tree of life painted on the back mirror to the narrow egg-shaped tables to the flouncy curtained walls and velvet banquettes, there is scarcely a detail left untouched and unflourished by the designer.

Even the waitresses were ornamented with little black purses that make them look as if they've stopped by your table fresh from a shopping spree at Talbot's. It is a pretentious touch that corresponds accurately to much of the service. I've had a few gracious, down-to-earth servers over the years. But just as often, I've been glanced with attitude, the occasional roll of the eyes, and a consistent "no" when asking for that prime table perched beside the windows. It may look open, but it's reserved for "friends of Neil's."

It isn't my only quibble with Rouge. At quieter moments, when the patrons are few and the weather serene, Rouge is indeed a lovely sidewalk balcony onto the park. More often than not, you will squeeze into tables beside a bar crowded three-deep

Or Try These

Here are three other restaurants with outdoor cafes near Rittenhouse Square.

Brasserie Perrier

1619 Walnut St., Philadelphia
(215) 568-3000

Georges Perrier's second restaurant offers top-notch upscale contemporary dining in back, and a more casual French brasserie menu (with funky fondues) in the lively front lounge and cafe.

Bleu

227 S. 18th St., Philadelphia
(215) 545-0342

Neil Stein's second parkside cafe has finally found its lower-key neighborhood niche and moved out from the style-conscious shadow of Rouge with good values for excellent bistro cooking.

Devon Seafood Grille

225 S. 18th St., Philadelphia
(215) 546-5940

This handsome vaulted ceiling seafooder has a large, accessible dining room and a slightly less tony crowd that gobbles up its hot sweet biscuits, but the fish is rarely more exciting than adequate.

with players crowing their remarkable success. ("I just sold my movie to Miramax," said one woman in front of us.)

There is nowhere to retreat but behind the gauzy curtains. So don't come if you already suffer from poor self-esteem or hearing issues. The room can be deafeningly loud, not only from patrons, but from the music that often pounds through the air like a nightclub.

These are major distractions for those who actually come here to eat. Even the fascinating decor becomes overwrought and gaudy as the fabulous people bubble and whirl about the bar. Without the draw of Yeaman's fabulous food to hold our focus, I could hardly blame that chauffeur from taking a little snooze.

■ **MENU HIGHLIGHTS** Tuna tartare; tuna potstickers; fritto misto; grilled shrimp salad; goat cheese ravioli with oxtail; braised short rib; cassoulet; lamb tenderloins with mushrooms; herb-crusted fluke; seared scallops with carrot risotto; grilled salmon with lobster and corn chowder; chocolate mousse-praline bombe; pear hazelnut tart; peach crisp.

■ **WINE LIST** A small but high-quality international selection of wines, ranging from a crisp South African sauvignon blanc to a rustic Spanish ribera del duero crianza.

■ **IF YOU GO** Lunch served every day noon-2:30 p.m. Dinner served Monday-Saturday 5 p.m.-1:30 a.m.; Sunday 5 p.m.-to 12:30 a.m. Sunday brunch served 11 a.m.-2:30 p.m.

■ **RESERVATIONS** Not accepted (except for "Friends of Neil's")

■ **CREDIT CARDS** All major cards but Discover.

■ **SMOKING** Restaurant is nonsmoking inside until 11 p.m.

■ **HANDICAP ACCESSIBLE** There are two steps at the entrance, but one bathroom is handicapped accessible.

■ **PARKING** Street parking only.

Rx

The old apothecary-turned-casual-contemporary offers creative, affordable updates on bistro food.

The story of Rx has been repeated countless times these last few years: Restaurant-deprived neighborhood attracts young talent to open ambitious, affordable BYOB.

In this case, the setting is deep in West Philadelphia, a residential area with grand houses that in recent years have begun to make a big comeback.

If the customers waiting around the coat racks for a table at Rx are any indication, the gentrification (or Penn-trification, to be more precise) is well under way. Weeknights bring the mostly neighborhood crowd that owner Greg Salisbury expected when he rehabbed Rx (pronounced Rex) from an old corner pharmacy: Penn students, tweedy academics, and a contingent of low-key locals who never gave up on the area.

VERY GOOD

4443 Spruce St.
Philadelphia
(215) 222-9590

NEIGHBORHOOD
West Philadelphia

CUISINE
French Bistro/
Comfort Food

Weekends, though, have seen an influx of designer sweaters, meticulous makeup, and pricey boutique wines, sure signs that news of Rx has stirred a buzz among the dinerati, who, before the recent bistro boom, would more likely have strolled Walnut Street or chic Old City than ventured into an area known mostly for bargain Ethiopian and Indian eats.

It's no small irony, since Rx chef Ross Essner made his name at Bleu, Neil Stein's tony cafe on Rittenhouse Square. The menu at Rx, which Salisbury calls "feel-good food," isn't all that different, mostly simple French-bistro-inspired comfort fare made with fresh local ingredients and priced at $17 or less an entree.

And when the kitchen is on its game, it captures just the right balance of style and unpretentious good cooking.

The grilled hanger steak is the centerpiece of one of the best steak frites in town. The charred slices of tender beef are stacked like dominoes over creamed spinach and crisp frites.

The seared salmon is somewhat plain, but its costars are intriguing: a mound of tasty lentils ringed with silky white cauliflower puree and a sweet-tart reduction of port and blood oranges.

Beneath a tricornered cap of puff pastry, escargots nestle with mushrooms and cubes of celery root in a buttery sauce studded with cloves of roasted garlic.

If Ross Essner's cooking is the invitation to come, Rx's bright little dining room offers a reason to stay.

At lunch, the turkey meat loaf was irresistible — tangy and moist with shredded apple.

If Essner's cooking is the invitation to come, Rx's bright little dining room offers a reason to stay. Previously a catering facility and before that a take-out shop, the space has been tastefully spruced up with banquettes set beside wide windows; gold-accented white moldings; and sheets of metallic fabric that billow beneath the ceiling lights.

A wall-length wooden case is crowned with etched glass panes that read "Rx," a handsome reminder of the room's origin as an apothecary. It's a motif played to the hilt, with nostalgic knickknacks scattered around the room, from the antique doctor's scale (in a restaurant? Yikes!) set between two tables to the glass beakers on the shelves.

The glass petri dishes filled with olive oil were a bit much, though. I wasn't about to be caught dipping my bread in what looked like a medical specimen.

That's not Rx's only flaw. The room gets so noisy that it's hard to carry on a conversation. And the wait for one of the restaurant's 32 seats can be unnerving, especially as Salisbury fretfully shuffles his tables for two like a Rubik's Cube to put together seating for four.

During my meals, the servers were well-meaning but off-kilter, forgetting to bring water, neglecting to offer a bread basket until we were halfway through our entrees, and knocking over great piles of dishes at regular intervals all evening. The grand finale was a crash inside the dessert case, which dashed hopes of sampling the carrot cake.

Essner's kitchen occasionally slipped up, too. One evening the Thai curried mussels were gloriously addictive, basking in a gently sweetened spicy coconut broth; another night they were sloppily piled with empty and broken shells, not to mention a stray rubber band.

An appetizer of pre-made gnocchi was disappointing, too gummy to compete with the many homemade versions around town. And my black cod, a trendy Asian-accented favorite inspired by New York's Nobu via Stephen Starr's restaurants, was far too sweet, lacquered with a treacly miso glaze and garnished with gingery mashed yams.

Still, most of the food was appealing. The meaty duck spring rolls and an appetizer of tempura-fried scallops with spicy mayonnaise got the Asian flavors just right. Some beautiful seared scallops were equally smart, evoking a Caribbean mood with their fragrant coriander crust and accompanying mango and avocado salad.

A pan-seared whole Pocono trout, stuffed with mashed potatoes and ringed with horseradish cream, looked a little blobbish on the plate. But the fresh taste of the delicate fish paired so well with the other flavors that it was hard to resist.

Nicely browned skate, the fish darling of the current bistro boom, was prepared with textbook care. The crisp ribbed fillets were stacked like cards atop a refreshing salad of shaved fennel and blood oranges.

The dessert case was a study of bake-sale homeyness, though some offerings were more inspired than others. I've never encountered a harder brownie than the one that arrived at our table, split and sandwiched around a scoop of ice cream. The individual chocolate bundt cake also was dry.

But the pineapple upside-down cake was lusciously moist with sticky fruit. The chocolate pot de creme was undeniably creamy and indulgent.

Or Try These

Here are three other restaurants in University City.

Nan

4000 Chestnut St., Philadelphia
(215) 382-0818

Elegant French-Thai fusion is served in a fairly priced BYOB with understated decor.

Pod

3636 Sansom St., Philadelphia
(215) 387-1803

Conveyor-belt sushi and light-changing booths are part of the gimmick at Stephen Starr's futuristic Asian fantasy, but good Japanese fusion fare is one of the better reasons to return.

White Dog Cafe

3420 Sansom St., Philadelphia
(215) 386-9224

A University City institution that blends social activism with creative organic cooking and a funky, homey atmosphere.

The warm peach cobbler had a soft, crumbly pie-spiced topping. And the Jewish apple cake was a study in the architecture of comfort — a humongous wedge of butter-crisped crust that yielded to a tender heart of sponge cake perfumed with fruit. If ever there was a "feel good" finale to a story you've heard before, this was it: one slice of cake — and a slice of West Philly — that I'd gladly visit again.

■ **MENU HIGHLIGHTS** Escargots; Thai curried mussels; duck spring rolls; turkey meat loaf; scallop tempura; grilled hanger steak; salmon with cauli-flower puree; crispy skate with blood-orange brown butter; pineapple upside-down cake; chocolate pot de creme.

■ **WINE LIST** BYOB.

■ **IF YOU GO** Breakfast: Tuesday-Friday, 8 a.m.-noon. Lunch: Tuesday-Friday, 11 a.m.-5 p.m.; Saturday, 2-5 p.m. Dinner: Tuesday-Thursday, 5:30-9 p.m.; Friday-Saturday, 5:30-10 p.m. Brunch: Saturday, 10 a.m.-2 p.m.; Sunday, 10 a.m.-3 p.m. Entrees: lunch, $4-$7; dinner, $12-$17; brunch, $4-$8.

■ **RESERVATIONS** Reservations accepted for parties of six or more.

■ **CREDIT CARDS** Visa and Master Card only.

■ **SMOKING** No smoking.

■ **HANDICAP ACCESSIBLE** There are two steps at the front door; rest room is wheelchair accessible.

■ **PARKING** Street parking only.

Sansom St. Oyster House

The bustling old-time fish house has remained vibrant.

Reinventing Philadelphia's century-old oyster house tradition isn't an easy thing to do. But when Sansom Street Oyster House transformed itself three years ago, it proved to be an undertaking well worthwhile.

So many of the great restaurant names have faded into history since the early 1900s, when the Delaware River basin was still pristine and every local parish had an oyster house. And of the few old fish houses that have remained, many have withered to a shadow of their former greatness.

How fortunate for Mary and "Pa" Kelly that the legacy of Kelly's on Mole Street, which they started in 1901, was left for a quarter century in the curatorial hands of David Mink.

It may be no coincidence that the cooking has slipped a bit since the meticulous Mink sold the restaurant two years ago to his protege, chef Cary Neff. But the Sansom Street Oyster House remains one of

VERY GOOD

1516 Sansom St.
Philadelphia
(215) 567-7683

NEIGHBORHOOD
Rittenhouse Square

CUISINE
Traditional Fish House

the last bastions of this truly Philadelphian brand of restaurants, and is still one of my favorites largely because Mink's rehab of the old place showed how tradition can evolve with grace when blended with just the right dose of progress.

Neff brought some fresh ideas to complement the old-time kitchen. A top designer brought color and light to the previously dreary brown dining rooms. And suddenly, amid the flurry of stylish new upstarts contending for our seafood dollar, Sansom Street stood out. Not only for value and consistent quality, but also for a real sense of living Philadelphia history.

Sansom Street Oyster House was begun 27 years ago, but descends directly from Kelly's, which Mink's father, Sam, purchased in 1947 and left for young David to run until the early '70s. After a break from the business, David reemerged on the out-of-the-way 1500 block of Sansom Street, trying to re-create that old Kelly's feeling.

Mink succeeded in many ways, wooing a loyal cadre of local aficionados and power brokers who continue to savor the superb raw bar and unpretentious fish cookery long after more famous spots have been abandoned to tourists and ghosts. Over the years, he honed the menu to his particular tastes, from the appealing seafood-friendly wine list to the exquisite family collection of gilt-edged antique oyster plates that still adorns the walls (on indefinite loan to Neff). The triumph of Sansom Street's big transformation, though, came from the ability to refine and modernize without compromising its identity.

Or Try These

Here are three other traditional seafood restaurants.

Bookbinder's Seafood House

215 S. 15th St., Philadelphia
(215) 545-1137

The last Bookbinder restaurant standing was always my preferred Bookbinder for fish-house fare like snapper soup and crab cakes, but the time-worn ambience desperately needs new life.

Snockey's Oyster and Crab House

1020 S. Second St., Philadelphia
(215) 339-9578

This 90-year-old Queen Village institution has kept its dining room bright and spiffy, and maintained workmanlike renditions of snapper soup and milky oyster stew.

Pearl's Oyster Bar

1136 Arch St., Philadelphia
(215) 627-7250

This fried fish counter in the Reading Terminal Market is fairly ordinary, except for its big fried oysters and the fact that it is among the last of a dying breed.

For the dining areas, designer Floss Barber worked wonders, enlarging the granite-topped bar and installing open cafe windows. The rear dining rooms, once cloistered and dark, were opened, warmed with walls of red and lime accented by the dark wood wainscoting, banquettes and spindle-backed chairs.

For the kitchen, Mink hired Neff, formerly of Cary, to give a modern edge to the classic menu, adding a few items with casual nods to Asian and contemporary flavors that weren't too fussy for the spirit of this fish house.

I was somewhat enthralled at the time of my initial three-bell review two years ago to savor a perfect rendition of sherried snapper soup one moment and then move on to something as smart as St. Peter's fish glazed with sweet and spicy chile.

The entrees at several recent visits, however, have brought the twinge of a letdown. Now that he is the owner, I've rarely seen Neff in the kitchen where his talents are most needed. And the cooking has become more ordinary than I came to expect from my earlier meals. The shrimp Siam presented skewers of scrawny crustaceans slathered in a treacly sweet sauce that evoked a tiki bar more than Thailand. Their rice garnish suspiciously resembled par-boiled Minute Rice, as did the grains added to an otherwise authentic Louisiana gumbo. The halibut topped with unripe tomatoes and olives did little to enhance the otherwise unseasoned fish. And what was the point, I wondered, in offering such a special fish as Copper River salmon if it was only to be unceremoniously broiled to death beneath a blush of paprika?

My disappointments have been muted only by the fact that I still love being here, especially at the bustling lunch hour, and that Sansom Street was never really about any pretensions of creativity. For the satisfaction of fish house classics, this kitchen is still unsurpassed.

Oyster lovers who can't decide among salty Chincoteagues, sweet Kumamotos, or briny European Belons can have them all with the "seafood plateau." For $24, a wide ice tray comes piled with three kinds of oysters, raw cherrystones, spicey u-peel shrimp and marvelous house-smoked mussels. The crab legs were also delicious, their sweet meat saturated with salty juice. A forkful of the vinegary cabbage pepper hash will wipe your palate clean.

The cooked seafood appetizers were as good as the raw ones. Sansom Street has the best oysters Rockefeller I've eaten outside of Antoine's in New Orleans, the topping pureed to a silky green cloak tinted with anise Pernod. Deep-fried rock shrimp with their Old Bay-scented crust and bleu cheese dip are basically impossible to stop eating.

The crab imperial was a wonder of simple old-time richness, mounded into two clam shells and dressed to the original Kelly's recipe, a creamy glaze of sherry, dry mustard and mayo. The wonderful soups are ladled from the cauldrons of history. The rusty brown snapper, deeply flavored yet delicately spiced, turned nutty with a splash of sherry. The oyster stews were milky and intense.

Fried oysters and chicken salad is the classic Philadelphia oysterhouse combination, a strange but uncannily good duo. The oysters' creamy interiors are a perfect echo to the mayonnaise dressing of the chicken salad.

The desserts are also relics of a bygone era. The hot apple brown Betty spiced with nutmeg and clove, homemade sweet potato pie and eggy creme caramels are decidedly un-chic. But these flavors are still so satisfyingly homemade, they also mark the Sansom Street Oyster House with yet another tasty sign of its unmistakable authenticity.

■ **MENU HIGHLIGHTS** Raw bar — oysters, clams, smoked mussels, peel-your-own shrimp; steamed Ipswich clams; oysters Rockefeller; popcorn shrimp; snapper soup; fried oysters with chicken salad; baked clams; broiled lobster; crab imperial; grilled St. Peter's fish with chile glaze; apple brown Betty; sweet potato pie.

■ **WINE LIST** Modest in size, but affordable, diverse and carefully selected to pair with the seafood-centric menu. Good beers on tap include an "oyster stout."

■ **IF YOU GO** Lunch served Monday-Saturday, 11 a.m.-3:30 p.m. Dinner Monday-Saturday 3:30-10 p.m. Closed Sunday.

■ **RESERVATIONS** Accepted for parties of six or more.

■ **CREDIT CARDS** All major cards.

■ **SMOKING** Smoking at the bar only.

■ **HANDICAP ACCESSIBLE** Yes.

■ **PARKING** Restaurant validates after 5 p.m. for a $5 discount at Central Parking garages at 15th and Sansom Streets and 1616 Sansom St.

Savona

Elegant seafood is inspired by the French Riviera, with fine service and top-notch wines.

I t seems an unlikely journey, escaping the Schuylkill Expressway traffic and emerging moments later at a Mediterranean villa. But Savona has become that vaunted destination, a culinary oasis a few left turns from the highway.

A curved driveway sweeps us up, around and away, depositing our car at the glassed-in entrance. The bones of this fieldstone building erected in 1765, the former home of Aaron Burr, are historic Pennsylvania.

But the atmosphere inside is pure South of France, from the terracotta-colored walls and tiled floors to the lilting French accents of the staff, many of whom greet you as you head into the dining room for an evening of splendid Riviera-inspired seafood.

Which side of the Riviera, though, has often puzzled me.

EXCELLENT

100 Old Gulph Rd.
Gulph Mills, Pa.
(610) 520-1200

NEIGHBORHOOD
Main Line

CUISINE
French Seafood

Savona's owner, Evan Lambert, has always posed the restaurant as the "spirit of the Italian Riviera." The name itself pays homage to an Italian port. But chef Dominique Filoni is a native of St. Tropez. And despite the affinities between the two countries, especially on the Mediterranean coast, Filoni's food is unabashedly French, from the pistou soup to the chocolate bombe.

This may cause confusion if you're looking for pasta, since there are only two on the menu. But Savona does so many other things right that it can be forgiven its geographic fudging. Few restaurants, in the suburbs or city, offer such a polished fine-dining experience.

The dining rooms are gorgeous, with luxury linens, heavy silver, and some of the sleekest white Bernardaud plates around. The highly trained staff moves seamlessly around the table, whether delivering tiny crocks of cool sweet pea froth for the evening's amuse-bouche, spooning sauce from little copper pots, or guiding diners through the excellent 1,000-bottle wine list. Don't skimp here. It's worth ordering just to watch the sommelier decant your bottle over a candle flame into the fine top-shaped crystal carafe.

Filoni's food is worth the pomp, building on the pure flavors of high-quality ingredients with inventive touches that capture the Mediterranean spirit. The lobster salad is a crimson-colored tail curling over a bloom of baby spinach, the tender meat shined with pistachio oil and topped with a dollop of avocado mousse. Two plump zucchini blossoms, still clinging to their slender little green squash, are stuffed with a mince of lobster and foie gras scented with Pernod.

The Riviera salad gives the traditional Nicoise new elegance, its bramble of frisee crisscrossed with fresh anchovies, crumbles of oil-poached tuna, baby artichokes, and scampi tails as sweet as seafood candy. A composition of ruby-rare tuna is slicked with truffled oil, an intriguing bass note that didn't overwhelm the pristine fish.

Some luxury ingredients weren't always used to best advantage. The lobster risotto was too rich and sticky, and the herb-crusted lobster tail, seasoned oddly with dill, had turned an unappetizing black. The agnolotti were another seemingly sure-fire indulgence that didn't quite work. Stuffed with molten foie gras, the large dumplings were too heavy and awkward to be eaten from a bowl of broth. The seared foie gras appetizer had a wonderful basil-peach compote but was overcooked.

But almost always, the kitchen's dishes were perfect. Many of the best celebrated the simple vibrance of fresh produce. The pistou soup's ham broth was emerald green with basil and brimming with zucchini, potatoes, beans, tomatoes and swirls of vermicelli. Braised baby artichokes barigoule were served with flair as the waiter spooned a delicious wine broth over an arrangement of tiny vegetables covered with two pasta diamonds, one tinted with cocoa, the other with chestnut flour.

Pasta seldom appears at Savona, and usually more for flourish than for substance, as the Italians would have it. The sole exception is the tagliatelle, whose ribbons make the perfect nest for crisp maitake mushrooms, bitter broccoli rabe, and sweet scampi tails.

Speaking of sole, I doubt anyplace else does a better rendition of the Dover fish than Savona, where it is boned tableside and spooned onto the plate with buttery artichokes, peas, and, if you're lucky to hit the season, snappy green coils of fiddlehead ferns.

Then again, all of Savona's fish were top-notch during my visits.

Or Try These

Here are three other fine-dining restaurants in the western suburbs.

Le Mas Perrier

503 W. Lancaster Ave., Wayne, Pa. (610) 964-2588

Georges Perrier's elegant suburban outpost offers a lovely Provencale ambience and much-improved service, but the new chef, while talented, has taken the menu in the less intriguing direction of Asian-fusion.

Birchrunville Store Cafe

Hollow and Flowing Spring Roads, Birchrunville, Pa. (610) 827-9002

A bucolic country store-turned-restaurant with seasonal French-inspired cooking.

Taquet

139 E. Lancaster Ave., Wayne, Pa. (610) 687-5005

Elegant French fine-dining with subtle Moroccan accents at the Wayne Hotel. Could use attention to details to fulfill its potential.

Meaty white fillets of John Dory came perfectly grilled alongside a coarse puree of zucchini and olive. Pan-seared branzino paired nicely with sweetly braised endive and fennel and an unusual pistachio puree. Browned scallops were poised over delicate white asparagus, tender fava beans, and bits of prosciutto. And Ligurian ciuppin, similar to bouillabaisse, was as delicate as any seafood stew I've tasted.

But after savoring medallions of succulent porcini-crusted lamb loin, set with whole morels around a pillow of truffled mashed potatoes, I can't help wondering why Filoni doesn't cook more meat.

There are fewer desserts than I might have expected, but perhaps Savona wants to show off its cheese cart, an exquisite Christofle chariot topped with a glass dome that disappears when it rolls open, releasing the fragrance of pungent Reblochon, Saint-Nectaire and raw-milk Camembert.

Still, it's worth saving room for the baked apple stuffed with nuts and dried fruit, or the funky white-chocolate bombe, whose ivory shell conceals mousses of milk chocolate and crunchy espresso.

But how could I pass up the sublime chocolate souffle, where the forces of light and darkness unite in a floating column of airy cocoa? A server cracks its surface and pours creme anglaise into its heart, and the souffle sighs upward before settling in.

Blissfully, I can only do the same.

■ **MENU HIGHLIGHTS** Pistou soup; ruby-red tuna; braised baby artichokes; lobster salad; zucchini blossoms stuffed with lobster and foie gras; scampi tagliatelle; Ligurian seafood stew; scallops; Dover sole with peas and artichokes; grilled black bass; porcini-dusted lamb; cheese cart; chocolate souffle; white and dark chocolate bombe.

Chocolate bombe

■ **WINE LIST** Savona has one of the area's outstanding wine programs, with a huge international cellar of 1,000 high-quality wines. Even better, the staff knows how to serve, with expert guidance from the sommelier, beautiful glassware, and dramatic tableside decanting.

■ **IF YOU GO** Dinner served Sunday-Thursday 5:30-10 p.m., Friday-Saturday 5:30-11 p.m. Entrees $28-$39.

■ **RESERVATIONS** Strongly recommended, especially on weekends.

■ **CREDIT CARDS** All major cards but Discover.

■ **SMOKING** Smoking in the bar only.

■ **HANDICAP ACCESSIBLE** Yes.

■ **PARKING** Free valet parking.

Shiao Lan Kung

The bare-bones nook has some of the brightest,
most consistent cooking in Chinatown.

Canton Man worked his wok with bare hands, a silver-haired blur of frayed chef's whites caught in the groove of perpetual motion.

He waved his ladle like a wand, tapping faucets, dipping sauces, stirring, flipping — *poof!* The heat of red flame brought life to the bleak monochrome metal of his kitchen, which, until the clouds of steam blew away, you'd never distinguish from any other Chinatown nook.

But when the smoke cleared and the dishes emerged into the tiny lilac dining room at Shiao Lan Kung (which means "man from Shiaolan," a village in south Canton), something was definitely different. It was not the menu itself, which is as familiar as it gets, from the wonton soup to the orange beef and kung po chicken.

EXCELLENT

930 Race St.
Philadelphia
(215) 928-0282

NEIGHBORHOOD
Chinatown

CUISINE
Chinese

What was different here were the flavors produced by Man Lee, the venerable chef-owner who sadly died of lung cancer more than a year ago. It was a challenge to this modest family business, and a blow to devoted fans like myself. Because Lee managed to coax such vivid tastes from his simple ingredients that he breathed life into a genre of Chinese cooking that, for me, had so long been muted in the mediocrity of take-out containers. Remarkably, under the tutelage of an old family friend, Siu Wai Chau, two of Lee's nephews, King Lun Au and Yuan Jun Au, have begun to reproduce the old family recipes to amazing perfection.

Salt-baked shrimp are sealed inside a micro-thin crust that crackles with five-spice flavor. Piqued by a mince of hot peppers, they are quenched by the collar of slivered oranges that rims the plate. Plump dumplings are shrink-wrapped in thin dough skins, their pork stuffing filled with a sweet cabbage mince that plays against the gingery garlic soy pooled beneath them.

Orange beef is not the typical deep-fried gristle in sticky sauce, but tender strips of meat and crunchy batons of scallion glazed in a mysterious dark sauce flared with the anise intrigue of dried tangerines.

And where else, I wonder, are the wontons made to order? The stuffing is seasoned at the last minute for maximum tenderness, then wrapped in skins so fine that the dumplings float like little Casper ghosts through the sesame-tinged broth.

Opened in 1987, the Lees' restaurant was as unassuming as it gets, a 42-seat cubbyhole that thrives from dinner until 3:30 in the morning, when a wave of post-nightclub munchers flows through the Race Street door. But even the early settings can become hectic. I've rarely seen such patience in the face of mayhem as Anna and her staff, handling the dining room with poise, helping diners with the menu, expediting dishes, smiling at the biggest mess a baby ever left.

When I say that Shiao Lan Kung redecorated (an enthusiastic cabbie alerted me to this), it was a lesson in relativity: They upgraded from dingy to modestly pleasant, with the acquisition of real plates their biggest coup.

The pale purple paint job, the marbleized tile wainscoting and the table flowers are nice. But nothing pleased me more than the disappearance of those worn-out plastic plates. Food this good deserves the respect of china.

This is not to say it's faultless. I've seen the occasionally greasy eggroll (that didn't stop it from being yummy). I've also come across the occasionally over-thickened sauce. The barbecue ribs were a little dry and tough.

But for standard Chinese cooking rendered with sharp, bright flavors and quality products, I've found few that can keep up with Shiao Lan Kung.

Slices of chicken were always tender, whether cloaked in smoky garlic black bean sauce or the warming spice of a plummy kung po studded with peanuts that pop with a fresh-roasted snap.

Sauces of all kinds come with distinct, dynamic flavors. Reddish Szechuan sauce takes sweet and sour to the next level, using the lees of aged homemade rice wine to give it swivel on the tongue. It is a perfect complement to the moist flesh of fried whole fish and the crunch of slivered scallions, but is also great with shrimp.

The Hunan tastes more of earthy dark pepper, glazing chicken or beef or garlic scallops in its complex tang.

Or Try These

Here are three other places to eat after midnight.

Tony Luke's

39 Oregon Ave, Philadelphia
(215) 551-5725

Nostalgists inevitably head to Ninth and Passyunk for late-night steaks at Pat's or Geno's, but this sassy Oregon Avenue steakerie tops it off with garlicky broccoli rabe until 2 a.m. on weekends.

Mayfair Diner

7373 Frankford Ave., Philadelphia.
(215) 624-8886

The stainless-steel classic rimmed with green neon still draws a devoted Northeast crowd for homey '50s-era fare 24 hours a day.

N. 3rd

801 N. Third St., Philadelphia.
(215) 413-3666

This Northern Liberties bar-restaurant has one of the city's most interesting cheap wine lists and serves updated comfort food, from ribs to corn-crusted catfish, until 1 a.m. on weekends.

The decor is unassuming, the food outstanding at Shiao Lan Kung.

Dragon and phoenix nest, presented in an edible basket of fried taro root, showed the power of a mild clear sauce to focus the flavors of the ingredients it covered. Tender curls of fresh shrimp, snappy florets of broccoli, crunchy snow peas, and butter-soft white-meat chicken suddenly seemed magnified in taste.

Sauteed greens are a specialty, too. I especially love the mound of leafy pea leaves. Softer than stalky Chinese broccoli, the leaves are a verdant chlorophyll cushion for the cloves of garlic nestled inside.

There were dishes that looked terrible but tasted great, such as the boneless fried lychee duck that was crisped to mahogany brown, then napped in fluorescent red jelly. Despite its tacky color, the sweet-and-sour sauce stopped just shy of cloying, the cool chunks of lychee fruit and pineapple on the side contrasted the gamy darkness of the nicely rendered duck.

Ma po bean curd was another, an unsightly plate of jiggling reddish mush that concealed a universe of textures and tangy flavors. Soft tofu squares, crumbly ground pork, snappy bamboo and water chestnuts, and woodsy shiitake mushrooms all evoked comfort from within this addictive slurry of hot red bean sauce.

If I could pick a cliche for dessert, it would be the fried banana. But it is the only dessert offered here, and so they do it well.

The fruit arrives in crisp cocoons of batter, glistening hot beneath a shine of molasses and sesame seeds. I crack it open, and it is amazingly light, a tube of half-melted fruit suspended in a pillow of its own sweetness. Again, I am surprised. Then again, I have come to expect this from the house of Canton Man, where his fiery hot wok taught me new respect for dishes I'd turned away from long ago.

The Chinatown Menu

Because so many Chinatown restaurants have similar menus, the key to unlocking the neighborhood's secrets is knowing which place does which dish best. Here are some of my favorites:

■ Salt-baked seafood and steamed dumplings with ginger sauce at **Shiao Lan Kung**, 930 Race St.

■ Peking duck rolls, E-Fu "long life" noodles, and wonton soup at **Sang Kee**, 238 N. Ninth St.

■ Sichuan turnip soup with shredded pork and all of the hot pots (especially the chicken with black pepper sauce) at **Lee How Fook**, 219 N. 11th St.

■ Roti canai pancakes with chicken curry dip, Malaysian spring rolls, and coconut prawns at **Penang**, 117 N. 10th St.

■ Fiery satay beef soup at **Nice Chinese Noodle House**, 1038 Race St.

■ Dynasty mock shrimp, emerald soup and salt-baked oyster mushrooms at **Cherry Street Chinese Vegetarian**, 1010 Cherry St.

■ The barbecue platter, spring rolls, and broken rice with charred pork at **Vietnam**, 221 N. 11th St.

■ Spicy crisped lentil cakes and flaky thousand-layer bread at **Rangoon**, 112 N. Ninth St.

■ The best (and most expensive) cup of coffee in the city ($8 for Jamaican Blue Mountain) at **Ray's Cafe & Tea House**, 141 N. Ninth St.

■ Made-to-order dim-sum at **Lakeside Chinese Deli**, 207 N. Ninth St.

■ **MENU HIGHLIGHTS** Hong Kong wonton soup; steamed dumplings; orange beef; salt-baked scallops and shrimp (request without shells); chicken in black bean sauce; steamed salted chicken; Hunan beef; fried whole fish in Szechuan sauce; steamed clams; spicy garlic scallops; kung po chicken; dragon and phoenix nest; lychee duck; snow pea leaves with garlic; fried bananas.

■ **WINE LIST** Go for the Tsing Tao beer.

■ **IF YOU GO** Dinner served Sunday-Thursday 4 p.m.-3 a.m., Friday-Saturday 4 p.m.-3:30 a.m. Entrees, $6.50-$16.95.

■ **RESERVATIONS** Accepted only for parties of 6 to 10 people.

■ **CREDIT CARDS** All major cards but Discover.

■ **SMOKING** There is no designated nonsmoking section.

■ **HANDICAP ACCESSIBLE** No. There is one step at the entrance and bathrooms are not handicapped equipped.

■ **PARKING** Street parking only.

Standard Tap

The hip neighborhood bar serves up gutsy yet sophisticated rustic fare with great seasonal ingredients and one of the best local beer selections in town.

I n the early 1980s, a Texas Monthly magazine writer named Jim Atkinson wrote a homage to the "bar bar" and its fight to survive the "wimpifying" influence of the fern bars sprouting up across the country.

The "bar bar," he wrote, was usually a dark, whiskey-drinking place where the arts of conversation, listening, killing time, and holding forth were still prized. And "if somebody knows where you are," he added, "you aren't in a bar bar."

The fern bar, meanwhile, was "about being there — being there to be seen." And its trappings were too horrible for Atkinson to bear: wine spritzers and piña coladas, fried zucchini sticks and fake Tiffany lamps, guys named Biff scoping out girls named Heather, and bartenders wielding computerized liquor guns to maximize profits.

VERY GOOD

901 N. Second St.
Philadelphia
(215) 238-0630

NEIGHBORHOOD
Northern Liberties

CUISINE
Updated Pub

What Atkinson described was only the beginning of the struggle between independent bars with character and corporate clones such as Bennigan's and Houlihan's. And the situation would get worse before it got better.

But get better it did. Not only have unique "bar bars" been thriving in Philadelphia, but some have begun cooking up a storm.

How about the New Wave Cafe in Queen Village, which, before its current chef arrived, was most noted as a waiting room for the restaurant across the street? Or the Black Sheep, near Rittenhouse Square? The crowd there can be a bit "ferny," but the owners earn points for opening an Irish pub sans shamrocks.

Perhaps the most "bar bar" of the new generation, though, is the Standard Tap in Northern Liberties. It's a place Atkinson would love, half-lit with the yellow glow of a gas chandelier that gives the occupants of the hand-built cherrywood bar and the dining room banquettes a moody air of "I'm not here."

The beautifully renovated building, which has been a Northern Liberties taproom for most of its two centuries, is set at the northernmost fringe of this burgeoning neighborhood. The crowd has an

The beautifully renovated building has been a Northern Liberties taproom for most of its two centuries.

edgy, effortlessly cool air — an artsy mix of salt-and-pepper Bohemians, restaurant industry insiders, and thirtysomethings with tattoos who make the Old City folks to the south look like trendy wannabes.

There is no television. So conversation is the sport of choice if you can surmount the din of the jukebox playing Tom Waits and Iggy Pop. That is, unless you play darts. In which case you'll be doing your damnedest not to hit one of the servers exiting the kitchen just a few inches left of the dart board's well-pocked wall.

There may not be quite enough whiskeys for Atkinson's, or my, taste. But the Standard Tap is a premier venue for local beers, with as many as 13 brews on draft and not a bottle of suds in sight. This commitment to fresh beer is no surprise since one of the Tap's two owners, William Reed, spent five years as a brewmaster at the now-closed Sam Adams Brewhouse on Sansom Street.

But the focus on local goes beyond the beer, from the wood that Reed and partner Paul Kimport used to build the bar and banquettes to the ingredients in the Tap's surprising food, which has continued to improve since former Fishmarket chef Carolynn Angle moved into the kitchen.

There is an austerity to the blackboard menus, which simply read "squid," "duck salad," "smelts," or the like. And those bony little pungent fish say "bar bar" as much as anything else.

Don't let the low-key menu fool you, though. This food is ambitious with an honest homemade quality that rises far above the potato-skin/nacho cliches that fern bars worked so hard to standardize.

Angle's seafood chowder is simply awesome, creamily rich and full of tender shrimp, oysters and chunks of fresh potatoes. The hearty chicken pie comes wrapped in a flaky turban of buttery pastry. And a bowl of spicy cream broth brings a clever "hash" of scallops and cuminy chorizo, each seared to a trompe l'oieul of lookalike brown disks.

The duck salad features one of the best legs of duck confit in town, steeped in a pot of its own fat and then crisped until the skin protects the soft, herb-infused flesh like salty brown parchment.

An appreciation of good ingredients is apparent in some of the other salads, too — the crimson mound of sweet roasted beets sided with a dollop of sour cream, or the slices of lusciously ripe heirloom tomatoes that are displayed liberally during late summer beneath shards of Locatelli cheese.

I saw only one dessert offered during my visits, but it was a nice rendition of the classic many restaurants flail at: a creme brulee with real vanilla and a still-warm caramel crust.

A few dishes were lacking. The beef stew was skimpy with meat on its second day served as a special. The burgers, while tasty, suffered from fancy-bun syndrome, with a chewy, flour-dusted roll that smooshed the beef to pieces before I managed to bite through it.

An upscale grilled cheese sandwich was also defeated by a poor choice of bread, a focaccia that overshadowed the tasty blend of jack cheeses inside.

Or Try These

Here are three other restaurants in Northern Liberties.

Pigalle

702 N. Second St., Philadelphia
(215) 627-7772

This French-inspired bistro has a polished and sultry style that is novel in Northern Liberties, and a new chef since the review.

Aden

614 N. Second St., Philadelphia
(215) 627-9844

This personable little cafe has an intimate, hand-painted ambience and an affordable Mediterranean menu that is best with simple comforts such as stuffed peppers.

N. 3rd

801 N. Third St., Philadelphia.
(215) 413-3666

This hip Northern Liberties bar-restaurant has one of the city's most interesting cheap wine lists and serves updated comfort food, from ribs to corn-crusted catfish, until 1 a.m. on weekends.

The Tap's kitchen, though, thrives on the rustic flavors that used to be reserved for European-style bistros, not neighborhood bars. There is a homemade breakfast sausage at Sunday brunch that at dinner occasionally finds its way into a creamy corn stew beneath a crisp fillet of red snapper. The paté is also made in-house; the night we ordered it, it was a slab of coarsely ground pork and venison ringed

Duck confit salad.

with smoky bacon. The soups have always been excellent, whether it is a bowl of thick lentil or an icy-cold vichyssoise.

And the roast pork sandwich is a monument to gusto, a mound of shredded tender meat on a bun swamped with fennel-scented juice.

As I laid roasted green chiles on top, the wonderfully sloppy mess came alive with the kind of heat that made me want to get up and dance. Or at least, throw darts in a genuine "bar bar."

■ **MENU HIGHLIGHTS** Beet salad; cold potato-leek soup; seafood chowder; duck salad; heirloom tomato salad; pork sandwich; softshell crabs; seared snapper with corn-sausage stew; scallop and chorizo hash; creme brulee.

■ **WINE LIST** There is a small selection of affordable wines, but the focus is on local draft beers from Yards, Victory, Stoudt's and others, including a wonderful ESB ale from Tröegs in Harrisburg.

■ **IF YOU GO** Dinner served daily 5 p.m.-1 a.m. Brunch served Sunday 11 a.m.-4 p.m. Dinner entrees $7-$16.

■ **RESERVATIONS** Not taken.

■ **CREDIT CARDS** Visa and MasterCard only.

■ **SMOKING** No nonsmoking section.

■ **HANDICAP ACCESSIBLE** Not wheelchair accessible.

■ **PARKING** Street parking only.

Strawberry Hill

The warm Lancaster tavern has ambitious eclectic cuisine and a great California wine cellar.

I t is hard to say what is more surprising about Strawberry Hill. That it has an amazing cellar of 1,400 wines, many of them California rarities seldom seen east of the Mississippi (let alone in Pennsylvania). Or that such a highbrow wine collection exists at all in Lancaster County, which is better known for its outlet malls and chicken buffets, not to mention Amish buggies.

For those who imagine such an important wine destination to be a bastion of pomp and snootiness, where tuxedoed captains dangle silver tasting cups from chains around their necks and arrive at your table spouting malolactic hyperbole, Strawberry Hill has a few other surprises. For instance, the sommelier — loquacious owner Dennis Kerek — is likely to greet you in a red T-shirt, jeans, and jogging shoes. His ponytailed son Chip is even mellower, a master of the soft sell who refers to many of the West Coast wine-makers on the list as "good buds."

EXCELLENT

128 W. Strawberry St.
Lancaster, Pa.
(717) 393-5544

NEIGHBORHOOD
Lancaster County

CUISINE
New American

As for the cellar itself, forget the polished glass and wrought-iron showcases of Center City's finest. You have to go through the men's room to get to the cramped basement nook where Strawberry Hill stores its treasure — a chilly, humid room filled with unceremonious stacks of anonymous wooden crates.

But what Strawberry Hill lacks in pretense it more than compensates for in substance. (And from the taste of Brent Hodge's impressive menu, its ambitions aren't limited to the cellar.) Inside those wooden boxes, though, are some of the best wines from Napa and Sonoma, not to mention some considerable Bordeaux. There are multi-vintage collections of sought-after producers such as Harlan, Heitz and Peter Michael, a complete selection of Robert Biale's opulent red zinfandels (my favorite is Black Chicken), and lesser-known labels such as Nickel & Nickel and August Briggs.

This is the kind of list that serious wine lovers will travel and pay dearly for, which is fortunate, since a trip to Strawberry Hill will likely demand they do both. It is a solid 90-minute haul from Philadelphia, and the wines, tailored to aficionados, really start to get interesting in the $60-plus zone. Expensive? Definitely. But the markups are pretty fair compared with some of Philly's best wine lists.

Chip (left) and Dennis Kerek have assembled one of the finest collections of California wines in Pennsylvania.

There are, thankfully, several excellent wines by the glass for those looking to spend less (around $8 a pour), including a bright New Zealand chardonnay and a fat red primitivo, the Italian zinfandel.

More important, Strawberry Hill's appeal goes beyond its wines.

It may not be the epitome of white-tablecloth gastronomy, but the restaurant is hardly unattractive. It sits high atop a five-point intersection in the historic Cabbage Hill neighborhood of Lancaster, in a turreted brick building with a long history as a speakeasy and tavern, most recently Obie Miller's. Its exposed brick walls and giant wine-barrel entranceway exude warmth with a soundtrack of jazz.

Like the wine list, Hodge's wide-ranging modern menu is a pleasant surprise, offering some of the most adventurous and vibrant food I've tasted in the hinterlands of Pennsylvania.

Hodge doesn't shy from exotic seasonings such as Jamaican jerk and Cajun spice, but it's his use of quality ingredients and local flavors, for which Kerek shops at Lancaster's Central Market, that really bolsters this food.

Wonderful wild mushrooms are everywhere. Crunchy fronds of maitake mushrooms mingle with green peas in a dark cabernet gravy, offering an earthy contrast to the ivory sweetness of giant scallops crusted with polenta. Snappy chanterelle caps punctuate the rich, beefy broth of a summer-vegetable soup filled with shreds of veal.

And orange-fleshed lobster mushrooms are mounded with sweet white corn and brown butter beneath a tail of sauteed lobster. A similar corn appetizer topped with jumbo shrimp gets an extra jolt of fire from spicy cherry peppers.

The cuts of beef provided by Kunzler Meats, a local butcher, were exceptional. The filet mignon was one of the best I've tasted, so tender that each bite was like falling into a down pillow. The massive strip steak was just as great, a plate-long slab of grilled succulence served alongside a moist bread pudding filled with wild mushrooms.

Hodge employs all the moves of trendy cooking, from drizzled sauces to edible flowers. But a few busy dishes could have used more fine-tuning. The vegetal delicacy of artichoke bisque was drowned out by the sharp tang of too much Maytag blue cheese. An ample slice of seared foie gras ringed by black-berry coulis would have been perfect had its pedestal of polenta been half as thick. The crab cakes were eclipsed by a heavy-handed dusting of spice. My guest's edible flower came with a resident bug.

We simply brushed it off. Hodge's food was most often a hit. A thick slice of herb-smoked Arctic char came over a clever bed of celery and shiitake mushrooms shaved into noodle-like strands. Cajun-seared tuna and scallops played the spice card just right, the beautiful seafood tossed with Asian-flavored noodles and crunchy clusters of maitake mushrooms.

The jerked duck was among the most intriguing dishes, the tender breast perfumed with a gingery Caribbean spice, then paired with a perfect leg of classic duck confit over a rich mound of barley risotto ringed by green cilantro oil. The chile-dusted salmon was surprisingly bland, but saved by a fabulous garnish of corn-filled flapjacks, herb-infused molasses, and a chunky mashed avocado.

Or Try These

Here are three other restaurants in and around Lancaster.

The Restaurant at Doneckers

333 N. State St., Ephrata, Pa. (717) 738-9501

A former Le Bec-Fin chef blends French haute cuisine with regional flavors at this upscsale Lancaster County shopping complex.

The Inn at Twin Lindens

2092 Main St., Churchville, Pa. (717) 445-7619

Donna Leahy's lovely inn, set amid rolling Lancaster farmland, serves more sophisticated delights than most bed and breakfasts could dream of, but the once-a-week Saturday dinners are also a treat.

Green Hills Inn

2444 Morgantown Rd., Reading, Pa. (610) 777-9611

This gracious inn with continental cuisine is a special-occasion standby.

No help was needed, though, for the juicy rack of lamb, which came with an unctuous creamy risotto filled with more of that sweet corn and excellent lobster mushrooms.

Hodge gets kitchen help from pastry chef Diana Koler, whose yeasty house-baked rolls are at least as much of a highlight as her satisfying renditions of desserts such as chocolate cheesecake, fruity cream-laced layer cakes, and streusel-topped sour-cream apple pie.

Even the proprietor gets involved in the kitchen, stewing a secret spaghetti meat sauce that, according to the menu, is "known only by members of the Kerek family."

I suspect that the otherwise fine server who took a knife to the fresh spaghetti (blasphemy!) while trying to split our order was not an official member of the Kerek family. But the dish was wonderful all the same, with sausage crumbles and homemade meatballs inside a tomatoey puree that unleashed a devilishly spicy, sneaky sting.

It did seem slightly strange to find such a homey dish on this strikingly modern menu, not to mention two-fisted spice amid the gentle blandness of Lancaster. But at Strawberry Hill, it was just one of many pleasant surprises.

■ **MENU HIGHLIGHTS** Shrimp with sweet corn; smoked Arctic char; cornmeal-crusted scallops; filet mignon; strip steak; jerk-spiced duck; homemade spaghetti; chocolate cheesecake.

■ **WINE LIST** This is one of the finest collections of California wines available in Pennsylvania, with selections from rarely seen wine-makers such as Robert Biale and August Briggs, and big-ticket cult wines from Harlan, Heitz and Peter Michael. Bargain-seekers should stick to wines by the glass. This list focuses on bottles costing $60 and above.

■ **IF YOU GO** Dinner served nightly, 5-11 p.m. Dinner entrees, $13-$32.

■ **RESERVATIONS** Suggested.

■ **CREDIT CARDS** All major cards but Diners Club.

■ **SMOKING** There is a nonsmoking section.

■ **HANDICAP ACCESSIBLE** There is a ramp on the side of the restaurant; rest rooms are not wheelchair accessible.

■ **PARKING** Free parking across the street in the school parking lot.

Striped Bass

Neil Stein's expensive seafood palace features
spectacular decor and talented chef Terence Feury.

The best restaurants are often defined by the deeds of great chefs. But until the arrival of Terence Feury three years ago, the story of Striped Bass had always been about a splashy dining room and the big fish.

Transformed in 1994 from a former Walnut Street brokerage house, the room's soaring beveled wood ceilings, its marble columns and muslin-draped windows make for what is easily the city's most spectacular dining space. To sit at one of the banquettes and slurp down an icy tray of gold-rate oysters with a splash of frozen black currant mignonette is to dine in a cathedral of nouveau riche glamour.

But try not to stare at the two salon-precious hairdos that slink by the tables of young traders in designer suits swilling their $200 bottles of wine. It's unbecoming to ogle the guests of owner Neil Stein. The two ladies were eating for free. Which is not a bad deal at one of the city's priciest restaurants.

I focus instead on another big fish, the 16-foot striped bass made of forged steel that leaps elusively over the flames of the restaurant's open kitchen, emphasizing, if you didn't already get it, a recurring theme here.

Yes, the menu is entirely seafood — or at least it was until recently, when the restaurant finally began experimenting with one daily meat dish. But Stein never ceases to polish his beloved Bass, taking care of meticulous details, from the spotless stemware to the gorgeous flowers at the entrance. Entrees may run anywhere from $28 to $50, but this is one restaurant that looks and feels the part.

EXCELLENT

1500 Walnut St.
Philadelphia
(215) 732-4444

NEIGHBORHOOD
Rittenhouse Square

CUISINE
New American Seafood

Whether it always acts the part is another question. The restaurant's service staff is capable of extraordinary service — I had such a meal recently, although I was certain the staff knew I was present. My waitress was lovely and always had good advice on the menu and wine list. The back staff seamlessly cared for the table. They need to be more consistent, though. On other visits last year, I went through long stretches of waiting for the staff to notice our dirty plates or crumb the tables or simply bring more water.

The restaurant's dessert list is good enough, with the requisite

The 16-foot striped bass made of forged steel that leaps elusively over the flames of the restaurant's open kitchen emphasizes a recurring theme.

molten chocolate cake and variations on mousse, but it has been more dynamic in the past. The appointment of talented Avenue B pastry chef Joseph Furgiuele to oversee the desserts at all of Stein's restaurants should improve these areas.

As for Feury, he has simply gotten better and better over the last three years, maturing into one of the city's finest chefs. When he first arrived from New York's Le Bernardin on the heels of Asian-influenced Allyson Thurber, and her celebrity predecessor, Alison Barshak, Feury was by comparison more subdued. The first-time head chef seemed more preoccupied with navigating the restaurant's incredible supply of world-class seafood in simple but consistent ways rather than anything daringly creative.

Over time, however, Feury has been able to refine a culinary vision, a Mediterranean-inspired palette that is both elegant and inventive.

At the apex of next summer's swelter, I will long for that vichyssoise Feury herbed with the tarragon kiss of fines herbes. My server poured it into my bowl, and the green broth pooled around an island of exquisitely rare lobster tail fanned over diced potatoes. It was ethereal.

A most unusual dish of braised squid caused a similar reaction. Normally flash-fried or quickly grilled, Feury cooked his squid gently for an hour and a half in olive oil, sundried tomatoes and olives. The calamari had plumped into pillowy tender brown rings, completely infused with piquant tang of their dark stew. Even the complimentary hors d'oeuvre was sublime, a bite-size puff of sweet lump crab napped with caviar-jeweled remoulade.

There was an era when this restaurant appeared to have run out of ways to cook its fish, relying on stock-based sauces that seemed determined to prove that fish should be treated like meat.

But Feury has since found an impressive range of other methods to showcase his bounty that harmonize, rather than overpower, the pristine ingredients. Crisply seared black bass came with an earthy puree of cauliflower that was a perfect compromise between sauce and starch, its ivory mousseline accented by sweet streaks of reduced Banyuls wine. A more assertive striped bass found an intriguing balance in the richness of a walnut cream. Perfectly rare tuna crowned a lightly spiced tomato ragu with marvelous homemade penne, an irresistible bowl of olive-oil-splashed zestiness that completely evoked the Mediterreanean.

It is a mood that Feury has alluded to with some of his best dishes in the past, including a prosciutto-wrapped halibut over polenta studded with figs, and a sauteed cod encircled by pureed olives.

When he steps into other regional influence, the flavors aren't always so convincing. A scallop ceviche, for example, had a one-dimensional marinade. But his Thai-themed swordfish steak was memorable, baked inside a banana leaf to an awesome succulence, then placed over a fragrant curried carrot puree —

Or Try These

Here are three other upscale restaurants that focus on seafood.

Morimoto

723 Chestnut St., Philadelphia
(215) 413-9070

Superstar chef Masaharu Morimoto brings cutting-edge Japanese cuisine to the undulating bamboo dining room of Stephen Starr's hip restaurant.

Savona

100 Old Gulph Rd., Gulph Mills, Pa. (610) 520-1200

Exquisite seafood inspired by the French Riviera, with fine service and top-notch wines.

McCormick & Schmick's

1 S. Broad St., Philadelphia
(215) 568-6888

This Portland-based chain brings an impressive dining room to a prime power lunch spot across from City Hall, although seafood has been inconsistent.

another vegetable-based sauce that achieved intensity without richness. Feury also dabbles with a potent Cuban sour orange mojo, but he found one of the few fish that could match the mojo's citrus kick, an intensely flavorful wild king salmon with flesh the deep-orange hue of brick.

If the kitchen has found new ways to think about luxury fish, so has wine guru Ed Murray, who was recently promoted to general manager. He inherited a fabulous cellar from predecessor Marnie Olds, but has continued to make it more accessible, finding excellent, lesser-known bottles for $50 and under to compliment the stash of big-ticket chardonnays, working the wines by the glass, and expanding into red grapes and regions one rarely thinks of with seafood. This list has everything from some earthy Spanish reds to an obscure but trendy Austrian gruener veltliner.

Of course, fine wine has always been one of this restaurant's great draws, just as the soaring room and its splendidly giant steel fish, and the flamboyant Mr. Stein have been magnets for the glamour dining set. But now at last, it is the talent of a great chef that finally defines Striped Bass.

■ **MENU HIGHLIGHTS** Raw bar oysters; vichysoisse with fines herbes and lobster; fresh penne with spiced tuna; slow-braised squid in sundried tomato sauce; black bass over cauliflower puree; striped bass with walnut sauce; red snapper with herbed rice; Thai curry-marinated swordfish; wild salmon with sour orange mojo; chocolate dream.

■ **WINE LIST** The large wine cellar has an international selection of excellent bottles — many under $50 — that includes but goes beyond the requisite fish-friendly chardonnays and sauvignon blancs to include versatile pinot noirs, merlot-based Bordeaux, several German rieslings, and some interesting but less common whites such as Austrian gruener veltliner and Spanish albarino. There is also an extensive list of quality wines by the glass.

■ **IF YOU GO** Lunch served Monday-Friday 11:30 a.m.-2:30 p.m. Dinner served Monday-Thursday 5-11 p.m., Friday-Saturday 5-11:30 p.m., Sunday 5-10 p.m. Sunday brunch, 11 a.m.-2:30 p.m.

■ **RESERVATIONS** Strongly recommended.

■ **CREDIT CARDS** All major cards but Discover.

■ **SMOKING** Permitted in the bar area only.

■ **HANDICAP ACCESSIBLE** Yes.

■ **PARKING** Valet parking costs $15.

Susanna Foo

Sublime French-Chinese fusion is served
in a dining room of understated elegance.

Asian fusion cooking has become so common in the last decade that the typical Center City bistro is more likely to serve seared tuna and spring rolls than spaghetti and meatballs.

If it isn't sushi-grade fish, we won't eat it. That crab cake had better be breaded with panko crumbs. And what are mashed potatoes without a little kick of wasabi?

But as with any trend that moves the exotic into the mainstream, there are a thousand imitators for every innovator, a league of dabblers who paint by number for every inspired chef who expresses new ideas through food with such natural ease that it becomes an extension of his or her personality. That ease is the enduring appeal of Susanna Foo.

SUPERIOR

1512 Walnut St.
Philadelphia
(215) 545-2666

NEIGHBORHOOD
Rittenhouse Square

CUISINE
Asian Fusion/Chinese

Foo was one of the first chefs to produce "French-Chinese" cuisine when she opened her eponymous restaurant on Walnut Street in 1987. And she remains one of the best, blending the flavors of her native China with French ideas, infusing sauces with wine and stock and plating food crafted from fresh, local ingredients with Western style.

When I first tasted her cuisine, it was as if someone had peeled back the layers of varnish laid by decades of mediocre Chinese food to reveal the true flavors of what this great tradition could be. The greaseless crunch of her spring roll awakened my slumbering palate from apathy. The bits of chicken, shrimp and sweet green cabbage tightly wrapped inside called through a dab of potent mustard with clean, distinct harmony. I spooned into a crystalline broth of wonton soup and closed my mouth around dumplings so delicate their nearly translucent wrappers seem to melt away. The seafood filling was soft and springy, with minced scallops, shrimp and water chestnuts.

From these rehabilitated classics, I turned to the complexity of sauces — spicy black bean with seasonal shad roe, fiery kung pao over diver scallops, and a caramelized orange potion that renders crispy prawns absolutely irresistible. These sauces raced across my tongue with swerving twists and turns, leaving tingles of spice and sour and sweetness before they lingered then faded.

Foo, who unlike many famous names actually still cooks, has done so much more than fancify the classics. These plates hold surprises that one might never expect in a so-called Chinese restaurant.

In Susanna Foo's cuisine, there is room for Italian polenta, vodka, foie gras, Mexican peppers, ketchup, and Jersey white corn — but they always make sense. And there are more than a few French techniques culled from her brief studies at culinary school and her associations with stellar executive chefs.

Bill Kim, a former sous-chef at Charlie Trotter's in Chicago who now heads the kitchen at the Inn on Blueberry Hill in Doylestown, helped organize her kitchen and polish presentations. Bruce Lim, the former owner of Ciboulette who now owns Red Chopstix on Locust Street, deepened her knowledge of French cuisine.

The choice of Patrick Feury as Lim's successor last year seemed an odd one at first. Feury, the brother of Striped Bass chef Terence Feury, who opened Avenue B after years in some of Manhattan's finest kitchens, was mostly experienced with Italian, French and Scandinavian cooking. But he has learned the ways of Foo at light speed, all the while helping to intensify flavors and add more substance to the previously petite plates.

He has nicely preserved the menu's spirit. Tiny croutons encrust the lusciously

The banana chocolate tart with rum sauce is one of the city's greatest desserts.

meaty crab cakes with the explosion of a "hundred corners." Tender dim-sum dumplings filled with veal bask in a spicy ancho chile sauce.

What may look like an average stir-fry turns out to be morsels of "Tung An" pheasant, artichoke hearts, and crunchy cloud-ear mushrooms that shimmer with a boldly spiced yet ethereal sauce. The bitter crunch of brussels sprout leaves plays against the sweetness of scallops and the butter-softness of filet mignon. Slivers of asparagus mingle with lookalike rings of jalapeno, igniting a sweet-and-sour sauce that glazes fried grouper deeply scored to resemble a pinecone.

Feury's creative contributions have been equally delicious. His ginger-and lemongrass-marinated venison with chestnut bread pudding is a fabulous Asian take on seasonal game, garnished with a baked lady apple that lends an intoxicating perfume. A pureed soup of celery root and Asian pear topped with a tiny rice cake and a refreshing dice of crunchy pear fruit for texture was one of the most intriguing bowls of soup I've tasted.

Susanna Foo isn't perfect. The pad Thai is still pretty ordinary. The usually wonderful tea-smoked duck with anise sauce was dry on my last visit. And for all its elegance, the restaurant still insists on using plastic chopsticks.

Still, it also is one of the most complete restaurants in town. The veteran service staff is among the most professional anywhere. And the dining room is a pretty haven of understated elegance. Light pours into the front of the restaurant, illuminating a suitcase of blooming orchids. Sand-colored walls and plush half-moon booths glow with the golden warmth of billowy silk lanterns.

The excellent cellar, like the cuisine, defies stereotypes that Asian food does not mix well with wine. The typically recommended whites from Alsace are eclipsed by a collection of big-name Bordeaux, Burgundies, and West Coast reds that stand up nicely to the menu's assertive spice.

Even the desserts here have always been inspired, ranging from mango panna cotta to coconut brulee, a caramelized round of coconut custard served with sauteed pineapple over a puddle of tapioca coconut cream. The sweet masterpiece, though, has always been the banana chocolate tart, which layers flaky phyllo rounds between chocolate banana ganache, a caramelized rosette of bananas, and frothy rum sabayon.

No, it may not be the familiar old Chinese, but I have to admit that I'm glad. Dinner at Susanna Foo not only restores my wonder in the flavors of Chinese cooking, but also reveals the exciting new possibili-

Or Try These

Here are three other upscale Chinese restaurants.

Margaret Kuo's Peking Restaurant

Granite Run Mall,
1067 W. Baltimore Pike,
Media, Pa., (610) 566-4110

Shockingly elegant for a mall restaurant, this pan-Asian gem highlights lesser-known regional cuisines from Shanghai and Beijing, as well as excellent sushi.

Chez Elena Wu

910 Haddonfield-Berlin Rd.,
Voorhees, N.J. (856) 566-3222

French and Cantonese cuisines coexist rather than mingle at this fine South Jersey venue, with separate chefs turning out the escargots and thin-skinned wonton soup.

Yangming

1051 Conestoga Rd.,
Bryn Mawr, Pa.
(610) 527-3200

Michael Wei's Bryn Mawr standby has been one of the trailblazers in blending East with West, but a recent meal didn't have the bright flavors of Cincin, its sister restaurant in Chestnut Hill.

ties that can emerge when its fresh, vibrant colors are unlocked by the creativity of an original master.

■ **MENU HIGHLIGHTS** Lobster dumplings; mushroom dumplings; veal dumplings; hundred corner crab cakes; wonton soup; hot and sour soup; stuffed lemon sole; grouper; scallops and filet mignon with brussels sprouts; grilled venison; Tuna An pheasant; mango panna cotta; coconut brulee; banana chocolate tart.

■ **WINE LIST** There are a few crisp, aromatic whites from Alsace, Germany and New Zealand, but generally, this impressive cellar ignores the cliches of matching those safe wines with Asian food, offering instead a collection of big-name Bordeaux, Burgundies, and West Coast reds that can stand up nicely to the menu's assertive spice. Bargains, though, are few.

■ **IF YOU GO** Lunch is served Monday-Friday, 11:30 a.m.-2:30 p.m. Dinner: Monday-Thursday, 5-10 p.m.; Friday-Saturday, 5-11 p.m.; Sunday, 5-9 p.m. Three-course lunch, $24.95. Dinner entrees, $17.50-$33.50.

■ **RESERVATIONS** Highly recommended.

■ **CREDIT CARDS** All major cards but Diners Club and Discover.

■ **SMOKING** Entire restaurant is nonsmoking, except the bar.

■ **HANDICAP ACCESSIBLE** There are three small steps at the entrance; rest rooms are accessible to the handicapped.

■ **PARKING** Valet parking at Walnut and Sydenham (in front of Circa) is $16 after 5 p.m.

Tangerine

Inventive Mediterranean-inspired cuisine is served in a Stephen Starr fantasy room fit for a harem.

The news hasn't been great lately over at Eighth and Market Streets, where dreams of a Disney paradise dissolved into a giant hole that has since become a parking lot.

But who needs Disney when we have Stephen Starr? The visionary vibemaster of the table has been converting Philadelphia into his own version of Epcot Center. A ratpack martini bar, a big Buddha pan-Asian hall, two celebrity chef venues, and a glittering French bistro set new standards for stylish concept dining. So when he took over the space at 232 Market Street three years ago, the question was: Which theme would be next?

There were more than a few late-night brainstorm pow-wows between Starr and his cohorts as they tried to conjure up the Next Big Thing. Would it be a giant hotel lobby? A re-created Havana street?

EXCELLENT

232 Market St.
Philadelphia
(215) 627-5116

NEIGHBORHOOD
Old City

CUISINE
Contemporary
Mediterranean

Maybe Indian? Brazilian? A restaurant where people eat in beds?

Whoa, boy.

Finally, it hit Starr while working out on the treadmill: Nouveau Moroccan!

My eyes begin to roll each time I hear what theme he plans to tackle next. But only on one occasion — with cold, futuristic Pod — has one of his restaurants been too gimmicky for me to embrace.

When 232 Market St. emerged as Tangerine, I was convinced that Starr's powers of restaurant magic were sharper than ever. He had transformed a hardware store into a fabric-draped Casbah of dining pleasure, where a dramatic flair touched every aspect of the experience, from the shimmering wall of votive candles to the inventive and beautiful food, which showed chef Chris Painter's talent for melding traditional North African flavors with wide-ranging contemporary ideas. The allure of this restaurant was impossible to deny. Part nightclub, part theme park, part culinary exploration, Tangerine was proof that serious restaurants can also be fun.

And you might not even know that it was there. Behind its inconspicuous frosted-glass doors, a sultry world of shimmering red scrims, woven kilim floors and hanging lamps give this rambling space the intimacy of a sultan's secret lair in the souk. World music throbs in the background. Filigreed lights spray the tented ceiling with a stardust of dappled lights.

The mood is still solidly ensconced in this exotic world. But the food has been taking a few strange detours of late, tiptoeing back from its Moroccan theme. And how did the occasional lotus chip, tempura lobster and miso-glazed sea bass manage to sneak their way in. It's happened in part because North African flavors haven't had as much staying power with regulars, apparently, as Starr's Asian-themed menus. But also, the ugly anti-Middle Eastern backlash that reared itself after 9/11 didn't help.

It would be a huge disappointment if such a distinctive kitchen continued to let itself be corrupted like that. But there is still, for now, more than enough moves here to keep me intrigued.

There is still an excellent rendition of traditional Moroccan chicken tagine, the slow-stewed chicken ladled over couscous, its meat penetrated by the gentle salt and sour of green olives and preserved lemons.

Starr and Painter always insisted, though, that the menu was not meant to faithfully represent authentic Moroccan food. Rather, North Africa and the Mediterranean are a source for its inspiration. And there are still several examples of these inventive fusions.

A delicious chickpea crepe filled with chicken and chanterelle mushrooms, for example, zigs with a sweet and sour zap of pomegranate sauce. The great phyllo-wrapped chicken bisteeya pie is gone, but there is a crab cake appetizer now that more than compensates. Gift-wrapped in a flaky sheet of brik pastry, a meaty lump crab cake towers over a wonderful potato salad studded with capers and ringed by rich lobster sauce.

Painter, a Pottsville native who worked at the French Laundry in Napa and L'Espinasse in Washington, makes his own ras al hanout, a complex spice blend that conveys the intricate flavors of mahgreb cooking throughout the menu. This mix of cinnamon, clove, ginger, allspice and smoked paprika, among other things, lends a musky pixie dust to

Or Try These

Here are three other restaurants with North African-inspired cooking.

La Boheme

246 S. 11th St., Philadelphia.
(215) 351-9901

This little storefront near Jefferson Hospital serves up bistro fare with a Moroccan accent, spicing calamari with fragrant ras el hanout and chicken tagine with olives and preserved lemon.

Spring Mill Cafe

164 Barren Hill Rd.,
Conshocken, Pa.
(610) 828-2550

There is a bucolic charm to this converted general store, where French country classics such as rabbit prune stew mingle with spicy lamb tagine and flaky chicken b'stilla pie.

Figs

2501 Meredith St., Philadelphia
(215) 978-8440

This Art Museum bistro is a cozy, pumpkin-colored corner room with an intriguing (albeit inconsistent) menu that blends contemporary cooking with North African accents.

crunchy calamari that make them absolutely devourable.

Painter's funky take on gnocchi, infused with harissa chile paste and glazed in a celery-root cream with bits of dates, is an inspired creation, an alliance of spice, tang and vegetal sweetness that hums in the mouth.

The seafood Afrique has gained some useful spice over the years, adding a subtle layer of heat to the dish's medley of flavors. Perfectly seared large shrimp and scallops were mounded around an intriguing fufu mash of gingered carrots and banana, an almond-steeped cream pebbled with sweet peas pooled at the bottom of the plate.

A harissa-fired sweet pepper puree was the ideal accent to seared snapper and dumplings filled with garlicky spinach. A mince of sour cherries helped to elevate a peppered filet mignon into something artful, tiered above a pedestal of truffled fingerling potatoes and a sauce lightly thickened with foie gras.

At a recent meal, a dust of green pistachios lent a distinctive nuttiness to perfectly rare breast of duck, which came atop creamed onions and a cosmic swirl of port sauce touched with a whiff of cinnamon.

If there has been one noticeable step backward, it has been with Tangerine's desserts. The ginger molasses spice cake with rum-infused apples was nice, as was the trilogy of chocolate. But none had the evocative powers of the sweet caravan that first passed through here. Chocolate pot de creme served in a Turkish ibrik. Hot mint tea poured onto lemon sorbet. And the twisty almond-phyllo tube known as "the snake," a baklava-like pastry that reminded why this cuisine has so much potential to transport Philadelphia diners.

By the time we'd polished it off and headed down the candle-lit corridor to the exit, we would pass only reluctantly through the frosted front doors. As we reemerged onto Market Street, we left behind an evocative world far more delicious than even Disney could create.

■ **MENU HIGHLIGHTS** Calamari ras al hanout; harissa gnocchi; chickpea crepes; crab cake in brik pastry; arugula salad; chicken tagine; mustard-crusted tuna; pistachio-crusted duck; filet mignon with sour cherries; shrimp and scallop afrique; ginger molasses spice cake.

■ **WINE LIST** A global cellar is well-selected to match the menu's exotic flavors, with plenty of interesting bottles between $40 and $70.

■ **IF YOU GO** Dinner served Sunday-Thursday 5-11 p.m., Friday-Saturday 5-midnight. Entrees, $18-$45.

■ **RESERVATIONS** Highly recommended.

■ **CREDIT CARDS** All major cards but Discover.

■ **SMOKING** No smoking in the dining rooms.

■ **HANDICAP ACCESSIBLE** Yes.

■ **PARKING** Valet costs $12.

For the Hands

Sandwiches

The cheesesteak is only part of the city's love affair with sandwiches. Here are some of my other, non-steak favorites:

■ The roast pork with spinach and provolone at **John's Roast Pork,** Snyder Avenue and Weccacoe Street (215) 436-1951.

■ The sloppy roast beef on kaiser at the original **Nick's Roast Beef,** 2149 S. 20th St. (215) 463-4114.

■ The chicken cutlet with spicy roasted peppers at **Shank's & Evelyn's Luncheonette,** 932 S. 10th St. (215) 629-1093.

■ Traditional Italian hoagies at **Ricci,** 1165 S. 11th St. (215) 334-6910; **Lombardi's Specialty Hoagies,** 1226 Ritner St. (215) 389-2220; and a small sandwich (the big ones have too much meat) at **Primo Hoagies,** 2043 Chestnut St. (215) 496-0540.

■ The awesomely satisfying vegetarian hoagie, with olive-oil roasted eggplant and salty crumbled cheese, at **Chickie's Italian Deli,** 1014 Federal St. (215) 462-8040.

■ Nouveau-style Italian Hoagies at **DelColle Market,** 222 W. Rittenhouse Square (215) 732-3838; and **Wolf's Market,** 1500 Locust St. (215) 735-2929.

■ The hot, thick-sliced New York-style corned beef from **Pastrami and Things,** 225 S. 15th St., (215) 545-4210, is sublime.

■ The cold, thin-sliced Philadelphia-style corned beef from **Koch's Deli,** 4309 Locust St. (215) 222-8662.

■ The grilled panini with mozzarella, basil, tomato and prosciutto at **Paninoteca,** 120 S. 18th St. (215) 568-0077.

■ The classique pan bagnat at **La Cigale,** 725 Walnut St. (215) 625-3666.

■ Baguette with paté and brie at **Cafe Lutecia,** 2301 Lombard St. (215) 790-9557.

■ Grilled lamb and brie sandwich at **Fireworks!** in the Reading Terminal Market (215) 592-9008.

■ The Countryside, a hot muffuletta taste-alike at **The Countryside Market & Delicatessen,** 514 Yale Ave., Swarthmore, Pa. (610) 604-4799.

■ The Vietnamese chicken hoagie at **Ba Le Bakery,** 606 Washington Ave. (215) 389-4350, has tender meat and spicy pickled veggies.

Burgers

Great burgers also abound. Here are some of the best:

■ The caramelized-leek and bleu cheese burger at **Monk's Cafe,** 264 S. 16th St. (215) 545-7005.

■ The fancy burger topped with apple-smoked bacon at **Bleu,** 227 S. 18th St. (215) 545-0342.

■ The English muffin burger at **London Grill,** 2301 Fairmount Ave. (215) 978-4545.

■ The triple sampler of three miniature burgers at **Copa Too,** 263 S. 15th St. (215) 735-0848.

■ The big, beefy steak-house burgers at the downstairs grill of **Smith & Wollensky,** Rittenhouse Hotel, 210 W. Rittenhouse Square (215) 545-1700; and at **Jolly's,** Latham Hotel, 135 S. 17th St. (215) 563-8200.

■ The upscaled burgers at **Standard Tap, Magazine, Happy Rooster** and **Morning Glory Diner** are also worth indulging.

■ It's hard to find a great burger for $5 or less, but you can still find a reliable one at **Tangier Restaurant,** 1801 S. 18th St. (215) 732-5006.

Pizza

Another food group not to be overlooked is this short list of prime pizzas:

■ Reserve your dough for the garlicky white pies and meat-lover pizzas laden with prosciutto and sausage, pulled from the immense brick oven at **Tacconelli's Pizzeria** in Port Richmond, 2604 E. Somerset St. (215) 425-4983. It is still the city's best.

■ Some of the best thin-crust pizzas and strombolis come from **By George** in the Reading Terminal Market, (215) 829-9391, and Ardmore Farmers Market (610) 649-4944.

■ I love the New York-style pies cooked with good ingredients in the coal-fired ovens at **Lombardi's,** 132 S. 18th St. (215) 564-5000.

■ For pizza simplicity, try the thin-crusted Margherita pizzas at **Girasole Ristorante,** 1305 Locust St. (215) 985-4659, and **Illuminare** at 2321 Fairmount Ave. (215) 765-0202.

■ Classic Philly-style pizza can be found in the heart of the Italian Market at **Lorenzo's Pizza,** 900 Christian St. (215) 922-2540.

■ For its wide variety of mix-and-match toppings and super crust, office-district workers rightly stand in line at **Joe's Pizza,** 122 S. 16th St. (215) 569-0898.

■ The no-cheese tomato pies of Trenton are famous, but **People's Pizza** in South Jersey makes a fine one (and hefty stuffed pizzas) just across the Ben Franklin Bridge, at 1500 Chapel Ave. (at Route 38), Cherry Hill (856) 665-6575.

■ Some of the most unusual pizzas are the gourmet wood-grilled pies at **Carambola,** 1650 Limekiln Pike, Dresher, Pa. (215) 542-0900, and the porcini flatbread with truffled potatoes and goat cheese at **Penne,** in the Inn at Penn, 3611 Walnut St. (215) 823-6222.

■ When it comes to the category of cheap-but-decent pizza, the massive, slightly sweet pizzas at **Lazaro's Pizza House,** 1743 South St. (215) 545-2775, have become a bargain staple for neighbors of Graduate Hospital.

Tierra Colombiana

Authentic Cuban and Colombian cooking is served in an inviting dining room on North Fifth Street.

Bathed in the red glow of neon dancers urging us to join the mambo club upstairs, Tierra Colombiana radiates the heat of life for a neighborhood that needs it. Just a few blocks south of Roosevelt Boulevard, its bright stucco walls and Spanish-tiled entrance pop out of the grim shadows of North Fifth Street like a sun-splashed island oasis.

Sure, you can find the sexy hybrid of "Nuevo Latino" cooking downtown, where plantain wings and ceviche fantasies woo Center City's dinerati. But at Tierra Colombiana, it's the viejo favorites that draw Latin cooking aficionados from across the region. Those who come searching for down-home Cuban and Colombian cooking — the corn-scented steam of an unwrapped tamale; the pork and pickle crunch of a hot-pressed Cuban sandwich; a dense spoonful of caramel custard flan — will find a good bet to bring the relatives when they visit from Miami.

VERY GOOD

4535 N. Fifth St.
Philadelphia
(215) 324-6086

NEIGHBORHOOD
North Philadelphia

CUISINE
Cuban/Colombian

Tierra offers a stark contrast to the scrappy streetscape that surrounds it. But in the 10 years since Jorge Mosquera moved his little restaurant from Sixth Street and Hunting Park Avenue, the southeast corner of Fifth and Raymond Streets has proved a winner, drawing everyone from Latino business lunchers to art museum field trips to an impassioned marriage workshop in the banquet room that turned into a field day for the roaming flower vendor.

The nightclub upstairs has become a lively weekend scene for the gyrating salsa set. And the main-floor dining rooms are as inviting as any downtown restaurant (including Mixto, Mosquera's very new venture on Pine Street), with rustic lanterns, white brick archways, and walls the color of a passion fruit batido shake.

The servers are sweet and attentive. And though it helps to speak a little Spanish, they are always eager to offer suggestions of their favorites from the large menu.

Mosquera's family is actually from Ecuador. The principally Cuban and Colombian menu reflects both the neighborhood clientele and the cooks in the kitchen, including Jose Perez, the semi-retired Cuban who comes in a few days a week to cook black beans and the secret

The Paella Marinera, which features lobster, mussels, clams and shrimp.

recipes for his traditional desserts.

Among the menu's other fine classics was stewed ropa vieja, brisket cooked so long its name means "old clothes," transformed into a tangy mince of beef as soft as silk threads. The paella Valenciana was a glorious mountain of moist yellow rice, brimming out of its wide earthen crock with perfectly cooked seafood, chicken, vegetables and sausage. The Cuban arroz con pollo was filled with tender morsels of chicken and cuminy chorizo, the rice tangy with a splash of beer.

Rice and beans are at the heart of Latin cooking, of course, and on most occasions, Tierra's were superb, a hearty side that comes with every entree. You can get them separate, mixed, and cooked together as moro (also known as congri). Or you can have the Colombian-style red beans that were pillowy soft and gently sweetened with chunks of calabaza pumpkin.

But they also give you starch with your starch here. Choose from additional sides of crisp fried yucca strips, fried green tostone plantain disks, or sweet dark plantain maduros.

But then, if you're a starch-aholic, there are always those delicious cheesy corn cakes from Nicaragua called arepas. A growing Puerto Rican clientele has rallied another addition to the pastry case by the bar — excellent pastelillo turnovers filled with ground meat and beans.

Tierra's corn-husk-wrapped Cuban tamales are imported from New York and are sufficiently fluffy inside. But the giant housemade Colombian tamales are the real prize. Unfold the banana-leaf wrapper and behold a meal in itself, steamed corn flour embedded with fistfuls of roasted pork, chicken, beef and vegetables.

While the kitchen had a tendency to overcook some items (like the garlic shrimp and boneless pork chops), some of its best entrees found their magic in the safe comfort of a nice stew. The muchacho relleno, or "stuffed boy," was one of my slow-cooked favorites, a beef roast stuffed with coriander-ground sausage and vegetables. Baked to melting softness, it arrives smothered in an irresistibly piquant tomato gravy of onions and peppers.

The octopus, which boils for a couple of hours before it is ready, was the base of an outstanding salad, its tender white chunks swathed in an oily marinade with olives and sweet pimento peppers.

The bacalao does for seafood what ropa vieja does for meat, transforming salt-cured cod (which is soaked for two days) into an unctuous fishy mash. Salt cod is definitely an acquired taste, but, splashed in the same sweet pepper and tomato gravy used for some of the meat dishes, its briny flavor and slightly chewy texture had found the perfect edgy match.

There are several beers and frothy batido fruit shakes to complement the exotic flavors, but Tierra also has a decent wine list of affordable red wines from Spain and Latin America. Our Marques de Caceres ($29) was a classic Spanish rioja that was well-balanced and rich.

"Rich" can only begin to describe the density of the desserts here — traditional confections that could slay even the most intense sugar craving. The tres leches cake oozes cream and sweetened milk every time your fork passes down for another slice. The dulce de leche is like eating caramelized cheese curds in brown sugar syrup. And as if the home-style custard flan were not rich enough (it is, by the way), the tocinillo del cielo is gravity on a spoon, infusing an impossibly thick custard with cinnamon, lime zest and vanilla.

By then, I needed a milky hot mug of cafe con leche, the fresh ground Cuban-style coffee that revived me just in time. Because, as our weekend meal ended, I began to feel the syncopation of the dance music upstairs. The vibrations of salsa, merengue and mambo filtered down through the ceiling, pulsing with the tempting glow of life after dinner.

Or Try These

Here are three other authentic Latino restaurants.

El Viejo San Juan

1176 N. Third St, Philadelphia
(215) 922-2376

A beautiful renovation evokes a Caribbean mood at this new Girard Avenue art gallery/restaurant, where the red beans and rice, and roasted pork with pickled plantains offer the real taste of San Juan.

El Bohio

2746 N. Fifth St., Philadelphia
(215) 425-5991

This gritty Puerto Rican corner eatery has anchored the Golden Mile for more than two decades with spicy fried chicken, adobo-smothered pork chops, and the best flan in town.

Cafe Habana

102 S. 21st St., Philadelphia
(215) 561-2822

The classic homestyle Cuban fare has been up and down, but this stylish Latin bar shakes a fabulous mojito.

■ **MENU HIGHLIGHTS** Arepas; empanadas; Colombian tamale; chorizo in white wine; octopus salad; sandwich Cubano; red beans; moro rice; ropa vieja; Cuban arroz con pollo; Argentine broiled skirt steak; muchacho relleno; paella Valenciana; fried yucca; maduros; tres leches; flan.

■ **WINE LIST** Small but afforadable list of Spanish and South American wines. Also try the Dominican beer, fruity batido shakes and cafe con leche.

■ **IF YOU GO** Breakfast, lunch, and dinner served Monday-Thursday, 7 a.m.-11 p.m., Friday-Saturday, 7 a.m.-12:30 a.m. Entrees, $7-29.95 (paella for two).

■ **RESERVATIONS** Recommended.

■ **CREDIT CARDS** All major cards.

■ **SMOKING** There is a nonsmoking section.

■ **HANDICAP ACCESSIBLE** Bathrooms are not equipped.

■ **PARKING** Street parking around restaurant is supervised by guard.

Tre Scalini

A South Philly BYOB serves up authentic central Italian home cooking.

Uno, due, tre . . . quattro?

I have to climb four little steps — not three — to enter the cedar-shingled storefront on South 11th Street that is Tre Scalini. Odd, I think, until owner and chef Franca DiRenzo sets me straight.

I'm counting in the wrong contintent.

The "three little steps" that Tre Scalini is named after can be found in Rome on the Piazza Navona — Tre Scalini is the popular sidewalk cafe there where the chocolate ice cream dessert tartufo apparently was invented. DiRenzo, who is from the nearby Molise region on Italy's central Adriatic coast, says she was enchanted by the cafe because "it is the place for friends, where everyone goes to meet."

VERY GOOD

1533 S. 11th St.
Philadelphia
(215) 551-3870

NEIGHBORHOOD
South Philadelphia

CUISINE
Italian Trattoria

It is an appropriate name for DiRenzo's cozy South Philadelphia restaurant. Its wood-beamed retro dining room seems to thrive with tables of old friends and regulars come to savor her homemade pasta, garlicky broccoli rabe, and succulent veal chop heaped with mushrooms.

A polished couple in crisp suits and gold jewelry exchange a kiss in the kitchen corner, beneath the sign that reads "la cucina." A foursome of post-hippie boomers dressed in black leather, jeans and mohair boas uncork their third bottle of (bring your own) wine, talking up their friendly server to find out his family connection. Nephew? Daughter? Daughter's boyfriend? Everyone who works here seems to be related, giving Tre Scalini a sense of familiar ease.

This can occasionally translate into a very slow dinner, like the one I experienced on a recent revisit. But it's also the kind of place that makes people feel at home — perhaps a little too comfortable in the case of one of my guests, a friend of a friend, and now a star on my Undesirable Guest List (a.k.a. UGLi). He bellowed throughout the evening to a room full of strangers, spouting his dubious views on movies and more than a few unsolicited details of his sex life.

We would have slid beneath the linen out of embarrassment had the food not been so good as to demand that we stay above table. It was a clinic in the powers of simple, rustic flavors. Rooted in the homecooking traditions of DiRenzo's native Molise, it is bolstered by the kitchen's admirably consistent hand.

Grilled triangles of soft polenta come topped with snappy broccoli rabe, a hint of green bitterness tempered by a whiff of sauteed garlic. Stewed cannellini beans are topped with plump curls of shrimp, which add a gentle sea flavor to the light marinara broth. Vegetarian lentil soup is as simple as it gets, but this soulful bowl of tiny disks, fresh tomato and olive oil is impossible not to finish.

A salad of buffalo mozzarella is soft and creamy, its basil-flecked tomatoes tasting ripe even in chilly March. A bed of thinly shaved fennel root meets the perfect antidote to anise crunch — a sweet round slice of orange citrus and a softening drizzle of vibrant green olive oil.

I ask DiRenzo about her cooking secrets. Why does she use pasta water to lighten her sauces? Why does she cook her marinara with the lid off? Why is it done when the oil rises to the surface? And her answer is always the same: "That's what my mother told me. Whatever I do, it's the way my mother taught me."

So I guess I ought to thank DiRenzo's mother, Adelina Scarduzio, for doing such a good job in passing down the family traditions.

My very favorite is the homemade pasta di casa, the square-cut spaghetti that DiRenzo hand-kneads then presses through a harplike loom of wires known as la chitarra, "the guitar." Twirled with a bright bolognese filled with finely minced beef and gently steeped tomatoes, a forkful of its al dente strands spring in the mouth with lusty homespun freshness.

Or Try These

Here are three other lively Italian BYOBs.

Porcini

2048 Sansom St., Philadelphia
(215) 751-1175

One of the first in a wave of no-frills trattorias in Center City, this closet-size BYOB remains one of the best, with homemade pastas and a dose of exuberant hospitality.

Spezia

614 W. Lancaster Ave., Bryn Mawr, Pa. (610) 526-0123

The little Main Line BYOB with the gold-painted tin ceiling offers a simple but stylish setting for an ambitious Italian-themed menu that focuses on good ingredients and deft cooking. The owners offer extra-fancy crystal for a supplement.

Il Cantuccio

701 N. Third St., Philadelphia
(215) 627-6573

This tiny corner room covered with painted vines embodies the funky, handcrafted spirit of Northern Liberties, and regional Italian dishes like white beans and sausage are finally evolving from sloppy to rustic.

The orecchiette are addictive in their garlicky oil sheen; the little pasta cups cradle bits of bitter broccoli rabe and crumbles of home-made sausage. And though the squid ink pappardelle are not house-made, they are still wonderful, jeweled with lumps of sweet crab and perfectly cooked shrimp.

I was less impressed by the lobster ravioli, which tasted more of cheese filling than anything crustacean. The grilled lamb chops were also overcooked.

Still, these missteps were exceptions to the rule — DiRenzo's other seafood and meat entrees were sent off without a hitch. The brodetto stew was brimming with perfectly cooked seafood and a marinara broth that focused their flavors. Her salmon was an inventive take on the ubiquitous fish, the fillet rolled into a thick coil around minced garlic and oregano. Seared brown on each end, the center was ringed by a stripe of soft pink flesh that glazed with olive oil, balsamic and lemon juice. A generous, flaky fillet of halibut came blanketed with a piquant collage of olives, tomatoes and capers.

The veal dishes were also divine, whether a thick chop or pillowy medallions of fillet. Each came beneath an avalanche of sauteed mushrooms — porcini, shiitake and portobellos — that moistened the meat with their woodsy, garlic juice.

Such soulful cooking makes me wish I had been in during one of the restaurant's other signature specials — the baby goat, quail or rabbit, or even sweet-and-sour chicken livers agrodolce.

Desserts at Tre Scalini such as tiramisu are sufficient to sate the sweet tooth, but given the homespun touch that transforms the rest of the meal, it's a disappointment that none are made in-house. The white pistachio and rum-raisin ice creams are nevertheless very tasty, the Bindi sorbets-in-a-fruit a little less so.

At the very least, though, DiRenzo could import some tartufo to honor the cafe that inspired the Tre Scalini name. Otherwise, four steps on 11th Street is four steps, right? Maybe we ought to be heading down to good old Quattro Scalini?

"Actually," she says in defense of her own stoop, "I have three steps and a landing."

■ **MENU HIGHLIGHTS** Grilled polenta with broccoli rabe; shrimp with cannelini beans; buffalo mozzarella and tomato salad; shaved fennel and orange salad; pasta di casa bolognese; black pappardelle with shrimp and crab; orechiette with broccoli rabe and sausage; garlic-stuffed salmon roulade; veal tenderloin; rum raisin and pistachio ice creams.

■ **WINE LIST** BYOB.

■ **IF YOU GO** Dinner served Tuesday-Saturday, 5-10 p.m., Sunday 3:30-9 p.m., closed Monday. Dinner entrees, $11.95-$21.95.

■ **RESERVATIONS** Highly recommended.

■ **CREDIT CARDS** All major cards but Discover and Diners Club.

■ **SMOKING** The second-floor dining room is nonsmoking.

■ **HANDICAP ACCESSIBLE** Not accessible. There are four steps to the front entrance.

■ **PARKING** Street parking only.

Vetri

A sublimely sophisticated homage to rustic Italian cuisine graces the tiny dining room of a legendary townhouse.

arc Vetri loves his meat slicer. And, if you're into that kind of thing, it's hard to deny she's a beauty.

With a gleaming steel blade and a body of burgundy enamel trimmed with gold, the old Berkel No. 21 (circa 1930s) sits like a queen at the center of the sunny yellow dining room beneath a window-paned mural of Tuscan mountains.

At least four diners would have been sitting in this space when Vetri opened almost four years ago, and at less than 40 seats, there weren't many to spare. But as the cook bounds in and out of the dining room to finish his antipasti tonight, adjusting the metal knobs, clamping the prosciutto in just right, spinning the crank and

SUPERIOR

1312 Spruce St.,
Philadelphia
(215) 732-3478

NEIGHBORHOOD
Avenue of the Arts

CUISINE
Upscale Italian

sending the ham-bearing carriage back and forth into the *whoosh* of its powerful glide, the extra diners are long forgotten.

He peels off impossibly thin slices of prosciutto that are folded into a delicate pink mound at the center of our antipasti, which is presented on vintage Limoges china ringed by a paean to the flavors of fall. Mustardy celery root salad. Cauliflower poached with saffron threads. Crunchy, char-edged brussels sprouts. Springy cubes of polenta. Crimson chunks of sweet beet.

A knife and fork is proper, I suppose. But by the end, I am popping each morsel into my mouth with fingers, marveling as one flavor complements the next, greedily moving faster and faster until I stop, suddenly, at the prosciutto. It unfolds like an exotic silk handkerchief, so fine you can almost see through it. Pliant, pink, salty and sheer, it wraps itself around my fingers and disappears, evaporating in a puff of hot breath.

At what moment did eating at Vetri become so sublime?

It was intriguing the moment it opened, when the Abington-born chef returned from his journeys in New York, California and Europe to occupy this famed Spruce Street townhouse — the birthplace of La Panetiere, Le Bec-Fin, Ciboulette and Chanterelles — and to conjure up visions of rustic Italy this city had yet to see.

From the start, his spinach gnocchi were one of my platonic foods, misty rounds of vibrant green, the velvet embodiment of spinach, swimming in ponds of brown butter and fastened beneath a lace of shaved ricotta cheese. His chestnut fettuccine with wild boar ragu and cocoa epitomized the incredible depth and elegance of country flavors. His house-aged rib chop seared with rock salt in a cast-iron pan remains one of the best slices of beef in town. And his chocolate polenta souffle brought the ingenious surprise of tiny grains to creamy hot chocolate.

These were the underpinnings of a promising new venture, but with plenty of room for improvement. So at what stage in its development did Vetri actually become magical, blossoming not only into Philadelphia's best Italian restaurant, but also its most seamless intimate dining room?

Was it when they expanded their wine cellar from 60 to 400 labels? Or the board of rare pecorinos scented with walnut leaves, white wine, tomato or juniper berries? Or the grappas, the imported polenta-papered menu covers or the antique china?

No, what has impressed me most has been a distinct leap forward in the kitchen. In becoming perhaps the most difficult restaurant in town to land a table at,

Wild boar ragu with cocoa.

Vetri and his crew have earned the liberty to create and polish. On Saturday evenings now, in fact, the restaurant serves only five-course tasting meals, with offerings that change every week, along with the colorful, hand-painted menus that Vetri himself crafts in the preceding days. The food that emerges seems new, but in fact, it is as rooted in the old ways as the coveted meat slicer, gliding at the peak of tradition, tuning the subtle dials of texture, temperature and presentation to render each dish personal, inventive and fresh.

Moments before dessert, the chef appears and pours a small carafe of hot olive oil over a cup sealed with a lid of chocolate. It liquefies the chocolate onto a scoop of rosemary ice cream. Herby but sweet, buzzing with the bittersweet shade of dark chocolate, each spoonful washes the oily fruit of olive into streams of hot and cold liquid that tangle my tastebuds into delicious confusion.

Vetri's kitchen often indulges in preparations that sometimes take days to complete. The stuffed pig's head sausage is a kind of elaborate and chunky rendition of scrapple, seared to a divinely salty crisp and set over Italian farro. In season, Vetri rolls wild salmon fillets into a ballantine that he then poaches in milk and layers between oily gravlax and crisp rounds of thin potato cake. A glazing of creme fraiche and caviar adds a glorious finish.

More recent meals have brought me the wonders of delicate sweetbread-stuffed ravioli garnished with a silky tan sauce of slow-stewed, pureed veal shoulder. Coarsely ground lamb sausage perched over shredded celery root and apples. Perfectly seared duck breast fanned over an unctuous mash of duck rillettes and pureed parsnips.

Vetri has a dish-specific stock for seemingly every creation. Whether it's for the guinea hen stuffed with foie gras and pistachios, or the cannelloni wrapped around a mousse of gently smoked capon, the stocks enrich the complexity of natural flavors.

Vetri's recent focus on desserts has also paid dividends. Creme caramel infused with butternut squash crackled with candied squash seeds scattered on top. Warm almond cake mingled with a scoop of honey and nut gelato, gathering a tiny dice of fresh apples in its path.

The most intriguing, though, was a plug of apple streusel that sat over a two-toned plate. On one side was an ivory pool of walnut-steeped cream, on the other, a thin amber rink of gelled apple cider. Each element was a delight on its own, but to eat them together, to feel the tangy jiggle of cider dissolve, the warm cream soaking through the pastry, the aroma of walnuts perfuming the air like an orchard, was a heavenly finale.

The magic of a 35-seat restaurant is its ability to focus on the efforts of individuals, a personal tone that rings especially true for a duo such as Vetri and his manager-partner Jeffrey Benjamin. They

Or Try These

Here are three other sophisticated Northern Italy-inspired restaurants.

Avenue B

260 Avenue of the Arts, Philadelphia, (215) 790-0705

An upscale Italian from Neil Stein and Gabe Marabella that has a corner on the Kimmel Center crowd, although it also has perpetual troubles in keeping a steady chef.

Le Castagne

1920 Chestnut St., Philadelphia (215) 751-9913

A sleek contemporary Northern Italian with excellent fresh pastas from the owners of La Famiglia.

Kristian's

1100 Federal St., Philadelphia (215) 468-0104

This renovated butcher shop has matured into South Philly's finest upscale Italian eatery, although the service doesn't match the finesse of young chef Kristian Leuzzi.

are an odd couple, the rebellious slow-food cook and the straitlaced front-house man, a soft-spoken refugee of corporate dining rooms, whom regulars often refer to (affectionately) as George Costanza in pinstripes.

But they've become one of the most effective and personable pairings around. Benjamin has organized the artista; Vetri has mellowed Mr. Meticulous. Benjamin's wonkish enthusiasm has become less awkward over the years and his photographic memory has channeled extraordinary rapport with clients.

Marc Vetri, for his part, has feverishly poured profits back into his project, polishing its pleasantly simple decor, settling deeper into his restaurant home. For the long term.

And it is as if this legendary space has decided to capitulate, resonating the flavors of each dish with the clarity of a prized violin, transforming a three-hour evening here into little more than a blink. The birthplace of so many great restaurants that have moved on seems now to have wrapped its bricks and dark wood planks around its latest tenant with a hopeful embrace that says: Maybe this is the one that will finally stay.

■ **MENU HIGHLIGHTS** Antipasti; eggplant terrine; pig's-head roll; crispy sweetbreads, sweetbread ravioli; spinach gnocchi; chestnut fettuccine with boar ragu; ricotta almond tortellini with truffle sauce; salmon ballantine; smoked capon cannelloni; sweet onion crepe; wilted green salad; langostini in spicy broth; guinea hen stuffed with foie gras; roasted turbot; rib steak seared in rock salt; cheese board; chocolate polenta souffle; rosemary ice cream with chocolate lid and hot olive oil; apple streusel with cider jelly and walnut cream.

■ **WINE LIST** With the addition of extra space, the largely Italian wine cellar has blossomed from a starter choice of 60 wines to its current list of 400. Older vintages are still scarce, but it is now deep in regional variety and price-points, and consistent in quality, whether sipping the excellent house wines by the glass (a lusciously drinkable Pio Cesare Barbera d'Alba) or indulging one of the more expensive bottles such as an earthy Taurasi from Campania ($85). Spirit lovers should try the excellent grappa selection.

■ **IF YOU GO** Dinner served Monday-Saturday, 6-11 p.m. Closed Sunday. Dinner entrees, $24-$37. Five-course tasting, $65. Seven-course tasting, $90. Saturday dinner is limited to the tasting menu.

■ **RESERVATIONS** Required.

■ **CREDIT CARDS** All major cards but Discover.

■ **SMOKING** Entire restaurant is nonsmoking.

■ **HANDICAP ACCESSIBLE** No. There are five steps up to the front door, and the bathrooms are not handicapped equipped.

■ **PARKING** Street parking only.

Vietnam

Delicious Vietnamese home cooking is served
in a sultry French colonial ambience.

Before you open your eyes to see the remarkable transformation of a pink linoleum box — for that is what the dining rooms at Vietnam Restaurant used to be — imagine bobbing across the South China Sea stuffed into a 35-foot boat with 190 other refugees.

For three days and three nights in 1979, this is how the journey from Vietnam began for the Lai family, stripped of its sandal factory, relieved of its home, crammed on a freedom boat without enough food or water. Fuel was running thin, too, just as a tanker came to the rescue, towing the boat to the safety of a Malaysian refugee camp.

By comparison, opening a restaurant in Philadelphia five years later seemed relatively easy. The price was cheap for this modest building, set on one of the lesser-traveled cross-streets of Chinatown. And red tape? What red tape? It was nearly three years before they even knew there was such a thing as a Health Department license.

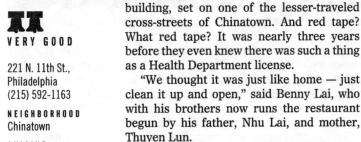

VERY GOOD

221 N. 11th St.,
Philadelphia
(215) 592-1163

NEIGHBORHOOD
Chinatown

CUISINE
Vietnamese

"We thought it was just like home — just clean it up and open," said Benny Lai, who with his brothers now runs the restaurant begun by his father, Nhu Lai, and mother, Thuyen Lun.

Having settled any fines long ago (the restaurant, by the way, is always spotless), the Lais turned their humble, virtually generic storefront into a veritable cult destination for reliable Vietnamese home cooking. The dining room was never much to look at — pink linoleum floors, Formica tables, and fluorescent lights — but one didn't come here to be dazzled.

I came for definitive and affordable versions of what I consider to be this city's benchmark for Vietnamese classics. The shattering crunch of fried spring rolls wrapped in a snappy cool leaf of lettuce with mint and pickled carrot. Bowls of springy noodles topped with stuffed grape leaves and lemongrass charred pork. All of it comes with dishfuls of clear nuoc mam on the side, the spicy sweet-and-sour liquid that gives Vietnamese food an edge of twists and turns.

Then one day, a Vietnam groupie told me about the Big Redecoration, pronouncing it "beautiful," and at the same time rolling his eyes: "Now they're probably going to raise the prices."

Benny Lai and his brothers run Vietnam, the restaurant begun by their parents.

There are redecorations and there are redecorations. This one comes with a capital R. Created by one of the restaurant's customers, designer Jesse Gardner, this is one of the most amazing metamorphoses I've witnessed. The old brick facade has been replaced by stucco cut to look like grand French colonial blocks; exotic striped canopies flutter in the breeze around antique-style windowpanes.

Inside, the fluorescent rooms have been transformed into a sultry set from *Indochine*. Wide-banded Australian hardwood floors give the little rooms coffee-colored warmth and softness. Palm fronds grow against dark wood wainscoting and honeyed yellow walls. Tiny lights lend a moody romance to the dating couples who dip their straws into flaming volcano cocktails, catching glances from tables of tweedy professorial types and large groups of young Asians who wrap the offerings of their BBQ platter in sheer white crepes of pliant rice paper.

Benny Lai hedged when I ask the price-hike question. It's true, he said, they're going up: a quarter for every entree.

Oh, the cheapskates can squirm, but I'm breathing a sigh of relief. This restaurant has kept a cool, even keel as it shed its Formica skin, emerging room by room into its new movie-star look. The all-family service staff remains a model of efficiency, attentive to details, courteous, and helpful in navigating the giant menu. And the kitchen, for the most part, has remained a delight.

The BBQ platter is an irresistible snapshot of some of the best bites — crackly skinned spring rolls, skewers of grilled grape leaves, meatballs and lemongrass chicken. There were also the soft-wrapper shrimp rolls, ready for a dunk in the hoisin dip, dark and unctuous, like some exotic chocolate sauce. The shaved raw flank-steak appetizer was one of my favorites, like a Vietnamese carpaccio marinated in sweetened lime, dusted with nuts and potent peppermint.

Rice flake noodles wrapped around a fine mince of sauteed pork and mushrooms like slippery ravioli packages. Wonton soup, brimming with tiny balls of crinkle-wrapped dumplings, filled the air with the intense aroma of fried garlic.

Cold "needle noodles" brought chewy twines of thick rice noodles tossed in cool coconut milk, shredded pork, and the subtle texture of roasted rice powder. And "broken rice" has become one of my new favorite starches — with the texture of couscous and the flavor of jasmine rice. Like the bowls of thin rice vermicelli noodles, broken-rice platters come with any topping you desire. I loved the cubes of country-style beef that come glazed in a brooding dark sauce. The crabmeat egg was also novel, a slice off a loaf-shaped omelet filled with crabmeat, bean thread noodles, and garlicky mushrooms.

While Vietnam has captured my affection, it is still a long way from perfection. Entrees such as the tender greens with pork, and chicken dishes glazed in spicy peanut satay or coconut turmeric curry were tasty. But many of the other entrees were uninspired stir-fries, stuffed with fillers like coarse-chopped pepper and onion and doused with sauces that are interesting but not great.

Or Try These

Here are three other Vietnamese restaurants.

Le Me Toujours

515 Route 73 South, Marlton, N.J. (856) 810-2000

This attractive South Jersey restaurant blends traditional Vietnamese and French flavors into beautiful and sophisticated contemporary dishes.

Pho 75

1122 Washington Ave., Philadelphia (215) 271-5866

Grab a flavorful meal in a bowl at the city's best (albeit very utilitarian) Vietnamese noodle soup hall, then shop for fish sauce at the vast Asian market next door.

Le Cyclo

606 Washington Ave., Philadelphia (215) 389-7844

Located behind the Ba Le Bakery, this sleek, modern room is a destination for hip, second-generation Vietnamese, where fresh sugar cane juice and bubble teas accompany the duck noodle soup and other modern takes on traditional dishes.

The coconut milk rice pudding dessert is, on occasion, pasty enough to hang wallpaper — but it has grown on me over time. Still, I prefer the frosty homemade ice creams, which taste like snowballs made of coconut or exotically floral jackfruit.

A cup of dark Vietnamese hot coffee mixed with sweetened condensed milk snaps the food-dazed diner back to life, sparking another tour through the newfound warmth of these dining rooms.

Beyond the sheer effect of the decor, I am struck by the sense of nostalgia captured in the sepia-toned photos that hang on the wall, which Gardner shot on his research missions to the Lais' hometown in Vietnam. Many of the subjects are the family's former neighbors, reminders, in a way, of both how far this modest restaurant has taken the Lais from the country they escaped 23 years ago, and how, in glow of their success, they have returned full circle again.

■ **MENU HIGHLIGHTS** BBQ platter — spring rolls, lemongrass chicken, grilled grapeleaves, meatballs; unfried shrimp rolls; raw flank steak with meat roll; wonton soup; rice vermicelli bowls with spring rolls and charbroiled pork; broken rice platter with country-style beef; char-grilled squid or pork or crabmeat egg; pork with tender greens; chicken in turmeric sauce; crispy red snapper in spicy basil sauce; rice pudding; coconut ice cream.

■ **WINE LIST** Stick with brisk and refreshing Vietnamese '33' beer, or go for the fun, high-octane cocktails like the Suffering Bastard or Volcano.

■ **IF YOU GO** Entire menu served Sunday-Thursday, 11 a.m.-9:30 p.m., Friday-Saturday, 11 a.m.-10:30 p.m. Entrees, $4.25-$14.95.

■ **RESERVATIONS** For banquets only.

■ **CREDIT CARDS** All major cards.

■ **SMOKING** Smoking allowed in the bar area only.

■ **HANDICAP ACCESSIBLE** No.

■ **PARKING** Street parking only.

White Dog Cafe

The University City institution blends social
activism with creative organic cooking and a
funky, homey atmosphere.

I saw Ken Starr the other day in the most unlikely place — or
rather, he saw me — at the White Dog Cafe.

The White Dog, that University City bastion of liberal
activism — where pesticide-free organics rule the kitchen, and
field trips to Cuba are one of the annual customer perks —
might be the last place one would expect to find the ex-spe-
cial prosecutor. But when I opened the bathroom door marked
"Democrats" (there is another marked "Republicans" across
the aisle), there was his head in mural form hovering over the comfort station, giant and bespectacled, his investigator's cheeks flush
with anticipation. "He's watching you," reads a message on the wall.

Wherever you stand on politics, the White Dog has always had a
rare sense of humor. That is part of what gives
this institution such a palatable feel, even
though they do wear a laundry list of causes
on their sleeve. Many of them are more than
worthy — supporting local farms, fighting cru-
elty to animals, fostering AIDS education, mul-
ticultural understanding, and Habitat for
Humanity, to name a few. And since its incep-
tion in 1983, owner Judy Wicks has proved
that a restaurant can be so much more than a
place to eat. This one is a center of social
change.

VERY GOOD

3420 Sansom St.
Philadelphia
(215) 386-9224

NEIGHBORHOOD
University City

CUISINE
New American/Organic

The restaurant is cozy in a homey, funky Victorian way, with mismatched oak tables scattered through several rooms, blue gingham
tablecloths, lace-curtained windows, and lots of warm wood accents.
But without a credible kitchen, White Dog's presence would have far
less importance than it does. In his nearly 16 years there, chef and
partner Kevin von Klause has established a model network of alternative food purveyors, tapping seasonal bounty from as many as 18
farmers.

His food is inspired by an eclectic palette of flavors, from tropical salsas and rum sauces to gingery Asian broths, Amish cheeses,
and Texas barbecue. But more than that, these dishes aptly reflect
the natural flavors of good ingredients — fresh squash blossoms
stuffed with cheese, crisp summer soft-shells, sprouts and heirloom

veggies everywhere, fistfuls of herbs infusing everything from home-made sheets of pasta to a cool puree of vichyssoise potato soup.

And virtually all of it, of course, is pesticide- and cruelty-free. Even the ravioli special was "free-form," never to suffer under the bondage of a crimped edge. Instead, its herb-printed sheets floated in a late-spring broth touched with lemon balm, earthy morels, feta cheese and broccoli.

Persistent inconsistencies in the kitchen and especially with service, though, have always held the White Dog back from reaching the next level. You don't expect to find "laissez-faire" service at a left-wing restaurant, but all of my visits over the last four years have been marked by painfully long waits. Our servers are usually pleasant and informed, but very distracted. In one case, we waited 45 minutes between courses, though the main dining room didn't seem overly busy

Much of the food was a success.

The guacamole was the cool, creamy green essence of that irresistible dip, tinged with an edge of garlic and cilantro. A spring soup of asparagus and Amish cheddar was rich and satisfyingly frothy. A stir fry of tender beef and snappy rock shrimp was tossed in a sweet and gingery soy broth, glazing a nest of soba noodles and watercress. Crab cakes were fresh and lumpy, their gentle cornmeal-dusted crust sparked with chunks of rock shrimp. Sweet chunks of roasted beets were delicious alongside rich Gorgonzola cheese and a refreshing shred of daikon radish. And sweet pea soup was one of the best I've ever tasted, a cool green puree thickened with potato and studded with the occasional snap of a whole pea.

Duck breast "steaks."

Sauteed bacon added a woodsy counterpoint to the fresh sea flavor of soft-shell crabs. And a rib-eye steak from Niman Ranch was supremely tender, complimented by a bundle of braised greens and a classic smoky barbecue sauce.

Consistently, though, the White Dog will deliver a handful of dishes that, frustratingly, seemed to be missing an attention to little details that kept good ideas from becoming great. An intriguingly Moroccan-spiced lamb burger was cooked dry and gray, even though it had been requested medium-rare. And the chile-glazed duck "steaks," which otherwise were fabulous with their sour cherry sauce and grainy prairie pilaf, have been over-charred more than once.

Desserts have usually followed the same path of good intentions with similar mixed results, with a luscious blueberry pie being overwhelmed by a potent streak of lemon or a strawberry eclair suffering from a gummy choux pastry crust.

On a recent visit, however, the desserts were the uncontested highlight of the meal.

A thick slice of strawberry-rhubarb pie sandwiched between a lattice crust brought the tart sweetness of early summer to an indulgent yellow scoop of buttermilk ice cream. And the milk chocolate mousse cake was a wonder, its dense chocolate custard layered between a fluff of whipped cream and a crust lined with fabulous peanut brittle.

It was more than enough to compensate for the disappearance of the Chiapas coffee cake I once enjoyed here, a rich little cake textured with the clever crunch of coffee grinds ringed by ripe tropical papaya and coffee ice cream.

Or Try These

Here are three other restaurants in University City.

Penne

The Inn at Penn, 3611 Walnut St., Philadelphia
(215) 823-6222

The Inn at Penn has made a vast improvement over the former Ivy Grille with this warm Italian concept, which features Roberta Adamo handcrafting pastas in the dining room to order, great thin-crust pizzas, and an Italian wine bar with more than 30 wines by the glass.

Nan

4000 Chestnut St., Philadelphia
(215) 382-0818

Elegant French-Thai fusion in a fairly priced BYOB with understated decor.

Pod

3636 Sansom St., Philadelphia
(215) 387-1803

Conveyor-belt sushi and light-changing booths are part of the gimmick at Stephen Starr's futuristic Asian fantasy, but good Japanese fusion fare is one of the better reasons to return.

Aside from its appealing caffeinate jolt, I was interested to note that the White Dog financed the harvest of its own coffee, advancing $20,000 to nonviolent Zapatista farmers in Mexico's volatile Chiapas region. It was certainly a delicious brew, and the arrangement sounded OK to me. But I'm sure Ken Starr would like to look into it if he ever makes it up to the dining room for dinner.

■ **MENU HIGHLIGHTS** Sweet pea soup; asparagus cheddar soup; salmon with horseradish-whipped cream; guacamole; crab cake with rock shrimp; duck "steaks"; grilled rib-eye; wok-seared striped bass with sweet pepper glaze; milk chocolate mousse cake over peanut brittle crust; strawberry rhubarb pie with buttermilk ice cream.

■ **WINE LIST** The medium-size all-American cellar has a nice selection under $40, including some organic wines.

■ **IF YOU GO** Lunch served Monday-Friday 11:30 a.m.-2:30 p.m. Dinner, Monday-Thursday 5:30-10 p.m., Friday-Saturday 5:30-11 p.m., Sunday 5-10 p.m. Bar and grill open Sunday-Thursday 2:30 p.m.-midnight, Friday-Saturday 2:30 p.m-1 a.m. Brunch served Saturday and Sunday 11 a.m.-2:30 p.m.

■ **RESERVATIONS** Highly recommended.

■ **CREDIT CARDS** All major cards.

■ **SMOKING** All dining rooms are nonsmoking, but smoking is allowed in bar and patio.

■ **HANDICAP ACCESSIBLE** Entrance off Moravian Court is wheelchair accessible, but rest rooms are not.

■ **PARKING** Street parking only.

Index

This index contains every restaurant mentioned in the book. The 76 favorites are denoted by ALL CAPS. Restaurants that have been formally reviewed are shown with their bell ratings. If a city and state are not listed, the restaurant is located in Philadelphia.

Bacchus Market

2300 Spruce St. (215) 545-6656
My favorite prepared foods store is a tiny corner shop near Fitler Square that offers just the right combination of homey cooking with a sophisticated touch. Fabulous soups, excellent fish, indulgent sides (creamed brussel sprouts) and bake-sale style desserts add-up to a satisfying dinner.

The Bards

2013 Walnut St. (215) 569-9585
Great brown bread, shepherd's pie and stuffed chicken anchor the updated Irish menu, and live Celtic music fills the Sunday morning air at this pleasant wood-trimmed pub.

Beau Monde

624 S. Sixth St. (215) 592-0656
A Queen Village cafe that offers authentic Breton-style buckwheat crepes in a beautiful room with gilt paneling, mosaic hearth and sidewalk seating.

Berlenga's Island

4926 N. Fifth St. (215) 324-3240
This obscure grotto bar and restaurant is a survivor from when the neighborhood was known as Little Lisbon, offering flaming sausage, grilled quails, and clam and pork stew.

Big George's Stop-N-Dine

285 S. 52d St. (215) 748-8200
It's best to visit the sunny cafeteria-style dining room on Sundays when the turn-over keeps the vast soul-food steam table, ranging from pig's feet to smothered pork chops, at its freshest.

BIRCHRUNVILLE STORE CAFE

Hollow and Flowing Spring Roads, Birchrunville, Pa. (610) 827-9002
A bucolic country-store-turned-restaurant with seasonal French-inspired cooking that has rustic charm to spare.

BISTRO ST. TROPEZ

Marketplace Design Center, 2400 Market St. (215) 569-9269
An upbeat bistro with a fantastic Schuylkill view, St. Tropez has a stylish, retro decor befitting its location in the Marketplace Design Center and a creative take on French cuisine at reasonable prices.

Bitar's

947 Federal St. (215) 755-1121
The original South Philadelphia market and sandwich shop (it now has branches in University City) is the innovator of the grilled falafel sandwich.

THE BLACK SHEEP

247 S. 17th St. (at Latimer) (215) 545-9473
Don't expect neon shamrocks in this handsomely upscale Irish pub, which brings the warmth of an antique hearth, creamy Guinness, and premium whiskeys to a beautifully restored townhouse near Rittenhouse Square. The pub fare is better than average.

Bleu

227 S. 18th St. (215) 545-0342
Neil Stein's parkside cafe has finally found its lower-key neighborhood niche and moved out from the style-conscious shadow of Rouge with good values for excellent bistro cooking, including an awesome signature burger.

BLUE ANGEL

706 Chestnut St. (215) 925-6889
The exquisite glass ceiling twinkles with a cinematic luster at this gorgeous Belle Epoque-style French bistro, where the classic bistro menu offers highly polished renditions of pure Gallic soul food.

The Blue Bell Inn
601 Skippack Pike, Blue Bell
(215) 646-2010.
Some modern dishes have been spotted here, but this American classic is still best for fried oysters, creamed spinach, fine wines and prime steaks finished with butter in cast-iron skillets. Some recent lumps in the bearnaise, though, hint at a careless kitchen.

Blue Danube Restaurant
538 Adeline St., Trenton (609) 393-6133
Rustic fabrics festoon the half-timbered dining room of this Hungarian eatery, where a shot of palinka and a plate of paprikash can make a Trenton neighborhood feel like the old country.

Blue Sage
772 Second Street Pike,
Southampton, Pa., (215) 942-8888
A casual strip mall bistro serving creative vegetarian cuisine that goes far beyond the cliches of twig-and-sprout cuisine.

Bookbinder's Seafood House
215 S. 15th St. (215) 545-1137
The last Bookbinder restaurant standing was always my preferred Bookbinder for classic fishhouse fare like snapper soup and crabcakes (and peanut butter pie), but the time-worn ambience desperately needs new life.

BRASSERIE PERRIER
1619 Walnut St. (215) 568-3000
Georges Perrier's second restaurant offers top-notch upscale contemporary dining in back, and a more casual French brasserie menu in the lively front lounge and cafe.

Bridgid's
726 N. 24th St. (215) 232-3232
A surprising menu of eclectic comfort food and a great beer selection make this an enticing and affordable neighborhood destination.

BUDDAKAN
325 Chestnut St. (215) 574-9440
Stephen Starr's first mega-restaurant in Old City remains wildly popular thanks to its giant golden Buddha and top-notch Asian fusion cuisine.

Bubble House
3404 Sansom St. (215) 243-0804
Trendy Asian bubble teas filled with chewy tapioca beads are served up with Asian fusion fare for the Penn crowd.

By George
Reading Terminal Market, 12th and Arch Streets, (215) 829-9391. Ardmore Farmers Market, Suburban Square, (610) 649-4944
This market standby serves up excellent brick-oven pizzas slices, hearty strombolis (including one filled with a cheesesteak), veggie hoagies and tasty pasta salads.

C

Cadence
300 S. Broad St. (215) 670-2388
The early months have proved shaky for the French-inspired brasserie inside the Kimmel Center, where the hours have gotten progressively more restrictive rather than more inviting. But stick with the raw bar (when it's open) and gaze up at City Hall from the spectacular balcony.

Cafe Habana
102 S. 21st St. (215) 561-2822
The homestyle Cuban fare has been up and down, but this stylish Latin bar shakes a fabulous mojito.

Cafe Lutecia
2301 Lombard St. (215) 790-9557
This pleasant corner cafe in the Fitler Square neighborhood is ideal for a simple baguette with paté and brie, hearty potato-leek soup or a fresh salad.

CAFE SPICE ■■

35 S. Second St. (215) 627-6273
This hip Indian bistro has contemporary decor, but classic dishes prepared with quality ingredients and sharp flavors.

Caffe Casta Diva

227 S. 29th St. (215) 496-9677
One of the newest Center City storefront Italians is an old burrito house transformed into a tranquil little room, where homemade pastas (try the spinach fettuccine with walnut pesto), interesting salads, and nice veal dishes are whimsically tied to an opera theme.

Caffe Monticello

236 Market St. (215) 627-0588
The menu at this stylish Old City bistro speaks mostly Italian, but with a Portuguese accent, evident in the caldo verde potato-kale soup and lemony steamed clams.

Campo's

214 Market St. (215) 923-1000
This spiffy branch of the Gray's Ferry original is by far the quaintest and friendliest steak shop in the city, but the slim sandwiches are also too polite, lacking much heft or flavor.

THE CAPITAL GRILLE ■■■

1338 Chestnut St. (215) 545-9588
This clubby steak house is one out-of-town chain that gets it right, from the consistently cooked chops to the outgoing service. It has become one of the city's favored spots for power dining.

CARAMBOLA ■■

1650 Limekiln Pike, Dresher, Pa. (215) 542-0900
A strip-mall find in the northern suburbs with fun atmosphere and surprisingly sophisticated eclectic fare, from great grilled pizzas to roast duck, phyllo-wound shrimp Carambola, and homemade gelati.

Caribou Cafe

1126 Walnut St. (215) 625-9535
This handsome cafe convenient to the theater district has had a steady string of inconsistent chefs. But the bar and sidewalk seating are irresistably attractive, and several recent menu items — smoked duck pastrami reuben, crab cakes — boded well for a promising pre-theater nibble.

Carlino's

2616 E. County Line Rd., Ardmore, Pa., (610) 649-4046
This Main Line prepared-foods institution specializes in excellent house-made pastas and sauces, pizzas, and a wide assortment of fine vinegars, oils, and other specialty products.

CARMINE'S

5 Brookline Blvd., Havertown, Pa. (610) 789-7255
Chef John Mims has re-created a New Orleans joint in the suburbs, converting a modest checkerboard-floor deli into a lively cafe that emphasizes bold-flavored Creole-plus cooking, and a recently expanded and improved decor.

Cassatt Lounge and Tea Room

The Rittenhouse Hotel, 210 W. Rittenhouse Square (215) 546-9000
Nibble afternoon sandwiches and scones with Devonshire cream in the civilized tranquility of the tea room and trellised garden at the Rittenhouse Hotel.

The Chef's Market

231 South St. (215) 925-8360
This Queen Village institution was one of Center City's first specialty foods retailers and prepared foods markets, and it remains a reliable standby - especially for catered parties. The smoked whitefish salad is a classic.

Cherry Street Vegetarian
1010 Cherry St. (215) 923-3663
One of the best of Chinatown's mock meat vegetarians, Cherry Street doesn't skimp on flavor with dishes like Dynasty mock shrimp and emerald soup and salt-baked oyster mushrooms.

Chez Elena Wu
910 Haddonfield-Berlin Rd., Voorhees, N.J. (856) 566-3222
This upscale Chinese restaurant brings a French influence to a largely Cantonese menu, with separate chefs for the superb wonton soup and the escargots.

Chick's Deli of Cherry Hill
906 Township Lane, Cherry Hill, N.J. (856) 429-2022
The chicken steaks are famous at this back-alley find off Route 70, but it was the beef steak that was recently worth noting, a perfect blend of flowing cheese, sweet onions and tender meat.

Chickie's Italian Deli
1014 Federal St. (215) 462-8040
This small corner deli in South Philadelphia turns out a fabulous olive oil-roasted vegetable hoagie sprinkled with salty white cheese.

Chink's Steaks
6030 Torresdale Ave. (215) 535-9405
Step into a time warp at this marvelously preserved soda shop where chocolate egg creams and frothy shakes are the ideal pairing for what may be the most succulent traditional soft-roll American cheese cheesesteak in town.

CHLÖE
232 Arch St. (215) 629-2337
Husband-and-wife chefs Dan Grimes and Mary Ann Ferrie have created a homey neighborhood gem in a tiny Old City space warmed by thistle brooms and votive lights, and a deftly rendered, affordable menu of international comfort food.

Chris' Jazz Cafe
1421 Sansom St. (215) 568-3131
Tucked into an obscure block across from the Union League, this unpretentious hideaway is a great place to catch jazz stars such as Jimmy Bruno in a late-night jam session. The menu isn't gourmet, but the ribs and crab cakes are respectable.

Cibucan
2025 Sansom St. (215) 231-9895
The tapas here are inconsistent, but this beautiful restaurant now has a liquor license and an upstairs bar worth a late-night mojito and snack.

CinCin
7838 Germantown Ave. (215) 242-8800
This sunny little sibling of Bryn Mawr's Yangming offers thoughtfullly upscaled Chinese food with good ingredients and French accented wine-infused sauces.

Circa
1518 Walnut St. (215) 545-6800
This converted bank building has a cavernous dining room (and a downstairs eat-in vault) that has long been one of the better bargains on Restaurant Row when it isn't too busy trying to be a trendy bar. Chef Tom Harkins keeps the tradition alive with surprisingly tasty New American fare.

CITRUS
8136 Germantown Ave. (215) 247-8188
A tiny bistro-bakery that offers modern seafood and vegetarian dishes with a light Asian touch and a heavy dose of animal-rights activism.

The Continental
138 Market St. (215) 923-6069
This Old City diner-turned-martini-bar is where Stephen Starr first found his restaurant mojo, serving global tapas to an endless supply of buff swingers in black.

Copa Too
263 S. 15th St. (215) 735-0848
This cramped multi-floor bar is known for great burgers, spicy Spanish fries, and addictive margaritas.

Corinne's Place   ✦✦
1254 Haddon Ave., Camden
(856) 541-4894
The homey pink dining room comes alive at Sunday brunch with one of the best soul-food buffets around, thanks in no small part to the cast-iron-skillet-fried chicken.

COUNTRY CLUB RESTAURANT   ✦✦✦
1717 Cottman Ave. (215) 722-0500
The region's best diner maintains its excellent Jewish and American comfort food while updating the kitchen with a new chef.

The Countryside Market & Delicatessen
514 Yale Ave., Swarthmore, Pa.
(610) 604-4799
Lunchers pack the dining room and patio at this excellent Swarthmore sandwich deli. Go for the hot house signature, a delicious muffuletta taste-alike called the Countryside, and a dessert of soft black licorice snips.

Criniti
2601 S. Broad St. (215) 465-7750
A classic neighborhood Italian, where opera plays over the stereo in a tiny paneled dining room and the homestyle food tastes like it is made with care.

Cuba Libre   ✦
10 S. Second St. (215) 627-0666
A fantasy dining room built to resemble an old Havana streetscape hosts an awesome rum list that makes this Old City nightspot worth a try, although the food has been inconsistent.

D

Dahlak
4708 Baltimore Ave. (215) 726-6464
This Ethiopian standby is a bit shabby these days, but the spicy tews and spongy njira bread are tasty, and the house-roasted ginger-flavored coffee is not to be missed.

Dalessandro's
Henry Avenue and Walnut Lane
(215) 482-5407
The staff couldn't be nicer at this Roxborough classic, but the tall berm of finely chopped mass-cooked beef tends to make a dry sandwich.

Dante & Luigi's
762 S. 10th St. (215) 922-9501
A century-old survivor that has slipped a bit, but is still a destination for stuffed brasciole, gnocchi and spaghetti with liver and onions.

Darbar Grill
319 Market St. (215) 923-2410
The all-u-can-eat Indian buffet genre has this new Old City entry, with a wide variety of freshly prepared classics, from tandoori chicken to cauliflower pakora, that seems slightly fresher than that of its University City counterparts.

The Dark Horse
421 S. Second St. (215) 928-9307
The new owners of the former Dickens Inn have struggled to bring the English fare here up to the level of their Black Sheep near Rittenhouse Square. But this handsome, rambling old pub is still a great destination for world-class single malt Scotch, darts and soccer-heads craving European football on the tube.

Davio's

111 S. 17th St. (215) 563-4810
This small Boston-based Italian chain has
a sleek second-floor perch in a former
Chestnut Street bank building, and excels
with classic steaks. The new chef comes
from Jake's

Deep Blue

111 W. 11th St., Wilmington
(302) 777-2040
This chic, contemporary restaurant
features seafood with international
influences and an excellent raw bar.

DelColle Market

222 W. Rittenhouse Square (Locust St.)
(215) 732-3838
This prepared-foods take-out near
Rittenhouse Square sells Superior Pasta
ravioli and high-quality condiments, and
makes one of the best Italian hoagies
anywhere.

Delilah's Southern Cafe

Reading Terminal Market, 12th and Arch
Streets, (215) 574-0929.
30th Street Station, 30th and Market
Streets, (215) 243-2440.
Before Delilah Winder attempted nouveau
soul food at her stylish Bluezette in Old
City, these casual food stands set decent
local benchmarks of the Southern
classics.

DEUX CHEMINEES

1221 Locust St. (215) 790-0200
Turn back the clock to an era of classic
French dining in an elegant 19th-century
townhouse, beautifully maintained by the
jovial and scholarly chef Fritz Blank,
whose cookbook library exceeds 12,000
volumes.

Devon Seafood Grill

225 S. 18th St. (215) 546-5940
This handsome seafooder has a large,
accessible dining room and a slightly less
tony crowd than the rest of Rittenhouse's
chic cafes that comes to gobble up its hot
sweet biscuits and fresh seafood that
lately has slipped from its impressive
opening form.

Di Palma

114 Market St. (215) 733-0545
This sleek Old City Italian has been a
showcase for ever-inventive Salvatore
DiPalma, who produces enough gems
to counter the occasional creative miss.

DiBruno Bros. House of Cheese

109 S. 18th St. (215)564-9339
930 S. Ninth St. (215) 922-2876
This Italian Market standby and its
bustling branch in the Rittenhouse area
are some of the finest cheese markets in
town, with an international selection of
curds, plus one of the best selections of
oils, vinegars, olives and cured meats.

DiBruno Bros. Pronto

103 S. 18th St. (215) 564-9339
Shop for your mozzarella and olive oil at
the cheese store two doors away, then
head to DiBruno's relatively new and
improving prepared foods store for the
rest of the meal, from rotisserie birds to a
variety of pastas, tasty panini and other
Italian specialties.

DILWORTHTOWN INN

1390 Old Wilmington Pike,
Village of Dilworthtown, West Chester, Pa.
(610) 399-1390
This Chester County classic is everything
a Colonial country inn should be, with a
first-class menu that melds classic and
contemporary, one of the region's finest
wine cellars, and gracious old-world
service to match the romantic intimacy
of its historic candle-lit setting.

DJANGO ✦✦✦
526 S. Fourth St. (215) 922-7151
The husband-wife team of Bryan Sikora
and Aimee Olexy sets a new standard for
the neighborhood restaurant in their
wildly popular BYOB, pulling off an
ambitious European-inspired menu
(including an awesome cheese plate) that
uses great local ingredients and keeps
prices moderate.

DMITRI'S ✦✦
Third and Catherine Streets,
(215) 625-0556; 23d and Pine Streets.
(215) 985-3680
Loyalists will debate the differences
between Dmitri Chimes' two Greek
seafooderies, with the Queen Village
original usually winning over Fitler
Square. But they both deliver consistently
good, satisyfingly simple seafood at
extremely fair prices.

Donkey's Place
1223 Haddon Ave., Camden
(856) 966-2616
Imitated to great acclaim by an eatery in
Manhattan, Donkey's specialty is a fistful
of flavor on a kaiser roll, as notable for its
generous mop-top of onions as it is for its
grease-dripping, salty punch.

Down Home Diner
Reading Terminal Market, 12th and Arch
Streets (215) 627-1955
Jack McDavid's Reading Terminal outlet
for hog-jowl soup and panfried chicken
could be so good if the food were more
consistent.

Downtown Cheese Shop
Reading Terminal Market, 12th and Arch
Streets (215) 351-7412
Jack Morgan has a talent for bringing the
most amazing and rare artisan cheeses to
this excellent market stand, which has
recently expanded into some other
sublime condiments, from Tuscan ham to
Greek yogurt.

E

East of Amara ✦✦
700 S. Fifth St. (215) 627-4200
This bright Queen Village sister to
crosstown Amara Cafe serves a mix of
deftly done Thai classics and more
unusual specialties such as jasmine rice
snowflake soup.

EFFIE'S ✦✦
1127 Pine St. (215) 592-8333
Classic Greek home foods, from moussaka
to baklava, can be savored in the lovely
brick patio or the cozy cottage behind
Effie's townhouse-turned-taverna.

El Bohio
2746 N. Fifth St. (215) 425-5991
This gritty Puerto Rican corner eatery has
anchored the Golden Mile for more than
two decades with spicy fried chicken,
adobo-smothered pork chops, and the
best flan around.

El Viejo San Juan ✦✦
1176 N. Third St. (215) 922-2376
A beautiful renovation evokes a Caribbean
mood at this new Girard Avenue art
gallery and restaurant, where roasted pork
with pickled green plantains, caldo santo
stew, and tamarind-glazed Cornish hens
offer the real taste of San Juan.

Emerald Fish
65 Barclay Farms Shopping Center, Route
70 East, Cherry Hill, N.J. (856) 616-9192
This colorful strip-mall BYOB has an
internationally inspired kitchen, with
great specials like Chilean sea bass
topped with miso-sweetened eggplant
paté.

ERNESTO'S 1521 CAFÉ   ⅩⅩ
1521 Spruce St. (215) 546-1521
This surprising spot in the shadow
of the Kimmel Center has evolved from
a minimalist coffee shop-gallery into a
full-blown trattoria that is one of the best
affordable pre-theater options around,
with fresh pastas, delicious salads and
homemade limoncello.

F

Fado Irish Pub
1500 Locust St. (215) 893-9700
Guiness owns this noisy Atlanta-based
pub chain, which is decorated to the hilt
with antiquey Irish kitsch, serves a decent
pub-plus menu that offers modern spins
on traditional boxty potato pancakes.

FELICIA'S   ⅩⅩ
1148 S. 11th St. (215) 755-9656
One of South Philly's best "post-red-
gravy" standbys remains as steady as its
great ricotta gnocchi despite the travails
of a seemingly endless renovation and a
recent fire that put it temorarily out of
commission.

Figs   Ⅹ
2501 Meredith St. (215) 978-8440
This Art Museum bistro is a cozy,
pumpkin-colored corner room with an
intriguing (albeit inconsistent) menu that
blends contemporary cooking with North
African accents.

Fireworks!
*Reading Terminal Market, 12th and Arch
Streets (215) 592-9008*
With its open-flame grill in the Reading
Terminal Market does decent burgers, but
specializes in grilled lamb and brie
sandwiches.

The Foodery Market
10th and Pine Streets (215) 928-1111
This corner market is the place to go for
that obscure can of trappiste ale; they
stock nearly every beer known to man.

FORK   ⅩⅩ
306 Market St. (215) 625-9425
The definitive Old City bistro has been
through a series of good chefs, but it is
the constant presence of co-owner Ellen
Yin that gives Fork its professional polish.

Founders
*Park Hyatt at the Bellevue, 200 S. Broad
St. (215) 790-2814*
The rotunda-topped dining room has
spectacular penthouse views, weekend
dancing, and some excellent upscale fare
(especially great crab cakes). Institutional
service, though, can make the *grande
dame* feel flat.

FOUNTAIN RESTAURANT   ⅩⅩⅩⅩ
*Four Seasons Hotel, 1 Logan Square
(215) 963-1500*
The city's most reliable palace of posh
redefines what hotel dining can be
through its creative, top-notch kitchen
and a seamless service staff that makes
everyone feel like royalty.

Frenchtown Inn   ⅩⅩ
*7 Bridge St., Frenchtown, N.J.
(908) 996-3300*
This historic inn beside the Delaware
River has a long tradition of sophisticated
dining, with an ambitious menu rooted in
seasonal French cooking, fine wines, and
cozy fireplace dining rooms.

FRIDAY SATURDAY SUNDAY   ⅩⅩ
261 S. 21 St. (215) 546-4232
The fluorescent chalkboard still glows
brightly at this "restaurant renaissance"
classic, where an eclectic menu rooted in
the '70s has gotten gentle updates from
the kitchen, and good values on the wine
list are a draw.

FUJI JAPANESE RESTAURANT   ⅩⅩⅩ
*404 Route 130 North, Cinnaminson, N.J.
(856) 829-5211*
Gritty Route 130 is an unlikely setting.
The restaurant itself is humble. But chef
Masaharu "Matt" Ito's Japanese tasting
"kaiseki" dinners offer some of the most
exquisite cooking around, making him one
of the region's best unsung chefs.

FuziOn

2960 Skippack Pike., Worcester, Pa.
(610) 584-6958

The team behind the now-closed Ly Michaels in Overbrook Park has brought its ambitious Asian-fusion cuisine farther west to a pretty little BYOB near Skippack Village.

G

Genji ⅡⅡ

1720 Sansom St. (215) 564-1720

It may have slipped a shade since the tragic death of its owner two years ago, but this remains Center City's most reliable venue for standard sushi.

Geno's Steaks

1219 S. Ninth St. (215) 389-0659

This South Philly institution easily bested rival Pat's on the day of our tasting, with steaks that were meaty (albeit slightly tough) and full of juicy drip. A splash of the killer hot sauce tastes like flame on a roll.

Gilmore's ⅡⅡ

133 E. Gay St., West Chester, Pa.
(610) 431-2800

A charming converted townhouse in downtown West Chester is now home to the French cuisine of former Le Bec-Fin lunch chef Peter Gilmore.

Girasole

1305 Locust St. (215) 985-4659

This darling of the Academy of Music crowd is a fine destination for standards such as carpaccio and homemade pasta. But its best dish may be the thin-crusted wood-oven margherita pizza.

Golden Gates

11058 Rennard St. (215) 677-9337

The Northeast's largest Russian-style nightclub banquet hall serves up chicken kiev, pelmeni dumplings, and the added spectacle of Russian showgirls.

Great Tea International

1724 Sansom St. (215) 568-7827

At this new basement tea room just below the Joseph Fox bookstore, the owner serves a classic Chinese tea ceremony with teas imported directly from Taiwan, along with pastries, steamed buns and dumplings.

Green Hills Inn

2444 Morgantown Rd., Reading, Pa.
(610) 777-9611

This gracious inn with classic French-inspired cuisine is a special-occasion standby.

Grilladelphia

Exxon Station, 2330 Aramingo Ave.
(215) 739-3801

It gets points for turning one end of an Exxon station convenience store into a serious steakerie. The hollowed-out round rolls are unusual, but the steaks themselves are satisfying fare.

The Grill ⅡⅡⅡ

Ritz-Carlton Philadelphia, 10 S. Broad St.
(215) 735-7700

There is nothing French about this mysteriously named restaurant, but the clubby dining room does offer an appealing contemporary update to the stuffy old hotel grill with gracious service and a sunny City Hall view.

H

H & J McNally's Tavern

8634 Germantown Ave. (215) 247-9736

Everything is made from scratch at this dark little tavern, from the lunch meat to the soups and desserts. But it's the Schmitter, a salami-cheesesteak fantasy on a kaiser roll, that makes it worth the trip.

H.K. Golden Phoenix
911 Race St. (215) 629-4988
One of Chinatown's first big Hong Kong-style dim sum houses in Chinatown isn't quite as good as it used to be, but is still a fair bet for a big assortment of competently done dumplings and heaps of garlicky greens.

HAPPY ROOSTER
118 S. 16th St. (at Sansom)
(215) 963-9311
This quirky bar-cum-restaurant offers surprisingly gourmet fare in a brass-railed, red booth hideaway for Market Street movers and restaurant insiders. The service can be spotty, but the sophisticated (and pricey) cooking makes it more than worthwhile.

High Street Caffe
322 S. High St., West Chester, Pa.
(610) 696-7435
The funky purple BYOB has ceiling lights fringed with Mardi Gras beads and the hearty Cajun menu indulges the full-octane flavors of Louisiana. The andouille gumbo was authentic, but the runny pecan pie went *splat* and the super-spicy voodoo crawfish is for double-dare flame-eaters only.

Hikaru
607 S. Second St. (215) 627-7110
Get your toro tuna fresh at this reliable Queen Village sushi standby, which recently underwent a handsome renovation with a riverstone paved entranceway and beautiful tatami booths for an intimate group dinner.

HORIZONS CAFE
101 E. Moreland Ave. (Routes 63 and 611), Willow Grove, Pa. (215) 657-2100
Giving tofu taste and seitan sizzle is a daunting task, but this casual vegan cafe usually succeeds nicely with a flavorful series of mock meat dishes that have exotic inspirations and attractive presentations.

Hotel DuPont
11th & Market Streets, Wilmington
(302) 594-3100
The soaring, oak-clad Green Room and the Wyeth-hung Brandywine make for dining rooms of unmatched classical grandeur. The service and the wine cellar are first-class, but the kitchens, while better than average, are rarely magical.

The House of Tea
720 S. Fourth St. (215) 923-8327
This is the city's best store devoted to serious loose teas, where everything from toasted Ecudorian yerba mate to fancy oolongs are scooped out of oversize tins.

Hunan
47 E. Lancaster Ave., Ardmore, Pa.
(610) 642-3050
This cozy Main Line standby may be run by Susanna Foo's in-laws, but the cooking is strictly traditional, featuring excellent hot-and-sour soup and scallion pancakes.

I

Il Cantuccio
701 N. Third St. (215) 627-6573
The tiny corner room covered with painted vines embodies the funky, handcrafted spirit of Northern Liberties, and regional Italian dishes like white beans and sausage are finally evolving from sloppy to rustic.

Il Tartufo
4341 Main St. (215) 482-1999
Alberto Delbello's "Roman-Jewish" trattoria is tight inside, but has a lovely sidewalk cafe from which to watch Main Street pass by while you nibble awesome fried artichokes, homemade mozzarella, and truffle-sauced veal scallopini.

Illuminare
2321 Fairmount Ave. (215) 765-0202
A gorgeously appointed dining room and patio features Italian-inspired cuisine with a special forte for brick-oven pizzas.

Indonesia
1029 Race St. (215) 829-1400
The spicy peanut curries and multicourse rice table feasts of Indonesia are served with care and affordable prices at this Chinatown newcomer.

Inn at Phillip's Mill   ✦✦
2590 River Rd., New Hope, Pa.
(215) 862-9919
The straightforward country French cuisine tastes all the better in the candlelit flicker of this historic Bucks County farmhouse.

The Inn at Twin Lindens   ✦✦
2092 Main St., Churchville, Pa.
(717) 445-7619
Donna Leahy's lovely inn, set amid the rolling Lancaster farmland, serves more sophisticated delights than most bed and breakfasts could dream of, but the once-a-week Saturday dinners are also a treat.

THE INN ON BLUEBERRY HILL   ✦✦✦
1715 S. Easton Rd., Doylestown, Pa.,
(215) 491-1777
This ambitious Bucks County inn has an exciting chef in Bill Kim, a Susanna Foo protege who is talented enough to make Blueberry Hill one of the region's premier dining destinations. The inn itself still has a generic charm, but the service is warm and professional.

Inn Philadelphia   ✦
251 S. Camac St. (215) 732-2339
The New American menu and service have sagged of late, but this hidden inn, tucked away in a historic enclave, has roaring fireplaces and a piano bar for a sense of country romance in the city.

International Cafe
113 Browns Mills Rd., Pemberton, N.J.,
(609) 893-9220
Come to this surprising haven in the Pinelands for massive portions of full-flavored Korean home cooking that thrives on special ingredients, from squash to chiles, that the owner grows in her backyard.

Ishkabibble's Eatery
337 South St. (215) 923-4337
This pink-and-black South Street take-out window is famous for its chicken steaks, but a recent sandwich was disappointingly dry.

J

Jack's Firehouse
2130 Fairmount Ave. (215) 232-9000
This renovated fire-house is a destination for exotic meats and nouveau down-home cooking, but has lost some buzz in recent years as chef Jack McDavid's media distractions mount. It's still a good bet for a shot of small-batch bourbon.

JAKE'S   ✦✦✦
4365 Main St. (215) 483-0444
A pioneer of Manayunk's fine-dining scene, Jake's is still the neighborhood's best bet after more than 15 years, offering the sleek clientele a stylish yellow dining room and a creative take on everything from mashed potatoes and calves' liver to the signature dessert cookie taco.

Jamaican Jerk Hut
1436 South St. (215) 545-8644
With steel drums and tall grass hedging in from the vacant lot next door, this South Street Jamaican has a shaded back patio (and the jerk sauce) to conjure a convincing Caribbean mood.

Jim's Steaks
431 N. 62d St. (215) 747-6615
The other branches got their black-and-white tile deco style from the original in West Philly. This Jim's has some of the best fried onions in town, but the meat leaves much to be desired.

Joe's Pizza
122 S. 16th St. (215) 569-0898
For its wide variety of mix-and-match toppings and super crust, office-district workers will rightly stand in line at this bright pizzeria.

JOHN'S ROAST PORK ★★★

Snyder Avenue and Weccacoe Street
(215) 463-1951

This relatively unknown luncheonette survived 70 years in the delicious obscurity of a South Philly shack until the hoards discovered it this year as the definitive practitioner of the sloppy roast pork and cheesesteak tradition. Don't expect tablecloths, but the picnic tables outside have one of the best views in the city.

Jolly's

135 S. 17th St. (215) 563-8200

This casual offshoot of the Prime Rib sits just below the Walnut Street sidewalk, offering a black-lacquer, piano lounge hideaway for top-notch American fare, from steaks and bugers to artichoke dip, at fair prices.

Jones ★★

700 Chestnut St. (215) 223-5663

Stephen Starr's latest venture reenvisions classics like fried chicken and waffles, turkey pot pie, and grilled cheese with tomato soup in a sunny, retro '70s room that also throbs with noise.

Jong Ka Jib Soft Tofu Restaurant

6600 N. Fifth St. (215) 924-0100

A relative newcomer to Olney's Koreatown, this handsome restaurant decorated with rice-paper walls and wooden booths specializes in spicy tofu soups that come in bubbling-hot cast-iron casseroles.

Joy Tsin Lau

1026 Race St. (215) 592-7228

This Chinatown classic is still decent for standard dim sum, but the well-worn dragon red dining room could use a sprucing-up.

JUDY'S CAFE ★★

627 S. Third St. (215) 928-1968

This affable Queen Village fixture is famous for stuffed meatloaf, cheese-cracker-crusted chicken, two-for-one coupons, and a gay-friendly atmosphere.

K

Kansas City Prime ★★

4417 Main St. (215) 482-3700

Derek Davis' chic local chophouse is satisfying as long as you stick with the excellent steaks; the rest is inconsistent and overpriced.

KHAJURAHO ★★

Ardmore Plaza, 12 Greenfield Ave.,
Ardmore, Pa. (610) 896-7200

The ancient arts of exotic food and sensuality are tastefully linked at this Main Line ethnic, where some of the region's finest Indian cuisine is served under the gaze of erotic sculptures from ancient Khajuraho.

Kim's

5955 N. Fifth St. (215) 927-4550

Traditional barbecued Korean meats are grilled at your table over real charcoal fires in this converted diner.

King of Falafel

16th and JFK

This little food cart parked across from Love Park at 16th and JFK fires up one of the most reliable falafels in town, as well as a delicious weekly special of oniony lentil rice called mjadra.

Kisso Sushi Bar

205 N. Fourth St. (215) 922-1770

A sleek, earth-toned sushi bar in Old City where inventive ideas such as the cooked tuna-wrapped raw tuna roll and the BYO-Sake policy have been a hit. (A Northern Liberties outpost called Kissen should open soon.)

Koch's Deli

4309 Locust St. (215) 222-8662

Devotees swear by the garlic-infused corned beef special at this cramped take-out deli as the definitive Philly style (cold, thin-sliced) corned beef. But the colorful counter-side banter and complimentary cold-cut noshes are also a draw.

Korea Garden

1720 E. Route 70, Cherry Hill, N.J.
(856) 751-7388

The table grills are gas-fired, but this is still a fine, upscale destination for South Jersey's Korean community, where good barbecued meats, fiery kimchee, and tasty jap chae noodles are highlights.

Krazy Kats   ★★

Route 100 and Rockland Road,
Montchanin, Del. (302) 888-2133

A wacky animal motif somehow fits in at this beautifully refurbished inn with adventurous New American cooking and a fine wine list. Service, though, was uncharacteristically spotty on a recent visit.

KRISTIAN'S   ★★

1100 Federal St. (215) 468-0104

This prettily renovated butcher shop has matured into South Philadelphia's finest upscale Italian eatery, although the service still can't match the finesse of young chef Kristian Leuzzi.

L

La Boheme

246 S. 11th St. (215) 351-9901

This little storefront BYOB near Jefferson Hospital serves up bistro fare with a North African accent, offering calamari spiced with Moroccan ras el hanout and chicken tagine with olives and preserved lemon.

La Buca

711 Locust St. (215) 928-0556

This downstairs grotto off Washington Square is an oft forgotten haven of black tie service, and specialties such as whole fish, grilled langostinos, pasta fagiole and other Italian classics executed with perfect simplicity.

La Calebasse

4519 Baltimore Ave. (215) 382-0555

The no-frills dining room is a favorite among African cab drivers for authentic Ivory Coast cuisine, including roast guinea hen with jolof rice, spicy mafe peanut sauce, and roasted lamb shank with onions.

La Cigale

725 Walnut St./1315 Walnut St./113
S. 18th St. (215) 625-3666;
(215) 546-4366; (215) 569-1970

This small sandwich shop cafe chain with a Southern French twist serves great Provencale-style sandwiches on crusty bread.

La Colombe Torrefaction

130 S. 19th St. (215) 563-0860

The hip Euro-Rittenhouse crowd lounges around the chessboards at this smoky, chic cafe where the baristas really know how to pull the best single shot of espresso in town.

LA ENCINA   ★★

2 Waterview Rd., East Goshen, Pa.
(610) 918-9715

Chef Javier Cuesta has brought a taste of his native Seville to this lovely Chester County BYOB, offering the region's finest authentic Spanish cuisine, from awesome tapas and gazpacho to salt-crusted fish.

La Famiglia

8 S. Front St. (215) 922-2803

This posh Old City institution for upscale Neopolitan cooking may no longer be our very best Italian eatery, but it still has the region's finest (and most expensive) wine cellar, with nearly 13,000 bottles on display behind cages downstairs.

La Lupe

1201 S. Ninth St. (215) 551-9920

The latest in a wave of authentic new taquerias serving South Philly's growing Mexican population brings great tacos with homemade tortillas to the heart of cheesesteak country.

La Veranda
Pier 3, N. Columbus Blvd. (215) 351-1898
Sit with a dockside view of a Delaware
River marina at this upscale, old-world
Italian restaurant, where salt-baked
whole fish and Tuscan wood-fired steaks
are the specialty, and the service plays
favorites with regulars.

Lacroix at the Rittenhouse
*210 W. Rittenhouse Square
(215) 790-2533*
Former Four Seasons guru Jean-Marie
Lacroix has already transformed the
cuisine at the old TreeTops in the
Rittenhouse Hotel, but a name change
and a lavish decor revamp this fall has
finally made it a major new player in the
fine-dining scene.

LAKESIDE CHINESE DELI
207 N. Ninth St. (215) 925-3288
This gritty Ninth Street nook has an
unglamourous bare-tile decor, but serves
great made-to-order dim sum and other
fine Cantonese classics.

L'Angolo
1415 W. Porter St. (215) 389-4252
Authentic Italian antipasti, veal with
mushrooms, and almond-crusted
cheesecake are among the highlights
at this lovely South Philadelphia corner
grotto.

Larry's Famous Steaks
2459 N. 54th St. (215) 879-1776
The home of the five-pound "belly filler"
overloads its flabby rolls with too much
food to enjoy.

LAS CAZUELAS
426-28 W. Girard Ave. (215) 351-9144
This colorful little eatery isn't fancy, but
the homespun specialties from mole-
loving Puebla are an irresistible draw,
making this affordable spot worth a visit
to Girard Avenue.

Lazaro's Pizza House
1743 South St. (215) 545-2775
When it comes to the search for cheap-
but-decent pizza, the massive, slightly
sweet pizzas at Lazaro's have become a
staple for neighbors of Graduate Hospital.

Le Bar Lyonnais
1523 Walnut St. (215) 567-1000
The no-reservation downstairs bar at
Le Bec-Fin is still one of the city's best
gourmet deals, where the a la carte
menu, from steak and frites to the
excellent cheese plate, more than
compensate for the claustrophobic room.

LE BEC-FIN
1523 Walnut St. (215) 567-1000
The city's high temple of French cuisine
has gone through a tumultuous year,
culminating in a major dining-room face-
lift and an exciting new executive chef.
Through it all, Georges Perrier's gold-rate
gem has remained our finest, most
ambitious gastronomic experience.

Le Bus
4266 Main St. (215) 487-2663
The eclectic fare at this bakery-cafe is a
lunchtime favorite for many, although for
a family-friendly place, the service has
often been snippy.

LE CASTAGNE
1920 Chestnut St. (215) 751-9913
This contemporary Northern Italian from
the owners of La Famiglia serves excellent
fresh pastas amid a sleek decor of
imported marble and cherrywood-paneled
walls.

Le Cyclo
606 Washington Ave. (215) 389-7844
Located behind the Ba Le bakery, this cool
modern room is a destination for hip,
second-generation Vietnamese, where
fresh sugar cane juice and bubble teas
accompany updated classics like duck
noodle soup.

Le Mas Perrier

503 W. Lancaster Ave. (610) 964-2588
Georges Perrier's elegant suburban
outpost offers a lovely Provencale
ambience and much-improved service,
but the new chef, while talented, has
taken the menu in the less intriguing
direction of Asian-fusion.

Le Me Toujours

515 Route 73 South, Marlton, N.J.
(856) 810-2000
This attractive South Jersey BYOB blends
traditional Vietnamese and French flavors
into beautiful and sophisticated
contemporary dishes.

LEE HOW FOOK

219 N. 11th St. (215) 925-7266
The family-owned Chinatown veteran
is still one of the neighborhood's most
dependable standbys for great hot pots,
restorative soups, crispy Buddha rollls,
and delicious whole fish at affordable
prices.

Lenny's Italian Deli

Ninth and Fayette Streets, Conshohocken,
Pa. (610) 825-4569
This spot was a personal favorite when it
was the pork sandwich haven known as
Mastrocola's. It has slipped under the new
owner.

Little Fish

600 Catharine St. (215) 413-3464
This Queen Village BYOB is one of the
smallest nooks in town, but the daily-
changing seafood menu has creative,
wide-ranging flavors and great desserts.

Little Thai Singha Market

Reading Terminal Market, 12th and Arch
Streets (215) 873-0231
This newly expanded stand has become
one of the best spots in the Reading
Terminal Market, where lunchers line up
for the fresh BBQ salmon and crab
dumplings topped with crunchy garlic.

Lombardi's Specialty Hoagies

1226 Ritner St. (215) 389-2220
A corner deli in deep South Philly that
serves hefty, flavorful Italian hoagies.

Lombardi's

132 S. 18th St. (215) 564-5000
This casual cafe just north of Rittenhouse
Square is a branch of the classic New York
pizzeria whose coal-fired hearth produces
excellent pies topped with quality
ingredients. Clam pies are a specialty.

LONDON GRILL

2301 Fairmount Ave. (215) 978-4545
A Fairmount institution that strikes the
ideal balance between the neighborhood
pub and ambitious fine dining, with a
kitchen that ranges from fabulous burgers
to Asian duck spring rolls.

Lorenzo's Pizza

900 Christian St., (215) 922-2540
This corner pizzeria and steak shop sits in
the heart of the Italian Market, dispensing
wide slices of prototypical Philly-style
pizza.

LOS CATRINES RESTAURANT
& TEQUILA'S BAR

1602 Locust St. (215) 546-0181
A upscale Mexican that offers a beautiful
art-filled decor to complement its
authentic cuisine and top-notch tequila
list.

Ludwig's Garten

1315 Sansom St. (215) 985-1525
The German fare at this quirky Sansom
Street brauhaus can be way too heavy
(especially the lunch buffet). But the
selection of yeasty, potent German brews
is among the best I've seen anywhere.

M

Magazine
2029 Walnut St. (215) 567-5000
Bar Noir impresario David Carroll has crafted a tiny hotspot that feels like an updated Victorian parlor with a bohemian edge, where the tony crowd comes for Peter Dunmire's seasonal bistro fare.

Mainland Inn
17 Main St. (Sumneytown Pike), Mainland, Pa. (215) 256-8500
This pleasant Montco inn delivers candle-lit rooms, classy service, fine wines, and New American cooking that thrives on quality seasonal ingredients and straightforward, traditional ideas.

Mallorca
119 South St. (215) 351-6652
An upscale Spanish restaurant with great tapas, champagne sangria, and old-world service, but also, expensive entrees that can be disappointing.

Mama's Pizzeria
426 Belmont Ave., Bala Cynwyd, Pa. (610) 664-4757
This Main Line darling has a frilly pink dining room and a secret blend of cheeses blended in abundance (sometimes too abundantly) into the finely shredded steaks.

Marco Polo
8080 Old York Rd., Elkins Park, Pa. (215) 782-1950
Ignore the old fern-bar decor and strip-mall location, the Chinese-born chef is a surprisingly gifted Italian cook specializing in fresh whole fish.

MARGARET KUO'S PEKING
Granite Run Mall, 1067 W. Baltimore Pike, Media, Pa. (610) 566-4110
Shockingly elegant for a mall restaurant, this pan-Asian gem highlights lesser-known regional cuisines from Shanghai and Beijing, as well as excellent sushi.

MAX'S
602 Route 130 North, Cinnaminson, N.J., (856) 663-6297
A quaint 19th-century Friends-meetinghouse-turned-restaurant has become one of South Jersey's finest dining destinations, with polished service and a talented young chef turning out contemporary fare with French and Italian accents.

Mayfair Diner
7373 Frankford Ave. (215) 624-8886
This stainless-steel classic rimmed with green neon still draws a devoted Northeast crowd for homey '50s-era fare.

McCormick & Schmick's
1 S. Broad St. (215) 568-6888
This Portland-based chain brings an upscale dining room to a prime power lunch spot across from City Hall, although the reasonably priced seafood menu has been inconsistent.

Melange Cafe
1601 Chapel Ave., Cherry Hill, N.J. (856) 663-7339
In a lively dining room decked with colorful prints and garden lattice, chef Joe Brown draws inspiration from Louisianian and Italian cooking for bountiful portions of hearty food.

Melrose Diner
1501 Snyder Ave. (215) 467-6644
This 24-hour South Philly standby with the coffee-cup clock and horseshoe booths has been beautifully restored, but the menu could be spruced up next.

Metropolitan Bakery
262 S. 19th St., 215-545-6655.
Philadelphia's best artisan baker now has several locations, but this corner shop just south of Rittenhouse Square is always packed with locals clamouring for its crusty baguettes and yeasty rounds of sourdough miche, as well as indulgent sweets, home-made matzo (in-season) and a small but fine selection of oils, cheeses and other locally grown edibles.

Mexico Lindo
3521 Federal St., Camden (856) 365-9004
Try the enchilada-sauced beef tacos on homemade tortillas and succulent roast chickens on the weekends at this humble but authentically tasty bungalow on the outskirts of Camden.

Mezza Luna
763 S. Eighth St. (215) 627-4705
This crisp, contemporary space has one of South Philly's more upscale dining rooms, as well as airy ricotta gnocchi in gorgonzola sauce, rabbit stew, and fine seafood are worth the trip.

Miel Patisserie
1990 Route 70 East, Marlton, N.J. (856) 424-6435
Former Le Bec-Fin pastry prince Robert Bennett has recreated a Parisian palace of sweets in South Jersey, where devotees flock for exquisite pastries, superb chocolates, ice creams, and sublime hot chocolate.

Mikado
2370 Route 70 West, Cherry Hill, N.J, (856) 665-4411
This Route 70 newcomer is giving local powerhouse Sagami a run for the South Jersey sushi crowd, especially those who crave Mikado's wildly busy maki rolls.

Minar Palace
1605 Sansom St. (215) 564-9443
While it does not have the very best Indian (although the vegetarian specialties are good), Minar Palace is so inexpensive and so impossibly quick, it has become one of Center City's best flavor-to-dollar delivery standbys.

Monk's Cafe
264 S. 16th St. (215) 545-7005
This busy bar is one of the city's finest destinations for incredible Belgian ales, great burgers and mussels. The only major downside is the smoke-heavy air.

Monte Carlo Living Room
150 South St. (215) 925-2220
This classic Northern Italian has a tradition of exquisite continental cuisine and expert service that has remained special. The kitschy decore was recently updated, but whether it will thrive despite the recent departure of its longtime culinary genius, Nunzio Patruno, remains to be seen.

MOONLIGHT
36 W. Mechanic St., New Hope, Pa. (215) 862-3100
An entire dining room and its 3-D re-creations of famous still lifes are sheathed in moonscape white, a startling canvas for the exciting New American cuisine of Matthew Levin.

MORIMOTO
723 Chestnut St. (215) 413-9070
Superstar chef Masaharu Morimoto brings cutting-edge Japanese cuisine to the undulating bamboo dining room of Stephen Starr's latest hip restuarant. The best seats are at the sushi bar.

MORNING GLORY DINER
735 S. 10th St. (215) 413-3999
Updated macaroni and other homemade diner favorites are served in this hip, flower-decked Bella Vista eatery. An improved dinner menu is one of the neighborhood's best nighttime bargains.

MS. TOOTSIE'S SOUL FOOD CAFE
1314 South St. (215) 731-9045
Traditional soul food finds a stylish home in this little Center City bistro, where brushed-copper walls add modern attitude, and the cheery staff sets a welcoming tone for great yams and rich gravy-smothered turkey chops.

Mustache Bill's Diner
Eighth and Broadway, Barnaget Light, N.J. (609) 494-0155
Summer on Long Beach Island wouldn't be complete without a visit to this beautiful deco diner where the seafood omelets and creamed chipped beef are first-rate.

N

N. 3rd
801 N. Third St. (215) 413-3666
This Northern Liberties bar-restaurant has one of the city's most interesting cheap wine lists and serves updated comfort food, from ribs to corn-crusted catfish, until 1 a.m. on weekends.

NAN
4000 Chestnut St. (215) 382-0818
Elegant French-Thai fusion from former Alouette chef Kamol Phutlek in a fairly priced BYOB with understated decor.

New Orleans Cafe
1 W. State St., Media, Pa. (610) 627-4393
Cajun and Creole cooking is served in a converted bank building.

New Phnom Penh
2301 S. Seventh St. (215) 389-2122
The hub of South Philadelphia's Cambodian community has this modest but tasty corner spot to savor noodle soups and cubed steak with lime and white pepper as an authentic reminder of home.

NEW WAVE CAFE
784 S. Third St. (215) 922-8484
Chef Ben McNamara has turned the bar that was once known as the unofficial waiting room for Dmitri's into one of the best gourmet bargains in town with a menu that ranges from Pernod-scented escargots to great buffalo wings and surprisingly refined desserts.

Nice Chinese Noodle House
1038 Race St. (215) 625-8393
This bustling Chinatown noodle house lives up to its name with a variety of hearty, flavorful noodle dishes served either "dry" in stir-fries, or floating in giant soups. The beef satay noodle is a personal favorite.

Nick's Roast Beef
2149 S. 20th St. (215) 463-4114
The original independent Nick's is still the best, a dark corner taproom where regulars pick their own cuts of the sublime roast beef, which comes served over a kaiser roll with deep, dark gravy.

Novelty
15 S. Third St. (215) 627-7885
The dark and handsome younger sibling of Jake's in Manayunk has become one of the neighborhood's finest, most sophisticated spots even though its kitchen seems in constant flux.

O

Ocean City
234 N. Ninth St. (215) 829-0688
This big Hong Kong dim-sum palace has become popular for banquets and multi-dumpling feasts from lunch until 3 a.m.

Old City Coffee
221 Church St. (215) 592-1897
Reading Terminal Market, 12th and Arch Streets (215) 629-9292
This local roaster and cafe is a fine place to catch your breath while touring the neighborhood galleries and sip a full-bodied cup of gourmet single-variety coffee.

OPUS 251
The Philadelphia Art Alliance, 251 S. 18th St. (215) 735-6787
Sophisticated New American cuisine with an accent on seasonality is served in a Rittenhouse Square mansion with a secret garden.

Otto's Brauhaus
233 Easton Rd., Horsham, Pa. (215) 675-1864
Don your liederhausen at this German outpost for schnitzel, brats and snapper soup. The big beer garden hops during Oktoberfest.

P

Pad Thai Shack
18 S. 20th St. (215) 564-1932
This charming take-out nook dedicated to Southeast Asian street food stir-fries is largely a lunch-hour Market Street draw.

Pagoda Noodle Cafe
125 Sansom Walk (215) 928-2320
This Old City offshoot of Chinatown's Sang Kee duck noodle house makes for a decent and affordable pre-movie noodle nosh, but also blends a wonderfully refreshing watermelon smoothie.

Paloma
6516 Castor Ave. (215) 533-0356
Chef Adan Saavedra's French-influenced "haute Mexican" has evolved one of the more intriguing menus around, but slow and inattentive service continues to hold the restaurant back.

Paninoteca
120 S. 18th St. (215) 568-0077
This wood-clad sandwich cafe just north of Rittenhouse Square specializes in grilled Italian sandwiches stuffed with mozzarella and prosciutto as well as other classically tasty combinations. The menu is limited, but delicious.

Paradise
8336 Bustleton Ave. (215) 742-9811
A Russian banquet-style night club with great Siberian dumplings, crispy roasted chicken, and live music.

¡PASION!
211 S. 15th St. (215) 875-9895
A gorgeous addition has doubled the size of this Nuevo Latino gem, where Guillermo Pernot has evolved into one of the region's most virtuosic culinary creators, specializing in ingenious ceviches.

Pastrami and Things
225 S. 15th St. (215) 545-4210
The sublime hot corned beef at this bustling little cafeteria is one of the best traditional deli sandwiches this side of Manhattan's Lower East Side, a fistful of thick-cut, steaming pickled beef on rye that I crave regularly. Ironically, the pastrami is just average.

Pat's King of Steaks
1237 E. Passyunk Ave. (215) 468-1546
The inventor of the steak is coasting on its reputation, serving up puny sandwiches at a famous corner that is getting a much needed facelift.

Pearl's Oyster Bar
Reading Terminal Market, 12th and Arch Streets (215) 627-7250
This fried-fish counter in the Reading Terminal Market is pretty ordinary, except for its big fried oysters and the fact that it is among the last of a dying breed.

PENANG
117 N. 10th St. (215) 413-2431
The Malaysian chain from New York serves authentic Southeast Asian fare in Chinatown's most stylish dining room. A new delivery service is a major hit for roti-loving homebodies in Center City.

Penne
The Inn at Penn, 3611 Walnut St. (215) 823-6222
The Italian concept is a vast improvement over the former Ivy Grille, with Roberta Adamo hand-crafting pastas in the dining room to order, thin-crust pizzas, and an Italian wine bar with more than 30 wines to choose from.

People's Pizza
1500 Chapel Ave., Cherry Hill, N.J. (856) 665-6575
The no-cheese tomato pies of Trenton are famous, but People's makes a fine one (as well as hefty stuffed pizzas) just across the Ben Franklin Bridge.

Pho 75
1122 Washington Ave. (215) 271-5866
Grab a flavorful meal in a bowl at the city's best (and very utilitarian) Vietnamese noodle soup hall, then shop for fish sauce at the vast Asian market next door.

Pho Xe Lua
907 Race St. (215) 627-8883
This tiny Chinatown soup house dishes out authentic Vietnamese noodle bowls and some fun Southeast Asian shakes — like the stinky durian or creamy avocado — that are definitely an acquired taste.

PIF
1009 S. Eighth St. (215) 625-2923
This charming little BYOB serves French bistro fare inspired by the chef's daily shopping in the nearby Italian Market. The prices have crept a little high recently, considering the no-frills decor.

Pigalle
702 N. Second St. (215) 627-7772
The French-inspired bistro has a polished and sultry style that is novel in Northern Liberties, and a new chef since the review.

Plough and the Stars
123 Chestnut St. (215) 733-0300
Great Guinness and Irish-accented French cuisine are the draws to this beautifully rehabbed, dramatic Old City bank space.

Pod

3636 Sansom St. (215) 387-1803
Conveyor-belt sushi and light-changing booths are part of the gimmick at this cool, futuristic spot, but good Japanese fusion fare is one of the better reasons to return.

Pompeii

121 S. Broad St. (215) 735-8400
Don't let the high-toned Roman decor and uptown address fool you. South Philly-style red gravy runs through the heart of Pompeii's fare, but at Broad Street prices that usually strike me as high. Special meal deals, though, are worth a try, especially the three-course $25 pre-theater menu.

PORCINI
2048 Sansom St. (215) 751-1175
One of the first in a wave of no-frills trattorias in Center City, the closet-size BYOB remains one of the best, with homemade pastas and a dose of exuberant hospitality.

Porky's Point
3824 N. Fifth St. (215) 221-6243
The North Philadelphia take-out stand is the Latino equivalent of Tony Luke's, where cars triple-park and the line grows long into the night with people hungry for homemade blood sausage, red beans with chopped pig ears, and one of the city's most tender and tasty pork sandwiches.

THE PRIME RIB

1701 Locust St. (in the Radisson Plaza Warwick Hotel) (215) 772-1701
Step back into the era of the steak-house supper club, where leopard-print carpeting, live jazz, stiff cocktails, and comfy leather chairs offer the ideal retro setting for a prime rib that is the region's single best slice of beef.

Primo Hoagie
2043 Chestnut St. (215) 496-0540
This uptown branch of the South Philadelphia original is a lunchtime powerhouse, with an assembly line to crank out tasty Italian hoagies bulging with quality meat (although often too much). Ask for a small.

R

Radicchio   ✗✗
314 York Ave. (215) 627-6850
Authentic Italian trattoria fare, from great
chicken paillard and smoked mozzarella
to expertly filleted Dover sole for $20 in a
noisy little cafe near the Ben Franklin
Bridge.

Ralph's
760 S. Ninth St. (215) 627-6011
South Philly's definitive red-gravy palace,
with century-old ambience, greens and
pastina soup, and classic, crisp-bottomed
veal parmesan.

Rangoon
112 N. Ninth St. (215) 829-8939
Pungent Burmese cuisine, from spicy
crisped lentil cakes to flaky thousand-
layer bread, anchor one of the most
flavorful menus in Chinatown.

Rat's
16 Fairgrounds Rd., Hamilton, N.J.
(609) 584-7800
J. Seward Johnson's gourmet restaurant
and sculpture park materializes outside
Trenton like a hybrid of Giverny and the
Twilight Zone, a picturesque setting for
ambitious (and occasionally inconsistent)
French cuisine and a first-class wine
cellar.

Ray's Cafe & Tea House
141 N. Ninth St. (215) 922-5122
Excellent Chinese dumplings and delicate
French pastries are but a prelude to the
amazing (and amazingly expensive) coffee
that emerges from Ray's elaborate
vacuum brewing rig of beakers and
bunson burners. It's worth the price.

Real Pizza
100 N. Narberth Ave., Narberth, Pa.
(610) 664-1700
The low-key neighborhood pizzeria turned
out a very respectable assortment of
steaks, the most interesting being, not
surprisingly, the pizza steak.

THE RED HEN CAFÉ   ✗✗
560 Stokes Rd., Medford, N.J.
(609) 953-2655
Traditional Eastern European specialties
are updated gently with good ingredients
and careful cooking at this warm strip-
mall bistro, where a husband-wife team
is creating new respect for the pleasures
of borscht.

Rembrandt's
741 N. 23d St. (215) 763-2228
This Fairmount bar and restaurant is
known for its psychic reading nights
and one of the better burgers in town.

RESTAURANT 821   ✗✗✗
821 N. Market St., Wilmington
(302) 652-8821
Across from Wilmington's Grand Opera
House, this sophisticated restaurant has
brought an exciting blend of foie-gras
decadence and wood-roasted gusto to
the credit-card city.

The Restaurant at Doneckers   ✗✗✗
333 N. State St., Ephrata, Pa.
(717) 738-9501
Former Le Bec-Fin-chef Greg Gable blends
French haute cuisine with regional flavors
at this upscale Lancaster County
shopping complex. The dinners are
considerably more interesting than the
shopper-friendly lunches.

Ricci
1165 S. 11th St. (215) 334-6910
The venerable hoagie emporium relies on
an efficient assembly line to churn out
traditional Italian sandwiches topped
with quality ingredients.

Rick's Steaks
*Reading Terminal Market, 12th and Arch
Streets (215) 925-4320*
The Reading Terminal steakerie descends
from the Olivieri family that founded
Pat's, but the water-steamed meat is
served in small, unseasoned portions.

Ristorante Panorama
Penn's View Hotel, 14 N. Front St.
(215) 922-7800
Luca Sena's Italian grill is a reliable destination for veal paillard and grilled romaine salads and some new northern specialties, but the main draw is the world-class wine-by-the-glass system, which offers flights and tastes of more than 120 wines.

Ristorante Valentino
1328 Pine St. (215) 545-6265
A charmingly decorated Italian BYOB with distressed walls and cherubs, it has been slightly inconsistent, but try the gnocchi and simple grilled fish.

RITZ SEAFOOD
Ritz Center, 910 Haddonfield-Berlin Rd., Voorhees, N.J. (856) 566-6650
This diminutive restaurant wraps diners in a natural ambience of waterfalls and swimming koi, a tranquil and homey setting for chef Daniel Hover's creative pan-Asian seafood menu with Korean accents.

Roller's
8705 Germantown Ave. (215) 242-1771
Paul Roller's glassed-in strip-mall cafe is a restaurant renaissance survivor that still serves a reliable eclectic menu of updated comfort foods, and an affordable wine list.

ROSE TATTOO CAFE
1847 Callowhill St. (215) 569-8939
This Fairmount institution is still a vibrant place to eat, with a globe-hopping menu (including some Big Easy favorites) and a plant-filled, quasi-New Orleans ambience that is warm and intimate, if a bit dated.

Roselena's Coffee Bar
1623 E. Passyunk Ave. (215) 755-9697
The quirky Victorian coffee parlor offers multicourse dinners upstairs, but the main attractions are the after-dinner desserts by lamplight in the charmingly old world downstairs rooms.

ROUGE
205 S. 18th St. (Rittenhouse Claridge)
(215) 732-6622
The poodle people and the glamour crowd come to nibble chef Michael Yeamans' surprisingly fine modern bistro fare, but the sights of Rittenhouse Square are the biggest assets to this see-and-be-seen cafe.

Roya Restaurant
1823 Sansom St. (215) 557-0808
The casual downstairs hideaway is one of the region's few destinations for authentic Persian kebabs and pilaf.

Roy's
124-34 S. 15th St. (215) 988-1814
An old bank has been beautifully transformed into a branch of this upscale Hawaiian-fusion chain, but the creative fare, from wasabi spaetzle to pork chops with plum sauce is a bit too inconsistent for these prices, and poor service makes matters worse.

RX
4443 Spruce St. (215) 222-9590
The old apothecary-turned-casual-contemporary corner spot offers creative and affordable updates on bistro food that is just what the doctor ordered for gentrifying West Philly.

S

Sagami
37 W. Crescent Blvd., Collingswood, N.J.
(856) 854-9773
One of the area's first and finest sushi haunts, this dark, wood-paneled restaurant keeps strictly to tradition, resisting trendy maki rolls in favor of pristine fish served in classic ways.

The Saloon
750 S. Seventh St. (215) 627-1811
This manly, wood-clad South Philadelphia power-dining spot serves expensive (and often unspectacular) Italian cuisine, but it is rightly best known for its awesome garlic-infused chops.

Samosa
1214 Walnut St. (215) 545-7776
The sunny, bare-bones vegetarian buffet can't be beat for its incredibly cheap and satisfying country cooking that stays fresh thanks to steady steam-table turnover.

Sang Kee
238 N. Ninth St. (215) 925-7532
Long a favorite for Peking duck and noodles, this humble institution underwent an ambitious renovation three years ago, doubling and renovating its dining rooms. It's looking worn again lately, but the food is still great.

Sansom Street Kabob House
1526 Sansom St. (215) 751-9110
This recently opened downstairs grill house prepares traditional Afghan skewered meats, scallion turnovers, pilafs, and tandoor oven-baked flat breads.

SANSOM STREET OYSTER HOUSE
1516 Sansom St. (215) 567-7683
The best of the old-time seafood houses has maintained a waning Philadelphia tradition, beatifully restoring its dining rooms and balancing classics with a modern touch. The cooking, though, hasn't been quite as sharp since longtime owner David Mink sold to chef Cary Neff.

SAVONA
100 Old Gulph Rd., Gulph Mills, Pa. (610) 520-1200
This elegant restaurant has matured into one of the region's best fine-dining destinations, with warm terra-cotta-colored dining rooms and exquisite seafood inspired by the French Riviera, fine service, and one of the region's best cellars.

Seafood Unlimited
270 S. 20th St. (215) 732-9012
The tiny seafood market/restaurant underwent a handsome renovation, and has recently acquired a new chef bent on going beyond the basic fish-house fare (steamed lobster, crab-stuffed flounder) that has made this a neighborhood fixture for an inexpensive and predictable meal.

Sergeantsville Inn
601 Rosemont-Ringoes Rd., Sergeantsville, N.J. (609) 397-3700
This cozy inn (circa 1734) has ambitious young owners and an adventurous fine-dining menu that ranges from lobster risotto to a fondness for exotic meats.

Serrano
20 S. Second St. (215) 928-0770
With one of the city's best folk clubs upstairs (the Tin Angel) and a romantic downstairs dining room warmed by a fireplace and art, Serrano offers an affordable evening of entertainment, even if the globe-hopping menu is erratic.

Shank's and Evelyn's Roast Beef
932 S. 10th St. (215) 629-1093
The all-woman staff at this tiny luncheonette dishes out counterside sass with the big flavors of cutlet sandwiches topped with hot roasted peppers, everything omelets, and excellent roast beef.

SHIAO LAN KUNG
930 Race St. (215) 928-0282
Don't expect anything fancy at my favorite Chinatown nook, a tiny, crowded room where the kitchen turns out some of the brightest renditions of standard Cantonese cooking, from steamed dumplings to salt-baked seafood, with a few spicy twists.

Simon Pearce on the Brandywine
🔔🔔

1333 Lenape Rd., West Chester, Pa.
(610) 793-0948

Watch the artisan glass-blowing, then head upstairs for creative regional American cooking with some Irish accents that has improved over time.

Sitar India

60 S. 38th St. (215) 662-0818

The best of the University City buffets keeps the bargain steam-table of tandoori chicken and curried stews reasonably fresh and cheap.

Smith & Wollensky 🔔

Rittenhouse Hotel, 210 W. Rittenhouse Square (215) 545-1700

The clubby New York steak-house chain in the Rittenhouse Hotel has been inconsistent for the prices, but the more casual downstairs grill makes a particularly tasty burger.

Snockey's Oyster and Crab House

1020 S. Second St. (215) 339-9578

This 90-year-old Queen Village institution has kept its dining room bright and spiffy, and maintained workmanlike renditions of classics such as snapper soup and milky oyster stew.

Sonny's Famous Steaks

216 Market St. (215) 629-4828

The owner of this Old City newcomer takes her traditional steak seriously, slicing the never-frozen domestic beef to order, and insisting on real Cheez Whiz (imagine!). But stick with the basic steaks — variations were disappointing.

Sonoma

4411 Main St. (215) 483-9400

Derek Davis' California-style kitchen went completely organic this year, but its best draw may be a bar with hundreds of vodkas.

South Street Souvlaki

509 South St. (215) 925-3026

The classic South Street taverna still serves a respectable selection of classic Greek fare, from massive moussaka platters to yogurt-laced souvlaki sandwiches.

Spezia 🔔🔔

614 W. Lancaster Ave., Bryn Mawr, Pa.
(610) 526-0123

The little BYOB with the gold-painted tin ceiling offers a simple but stylish setting for an ambitious Italian-themed menu that focuses on good ingredients and deft cooking. The owners offer extra-fancy crystal for a supplement.

Spring Mill Cafe

164 Barren Hill Rd., Conshohocken, Pa.
(610) 828-2550

There is a bucolic charm to this converted general store, where French country classics such as rabbit prune stew mingle with North African flavors such as spicy lamb tagine and flaky chicken b'stilla pie.

STANDARD TAP 🔔🔔

901 N. Second St. (215) 238-0630

The hip neighborhood bar is redefined at this handsome historic tavern where gutsy yet sophisticated rustic fare is served with great seasonal ingredients and one of the best local beer selections in town.

Steve's Prince of Steaks

2711 Comly Rd. (215) 677-8020

This outpost of the Northeast chain just off Roosevelt Boulevard is a stainless-steel food bar where you can watch them cook thick-cut pads of excellent steak behind a bulletproof glass viewing window. Very tasty, with a particularly oozy white American cheese and good, spicy condiments.

STRAWBERRY HILL

128 W. Strawberry St., Lancaster, Pa,
(717) 393-5544

This warm tavern offers a surprising slice of California wine country in historic Lancaster, with an extraordinary cellar of 1,400 wines and a creative contemporary menu that uses excellent local ingredients.

STRIPED BASS

1500 Walnut St. (215) 732-4444

Neil Stein's expensive seafood palace features spectacular decor, fabulous wines, and the exciting cuisine of talented chef Terence Feury. It only needs more consistent service to step up to the highest tier.

Sukhothai

225 S. 12th St. (215) 627-2215

A pleasant Thai-inspired eatery in the contemporary space of the former Pamplona is owned by six Hmong brothers all nicknamed Chuck.

SUSANNA FOO

1512 Walnut St. (215) 545-2666

Susanna Foo's exquisite French-Chinese cuisine sets the city's benchmark for creative but natural fusion cooking in a dining room of understated elegance. Executive chef Patrick Feury continues to refine the concept, also adding more substance to previously petite portions.

Sushikazu

920 Dekalb Pike, Blue Bell, Pa.
(610) 272-7767

The smartly renovated little bungalow is home to a surprisingly creative sushi counter, where premium ingredients, from toro to live scallops, are sliced with great skill. Try off-the-menu specials such as the spicy tuna over crunchy rice or the Area 51 roll.

Swann Lounge

1 Logan Square (215) 963-1500

The Four Seasons' casual dining room cafe offers the hotel's grand luxury at bargain prices, with an excellent price-fixed lunch buffet, formal tea, a Viennese dessert table, and one of the city's best-outfitted bars.

Syrenka Luncheonette

3173 Richmond St. (215) 634-3954

The steam-table service can be gruff, but the Polish specialties are pure comfort, from the thick potato pancakes to the delicious breaded pork chops, hearty bigos stew, and mashed beets.

T

Tacconelli's Pizzeria

2604 E. Somerset St. (215) 425-4983

Reserve your dough for the garlicky white pies and meat-lover pizzas laden with prosciutto and sausage that are pulled from the immense brick oven. This Port Richmond institution still bakes the area's best pies.

TANGERINE

232 Market St. (215) 627-5116

Stephen Starr's fantasy casbah is a Moroccan-inspired room draped in billowing fabrics and shimmering votive lights. The kitchen's inventive fare blends North African and pan-Mediterranean themes, proving that serious restaurants can also be fun.

Tangier Restaurant

1801 S. 18th St. (215) 732-5006

It's hard to find a great burger for $5 or less, but it comes char-broiled and juicy at this reliable neighborhood bar.

Taqueria Moroleon
Newar Road Shopping Center, 15 New Garden, Kennett Square, Pa.
(610) 444-1210
This strip-mall surprise serves authentic gorditas and taco platters to the largely Mexican workforce that has settled around the mushroom farms of Kennett Square.

Taquet
139 E. Lancaster Ave., Wayne, Pa.
(610) 687-5005
This elegant old hotel restaurant with sunny banquettes and a gracious porch offers French cuisine with subtle Moroccan accents, but could pay more attention to the details of fine-dining.

Tartine
701 S, Fourth St. (215) 592-4720
The Queen Village newcomer takes the neighborhood bistro to new minimalist heights, with a stark decor that puts the emphasis on classic Gallic flavors, from boiled beef salad to fish meuniere, from a veteran French chef. Service, though, could be warmer.

Tashkent
842 Red Lion Rd. (215) 464-0106
An authentic grill house that specializes in the distinctive shish kebabs of Uzbekistan.

333 Belrose
333 Belrose Lane, Radnor, Pa.
(610) 293-1000
Carlo deMarco's New American grill in Radnor has some vibrant tropical flavors and one of the Main Line's liveliest bar scenes.

TIERRA COLOMBIANA
4535 N. Fifth St. (215) 324-6086
Mambo up to North Philly, where this happening destination lights up Fifth Street with authentic Latino cooking, an attractive dining room, and good values. Dance your tamales off at the nightclub upstairs.

Tir Na Nog
The Phoenix 1600 Arch St. (267) 514-1700
This handsome Irish chain out of New York brings a sprawling, upscale wood-clad decor and traditional pub menu to the ground-floor of one of Center City's toniest new apartment buildings.

Tony Luke's
39 Oregon Ave. (215) 551-5725
The homemade rolls elevate the broccoli rabe-topped steak Italian and pork sandwich at this Oregon Avenue take-out (which also has an open-air seating shelter), making this branch the best of the famous big-crowd steak emporiums.

Trax Cafe
27 W. Butler St., Ambler, Pa.
(215) 591-9777
This bright little dining room has the charm of a small-town junction converted into a pleasant cafe, with trackside outdoor eating and an ambitous menu that ranges from house-smoked ribs to porcini-dusted salmon.

TRE SCALINI
1533 S. 11th St. (215) 551-3870
Authentic central Italian home cooking, from fresh pasta to grilled polenta and veal with mushrooms, is served with familial warmth in a bi-level BYOB.

Trust
13th and Sansom Streets (215) 629-1300
The first piece in developer Tony Goldman's plan to revitalize 13th Street is a trendy, rehabbed bank space serving Mediterranean-inspired tapas. Early difficulties with inconsistent cooking have smoothed out under a new chef, and the service isn't quite as rude. The impressive bar scene here remains as lively as ever.

12th Street Cantina

Reading Terminal Market, 12th and Arch Streets; the Food Court Downstairs at the Bellevue, Walnut and South Broad Streets, (215) 625-0321; (215) 790-1578
A Mexican food stand that goes far beyond the expectations of a food-court vendor with authentically inspired casseroles, torta sandwiches, and salads.

Twenty Manning

261 S. 20th St. (215) 731-0900
Audrey Taichman's corner magnet for the urban chic blends solid Asian bistro fusion fare with a loungey decor of black leather couches for trendy people who don't mind the deafening noise.

Twenty21

2005 Market St. (215) 851-6262
The old Cutter's has been purchased by its former managers and redesigned into an upscale American grill with Irish accents, from barley risotto to whiskey-oatmeal creme brulee. The room is huge, but great service and an excellent bar soften the corporate edge.

V

VETRI

1312 Spruce St. (215) 732-3478
Marc Vetri's townhouse homage to rustic regional Italian cooking has become not simply the city's best Italian restaurant, but the region's most seamless small-dining-room experience, achieving intimate elegance without formal fuss.

VIETNAM

221 N. 11th St. (215) 592-1163
A beautiful renovation transformed this favorite Vietnamese haunt into a restaurant with real ambience, complete with moody French colonial accents. The polished look, though, has not compromised the delicious Vietnamese home cooking.

Villa di Roma

932-36 S. Ninth St. (215) 592-1295
The red-tiled facade marks the retro heart of the Italian Market, and the bustling low-frills dining rooms remain an unpretentious draw for families craving cheap chianti and fried asparagus, garlicky mussels, broiled sausage, and chicken Sicilian buried under cherry peppers.

Vivo Enoteca

110 N. Wayne Ave., Wayne, Pa. (610) 964-8486
Stylish Old City meets the Main Line at this modern Italian hot spot, which has undergone a stunning transformation from its days as upscale Fourchette 110, Fellini films now play in the lounge and servers in black boots serve Christopher Todd's small-plate Italian fare upstairs.

W

Warsaw Cafe

306 S. 16th St. (215) 546-0204
The tiny, windowpaned bistro that sits behind the Kimmel Center is a charming old spot, but the pan-Eastern European menu has seen better days.

WHITE DOG CAFÉ

3420 Sansom St. (215) 386-9224
Judy Wicks is the force behind this trailblazing University City institution, which blends social activism with creative organic cooking and a funky, homey atmosphere. Nagging inconsistencies in the kitchen and with service keep it from reaching its true potential.

White House Sub Shop

Mississippi and Arctic Avenues, Atlantic City (609) 345-8599
The light and crusty roll makes the steak and subs at this casino-city institution, but it's the sprinkling of sweet-hot pepper relish and the people-watching that give its sandwiches real panache.

Wolf's Market

1500 Locust St. (215) 735-2929
Joe Wolf has converted a WaWa into a
sleek prepared-foods hub, where high-
rise-apartment dwellers and Center City
workers flock for high-quality take-out,
from great mini-meatloafs to trendy
seared tuna, crisp gourmet pizzas, and
excellent locally made sweets.

Wooden Iron   ♟

*118 N. Wayne Ave., Wayne, Pa.
(610) 964-7888*
This is the hot hangout for the brass-
button-and-pinstripe crowd, where the
upscale bar and clubby dining room are
accented with a strong golf motif and a
conservative chophouse menu.

X

Xochimilco

*6560 Market St., Upper Darby, Pa.
(610) 352-2833*
Upper Darby has a charming BYOB in this
colorful Mexican, where the tortilla soup is
tangy and the ebullient singing owner will
serenade your meal.

Y

Yangming

*1051 Conestoga Rd., Bryn Mawr, Pa.
(610) 527-3200*
Michael Wei's Bryn Mawr standby has
been one of the trailblazers in blending
East with West, but my most recent meal
didn't have the bright flavors of CinCin,
its sister restaurant in Chestnut Hill.

Z

Zanzibar Blue   ♟♟

200 S. Broad St. (215) 732-4500
The Bynum brothers' slick downstairs jazz
club has upped its standing as a fine-
dining venue with the addition of chef Al
Paris, who delivers some inspired global
cuisine. The club must still reconcile noise
conflicts between serious food and music.

Zen Tea House

225 N. 11th St. (215) 629-4848
Nibble Italian pastries with your
Technicolor bubble tea shakes at this tiny
cafe, which brings a pint-size stroke of
cool, modern design to Chinatown.

Zocalo   ♟♟

3600 Lancaster Ave. (215) 895-0139
Jackie Pestka's kitchen offers house-made
tortillas and a contemporary take on
authentic Mexican flavors, from the pre-
Colombian dip to the guacamole, that
help this colorful, upscale restaurant
remain a draw to Powelton Village.

Zorba's Taverna

2230 Fairmount Ave., 215-978-5990.
A Fairmount neighborhood standby with
its steam-table stocked full of steady
Hellenic favorites like braised lamb
shank.

By Category

These lists organize all the restaurants mentioned in the book by a number of different categories. The 76 favorites are denoted by ALL CAPS.

Cuisine

Asian Fusion

BUDDAKAN
FuziOn
THE INN ON BLUEBERRY
  HILL
Pod
RITZ SEAFOOD
Roy's
SUSANNA FOO
Twenty Manning

Belgian

Monk's Café

Cajun/Creole

CARMINE'S
High Street Caffe
Melange Café
New Orleans Café

Chinese

Cherry Street Vegetarian
Chez Elena Wu
CinCin
H.K. Golden Phoenix
Hunan
Joy Tsin Lau
LAKESIDE CHINESE DELI
LEE HOW FOOK
MARGARET KUO'S PEKING
Nice Chinese Noodle House
Ocean City
Pagoda Noodle Café
Ray's Café & Tea House
Sang Kee
SHIAO LAN KUNG
SUSANNA FOO
Yangming

Coffee

La Colombe Torrefaction
Old City Coffee
Ray's Café & Tea House

Comfort Food

Bridgid's
Down Home Diner
Jones
JUDY'S CAFÉ
MORNING GLORY DINER
N. 3rd
Roller's
RX

Diner

COUNTRY CLUB
  RESTAURANT
Mayfair Diner
Melrose Diner
Mustache Bill's Diner

Ethiopian

Dahlak

Eastern European

Blue Danube Restaurant
Golden Gates
Paradise
THE RED HEN CAFÉ
Syrenka Luncheonette
Tashkent
Warsaw Café

French

Beau Monde
BIRCHRUNVILLE STORE
  CAFÉ
BISTRO ST. TROPEZ
Bleu
BLUE ANGEL

BRASSERIE PERRIER
Cadence
Café Lutecia
Caribou Café
Chez Elena Wu
DEUX CHEMINEES
Gilmore's
Green Hills Inn
Inn at Phillip's Mill
La Boheme
Lacroix at the Rittenhouse
Le Bar Lyonnais
LE BEC-FIN
Le Mas Perrier
Le Me Toujours
Mainland Inn
MAX'S
Miel Patisserie
NAN
Paloma
PIF
Pigalle
Plough and the Stars
Rat's
The Restaurant at
  Doneckers
RX
SAVONA
Spring Mill Café
Taquet
Tartine

German

Ludwig's Garten
Otto's Brauhaus

Greek

DMITRI'S
EFFIE'S
South Street Souvlaki
Zorba's Taverna

High Tea

Cassatt Lounge and Tea
  Room
Ritz-Carlton
Swann Lounge

Iberian

Berlenga's Island
Caffe Monticello
LA ENCINA
Mallorca

Indian

CAFÉ SPICE
Darbar Grill
KHAJURAHO
Minar Palace
Samosa
Sitar India

Irish

The Bards
THE BLACK SHEEP
Fado Irish Pub
Plough and the Stars
Simon Pearce on the
  Brandywine
Twenty21

Italian

Anastasi Seafood
Avenue B
Caffe Casta Diva
Caffe Monticello
Criniti
Dante & Luigi's
Di Palma
ERNESTO'S 1521 CAFÉ
FELICIA'S
Girasole
Il Cantuccio
Il Tartufo
Illuminare
KRISTIAN'S
La Buca
La Famiglia
La Veranda
L'Angolo
LE CASTAGNE

Marco Polo
MAX'S
Melange Café
Mezza Luna
Monte Carlo Living Room
Penne
Pompeii
PORCINI
Radicchio
Ralph's
Ristorante Panorama
Ristorante Valentino
Roselena's Coffee Bar
The Saloon
Shank's and Evelyn's Roast
  Beef
Spezia
TRE SCALINI
VETRI
Villa di Roma
Vivo Enoteca

Jamaican

Jamaican Jerk Hut

Japanese

Anjou
FUJI JAPANESE
  RESTAURANT
Genji
Hikaru
Kisso Sushi Bar
Mikado
MORIMOTO
Sagami
Sushikazu

Korean

Anjou
International Café
Jong Ka Jib Soft Tofu
  Restaurant
Kim's
Korea Garden

Latino

ALMA DE CUBA
AZAFRAN
Café Habana
Cibucan

Cuba Libre
El Bohio
El Viejo San Juan
¡PASION!
Porky's Point
TIERRA COLOMBIANA

Mediterranean

Aden
AUDREY CLAIRE
TANGERINE
Trust

Mexican

La Lupe
LAS CAZUELAS
LOS CATRINES &
  TEQUILA'S BAR
Mexico Lindo
Paloma
Taqueria Moroleon
12th Street Cantina
Xochimilco
Zocalo

Middle Eastern

Bitar's
King of Falafel
Roya Restaurant
Sansom Street Kabob
  House

New American

Astral Plane
AUDREY CLAIRE
The Blue Bell Inn
Blue Sage
Bridgid's
CARAMBOLA
CHLÖE
Circa
CITRUS
The Continental
Deep Blue
Devon Seafood Grill
DILWORTHTOWN INN
DJANGO
Emerald Fish
Figs
FORK

Red-Gravy Italian

Ralph's, *760 S. Ninth St. (215) 627-6011*

It has become fashionable among local food snobs to look down on old-time red-gravy joints such as Ralph's Italian Restaurant.

The wonders of regional Italian cooking that have been revealed over the last decade — the gnocchi and porcini risottos, the arugulas and extra-virgin olive oils — are suddenly what matters. It's Tuscan that's tony. The more balsamic, the better.

Forget the down-home parmigiana- and meatball-laden spaghetti bowls that have long been the trademark of Ralph's, the nearly 103-year-old Italian Market institution where you are best advised to wear a tomato-colored shirt.

There in its lively mosaic-floored rooms, the gravy flows in torrents over mussels, squid, veal and noodles. And it is almost always red, whether it's the "marinara" (vegetarian with a hint of oregano) or the "tomato sauce" (stewed with tiny bits of veal, beef and pork).

I've always resisted the urge to leave this Italian-American Philadelphia tradition behind, especially when it comes to Ralph's, which for my money makes the definitive crisp-bottomed veal parmigiana, restorative greens-and-pastina soup, and gently stewed veal cacciatore. One big reason is the gravy — tangy but balanced with the sweetness of onions (not sugar), fresh and herby yet complex with slow steeped flavors.

The recent invasion of chains such as Buca di Beppo and Maggiano's, which clutter their prefab noodle halls with Little Italy kitsch, has only made me relish our heritage more. Why settle for imitations when we have the real thing?

■ Here are three other red-gravy restaurants in South Philadelphia:

Criniti, *2601 S. Broad St. (215) 465-7750*
With its plastic tablecloths, wood-paneled walls, and blaring opera soundtrack, this is my idea of a Italian neighborhood joint, with warm service and specialties such as rigatoni Mamma Mia, clams casino, and veal parmigiana that still taste homemade.

Dante & Luigi's, *762 S. 10th St. (215) 922-9501*
A centurion oldie, like Ralph's, but with relatively new ownership, this classic is still a destination for those seeking out veal braciola, tender gnocchi, and spaghetti with chicken livers. Recent meals have not been as sharp as in years past.

Villa di Roma, *932-36 S. Ninth St. (215) 592-1295*
The red-tiled facade marks the retro heart of the Italian Market, and the bustling low-frills dining rooms remain an unpretentious draw for families craving buttery fried asparagus, garlicky mussels, broiled sausage, and wine-laced chicken Sicilian buried under cherry peppers.

New American

It has become increasingly difficult these days to define the cooking one finds in most new mainstream restaurants as having one particular ethnic bent or another. I have opted for as many specific labels as possible here (Italian trattoria, say, updated Irish pub or French bistro) when an influence was obvious enough. But just as often, I've found American chefs with a natural impulse to travel with their pans, to borrow flavors from around the world and blend them with local ingredients, to sear them over California-style grills, roast them in the tandoor oven, or toss them over pasta and then sauce it all with French demiglace or a Japanese miso glaze. This mishmash of ingredients and techniques sometimes turns to chaos, but often unlocks remarkable creativity. I have called these menus many things over the years: contemporary, modern, eclectic, nouveau, nuevo or fusion. But for the purpose of clarity in this book, I've decided to settle on New American, because it has indeed become the prevailing idiom of modern cooking in the United States.

Founders
FOUNTAIN RESTAURANT
Frenchtown Inn
FRIDAY SATURDAY SUNDAY
The Grill
HAPPY ROOSTER
HORIZONS CAFE
Hotel DuPont (Green and
 Brandywine Rooms)
The Inn at Twin Lindens
Inn Philadelphia
Jack's Firehouse
JAKE'S
Krazy Kats
Le Bus
Little Fish
LONDON GRILL
Magazine
Mainland Inn
McCormick & Schmick's
MOONLIGHT
N. 3rd
NEW WAVE CAFÉ
Novelty
OPUS 251
Rembrandt's
RESTAURANT 821
Roller's

ROSE TATTOO CAFE
ROUGE
Seafood Unlimited
Sergeantsville Inn
Serrano
Simon Pearce on the
 Brandywine
Sonoma
STRAWBERRY HILL
STRIPED BASS
Swann Lounge
333 Belrose
Trax Café
Twenty21
WHITE DOG CAFÉ

North African

Figs
La Boheme
Spring Mill Cafe
TANGERINE

Pizza

By George
CARAMBOLA
Carlino's
Girasole

Illuminare
Joe's Pizza
Lazaro's Pizza House
Lombardi's
Lorenzo Pizza
Penne
People's Pizza
Real Pizza
Tacconelli's Pizzeria

Prepared Foods

Bacchus Market
DiBruno Bros. House of
 Cheese
DiBruno Bros. Pronto
Downtown Cheese Shop
The Chef's Market
Wolf's Market

Pubs

THE BLACK SHEEP
Chris' Jazz Café
Copa Too
Fado Irish Pub
H & J McNally's Tavern
LONDON GRILL
NEW WAVE CAFÉ

Rembrandt's
STANDARD TAP
Tangier Restaurant

Sandwiches

Abner's
Café Lutecia
Campo's
Chick's Deli of Cherry Hill
Chickie's Italian Deli
Chink's Steaks
The Countryside Market &
  Delicatessen
Dalessandro's
DelColle Market
Donkey's Place
Fireworks!
Geno's Steaks
Grilladelphia
H & J McNally's Tavern
Ishkabibble's Eatery
Jim's Steaks
JOHN'S ROAST PORK
Koch's Deli
La Cigale
Larry's Famous Steaks
Lenny's Italian Deli
Lombardi's Specialty
  Hoagies
Mama's Pizzeria
Nick's Roast Beef
Pastrami and Things
Pat's King of Steaks
Primo Hoagie
Real Pizza
Ricci
Rick's Steaks
Shank's and Evelyn's Roast
  Beef
Sonny's Famous Steaks
Steve's Prince of Steaks
Tony Luke's
White House Sub Shop

Seafood

Bookbinder's Seafood
  House
CITRUS
Deep Blue
Devon Seafood Grill

DMITRI'S
Emerald Fish
Little Fish
McCormick & Schmick's
Pearl's Oyster Bar
RITZ SEAFOOD
SANSOM ST. OYSTER HOUSE
SAVONA
Seafood Unlimited
Snockey's Oyster and Crab
  House
STRIPED BASS

Soul Food

Big George's Stop-N-Dine
Corinne's Place
Delilah's Southern Café
MS. TOOTSIE'S SOUL FOOD
  CAFÉ

Southeast Asian

Indonesia
New Phnom Penh
Pad Thai Shack
PENANG
Rangoon

Steak House

The Blue Bell Inn
THE CAPITAL GRILLE
Davio's
Jolly's
Kansas City Prime
THE PRIME RIB
The Saloon
Smith & Wollensky
Wooden Iron

Tea

Bubble House
Great Tea International
The House of Tea
Zen Tea House

Thai

East of Amara
Little Thai Singha Market
NAN
Sukhothai

Vegetarian

Blue Sage
Cherry Street Vegetarian
CITRUS
HORIZONS CAFE

Vietnamese

Ba Le Bakery
Le Cyclo
Le Me Toujours
Pho 75
Pho Xe Lua
VIETNAM
DelColle Market

West African

La Calebasse

Location

PHILADELPHIA

Avenue of the Arts

Avenue B
Cadence
THE CAPITAL GRILLE
Chris' Jazz Café
ERNESTO'S 1521 CAFÉ
Founders
Girasole
The Grill
McCormick & Schmick's
Pompeii
Trust
VETRI
Zanzibar Blue

Chestnut Hill

CinCin
CITRUS
H & J McNally's Tavern
Roller's

Chinatown

Cherry Street Vegetarian
H.K. Golden Phoenix
Indonesia

Joy Tsin Lau
LAKESIDE CHINESE DELI
LEE HOW FOOK
Nice Chinese Noodle House
Ocean City
PENANG
Pho Xe Lua
Rangoon
Ray's Café & Tea House
Sang Kee
SHIAO LAN KUNG
VIETNAM
Zen Tea House

Delaware Avenue

La Veranda

Fairmount

Bridgid's
Figs
Illuminare
Jack's Firehouse
LONDON GRILL
Rembrandt's
ROSE TATTOO CAFE
Zorba's Taverna

Fitler Square

Bacchus Market
Café Lutecia

Graduate Hospital

Astral Plane
Lazaro's Pizza House
Tangier Restaurant

Logan Square

FOUNTAIN RESTAURANT
Swann Lounge

Manayunk/ Roxborough

Dalessandro's
Il Tartufo
JAKE'S
Kansas City Prime
Le Bus
Sonoma

Market Street West

BISTRO ST. TROPEZ
King of Falafel
LE CASTAGNE
Pad Thai Shack
Primo Hoagie
Twenty21

North Philadelphia

Berlenga's Island
El Bohio
Jong Ka Jib Soft Tofu
  Restaurant
Kim's
Porky's Point
TIERRA COLOMBIANA

Northeast Philadelphia

Chink's Steaks
COUNTRY CLUB
  RESTAURANT
Golden Gates
Mayfair Diner
Paloma
Paradise
Steve's Prince of Steaks
Tashkent

Northern Liberties

Aden
El Viejo San Juan
Il Cantuccio
LAS CAZUELAS
N. 3rd
Pigalle
STANDARD TAP

Old City

Anjou
BUDDAKAN
CAFÉ SPICE
Caffe Monticello
Campo's
CHLÖE
The Continental
Cuba Libre
Darbar Grill

Di Palma
FORK
Kisso Sushi Bar
La Famiglia
Novelty
Old City Coffee
Pagoda Noodle Café
Plough and the Stars
Radicchio
Ristorante Panorama
Serrano
Sonny's Famous Steaks
TANGERINE

Port Richmond

Grilladelphia
Syrenka Luncheonette
Tacconelli's Pizzeria

Queen Village

AZAFRAN
Beau Monde
The Chef's Market
DMITRI'S
East of Amara
Hikaru
The House of Tea
JUDY'S CAFÉ
Little Fish
Monte Carlo Living Room
MORNING GLORY DINER
NEW WAVE CAFÉ
Snockey's Oyster and Crab
  House
Tartine

Reading Terminal Market

By George
Delilah's Southern Café
Down Home Diner
Downtown Cheese Shop
Fireworks!
Little Thai Singha Market
Pearl's Oyster Bar
Rick's Steaks
12th Street Cantina

Rittenhouse Square

ALMA DE CUBA
AUDREY CLAIRE
The Bards
THE BLACK SHEEP
Bleu
Bookbinder's Seafood House
BRASSERIE PERRIER
Café Habana
Caffe Casta Diva
Cassatt Lounge and Tea Room
Cibucan
Circa
Copa Too
Davio's
Devon Seafood Grill
DiBruno Bros. House of Cheese
DiBruno Bros. Pronto
Fado Irish Pub
FRIDAY SATURDAY SUNDAY
Genji
Great Tea International
HAPPY ROOSTER
Joe's Pizza
Jolly's Bar and Grill
La Colombe Torrefaction
Lacroix at the Rittenhouse
Le Bar Lyonnais
LE BEC-FIN
LE CASTAGNE
Lombardi's
LOS CATRINES RESTAURANT & TEQUILA'S BAR
Magazine
Metropolitan Bakery
Minar Palace
Monk's Café
OPUS 251
¡PASION!
Pastrami and Things
PORCINI
THE PRIME RIB
Primo Hoagie
ROUGE
Roya Restaurant

Roy's
Sansom Street Kabob House
SANSOM STREET OYSTER HOUSE
Seafood Unlimited
Smith & Wollensky
STRIPED BASS
SUSANNA FOO
Twenty Manning
Warsaw Café
Wolf's Market

South Philadelphia

Anastasi Seafood
Ba Le Bakery
Bitar's
Chickie's Italian Deli
Criniti
Dante & Luigi's
DiBruno Bros. House of Cheese
FELICIA'S
Geno's Steaks
JOHN'S ROAST PORK
KRISTIAN'S
La Lupe
L'Angolo
Le Cyclo
Lombardi's Specialty Hoagies
Lorenzo's Pizza
Melrose Diner
Mezza Luna
New Phnom Penh
Nick's Roast Beef
Pat's King of Steaks
Pho 75
PIF
Ralph's
Ricci
Roselena's Coffee Bar
Shank's and Evelyn's Roast Beef
The Saloon
Tony Luke's
TRE SCALINI
Villa di Roma

South Street

AZAFRAN
Beau Monde
The Chef's Market
DJANGO
Ishkabibble's Eatery
Jamaican Jerk Hut
Jim's Steaks
Mallorca
Monte Carlo Living Room
MS. TOOTSIE'S SOUL FOOD CAFÉ
South Street Souvlaki

University City/ West Philadelphia

Abner's
Big George's Stop-N-Dine
Bubble House
Dahlak
Jim's Steaks
Koch's Deli
La Calebasse
NAN
Penne
Pod
Rx
Sitar India
WHITE DOG CAFÉ
Zocalo

Washington Square

BLUE ANGEL
Caribou Café
DEUX CHEMINEES
EFFIE'S
The Foodery Market
Inn Philadelphia
Jones
La Cigale
La Boheme
La Buca
Ludwig's Garten
MORIMOTO
Ristorante Valentino
Samosa
Sukhothai

SUBURBS

Chester County

BIRCHRUNVILLE STORE
 CAFÉ
DILWORTHTOWN INN
Gilmore's
High Street Caffe
LA ENCINA
Simon Pearce on the
 Brandywine
Taqueria Moroleon

Delaware County

CARMINE'S
The Countryside Market &
 Delicatessen
MARGARET KUO'S PEKING
New Orleans Café
Xochimilco

Jersey Shore

Mustache Bill's Diner
White House Sub Shop

Lancaster/Berks

The Inn at Twin Lindens
STRAWBERRY HILL
The Restaurant at
 Doneckers
Green Hills Inn (Berks)

Main Line

Carlino's
Hunan
KHAJURAHO
Larry's Famous Steaks
Lenny's Italian Deli
Le Mas Perrier
Mama's Pizzeria
Real Pizza
SAVONA
Spezia
Spring Mill Café
Taquet
333 Belrose
Vivo Enoteca
Wooden Iron
Yangming

New Hope/ Lambertville

Blue Danube Restaurant
Frenchtown Inn
Inn at Phillip's Mill
MOONLIGHT
Sergeantsville Inn

Northern Suburbs

The Blue Bell Inn
Blue Sage
CARAMBOLA
FuziOn
HORIZONS CAFE
THE INN ON BLUEBERRY
 HILL
Mainland Inn
Marco Polo
Otto's Brauhaus
Trax Café

South Jersey

Chez Elena Wu
Chick's Deli of Cherry Hill
Corinne's Place
Donkey's Place
Emerald Fish
FUJI JAPANESE
 RESTAURANT
International Café
Korea Garden
Le Me Toujours
MAX'S
Melange Café
Mexico Lindo
Miel Patisserie
Mikado
People's Pizza
Rat's
THE RED HEN CAFÉ
RITZ SEAFOOD
Sagami

Wilmington

Deep Blue
Hotel DuPont (Green and
 Brandywine Rooms)
Krazy Kats
RESTAURANT 821

Romantic

Aden
ALMA DE CUBA
Astral Plane
AUDREY CLAIRE
Avenue B
AZAFRAN
The Bards
Beau Monde
Berlenga's Island
BIRCHRUNVILLE STORE
 CAFÉ
BISTRO ST. TROPEZ
Bleu
BLUE ANGEL
BRASSERIE PERRIER
BUDDAKAN
Café Habana
CAFÉ SPICE
Caffe Casta Diva
Caribou Café
Chez Elena Wu
Chink's Steaks
CHLÖE
Cibucan
CinCin
Circa
Cuba Libre
DEUX CHEMINEES
Di Palma
DILWORTHTOWN INN
DJANGO
EFFIE'S
ERNESTO'S 1521 CAFÉ
FORK
Founders
FOUNTAIN RESTAURANT
Frenchtown Inn
FRIDAY SATURDAY SUNDAY
FUJI JAPANESE
 RESTAURANT
Gilmore's
Green Hills Inn
HAPPY ROOSTER
Hotel DuPont (Green and
 Brandywine Rooms)
Il Tartufo
Illuminare

Inn at Phillip's Mill
The Inn at Twin Lindens
THE INN ON BLUEBERRY
  HILL
Inn Philadelphia
JAKE'S
Kansas City Prime
Krazy Kats
KRISTIAN'S
LA ENCINA
La Famiglia
La Veranda
Lacroix at the Rittenhouse
L'Angolo
LE BEC-FIN
Le Mas Perrier
Le Me Toujours
LOS CATRINES &
  TEQUILA'S BAR
Mainland Inn
Mallorca
MAX'S
Mezza Luna
MOONLIGHT
Novelty
OPUS 251
Paloma
¡PASION!
Pigalle
THE PRIME RIB
THE RED HEN CAFÉ
RESTAURANT 821
The Restaurant at
  Doneckers
Ristorante Panorama
RITZ SEAFOOD
ROSE TATTOO CAFE
Roselena's Coffee Bar
Roy's
The Saloon
SAVONA
Sergeantsville Inn
Spezia
Spring Mill Café
STRAWBERRY HILL
STRIPED BASS
SUSANNA FOO
TANGERINE
Taquet
TRE SCALINI

VETRI
VIETNAM
Vivo Enoteca
Warsaw Café
WHITE DOG CAFÉ

Open Late

**Kitchen is open
after 11 p.m. (Some
are weekends only)**

ALMA DE CUBA
Anjou
The Bards
Berlenga's Island
THE BLACK SHEEP
Bleu
The Blue Bell Inn
BRASSERIE PERRIER
Bubble House
BUDDAKAN
Café Habana
CAFÉ SPICE
Caffe Monticello
Caribou Café
Chris' Jazz Café
Cibucan
The Continental
Copa Too
Corinne's Place
Cuba Libre
Deep Blue
Devon Seafood Grill
El Bohio
Fado Irish Pub
FORK
Geno's Steaks
Golden Gates
Grilladelphia
H & J McNally's Tavern
H.K. Golden Phoenix
HAPPY ROOSTER
Inn Philadelphia
Ishkabibble's Eatery
Jack's Firehouse
Jim's Steaks
Jones
Joy Tsin Lau

JUDY'S CAFÉ
Kansas City Prime
La Lupe
La Veranda
Lacroix at the Rittenhouse
Larry's Famous Steaks
LONDON GRILL
LOS CATRINES &
  TEQUILA'S BAR
Mayfair Diner
McCormick & Schmick's
Melrose Diner
Monk's Café
MORIMOTO
MS. TOOTSIE'S SOUL FOOD
  CAFÉ
N. 3rd
NEW WAVE CAFÉ
Novelty
Ocean City
Paradise
Pat's King of Steaks
PENANG
Pigalle
Porky's Point
ROSE TATTOO CAFE
ROUGE
Sang Kee
SHIAO LAN KUNG
STANDARD TAP
Sukhothai
Swann Lounge
TANGERINE
Tashkent
TIERRA COLOMBIANA
Tony Luke's
Twenty Manning
WHITE DOG CAFÉ
White House Sub Shop
Wooden Iron
Zanzibar Blue

Trendy

ALMA DE CUBA
Anjou
AUDREY CLAIRE
Avenue B
THE BLACK SHEEP

BLUE ANGEL
BRASSERIE PERRIER
Bubble House
BUDDAKAN
Café Habana
CAFÉ SPICE
THE CAPITAL GRILLE
CARAMBOLA
Cibucan
Circa
The Continental
Cuba Libre
DJANGO
DMITRI'S
EFFIE'S
FORK
Gilmore's
HAPPY ROOSTER
Il Tartufo
JAKE'S
Jones
Kansas City Prime
La Colombe Torrefaction
Le Cyclo
LOS CATRINES
  RESTAURANT & TEQUILA'S
  BAR
Magazine
MOONLIGHT
MORIMOTO
MORNING GLORY DINER
Novelty
¡PASION!
PENANG
PIF
Pigalle
Plough and the Stars
Pod
Radicchio
RITZ SEAFOOD
ROUGE
RX
Sonoma
Spezia
STANDARD TAP
STRIPED BASS
TANGERINE
Tartine
333 Belrose
TIERRA COLOMBIANA

Trust
Twenty Manning
VETRI
Vivo Enoteca
Wooden Iron

Expense Accounts

ALMA DE CUBA
Avenue B
BLUE ANGEL
Bookbinder's Seafood
  House
BRASSERIE PERRIER
BUDDAKAN
THE CAPITAL GRILLE
Circa
Davio's
DEUX CHEMINEES
Di Palma
DILWORTHTOWN INN
FORK
Founders
FOUNTAIN RESTAURANT
Frenchtown Inn
FUJI JAPANESE
  RESTAURANT
Genji
Green Hills Inn
The Grill
HAPPY ROOSTER
Hotel DuPont (Green and
  Brandywine Rooms)
THE INN ON BLUEBERRY
  HILL
JAKE'S
Kansas City Prime
KRISTIAN'S
La Famiglia
La Veranda
Lacroix at the Rittenhouse
LE BEC-FIN
LE CASTAGNE
Mainland Inn
Mallorca
MAX'S

McCormick & Schmick's
Mezza Luna
Mikado
MOONLIGHT
MORIMOTO
Novelty
OPUS 251
¡PASION!
Pod
Pompeii
THE PRIME RIB
RESTAURANT 821
The Restaurant at
  Doneckers
Ristorante Panorama
ROUGE
Roy's
Sagami
The Saloon
SANSOM STREET OYSTER
  HOUSE
SAVONA
Sergeantsville Inn
Simon Pearce on the
  Brandywine
Smith & Wollensky
Sonoma
Spezia
STRAWBERRY HILL
STRIPED BASS
SUSANNA FOO
Swann Lounge
TANGERINE
Taquet
Twenty21
VETRI
Wooden Iron

Brunch

**Serves brunch on
weekends. (Some
are Sunday only)**

Anastasi Seafood
Astral Plane
Avenue B
The Bards
Beau Monde

Big George's Stop-N-Dine
THE BLACK SHEEP
Bleu
The Blue Bell Inn
BRASSERIE PERRIER
Cadence
Café Lutecia
CAFÉ SPICE
Caribou Café
Cherry Street Vegetarian
CITRUS
The Continental
Copa Too
Corinne's Place
COUNTRY CLUB
  RESTAURANT
The Countryside Market &
  Delicatessen
Cuba Libre
Devon Seafood Grill
Down Home Diner
ERNESTO'S 1521 CAFÉ
Fado Irish Pub
Figs
FORK
Founders
FOUNTAIN RESTAURANT
Frenchtown Inn
Golden Gates
The Grill
Hotel DuPont (Green and
  Brandywine Rooms)
Illuminare
Indonesia
The Inn at Twin Lindens
Inn Philadelphia
Jack's Firehouse
JAKE'S
Jones
Joy Tsin Lau
JUDY'S CAFÉ
Kim's
Kisso Sushi Bar
La Buca
La Famiglia
Lacroix at the Rittenhouse
Larry's Famous Steaks
LAKESIDE CHINESE DELI
LAS CAZUELAS
Le Bus

Le Cyclo
Le Mas Perrier
LEE HOW FOOK
Lenny's Italian Deli
Little Thai Singha Market
Lombardi's Specialty
  Hoagies
Lombardi's
LONDON GRILL
Lorenzo's Pizza
Mainland Inn
Mallorca
Mayfair Diner
Melrose Diner
Minar Palace
Monk's Café
MORNING GLORY DINER
Mustache Bill's Diner
N. 3rd
New Orleans Café
New Phnom Penh
Nice Chinese Noodle House
Nick's Roast Beef
Ocean City
OPUS 251
Pagoda Noodle Cafe
Pastrami and Things
Pat's King of Steaks
Pearl's Oyster Bar
People's Pizza
Pho Xe Lua
Radicchio
Ralph's
Rangoon
Ray's Café & Tea House
Real Pizza
Rembrandt's
Ricci
RITZ SEAFOOD
Roller's
ROSE TATTOO CAFE
Roselena's Coffee Bar
ROUGE
Roya Restaurant
RX
Samosa
Sang Kee
Sansom Street Kabob
  House

SANSOM STREET OYSTER
  HOUSE
Seafood Unlimited
Shank's and Evelyn's Roast
  Beef
SHIAO LAN KUNG
Simon Pearce on the
  Brandywine
Sitar India
Snockey's Oyster and Crab
  House
Sonny's Famous Steaks
Sonoma
South Street Souvlaki
Spring Mill Café
STANDARD TAP
Steve's Prince of Steaks
STRIPED BASS
Swann Lounge
Syrenka Luncheonette
Tangier Restaurant
Taqueria Moroleon
Taquet
Tashkent
TIERRA COLOMBIANA
Tony Luke's
Trax Café
Trust
VIETNAM
Warsaw Café
WHITE DOG CAFÉ
White House Sub Shop
Zanzibar Blue
Zocalo
Zorba's Taverna

Family Friendly

Abner's
Anastasi Seafood
AUDREY CLAIRE
Ba Le Bakery
Beau Monde
Berlenga's Island
Big George's Stop-N-Dine
Bitar's

THE BLACK SHEEP
Bleu
The Blue Bell Inn
Blue Danube Restaurant
Blue Sage
Bookbinder's Seafood House
By George
Café Lutecia
Campo's
THE CAPITAL GRILLE
CARAMBOLA
Caribou Café
CARMINE'S
Cherry Street Vegetarian
Chez Elena Wu
Chick's Deli of Cherry Hill
Chickie's Italian Deli
Chink's Steaks
The Continental
Copa Too
COUNTRY CLUB
  RESTAURANT
The Countryside Market &
  Delicatessen
Criniti
Dalessandro's
Dante & Luigi's
Darbar Grill
Davio's
Deep Blue
Delilah's Southern Café
Devon Seafood Grill
Donkey's Place
Down Home Diner
East of Amara
El Bohio
El Viejo San Juan
Emerald Fish
Fado Irish Pub
FELICIA'S
Figs
Fireworks!
FORK
Founders
FOUNTAIN RESTAURANT
FuziOn
Genji
Geno's Steaks
Golden Gates
The Grill

H & J McNally's Tavern
H.K. Golden Phoenix
HAPPY ROOSTER
High Street Caffe
Hikaru
HORIZONS CAFE
Hotel DuPont (Green and
  Brandywine Rooms)
Il Tartufo
Illuminare
Indonesia
THE INN ON BLUEBERRY
  HILL
International Café
Ishkabibble's Eatery
Jack's Firehouse
Jamaican Jerk Hut
Jim's Steaks
Joe's Pizza
JOHN'S ROAST PORK
Jones
Jong Ka Jib Soft Tofu
  Restaurant
Joy Tsin Lau
JUDY'S CAFÉ
Kansas City Prime
KHAJURAHO
Kim's
Koch's Deli
Korea Garden
La Cigale
La Lupe
Lacroix at the Rittenhouse
LAKESIDE CHINESE DELI
L'Angolo
Larry's Famous Steaks
LAS CAZUELAS
Lazaro's Pizza House
LE BEC-FIN
Le Bus
Le Cyclo
Le Mas Perrier
Le Me Toujours
LEE HOW FOOK
Lenny's Italian Deli
Little Fish
Lombardi's Specialty
  Hoagies
Lombardi's
LONDON GRILL

Lorenzo Pizza
LOS CATRINES &
  TEQUILA'S BAR
Ludwig's Garten
Mallorca
Mama's Pizzeria
Marco Polo
MARGARET KUO'S PEKING
Mayfair Diner
Melange Café
Melrose Diner
Mexico Lindo
Minar Palace
Monk's Café
MORNING GLORY DINER
Mustache Bill's Diner
New Orleans Café
New Phnom Penh
NEW WAVE CAFÉ
Nice Chinese Noodle House
Ocean City
Old City Coffee
Otto's Brauhaus
Pad Thai Shack
Pagoda Noodle Café
Paradise
Pastrami and Things
Pat's King of Steaks
PENANG
People's Pizza
Pho 75
Pho Xe Lua
Pigalle
Pod
Porky's Point
THE PRIME RIB
Primo Hoagie
Radicchio
Ralph's
Ray's Café & Tea House
Real Pizza
The Restaurant at
  Doneckers
Ricci
Rick's Steaks
Ristorante Valentino
RITZ SEAFOOD
Roller's
Roselena's Coffee Bar
ROUGE

Roya Restaurant
Roy's
RX
Sagami
The Saloon
Samosa
Sang Kee
Sansom Street Kabob
 House
SANSOM STREET OYSTER
 HOUSE
Seafood Unlimited
Shank's and Evelyn's Roast
 Beef
SHIAO LAN KUNG
Simon Pearce on the
 Brandywine
Sitar India
Smith & Wollensky
Snockey's Oyster and Crab
 House
Sonny's Famous Steaks
Sonoma
South Street Souvlaki
Spring Mill Café
STANDARD TAP
Steve's Prince of Steaks
Sushikazu
Swann Lounge
Syrenka Luncheonette
Tacconelli's Pizzeria
Taqueria Moroleon
Taquet
Tartine
Tashkent
333 Belrose
TIERRA COLOMBIANA
Tony Luke's
TRE SCALINI
12th Street Cantina
VIETNAM
Villa di Roma
Warsaw Café
WHITE DOG CAFÉ
White House Sub Shop
Xochimilco
Yangming
Zen Tea House
Zocalo
Zorba's Taverna

Noisy

ALMA DE CUBA
AUDREY CLAIRE
Avenue B
AZAFRAN
The Bards
Beau Monde
BIRCHRUNVILLE STORE
 CAFÉ
BISTRO ST. TROPEZ
THE BLACK SHEEP
Bleu
BLUE ANGEL
BRASSERIE PERRIER
Bridgid's
BUDDAKAN
Café Habana
CAFÉ SPICE
Caffe Monticello
THE CAPITAL GRILLE
CARAMBOLA
CARMINE'S
CHLÖE
Cibucan
Circa
CITRUS
The Continental
Copa Too
COUNTRY CLUB
 RESTAURANT
The Countryside Market &
 Delicatessen
Criniti
Cuba Libre
DILWORTHTOWN INN
DJANGO
DMITRI'S
EFFIE'S
El Viejo San Juan
Emerald Fish
ERNESTO'S 1521 CAFÉ
FELICIA'S
Figs
FORK
FRIDAY SATURDAY SUNDAY
Girasole
Golden Gates
HAPPY ROOSTER

HORIZONS CAFE
Il Cantuccio
Il Tartufo
Inn Philadelphia
Jones
JUDY'S CAFÉ
Kansas City Prime
KHAJURAHO
KRISTIAN'S
La Boheme
La Colombe Torrefaction
LA ENCINA
LAKESIDE CHINESE DELI
L'Angolo
Larry's Famous Steaks
LAS CAZUELAS
Le Cyclo
LEE HOW FOOK
Little Fish
Lombardi's
LONDON GRILL
LOS CATRINES
 RESTAURANT & TEQUILA'S
 BAR
Melange Café
Monk's Café
MORIMOTO
MORNING GLORY DINER
MS. TOOTSIE'S SOUL FOOD
 CAFÉ
N. 3rd
NEW WAVE CAFÉ
Novelty
Paradise
¡PASION!
PENANG
Pho 75
PIF
Pigalle
PORCINI
Radicchio
Ralph's
Rembrandt's
RESTAURANT 821
The Restaurant at
 Doneckers
Ristorante Valentino
RITZ SEAFOOD
ROSE TATTOO CAFE
ROUGE

Roy's
RX
SANSOM STREET OYSTER
  HOUSE
Seafood Unlimited
Shank's and Evelyn's Roast
  Beef
SHIAO LAN KUNG
Simon Pearce on the
  Brandywine
Smith & Wollensky
Sonoma
South Street Souvlaki
Spezia
STANDARD TAP
STRIPED BASS
Sukhothai
TANGERINE
Tangier Restaurant
Tartine
333 Belrose
TRE SCALINI
Trust
Twenty Manning
VIETNAM
Villa di Roma
Vivo Enoteca
WHITE DOG CAFÉ
White House Sub Shop
Wooden Iron
Zocalo

Private Parties

Takes reservations for parties of 15 or more people. Restaurants that a private room are indicated by (P.R.)

ALMA DE CUBA (P.R.)
Anjou (P.R.)
Avenue B
Beau Monde
Berlenga's Island (P.R.)

Big George's Stop-N-Dine
  (P.R.)
BIRCHRUNVILLE STORE
  CAFÉ (P.R.)
BISTRO ST. TROPEZ (P.R.)
THE BLACK SHEEP (P.R.)
Bleu (P.R.)
BLUE ANGEL
The Blue Bell Inn (P.R.)
Blue Danube Restaurant
  (P.R.)
Blue Sage
Bookbinder's Seafood
  House (P.R.)
BRASSERIE PERRIER (P.R.)
Bridgid's (P.R.)
Bubble House (P.R.)
BUDDAKAN
Cadence
CAFÉ SPICE
Caffe Casta Diva (P.R.)
Caffe Monticello
THE CAPITAL GRILLE (P.R.)
CARAMBOLA
Caribou Café (P.R.)
Carlino's
CARMINE'S (P.R.)
Cherry Street Vegetarian
  (P.R.)
Chez Elena Wu (P.R.)
Chickie's Italian Deli
Chris' Jazz Café (P.R.)
Cibucan (P.R.)
CinCin (P.R.)
Circa (P.R.)
The Continental (P.R.)
COUNTRY CLUB
  RESTAURANT (P.R.)
The Countryside Market &
  Delicatessen
Cuba Libre (P.R.)
Dante & Luigi's (P.R.)
Darbar Grill
Davio's (P.R.)
Deep Blue
DEUX CHEMINEES (P.R.)
Devon Seafood Grill
Di Palma (P.R.)
DILWORTHTOWN INN (P.R.)
East of Amara

EFFIE'S (P.R.)
El Viejo San Juan (P.R.)
Emerald Fish
Fado Irish Pub (P.R.)
FELICIA'S
Figs
Founders (P.R.)
FOUNTAIN RESTAURANT
  (P.R.)
Frenchtown Inn (P.R.)
FRIDAY SATURDAY SUNDAY
  (P.R.)
FUJI JAPANESE
  RESTAURANT
FuziOn
Genji (P.R.)
Gilmore's (P.R.)
Golden Gates
Green Hills Inn (P.R.)
H.K. Golden Phoenix (P.R.)
HAPPY ROOSTER (P.R.)
Hikaru
Hotel DuPont (Green and
  Brandywine Rooms) (P.R.)
Il Tartufo
Illuminare
Indonesia
Inn at Phillip's Mill
The Inn at Twin Lindens
  (P.R.)
THE INN ON BLUEBERRY
  HILL (P.R.)
Inn Philadelphia (P.R.)
Jack's Firehouse (P.R.)
Jamaican Jerk Hut (P.R.)
Jong Ka Jib Soft Tofu
  Restaurant (P.R.)
Joy Tsin Lau (P.R.)
Kansas City Prime (P.R.)
Kisso Sushi Bar
Korea Garden (P.R.)
Krazy Kats (P.R.)
KRISTIAN'S
La Buca
LA ENCINA
La Famiglia (P.R.)
La Lupe
La Veranda (P.R.)
Lacroix at the Rittenhouse
  (P.R.)

LAKESIDE CHINESE DELI
L'Angolo
Larry's Famous Steaks
LE BEC-FIN (P.R.)
Le Mas Perrier (P.R.)
Le Me Toujours (P.R.)
LEE HOW FOOK
Little Fish
LONDON GRILL (P.R.)
LOS CATRINES & TEQUILA'S
  BAR (P.R.)
Ludwig's Garten (P.R.)
Mainland Inn (P.R.)
Mallorca (P.R.)
Marco Polo
MARGARET KUO'S PEKING
  (P.R.)
MAX'S (P.R.)
McCormick & Schmick's
  (P.R.)
Melange Café
Mezza Luna (P.R.)
Mikado (P.R.)
Monte Carlo Living
  Room (P.R.)
MOONLIGHT (P.R.)
NAN
New Orleans Café (P.R.)
NEW WAVE CAFÉ
Novelty (P.R.)
Ocean City (P.R.)
OPUS 251 (P.R.)
Otto's Brauhaus (P.R.)
Pagoda Noodle Cafe
Paradise
¡PASION!
PENANG
Penne (P.R.)
Pod (P.R.)
Pompeii (P.R.)
THE PRIME RIB (P.R.)
Ralph's (P.R.)
Ray's Café & Tea House
RESTAURANT 821
The Restaurant at
  Doneckers (P.R.)
Ristorante Panorama (P.R.)
ROSE TATTOO CAFE (P.R.)
Roselena's Coffee Bar
  (P.R.)

Roy's (P.R.)
RX
The Saloon (P.R.)
SAVONA (P.R.)
Sergeantsville Inn (P.R.)
Serrano (P.R.)
Simon Pearce on the
  Brandywine (P.R.)
Sitar India
Smith & Wollensky (P.R.)
Snockey's Oyster and Crab
  House (P.R.)
Sonoma (P.R.)
Spring Mill Café (P.R.)
STRAWBERRY HILL (P.R.)
STRIPED BASS
Sushikazu
Tacconelli's Pizzeria (P.R.)
TANGERINE (P.R.)
Taqueria Moroleon
Taquet (P.R.)
Tartine (P.R.)
333 Belrose (P.R.)
TIERRA COLOMBIANA (P.R.)
TRE SCALINI (P.R.)
Trust
Twenty21 (P.R.)
Twenty Manning
Villa di Roma
Vivo Enoteca (P.R.)
Warsaw Café
WHITE DOG CAFÉ (P.R.)
Yangming (P.R.)
Zanzibar Blue
Zen Tea House
Zocalo (P.R.)
Zorba's Taverna

BYOB

Aden
AUDREY CLAIRE
AZAFRAN
BIRCHRUNVILLE STORE
  CAFÉ
Blue Sage
Bubble House
Café Lutecia
Caffe Casta Diva

Campo's
CARAMBOLA
CARMINE'S
Cherry Street Vegetarian
Chez Elena Wu
CHLÖE
CITRUS
COUNTRY CLUB
  RESTAURANT
The Countryside Market &
  Delicatessen
Darbar Grill
DJANGO
DMITRI'S (Queen Village
  only)
East of Amara
EFFIE'S
El Bohio
Figs
FUJI JAPANESE
  RESTAURANT
FuziOn
Gilmore's
Golden Gates
High Street Caffe
HORIZONS CAFE
Il Cantuccio
Indonesia
Inn at Phillip's Mill
International Café
Jamaican Jerk Hut
KHAJURAHO
Kisso Sushi Bar
Koch's Deli
La Boheme
La Calebasse
LA ENCINA
LAKESIDE CHINESE DELI
LAS CAZUELAS
L'Angolo
Le Cyclo
Le Me Toujours
Little Fish
Lombardi's
MAX'S
Melange Café
Mikado
MORNING GLORY DINER
NAN
Nice Chinese Noodle House

Acknowledgements

eing a restaurant critic is one of the world's great dream jobs, but it demands a great support crew. I'd like to thank everyone who has shared a review dinner over the years for letting me tell them what to eat, and then letting me get first dibs. But I could never have done this without my wife, Elizabeth, who, more times than I can count, stayed behind eating take-out with our wonderful kids, Alice and Arthur, while I breezed off for yet another review meal. On the occasions they accompanied me, they kept me honest and down to earth, reminding me that dinner isn't always about the fine points of flavor and technique, but about being together, having fun, and enjoying the little things that can make any place special. Even as she grumbled while I forced her to order something she truly didn't want, Elizabeth — a lover of fountain soda, red sauce and Caesar croutons — never let me stray too far into the world of the snob.

Thanks especially to my parents who have always supported me unconditionally, and gave me the opportunities to discover what I was meant to do, even if it meant crossing the ocean. My mother, Joyce, taught me early on with her own good cooking the pleasures of food. My father, Myron, showed me it was possible to make a career out of something you love, and turn hard work into its own reward. And thanks to my mother-in-law, Barbara Trostler, a true friend and wonderful neighbor.

I'd like to thank everyone at The Philadelphia Inquirer who has supported me with the resources and independence to do this job right. Thanks to Robert Rosenthal, Lillian Swanson and Julie Busby for bringing me from New Orleans. Thanks to Anne Gordon, Tom McNamara, Nancy Cooney, Walker Lundy and Bob Hall for their continued support. Thanks to food editor Barbara Sadek and former food editor Gerald Etter for molding my raw copy into stories that make sense. Thanks to the many designers and photographers for making the reviews look beautiful — especially Eric Mencher, who is becoming a gourmand despite himself. And thanks to my friends and colleagues who have been mentors, friends, food scouts, sounding boards, dining companions, and faithful protectors of my identity — especially food guys Rick Nichols and Michael Klein. Thanks to my friends Jennifer Weiner and Adam Bonin, who have a talent for finding the right extra guest. And many thanks to Dick Cooper, Matt Ericson, Emmet Linn and Dan Loielo for making this book project a reality.

So many others along the way have taught me lessons I still hold close. Thanks to Anne Willan at La Varenne Ecole de Cuisine, and her chefs, Fernand Chambrette and Claude Vauguet, for making my entrance into the food world one of fortuitous magic. Thanks to the professors at Columbia Graduate School of Journalism — Dick Blood, Sam Freedman and Judith Crist — who gave me the tools to pursue journalism with integrity and standards. And thanks to the many writers and editors along the way who gave me a break and a push in the right direction, Corby Kummer, Julie Mautner, Barbara Mathews-Bowen, Paul Jablow, Jeff Weinstein, Gene Bourg and Karen Taylor-Gist. And Jim Amoss at the Times-Picayune, who opened the door for me to return to food writing in the Crescent City.

There are not many cities that could follow a food town like New Orleans. But Philadelphia has more than held its own. It is blessed with a passionate dining public that never hesitates to write me with a tip or bone of contention. But I am most indebted to the chefs and restaurateurs who have made these last few years an amazingly delicious adventure. They are the ones who perform every night, and they are the ones who have filled these pages with the tastes of wonder. How lucky I am to report on their magic.

— *Craig LaBan, November 2002*

About the Author

Craig LaBan is the restaurant critic for The Philadelphia Inquirer. He has a bachelor's degree in French from the University of Michigan, a master's degree in journalism from Columbia University Graduate School of Journalism and a culinary degree from Ecole de Cuisine La Varenne in France. Before coming to The Philadelphia Inquirer in 1998 as a staff writer, he worked for The Times-Picayune in New Orleans, The Inquirer's correspondent program, The Princeton Packet, and contributed to several national food magazines and regional publications in Boston and New Jersey.

LaBan has written about food and restaurants from New England to Louisiana. He has contributed to National Public Radio's All Things Considered and covered controversy in the jazz world. He won the 2000 James Beard Foundation Award for Best Newspaper Restaurant Reviews.

He is married and lives with his spouse, Elizabeth, daughter, Alice, and son, Arthur, in Philadelphia.